S0-ATZ-021

The IDG Books Advantage

We at IDG Books Worldwide created *Upgrade Your Own PC* to meet your growing
need for quick access to the most complete and accurate computer information
available. Our books work the way you do: They focus on accomplishing specific
tasks — not learning random functions. Our books are not long-winded manuals
or dry reference tomes. In each book, expert authors tell you exactly what you
can do with your PC and how to do it. Easy to follow, step-by-step sections;
comprehensive coverage; and convenient access in language and design — it's
all here.

The authors of IDG books are uniquely qualified to give you expert advice as
well as to provide insightful tips and techniques not found anywhere else. Our
authors maintain close contact with end users through feedback from articles,
training sessions, e-mail exchanges, user group participation, and consulting
work. Because our authors know the realities of daily computer use and are
directly tied to the reader, our books have a strategic advantage.

Our authors have the experience to approach a topic in the most efficient
manner, and we know that you, the reader, will benefit from a "one-on-one"
relationship with the author. Our research shows that readers make computer
book purchases because they want expert advice. Because readers want to
benefit from the author's experience, the author's voice is always present in an
IDG book.

You will find what you need in this book whether you read it from cover to
cover, section by section, or simply one topic at a time. As a computer user, you
deserve a comprehensive resource of answers. We at IDG Books Worldwide are
proud to deliver that resource with *Upgrade Your Own PC.*

Brenda McLaughlin
Vice President and Group Publisher

Internet: YouTellUs@idgbooks.com

Upgrade Your Own PC

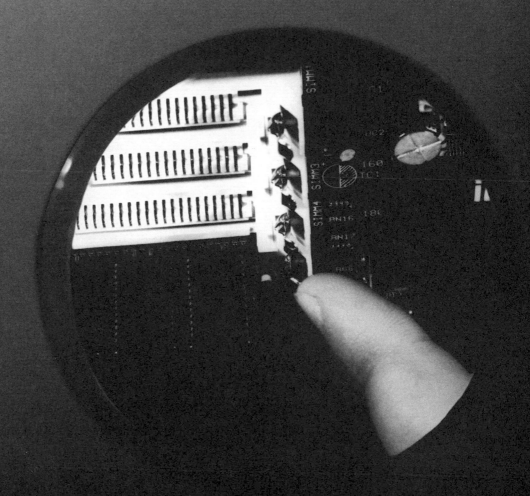

Upgrade Your Own PC

by Linda Rohrbough

IDG Books Worldwide, Inc.
An International Data Group Company

Foster City, CA ♦ Chicago, IL ♦ Indianapolis, IN ♦ Dallas, TX

Upgrade Your Own PC

Published by
IDG Books Worldwide, Inc.
An International Data Group Company
919 E. Hillsdale Blvd.
Suite 400
Foster City, CA 94404
www.idgbooks.com (IDG Books Worldwide Web Site)
http://www.dummies.com (Dummies Press Web Site)

Copyright © 1996 IDG Books Worldwide, Inc. All rights reserved. No part of this book, including interior design, cover design, and icons, may be reproduced or transmitted in any form, by any means (electronic, photocopying, recording, or otherwise) without the prior written permission of the publisher.

Library of Congress Catalog Card No.: 96-75294

ISBN: 1-56884-831-5

Printed in the United States of America

10 9 8 7 6 5 4 3 2 1

1E/SQ/QY/ZW/IN

Distributed in the United States by IDG Books Worldwide, Inc.

Distributed by Macmillan Canada for Canada; by Contemporanea de Ediciones for Venezuela; by Distribuidora Cuspide for Argentina; by CITEC for Brazil; by Ediciones ZETA S.C.R. Ltda. for Peru; by Editorial Limusa SA for Mexico; by Transworld Publishers Limited in the United Kingdom and Europe; by Academic Bookshop for Egypt; by Levant Distributors S.A.R.L. for Lebanon; by Al Jassim for Saudi Arabia; by Simron Pty. Ltd. for South Africa; by Pustak Mahal for India; by The Computer Bookshop for India; by Toppan Company Ltd. for Japan; by Addison Wesley Publishing Company for Korea; by Longman Singapore Publishers Ltd. for Singapore, Malaysia, Thailand, and Indonesia; by Unalis Corporation for Taiwan; by WS Computer Publishing Company, Inc. for the Philippines; by WoodsLane Pty. Ltd. for Australia; by WoodsLane Enterprises Ltd. for New Zealand. Authorized Sales Agent: Anthony Rudkin Associates for the Middle East and North Africa.

For general information on IDG Books Worldwide's books in the U.S., please call our Consumer Customer Service department at 800-762-2974. For reseller information, including discounts and premium sales, please call our Reseller Customer Service department at 800-434-3422.

For information on where to purchase IDG Books Worldwide's books outside the U.S., please contact our International Sales department at 415-655-3172 or fax 415-655-3295.

For information on foreign language translations, please contact our Foreign & Subsidiary Rights department at 415-655-3021 or fax 415-655-3281.

For sales inquiries and special prices for bulk quantities, please contact our Sales department at 415-655-3200 or write to the address above.

For information on using IDG Books Worldwide's books in the classroom or for ordering examination copies, please contact our Educational Sales department at 800-434-2086 or fax 817-251-8174.

For authorization to photocopy items for corporate, personal, or educational use, please contact Copyright Clearance Center, 222 Rosewood Drive, Danvers, MA 01923, or fax 508-750-4470.

LIMIT OF LIABILITY/DISCLAIMER OF WARRANTY: AUTHOR AND PUBLISHER HAVE USED THEIR BEST EFFORTS IN PREPARING THIS BOOK. IDG BOOKS WORLDWIDE, INC., AND AUTHOR MAKE NO REPRESENTATIONS OR WARRANTIES WITH RESPECT TO THE ACCURACY OR COMPLETENESS OF THE CONTENTS OF THIS BOOK AND SPECIFICALLY DISCLAIM ANY IMPLIED WARRANTIES OF MERCHANTABILITY OR FITNESS FOR A PARTICULAR PURPOSE. THERE ARE NO WARRANTIES WHICH EXTEND BEYOND THE DESCRIPTIONS CONTAINED IN THIS PARAGRAPH. NO WARRANTY MAY BE CREATED OR EXTENDED BY SALES REPRESENTATIVES OR WRITTEN SALES MATERIALS. THE ACCURACY AND COMPLETENESS OF THE INFORMATION PROVIDED HEREIN AND THE OPINIONS STATED HEREIN ARE NOT GUARANTEED OR WARRANTED TO PRODUCE ANY PARTICULAR RESULTS, AND THE ADVICE AND STRATEGIES CONTAINED HEREIN MAY NOT BE SUITABLE FOR EVERY INDIVIDUAL. NEITHER IDG BOOKS WORLDWIDE, INC., NOR AUTHOR SHALL BE LIABLE FOR ANY LOSS OF PROFIT OR ANY OTHER COMMERCIAL DAMAGES, INCLUDING BUT NOT LIMITED TO SPECIAL, INCIDENTAL, CONSEQUENTIAL, OR OTHER DAMAGES.

Trademarks: All brand names and product names used in this book are trade names, service marks, trademarks, or registered trademarks of their respective owners. IDG Books Worldwide is not associated with any product or vendor mentioned in this book.

 is a trademark under exclusive license to IDG Books Worldwide, Inc., from International Data Group, Inc.

About the Author

Linda Rohrbough has twice been honored by the Computer Press Association for her work in writing about the computer industry. *Mailing List Services On Your Home-Based PC* won "Best Nonfiction Computer Book" in 1994; in 1993, she won "Best On-Line Publication" for her work as COMDEX crew chief for an international, high-tech news service.

She is on the faculty at Collin County Community College, where she teaches computer repair, courses on the Internet, and courses on how to start a business using your computer. She is also the author of *Start Your Own Computer Repair Business*.

Linda lives in Dallas, Texas, with her husband, Mark, and her two daughters, Jessica and Margaret.

ABOUT IDG BOOKS WORLDWIDE

WINNER
Eighth Annual
Computer Press
Awards ≥ 1992

WINNER
Ninth Annual
Computer Press
Awards ≥ 1993

IDG BOOKS
WORLDWIDE

Welcome to the world of IDG Books Worldwide.

IDG Books Worldwide, Inc., is a subsidiary of International Data Group, the world's largest publisher of computer-related information and the leading global provider of information services on information technology. IDG was founded more than 25 years ago and now employs more than 8,500 people worldwide. IDG publishes more than 270 computer publications in over 75 countries (see listing below). More than 90 million people read one or more IDG publications each month.

Launched in 1990, IDG Books Worldwide is today the #1 publisher of best-selling computer books in the United States. We are proud to have received eight awards from the Computer Press Association in recognition of editorial excellence and three from *Computer Currents*' First Annual Readers' Choice Awards. Our best-selling ...*For Dummies*® series has more than 25 million copies in print with translations in 30 languages. IDG Books Worldwide, through a joint venture with IDG's Hi-Tech Beijing, became the first U.S. publisher to publish a computer book in the People's Republic of China. In record time, IDG Books Worldwide has become the first choice for millions of readers around the world who want to learn how to better manage their businesses.

Our mission is simple: Every one of our books is designed to bring extra value and skill-building instructions to the reader. Our books are written by experts who understand and care about our readers. The knowledge base of our editorial staff comes from years of experience in publishing, education, and journalism — experience which we use to produce books for the '90s. In short, we care about books, so we attract the best people. We devote special attention to details such as audience, interior design, use of icons, and illustrations. And because we use an efficient process of authoring, editing, and desktop publishing our books electronically, we can spend more time ensuring superior content and spend less time on the technicalities of making books.

You can count on our commitment to deliver high-quality books at competitive prices on topics you want to read about. At IDG Books Worldwide, we continue in the IDG tradition of delivering quality for more than 25 years. You'll find no better book on a subject than one from IDG Books Worldwide.

John J. Kilcullen

John Kilcullen
President and CEO
IDG Books Worldwide, Inc.

IDG Books Worldwide, Inc., is a subsidiary of International Data Group, the world's largest publisher of computer-related information and the leading global provider of information services on information technology. International Data Group publishes over 276 computer publications in over 75 countries. Ninety million people read one or more International Data Group publications each month. International Data Group's publications include: **ARGENTINA:** Annuario de Informatica, Computerworld Argentina, PC World Argentina; **AUSTRALIA:** Australian Macworld, Client/Server Journal, Computer Living, Computerworld, Computerworld 100, Digital News, IT Casebook, Network World, On-line World Australia, PC World, Publishing Essentials, Reseller, WebMaster; **AUSTRIA:** Computerwelt Osterreich, Networks Austria, PC Tip; **BELARUS:** PC World Belarus; **BELGIUM:** Data News; **BRAZIL:** Annuário de Informática, Computerworld Brazil, Connections, Super Game Power, Macworld, PC Player, PC World Brazil, Publish Brazil, Reseller News; **BULGARIA:** Computerworld Bulgaria, Networkworld/Bulgaria, PC & MacWorld Bulgaria; **CANADA:** CIO Canada, Client/Server World, ComputerWorld Canada, InfoCanada, Network World Canada; **CHILE:** Computerworld Chile, PC World Chile; **COLOMBIA:** Computerworld Colombia, PC World Colombia; **COSTA RICA:** PC World Centro America; **THE CZECH AND SLOVAK REPUBLICS:** Computerworld Czechoslovakia, Elektronika Czechoslovakia, Macworld Czech Republic, PC World Czechoslovakia; **DENMARK:** Communications World, Computerworld Danmark, Macworld Danmark, PC Privat Danmark, PC World Danmark, PC World Danmark Supplements, TECH World; **DOMINICAN REPUBLIC:** PC World Republica Dominicana; **ECUADOR:** PC World Ecuador; **EGYPT:** Computerworld Middle East, PC World Middle East; **EL SALVADOR:** PC World Centro America; **FINLAND:** MikroPC, Tietoverkko, Tietoviikko; **FRANCE:** Distributique, Golden, Hebdo·Distributique, Info PC, Le Guide du Monde Informatique, Le Monde Informatique, Reseaux & Telecoms; **GERMANY:** Computer Partner, Computerwoche, Computerwoche Extra, Computerwoche Focus, I/M Information Management, Macwelt, PC Welt; **GREECE:** GamePro, Multimedia World; **GUATEMALA:** PC World Centro America; **HONDURAS:** PC World Centro America; **HONG KONG:** Computerworld Hong Kong, PCWorld Hong Kong, Publish in Asia; **HUNGARY:** ABCD CD-ROM, Computerworld Szamitastechnika, PC & Mac World Hungary, PC-X Magazine; **ICELAND:** Tolvuheimur/PC World Island; **INDIA:** Information Systems Computerworld, PC World India, Publish in Asia; **INDONESIA:** InfoKomputer PC World, Komputek Computerworld, Publish in Asia; **IRELAND:** ComputerScope, PC Live!; **ISRAEL:** People & Computers; **ITALY:** Computerworld Italia, Computerworld Italia Special Editions, Macworld Italia, Networking Italia, PC Shopping, PC World Italia, PC World/Walt Disney; **JAPAN:** DTP World, HP Open World Japan, Macworld Japan, Nikkei Personal Computing, Open World Japan, OS/2 World Japan, SunWorld Japan, Windows World Japan; **KENYA:** East African Computer News; **KOREA:** Hi-Tech Information/Computerworld, Macworld Korea, PC World Korea; **MACEDONIA:** PC World Macedonia; **MALAYSIA:** Computerworld Malaysia, PC World Malaysia, Publish in Asia; **MEXICO:** Computerworld Mexico, Macworld, PC World Mexico; **MYANMAR:** PC World Myanmar; **NETHERLANDS:** Computer! Totaal, LAN Magazine, LanWorld Buyers Guide, Macworld, Net Magazine, Totaal! Beurskrant; **NEW ZEALAND:** Absolute Beginner's Guide, Computer Buyer, Computer Industry Directory, Computerworld New Zealand, MTB, Network World, PC World New Zealand; **NICARAGUA:** PC World Centro America; **NIGERIA:** PC World Nigeria; **NORWAY:** Computerworld Norge, Computerworld Privat (Datamagasinet), CW Rapport Norge, IDG's KURSGUIDE, Macworld Norge, Multimediaworld, PC World Ekspress, PC World Nettverk, PC World Norge, PC World's Produktguide, Windows World Spesial; **PAKISTAN:** Computerworld Pakistan, PC World Pakistan; **Panama:** PC World Panama; **P. R. OF CHINA:** China Computer Users, China Computerworld, China Infoworld, China Telecom World Weekly, Computer & Communication, Electronic Design China, Electronics Today, Electronics Weekly, Game Camp, Game Soft, Network World China, PC World China, Popular Computer Weekly, Software Weekly, Software World, Telecom World; **PERU:** Computerworld Peru, PC World Profesional Peru, PC World Peru; **PHILIPPINES:** Computerworld Philippines, PC World Philippines, Publish in Asia; **POLAND:** Computerworld Poland, Computerworld Special Report, Macworld, Networld, PC World Komputer; **PORTUGAL:** Cerebro/PC World, Computerworld/Correio Informático, Dealer World Portugal, MacIn/PCIn, Multimedia World Portugal; **PUERTO RICO:** PC World Puerto Rico; **ROMANIA:** Computerworld Romania, PC World Romania, Telecom Romania; **RUSSIA:** Computerworld Russia, Mir PK, Sety; **SINGAPORE:** Computerworld Singapore, PC World Singapore, Publish in Asia; **SLOVENIA:** MONITOR; **SOUTH AFRICA:** Computing S.A., InfoWorld S.A., Network World S.A., Software World; **SPAIN:** Computerworld España, COMUNICACIONES WORLD, Dealer World, Macworld España, PC World España; **SWEDEN:** CAP&Design, Computer Sweden, Corporate Computing, MacWorld, Maxi Data, MikroDatorn, Nätverk & Kommunikation, PC/Aktiv, PC World, Windows World; **SWITZERLAND:** Computerworld Schweiz, Macworld Schweiz, PCtip; **TAIWAN:** Computerworld Taiwan, Macworld Taiwan, PC World Taiwan, Publish Taiwan, Windows World; **THAILAND:** Thai Computerworld, Publish in Asia; **TURKEY:** Computerworld Turkiye, MACWORLD Turkiye, PC WORLD Turkiye; **UKRAINE:** Computerworld Kiev, Computers & Software, Multimedia World Ukraine, PC World Ukraine; **UNITED KINGDOM:** Acorn User, Amiga Action, Amiga Computing, Appletalk, Computing, GamePro, Macworld, Network News, Parents and Computers, PC Advisor, PC Home, PSX Pro UK, The WEB; **UNITED STATES:** Cable in the Classroom, CD Review, CIO Magazine, Computerworld, Computerworld Client/Server Journal, Digital Video Magazine, DOS World, Federal Computer Week, GamePro, InfoWorld, I-Way, JavaWorld, Macworld, Multimedia World, Netscape World Online, Network World, PC Entertainment, PC World, Publish, SunWorld Online, SWATPro Magazine, Video Event, WebMaster; **URUGUAY:** PC World Uruguay; **VENEZUELA:** Computerworld Venezuela, PC World Venezuela; and **VIETNAM:** PC World Vietnam. 7/16/96

Dedication

To Mark, Jessica, and Margaret.

To Mom and Dad.

Acknowledgments

It's tough, on a book this size, to thank everyone who had a part in making it come about. However, there are some specific names that have come to mind.

At IDG Books, I'd like to thank Greg Croy, Acquisitions Manager, for being this book's champion. Others who deserve thanks include Sue Pines, Development Editor and Virtuoso of Clever E-mail; Ellen Camm, Acquisitions Editor; Andy Cummings, Managing Editor; Nate Holdread, Kerrie Klein, and Judy Brunetti, Copy Editors; Barry Childs-Helton, Copy Edit Coordinator; Debbie Sharpe, Project Coordinator; and Shelley Lea, Design & Graphics Supervisor. I felt fortunate to be working with such a charming group of smart people.

In addition, I'd like to thank IMS Computers, headquartered in Carrollton, Texas, and owner Sid Saver for allowing me to do "live" research as a technician. Also thanks to staffer Kenneth Gray and Dana Bacom, the Plano store manager.

Finally, I appreciate the students and staff of Collin County Community College, and Mark Rohrbough, for being intermediate computer user guinea pigs.

(The publisher would like to give special thanks to Patrick J. McGovern, without whom this book would not have been possible.)

Credits

Senior Vice President & Group Publisher
Brenda McLaughlin

Acquisitions Manager
Gregory Croy

Acquisitions Editor
Ellen L. Camm

Software Acquisitions Editor
Tracy Lehman Cramer

Brand Manager
Melisa M. Duffy

Managing Editor
Andy Cummings

Editorial Assistant
Timothy J. Borek

Production Director
Beth Jenkins

Supervisor of Project Coordination
Cindy L. Phipps

Project Coordinator
Debbie Sharpe

Supervisor of Page Layout
Kathie Schutte

Reprint Coordination
Tony Augsburger
Theresa Sanchez-Baker
Todd Klemme
Elizabeth Cardenas-Nelson

Blueline Coordination
Patricia R. Reynolds

Media/Archive Coordination
Leslie Popplewell
Melissa Stauffer
Jason Marcuson

Development Editor
Susan Pines

Copy Editors
Nate Holdread
Kerrie Klein
Judy Brunetti

Technical Reviewer
Stephen J. Bigelow
President, Dynamic Learning Systems

Production Staff
Brett Black
Dominique DeFelice
Jane E. Martin
Drew Moore
Mark C. Owens
Anna Rohrer
Brent Savage
Gina Scott
Kate Snell
Michael Sullivan

Proofreaders
Christine D. Berman
Michael D. Bolinger
Nancy Price
Robert Springer
Carrie Voorhis
Karen York

Indexer
Richard T. Evans

Cover Design
Tobi Designs

Cover Illustration
Cover Illustration © Dave Cutler/SIS

Contents at a Glance

Introduction 1

Chapter 1: Before You Begin 9

Chapter 2: The Shocking Truth about Protecting Your Upgrade 21

Chapter 3: Upgrading Your Keyboard or Pointing Device 31

Chapter 4: Installing a Second Floppy Disk Drive or Tape Backup Drive 65

Chapter 5: Installing a Hard Disk Drive 117

Chapter 6: Memory Upgrades 165

Chapter 7: Processor Upgrades 197

Chapter 8: Low-Budget Upgrades 227

Chapter 9: Fax/Modem Upgrades to Get You on
    the Information Superhighway 279

Chapter 10: Upgrading Your Power Supply or Battery 309

Chapter 11: Multimedia Upgrades 339

Chapter 12: Replacing Your Motherboard 363

Chapter 13: Operating System Issues, Upgrades,
    Dual Boots, and Multiple-Boot Configurations 387

Chapter 14: Connectivity on the Cheap 419

Chapter 15: Printer Upgrades 435

Appendix A: Resources for Tools and Products 453

Appendix B: Glossary 459

Index **467**

Table of Contents

Introduction 1
  Why Upgrade Your Own PC? 2
  Who This Book Is For 2
  What This Book Covers 3
    The most common upgrades 3
    DOS and Windows 3.*x* 3
    Windows 95 4
    Plug and Play 4
  How This Book Is Organized 4
    Step-by-step instructions 4
    Detailed illustrations 4
    Case studies 5
    Commonly asked questions and the answers 5
    Troubleshooting practice 5
    A synopsis of each chapter 5
  Icons Used in this Book 7
  What You Need to Be Able to Do 8
  Final Words 8

Chapter 1: Before You Begin 9
  Deciding to Upgrade 9
  What You Should Watch For 10
    Proprietary hardware 10
    Special versions of the operating system 12
    The age of your PC 12
    Bang-for-the-buck issues 13
  What You Should Know 13
    README files 13
    Diagnostic tools you already have 13
      Discover your components using MSD 13
    Your ROM BIOS and how to get into it 15
      How to get to the CMOS settings 16
      Navigating the CMOS setup screen 17
      How to exit your CMOS 19
  What You Should Do 19

**Chapter 2: The Shocking Truth about
Protecting Your Upgrade** 21
  Operating System Upgrades, Dual Boots, and Multiple
    Boot Configurations 21
  What Happens when Components Are Damaged? 22

The Wrist Grounding Strap 22
What Is an Earth Ground? 25
How to Test for an Earth Ground 26
ESD Protection in Review 26
Other ESD Protection Devices 26
    Antistatic mat 28
    Antistatic spray 28
Power Surge Protectors 28
ESD Transportation Protection for Components 29

Chapter 3: Upgrading Your Keyboard or Pointing Device 31

Keyboards 32
    Preparation 32
        Noise level 33
        Key placement 33
        Types of keyboards 34
        Keyboard connectors 38
        Keyboard adapters 38
    Installation 40
    Troubleshooting 41
        Things to look for 41
        Common mistakes checklist 41
Pointing Devices 41
    Preparation 42
        Types of pointing devices 42
        Resolution (or sensitivity) 43
        Pointing device connectors 44
        PS/2 mouse connector 44
        Pointing device adapters 47
    Installation 51
        Precautionary measures 51
        Connecting the pointing device 51
        Installing the software 51
        Installation in review 59
    Troubleshooting 60
        Common mistakes checklist 61
Wireless Pointing Devices 61
    Preparation 61
    Installation 61
    Troubleshooting 62
Troubleshooting Practice: What's Wrong
in This Photo? 63

Chapter 4: Installing a Second Floppy Disk Drive or Tape Backup Drive 65

Adding a Second Floppy Disk Drive 66
  Preparation 67
    Determining the type of floppy disk drive to add 67
    Checking the BIOS 69
    Checking the case 72
    Purchase checklist 78
  Installation 79
    Connecting the cable to the floppy disk controller card 79
    Connecting the cable to the floppy disk drives 80
    Connecting the power supply to the new drive 81
    Telling the BIOS about the new drive 82
    Testing the floppy drives 83
    Installing the new drive in the case 84
    Burning in the new drive 85
    Installation in review 86
  Troubleshooting 87
Swapping Your Floppy Drives (So the B is the A) 88
  Looking for swap floppies in the CMOS setup 88
  What to do if there's no CMOS swap function 89
Adding an Internal Tape Backup Drive 90
  Preparation 90
    Checking the case for a free drive bay 90
    Checking for an unused power supply cable 91
  Installation 91
    Connecting the tape drive 91
    Installing the software and testing the tape drive 94
    Placing the tape drive securely in the case 96
    Final testing the tape drive and floppy disk drives 96
    Special instructions for Windows 95 96
    Installation in review 98
  Troubleshooting 98
Adding an External Tape Backup Drive 101
  Preparation 102
  Installation 102
    Installing the software for parallel port tape backup drives .. 103
    Windows 95 software for parallel port tape drives 105
    Installation in review 106
  Troubleshooting 107
Troubleshooting Practice: What's Wrong in These Photos? 110

Chapter 5: Installing a Hard Disk Drive 117

Upgrading Your Hard Disk Drive 117
  Preparation 118
    Back up your current hard drive 123
    Make a bootable floppy disk 123

Check the BIOS 125
Check inside the PC 129
Installation 130
Physical connection of the hard disk drive 131
Configure the new drive in the CMOS 132
Boot from the bootable floppy 135
Partition the drive using FDISK 135
Format the hard disk drive as a system disk 136
Test the new hard disk drive 137
Mount the drive into the case 138
Restore your data 138
Burn-in your hard drive 139
Installation in review 139
Troubleshooting 140
Installing a Second Hard Disk Drive 144
Preparation 144
Look for room in the case 144
See if you need adapters or mounting rails 145
Obtain a two-drive 40-pin ribbon cable 145
Check to see if you need a splitter or power cable adapter ... 145
Installation 146
Set your new hard disk drive to slave mode 146
Connect the cables to the drives 148
Change the CMOS settings to reflect both drives 149
Test the drives 149
Install the new drive in the case 155
Test again before you close the case 155
Installation in review 156
Troubleshooting 157
Check the jumper settings 157
Look for undocumented jumpers 157
When it still doesn't work 158
Swap the drives so that the new hard drive is drive C 158
Get the jumper settings for your old hard disk drive 159
Change the jumpers and the cabling 159
Common Mistakes Checklist 160
Troubleshooting Practice: What's
Wrong in These Photos? 161

Chapter 6: Memory Upgrades **165**
Preparation 166
What is memory? 166
The kitchen analogy 166
Virtual memory 167
The memory barrier 167
Types of memory and other memory issues 169
Physical formats 170
Logical formats: Fast Paging Mode versus EDO 176

Finding the amount of memory you can add
to your system 177
Determining how much memory you have now 177
Looking at your system documentation 177
Looking inside your PC 181
Proprietary memory 183
Buying tips 186
What to look for in good quality DRAM 186
Testing the memory 186
Installation 187
Removing SIMMs (optional step) 187
Placing the SIMM in the slot correctly 188
Testing 191
Installation in Review 191
Troubleshooting 192
Troubleshooting Practice: What's
Wrong in This Photo? 194

Chapter 7: Processor Upgrades 197

Preparation 198
What is a CPU? 198
The math coprocessor 198
The wheelbarrow analogy 199
Low-voltage processors 199
The heat sink 201
CPU cooling fans 201
Interposers 201
Upgradeable CPUs 202
The PC bus and the processor 204
Determining what CPU you have now 206
Looking for information during the boot process 206
How to find the CPU inside your PC 206
How to read CPU chip numbers 209
Looking at your CPU socket 210
Discovering what CPU upgrade you can add 211
Upgrades for 286 or 386 processors 211
Upgrades for 486 processors 213
Upgrades for Pentium processors 213
Jumper settings 214
The CPU cooling fan 214
Installation 215
Removing the old CPU 215
Removing a CPU from a LIF socket 215
Removing a CPU from a ZIF socket 216
Installing the new CPU 216
Installing the cooling fan on the new processor 216
Installing the new processor in the socket 217
Connecting the power to the cooling fan 219

Setting the jumper settings (optional) 220
Testing 222
Installing a third-party CPU upgrade 222
Installation in review 222
Troubleshooting 223
Troubleshooting Practice: What's
Wrong in These Photos? 224

Chapter 8: Low-Budget Upgrades 227

Section I — Video Card Upgrades 228
Preparation 228
What is a video card? 228
Video terminology 228
Why video cards need their own memory 232
Types of video cards 233
How to find out what you have now 233
Seeing what expansion slots you have 234
Buying tips 239
Backing up your system...240
Installation 241
Selecting a vanilla video driver under Windows 3.x 241
Removing your old video card 242
Installing the new video card 243
Installing PCI cards 244
Testing the new video card 244
Installing the drivers for the new video card 245
Installation in review 251
Troubleshooting 254
Section II — Hard Disk Controller Upgrades 261
Preparation 262
What is a hard disk controller? 262
Taking a look inside your PC 265
Looking for show stoppers 265
Buying tips 266
Backing up your system.. 266
Making a bootable floppy diskette 266
Recording your hard disk drive parameters 267
Multi-I/O card preparation.. 267
PCI multi-I/O cards 267
Installation 267
Removing your old controller card 268
Setting the ports and controllers on the new card 268
Connecting the ribbon cable(s) 269
Installing the new card 271
Changing the CMOS settings 271

Controller cards with their own BIOS 271
Installation in review 273
Software installation 274
Troubleshooting 275
Troubleshooting Practice: What's Wrong In
These Photos? 276

Chapter 9: Fax/Modem Upgrades to Get You on the Information Superhighway 279

Preparation 280
What is a modem? 280
Baud rate 281
Fax baud rates 281
What's a COM port? 282
The relationship between modems and COM ports 284
Why you should avoid COM3 and COM4 284
How to find out what COM ports you have 284
Finding your serial ports 284
Looking at your PC's BIOS configuration 285
Looking for a Plug and Play (PnP) BIOS 287
How to use MSD under DOS/Windows 3.x 288
How to use the Windows 95 Device Manager 289
Points to consider when buying a modem 291
How to decide between an internal or external modem 291
Plug and Play internal modems 293
Fax/modem considerations 293
Dual voice and data capability (DSVD) 294
Installation 294
Installing an external modem 294
Installing an internal modem 296
Testing 298
DOS/Windows 3.x testing 298
Windows 95 testing 300
Installation in review 303
Troubleshooting 304
Troubleshooting Practice: What's Wrong
in This Photo? 307

Chapter 10: Upgrading Your Power Supply or Battery 309

Power Supply Upgrades 310
What is a power supply? 310
The power connections 311
Preparation 311
Determining the wattage of your current power supply 311
Determining the wattage you need 313
What can happen if the system is underpowered 314

Testing the voltage 315
Proprietary power supplies 316
Buying tips 318
Installation 319
Removing your old power supply 319
Installing the new power supply 321
Testing the new power supply 323
Installation in review 324
Troubleshooting 324
Battery Upgrades 325
Preparation 325
Determining the type of battery you have now 325
Proprietary batteries 328
How to measure the voltage from your battery 329
How to determine if you should replace the battery 329
What to look for if the battery is soldered onto the
   motherboard 330
Recording your CMOS settings 331
Battery buying tips 332
Installation 332
Installing a coin battery 332
Installing the battery pack upgrade 333
Installation in review 335
Troubleshooting 336
Troubleshooting Practice: What's Wrong in These Photos? 337

Chapter 11: Multimedia Upgrades **339**

Preparation 340
The sound card 340
Sound terminology 340
Sound card jacks and connectors 340
Sound card memory address and IRQ issues 341
Software drivers for the sound card 341
Upgradeable sound cards 342
Sound cards with an IDE interface 342
Audio out 342
The CD-ROM drive 343
The CD-ROM drive interface 343
Direct memory access (DMA) 343
Software drivers for the CD-ROM drive 344
The MIDI connector 346
Looking inside your system 347
Buying tips 347
Software requirements 349
Compatibility 349
CD-ROM purchase tips 349

Plug and Play advice 349
Return policy 350
Installation 351
Installing the sound card and CD-ROM drive 351
Installing the software under DOS/Windows 3.x 353
Installing a sound card under Windows 95 353
Testing 354
Securing the CD-ROM drive into the case 354
Performing a system-wide test 355
Installation in review 355
Troubleshooting 359
Troubleshooting Practice: What's Wrong in These Photos? 361

Chapter 12: Replacing Your Motherboard **363**

Preparation 364
What is a motherboard? 364
Determining if a new motherboard will work in
your PC's case 365
Considerations when buying a motherboard 366
Processor 367
Chipsets 367
Integrated controllers and ports 368
Expansion slots 368
BIOS features to look for 369
Materials for installation 369
Buying a new case 370
Installation 371
Removing the old components 371
Disconnecting peripherals 371
Disconnecting ribbon cables inside the PC 372
Removing cards in expansion slots 372
Disconnecting wires to case switches 372
Removing the old motherboard 373
Checking the settings on the new motherboard 374
Installing the new motherboard 374
Connecting the case switches 378
Installing the basic components 379
Testing 379
Installing the rest of the components, one at a time 379
Testing again 382
Installation in review 382
Troubleshooting 384
Troubleshooting Practice: What's Wrong in These Photos? 385

Chapter 13: Operating System Issues, Upgrades, Dual Boots, and Multiple-Boot Configurations 387

Preparation 388
What's an operating system? 388
DOS version issues 389
What happens when the PC boots 390
The role the environment files play 390
Creating a rescue diskette 391
Creating a DOS rescue diskette 391
Creating a bootable diskette 391
Copying critical programs to the diskette 392
Copying the environment files to the diskette 392
Copying the drivers to the bootable diskette 392
Labeling the bootable diskette 394
Creating a Windows 3.x rescue diskette 394
Creating a Windows 95 startup diskette 394
Installation in review 398
Editing environment files 399
How to use EDIT under DOS 400
How to use SYSEDIT under Windows 3.x and Windows 95 401
Tricks for troubleshooting environment files 403
Clean boot 403
Executing the environment files one line at a time 403
"Comment out" commands 403
Researching back to the source of the command 404
Upgrading to Windows 95 406
Hardware requirements 406
Watch out for antivirus software and RAM-doubling utilities 406
Setting up a DOS/Windows 3.x and Windows 95 dual boot 407
Setting up a multiple-boot configuration 408
Setting up a multiple-boot configuration in DOS 408
Common mistakes checklist 412
Setting up a multiple-boot configuration in Windows 95 413
Deleting a hardware profile 415
The Futz Factor 415
Troubleshooting Practice: What's Wrong in These Photos? 416

Chapter 14: Connectivity on the Cheap 419

Direct Connection Using Windows 95 420
Requirements for direct connection 420
Looking for the Direct Cable Connection utility 420
How to install the Direct Cable Connection utility 421

How to configure for connection 421
   Determining the host and guest PCs 422
   Connecting the cable 422
   Configuring the guest PC 422
   Configuring the host PC 422
   Naming the host 424
   Setting up shared resources on the host 424
   Connecting for the first time 426
   Restarting Direct Cable Connection 426
   Changing the host and guest designations 426
  Troubleshooting 426
Updating Files between Two PCs 428
  How to add files to Briefcase 429
  How to edit Briefcase files on the guest 430
  How to tell whether your Briefcase files need to be synchronized 430
  How to synchronize (update) Briefcase files 430
  Splitting files and orphans 431
  Troubleshooting 432
Troubleshooting Practice: What's
  Wrong in These Photos? 432

Chapter 15: Printer Upgrades **435**

Preparation 436
  What to know about each type of printer 436
   Laser printers 436
   Other types of printers 438
  Software drivers for printers 438
   DOS, Windows, and printer drivers 438
   Emulation 439
  Get the right cable 439
  Know your ports 441
Installation 442
  Windows 3.*x* printer driver installation 443
  Windows 95 printer driver installation 444
  What to do if your printer is not listed 447
  Installation in review 447
Troubleshooting 448
Adding Memory to a Laser Printer 450
Multiple PCs and Printers 451
  Using switch boxes 451
  Connecting a second printer by using the serial ports 451

Appendix A: Resources for Tools and Products **453**

Appendix B: Glossary **459**

Index: **467**

Introduction

This book is a bridge. It's intended to fill the gap between the books for beginners on PC upgrading (the popular . . .*For Dummies* series by IDG Books) and the mega-sized technical books that are aimed at people who need reference manuals. I wrote this book because, frankly, I couldn't find a book like it. Let me tell you my story.

I got into working on my own PC because I wanted to save money and because I like tinkering with gadgets. As I watched the people who worked on my PC, I began to realize that, with a little help, I could do this myself. I took some programming and math courses in college, which I thought would help me. As it turns out, my college experience didn't help me much at all. However, I quickly began to realize that PCs are built in a modular fashion and that the actual engineering work has already been done.

I started hanging out at computer user group meetings and computer swaps. I bought all the repair and upgrading books I could find and read through them. I hovered around PC technicians, listened to them swap stories, and tried to learn the lingo. Eventually, I worked up the courage to try it myself. What I found is that there are things that everyone seems to know, but that no one has bothered to write down. I learned some of these things by trial and error, some by watching other people, some from hardware vendors, some from hovering, and some by reading. It took me several years to become comfortable with PC upgrades.

I figured someone else would write a book for intermediate users, such as I was when I started. Back then, I was looking for a book that used many clear illustrations, included tips on what to watch out for, helped me with mistakes, and didn't assume that I already knew all the unspoken rules. (In the meantime, I wrote two books about starting a business using a PC and thousands of articles on the computer industry.) I even started teaching computer upgrading courses at a local college to students who were just like me when I started upgrading. After a while, I decided that no one was going to write such a book, and I should write it myself.

Why *Upgrade Your Own PC*?

I learn best by seeing things done. I've found in my computer courses that others learn in much the same way I do. If a picture says 1,000 words, an example says 10,000. And the neat thing about learning how someone else did it is that you transfer the information you gain to other, similar situations.

I also noticed something else: In course after course, the same problems and questions came up. There were different faces and some new problems, but a major portion of the problems were similar, so we started doing real-world upgrades in class that addressed the most common problems. When students saw how a hard disk drive or memory went into a PC, they often were able to go home and do it themselves.

Frequently, I was able to go straight to the source of a problem that a student had been working on for hours. I often heard things such as, "How did you know that?" and "How did you see that?" I realized that I needed to teach my students how to see the way I did, so that they could ignore the visual "noise" inside a PC and focus on what was important. I tried to do just that.

My students' favorite part of the course was when I took several PCs and simulated problems and then let the students go from machine to machine and solve the problems. This troubleshooting enabled them to see what happens when real problems occur, and it showed them how to solve the problems.

I can't teach a course big enough to include everyone who may want to take it, but I can let you see through my eyes by using a camera and teach you the most common problems by showing examples. This book is filled with examples of how these upgrades are accomplished. Sections at the end of almost every chapter let you sharpen your troubleshooting skills by practice, in much the same way students in my courses do.

And to make sure that I was covering the most common upgrade situations, I worked without pay for a period of time as a technician in a very successful local computer chain. (Thank you, IMS.)

Who This Book Is For

This book is aimed at the intermediate PC user. What is intermediate? An intermediate user is not a novice or first-time computer user. Millions of people have purchased a PC for the first time in the last few years, and frankly, the newness has worn off. Not that it's not fun anymore, it's not new anymore. That's an intermediate user.

Following is a list of questions. If you can say *yes* to these four questions, then this book is for you.

1. Do you feel comfortable turning on your own PC?

2. Do you know a floppy disk drive from a CD-ROM drive?

3. Do you know what it means to copy a file?

4. Do you understand what a directory is?

This book may be useful if you're more than an intermediate user. If you've been involved in computing but haven't upgraded or repaired PCs, this book will help. If you're a technician, you may find this book to be useful as well. Most knowledgeable PC users have other users pestering them all the time for information and often end up in training situations. This book could be helpful if you're in that situation, because you can hand it to trainees and let them work through it. This is the book I wish I'd had for my courses, so I believe it will be a useful tool for anyone who has to teach.

What This Book Covers

In fifteen chapters, an appendix, and a glossary, I cover the most common upgrade scenarios. I also include the information you need for various upgrades from a DOS, Windows 3.*x*, and Windows 95 viewpoint. I must cover this information because you cannot talk about upgrading a computer without including information on the operating system used by that computer.

The most common upgrades

Obviously, a book this size cannot cover everything. You wouldn't want to read it if it did. But, as they say, after you've seen a few floppy disk drive installations or hard disk upgrades, you've seen them all. Some technicians may argue this point, but frankly, you'll catch on to the conventions and the manner in which computer upgrades are done. When you have that information, you'll be able to apply it to situations that are not as commonplace.

DOS and Windows 3.*x*

When I talk about DOS and Windows 3.*x*, I spend most of my time on MS-DOS Version 5.0 and higher. When I say Windows 3.*x*, I mean Windows 3.0, Windows 3.1, and Windows 3.11. Most of the information in this book that pertains to Windows 3.*x* also work for Windows for Workgroups.

Windows 95

Windows 95 is a world of its own. Although it is similar to DOS and Windows 3.x, it is different enough to justify separate treatment. I treat it separately where appropriate, and I include new functions in Windows 95 when applicable.

Plug and Play

Technically, Plug and Play pertains to Windows 95 and the hardware of the PC, but many hardware vendors are starting to refer to Plug and Play in DOS and Windows 3.x, as well. Plug and Play is starting to mean that you insert the hardware, and a software program sets it up for you. Sometimes this works and sometimes it doesn't, but this book helps you to get your new hardware working either way.

How This Book Is Organized

Like the PC, I tried to make the book modular. As much as possible, I attempted to make each chapter a unit so that you can simply turn to that chapter and perform the upgrade there. In some places, this wasn't possible, so if you need information from another chapter, I tell you where to look.

I recommend that you start with upgrades in the beginning of the book before attempting upgrades in Chapters 8 through 13. Success with easier upgrades will help prepare you for the more challenging ones.

Two chapters you should read no matter what are Chapters 1 and 2. Your odds of success plummet without the information in these two chapters. Also, they're short and well worth the time you'll spend there.

Step-by-step instructions

Each chapter contains illustrations that let you "see" like a technician. In addition, you find step-by-step instructions, illustrations, and tips to help you avoid problem areas. Tips that the pros use are included as well.

Detailed illustrations

I want you to see what I see when I'm looking at a PC, so I include illustrations that are clear and detailed. Photos, line drawings, and screen shots help guide you through the upgrades.

Case studies

I have many stories of typical upgrade scenarios, and I share them with you. The names have been changed to protect those involved (no one wants mistakes pointed out). Some case studies are about mistakes, and others explain struggles through difficult circumstances, but each tells what the problem was and how it was resolved. You'll find these case studies encouraging and enlightening.

Commonly asked questions and the answers

Where it makes sense, I include the most commonly asked questions and the answers. If you come up with a question that wasn't asked or answered, feel free to e-mail it to me. My e-mail address is at the end of the introduction.

Troubleshooting practice

At the end of each chapter, I include troubleshooting information. In almost every chapter, I also provide a section called "Troubleshooting Practice: What's Wrong in these Photos?" If you can't see what is wrong, the answers are provided. Not only does this help sharpen your skills, but it's also fun.

A synopsis of each chapter

Here's a chapter-by-chapter synopsis of the book.

Chapter 1 is aimed at helping you get the most out of your upgrade. It introduces you to the inside scoop on upgrading, how to avoid common mistakes, things you should know before upgrading, what to watch out for, and things you should do. It includes information on how to get into and out of critical areas of your PC, and it shows you upgrade tools that you already have.

Chapter 2 is all about how you can protect your upgrade from forces found in your home or office that can destroy the components before you even put them in. Static electricity, with an average discharge of about 10,000 volts, is a constant danger, but there are some inexpensive ways to thwart it. This chapter outlines the dangers of *electrostatic discharge* (ESD) to electronic equipment, explains grounding, tells you how to determine if a true earth ground exists, and explains the use of a grounding antistatic wrist strap.

In **Chapter 3,** you learn the ins and outs of upgrading your keyboard or pointing device. Although seemingly simple, there's more to these upgrades than meets the eye, especially with the new products that are entering the market.

Chapter 4 concerns installation of a second floppy disk drive or a tape backup drive, both of which are similar operations. You learn the types of drives available, how to determine if your system will support a second floppy disk drive or tape backup drive, and how to perform the installation.

Installation of a larger or second hard disk drive is one of the most common upgrades, and the focus of **Chapter 5**. In this chapter, you see the steps necessary to determine what size and type drive your system supports, tips on selecting a drive, and installation instructions for both a new drive and a second hard drive.

Adding more memory is the focus of **Chapter 6.** You can tell how much more memory you may add to your system, what to look for when purchasing memory, how to use the memory, and how to get your PC to recognize its new memory.

Chapter 7 focuses on processor upgrades. By using this chapter, you can determine when upgrading your processor makes sense, decide what replacement processor will work in your system, and learn how to perform the installation.

If you want to get more bang for just a few bucks, **Chapter 8** is for you. This chapter shows how upgrading your hard disk drive controller and/or your video card are low-budget ways to get a substantial boost out of an older computer. This chapter, divided into two sections, explains the benefits of these upgrades and how to do them. These upgrades often can be done for $100 to $200 (or less).

Chapter 9 helps you get onto the information superhighway. Adding a modem to your system is essential for getting into cyberspace, and this chapter discusses the types of modems and fax/modems, what to look for in purchasing a modem, how to tell if a modem will work in your system, and how to perform the installation.

Chapter 10 lets you in on why your power supply or battery are some of the more common components to fail. You learn how to check for potential problems and how to upgrade when necessary.

Chapter 11 is about adding multimedia capability in the form of a sound card or CD-ROM drive to your PC. Information on Windows 95 Plug and Play is included as well as insider tips on how to make your upgrade work.

There are times when replacing your motherboard is the only option that makes sense. **Chapter 12** defines when this is the right move, what to look for in a new motherboard, and how to install the motherboard.

Chapter 13 covers what you need to know about upgrading to Windows 95, as well as how to protect your PC, how to accomplish a dual boot configuration under DOS/Windows 3.*x* and Windows 95, how to make a rescue diskette, and how to troubleshoot problems in your system's start-up sequence.

Chapter 14 shows you how to use Windows 95 to connect two PCs and share files or printers for only the cost of a cable. You also learn how to set up My Briefcase so that you can automatically update files from one PC to another.

Chapter 15 lets you in on how to upgrade your printer. You learn what you need to know about installing the newest printers, and sharing a printer, and you learn other printer tips.

As you'll soon discover, **Appendix A** is an invaluable source of contact information for the most popular suppliers of computer hardware and components. Internet addresses, faxback numbers, and bulletin board system numbers are included as well, so you can get information you need 24 hours a day, 7 days a week.

Finally, no book like this would be complete without a glossary, which is **Appendix B.** This reference of terms that you are introduced to in the text gives you a quick refresher when you need it.

Icons Used in this Book

To help you identify important points, several icons are used throughout the book.

This icon alerts you to helpful shortcuts, tips the pros use, and other especially useful items.

This icon alerts you to an important point that is a danger to the upgrade.

This icon appears with commonly asked questions and answers in the text.

To help those of you who like lists, this icon designates the numbered steps to perform a procedure.

This icon denotes special functionality or characteristics found in Windows 95.

When an upgrade scenario is included in the text, this icon alerts you to it.

This icon points out a tip that saves you some cash.

The check mark icon flags the "Common Mistakes Checklist."

What You Need to Be Able to Do

The one task that you must be able to accomplish that I don't help you with is how to open the case on your PC. There are so many variations on getting into PC cases these days that it isn't possible to cover them all, and doing so would take precious room in this book that can be spent on things that you care much more about. You can probably figure out how to open the case on your PC by yourself, but you can also ask the retailer where you purchased the computer, look in the manuals that came with the computer, or ask a knowledgeable friend to help.

Final Words

In all, I've tried to make this a cut-to-the-chase book that values your time as a reader. To that end, I'm always interested in hearing what you think. If this book worked (or didn't work) for you, or you have an idea, comment, or suggestion, feel free to contact me in care of IDG Books Worldwide or via e-mail on the Internet at 75570.3235@ compuserve.com.

Here's to you. May you save money, make your PC better, and maybe have fun — all at the same time!

CHAPTER 1

Before You Begin

In This Chapter

✦ Essential steps to take before upgrading

✦ Investigating an upgrade to get the best deal

✦ Determining if your PC is a good candidate for an upgrade

✦ Uncovering tools you already have to help with upgrades

✦ Discovering the BIOS and CMOS setup menu — critical areas of your PC

✦ Learning how to enter, navigate, and exit critical areas of your PC

E veryone has heard an upgrade horror story. Yet everyone knows at least two or three teenagers who used to mow lawns and are now working in a retail outlet upgrading computers. Although lawn mowing can be strenuous, computer upgrades obviously require more know-how than muscle. That's what this book will provide to you.

The purpose of this chapter is to introduce you to the inside scoop on upgrading so that you can avoid common mistakes and get the most bang for your buck. This chapter covers basic information that you should know before you upgrade, including things you should watch out for and things you should do.

Deciding to Upgrade

Most of the time, the decision to upgrade a computer is a practical one — some new functionality is needed in order to perform a specific task. Although you can buy a new computer to get this functionality, it can be significantly less expensive to upgrade the computer you already have. Not to mention that upgrading can be fun and a time-saver as you can continue using the machine that you are already familar with and that you have software on.

Adding new capability may allow you to enjoy your computer more, such as installing a more comfortable keyboard or mouse, or installing a better video card. New capability may also be important to a job you want to get done. Memory upgrades, adding floppy disk drives, hard disk drive upgrades, multimedia upgrades, and others often fall into this category. A component you add for one task is also available for other tasks, so if you add more memory for your accounting software, you can also use that same memory to play the latest PC games.

When you're considering an upgrade, preparation helps you get the most for your money. Here are some tips on what to watch for.

What You Should Watch For

When you decide what you want to upgrade, you must take a closer look at your system. Although each chapter is designed to help you upgrade a specific component, you can get an idea of how involved the process will be by looking at a few basic items. These items include how proprietary your PC hardware is, a proprietary version of your operating system, the age of your PC, and bang-for-the-buck issues. I explain each item in the following sections.

Proprietary hardware

Often, an upgrade means that you're going to replace one component with another, but that can get sticky if your system is a proprietary one. PCs are modular, but the parts are not necessarily interchangeable. Before you buy a component, you must check your system to see if the component you want to replace is a proprietary one. Let me explain.

Proprietary components range from specialized power supply connections and switches to entirely customized cases, motherboards in unusual shapes to fit the customized cases, drives with special interfaces, and specialty connectors. If the company that makes the PC comes up with a configuration unlike that used by the rest of the market, it feels it can legally protect that configuration, hence the term *proprietary*.

An extreme example of proprietary hardware is the IBM PS/2 Model 70 system shown with the case open in Figure 1-1. Notice the unusual shape and position of the power supply. Also, the floppy disk drive connector is different than most systems, as is the hard disk drive connector shown in Figure 1-2. The one thing about this system that is compatible is the memory, which is in the form of 72-pin SIMMs.

Upgrades for this PC are very expensive, if you can get them at all. A single component can cost half the price of a new PC.

Figure 1-1: One clue that this IBM PS/2 Model 70 is a proprietary system is the unusual shape and position of the power supply. You can also see that the floppy disk drives connect differently compared to those shown in Chapter 4.

Figure 1-2: The hard disk drive has a proprietary connector compared to the drives shown in Chapter 5.

The only way to tell what's proprietary is to check on a case-by-case basis, which is why it's so important that you read the chapter on the component you want to upgrade before you buy anything.

During investigation, you may discover that the upgrade you had in mind isn't worthwhile, but another upgrade is more than worth it. For example, just because you can't upgrade the power supply in your PC to support multimedia doesn't mean it's not worthwhile to upgrade the processor or soup-up the video so that it runs Windows faster. Having a PC that's proprietary, doesn't mean that you can't get lots of use out of it. You just may have to change your plans.

You don't want to buy a component before you're sure it will fit in your system for two reasons. One is to save time so that you don't have to make numerous trips to the store to get the right component. The other reason is that some suppliers do not accept returns on components — you could get stuck with an expensive component.

Special versions of the operating system

If you own an IBM, Dell, Compaq, or other brand-name computer, you may possibly have a special version of the DOS or Windows operating system. PC manufacturers can purchase a license for MS-DOS or Windows from Microsoft, and then make changes to the operating system to suit their own agenda. This change tends to happen more with DOS than Windows. Microsoft calls a special version an *OEM* version and refers to these versions in a group it terms *OEM-DOS* or *OEM-Windows*. (OEM stands for *Original Equipment Manufacturer*.)

The OEMs (the vendors) like to add special functions that work with their own hardware. For example, you may be able to turn on a "sleep" power-saver mode with a keystroke combination or bring up a special function to support a second monitor or display screen.

If you have a special version of the operating system, you may have some proprietary hardware, as well as concerns in upgrading your operating system. You can find out what version is running at the DOS prompt by typing the VER command, which gives you the version of DOS running on your PC. In Windows 3.*x*, the opening screen may tell you, but you can also look in Program Manager by selecting Help⇨About to see the version. If you find you have a special version of DOS or Windows, contact your vendor before attempting a video or operating system upgrade to make sure that the upgrade you have in mind will work.

The age of your PC

Your PC's age may affect your upgrade. What was popular architecture and plentiful when your PC was built may not be available anymore. Standards in the PC industry change frequently, which is why most PC repairs end up being upgrades. Not only is the component not available, but you have to make changes to your system to support what is available.

Bang-for-the-buck issues

As I previously mentioned, you can certainly upgrade an older PC. Whether upgrading is a good buy depends on how much of the old PC you can reuse. If the answer to that question is *not much* (maybe you can only reuse only the floppy disk drive and the case), then it's usually cheaper to buy a new PC.

To save money, shop carefully and look at the total cost of what you want to do. (If you read the material first, you'll be able to maximize your ability to upgrade and avoid expensive problems later.)

What You Should Know

You should understand how to perform some basic tasks that go along with most PC upgrades. These tasks include looking for README files, knowing how to use diagnostic tools built into the operating system, and understanding the ROM BIOS. Each of these tasks is explained next.

README files

A convention in the computer industry is for OEMs to put a file on the diskette that has very specific information designed to solve problems for you, the installer. This file contains information about last-minute changes to the video card or software, known bugs, known incompatibilities with other software programs or operating systems, and ways to work around problems (known as *workarounds*). Normally, this is a text-only file and is named something like READ.ME, README., or README.TXT.

Check the diskette that came with your video card for a READ.ME or a README.TXT file using the DOS directory command by typing **DIR A:** and pressing Enter. When you've determined that the readme file is there, you can use the DOS EDIT program described in Chapter13 to read it.

Diagnostic tools you already have

Besides the DOS EDIT tool, you have other tools that you can use for diagnostics. These tools are mentioned later in the book when you need them, but there's one that's helpful overall — the Microsoft Diagnostic, or MSD. MSD is available on most systems running DOS 5.0 or higher and can help you describe what's in your system before you open the case.

Discover your components using MSD

If you don't already know what components you have in your system, you can get this information from MSD. Start MSD from the DOS prompt. (If you're running Windows, quit Windows first. If you're running Windows 95, see the information about running

MSD under Windows 95.) Type **C:\MSD** and press Enter. The screen for the Microsoft Diagnostic appears on your monitor looking something like the example in Figure 1-3. (MSD is located in the DOS directory, so you may have to type **C:\DOS\MSD** and press Enter to start it.)

MSD looks at your system and attempts to give you a list of what makes up your particular system. It is not always 100 percent accurate, however, but it provides you with valuable information that you can verify as you go along.

If you don't understand all the terminology that MSD is throwing at you, don't worry. Terminology is covered here, and you learn what you're looking for when you need the information.

Using MSD under Windows 95

Some Windows 95 installations have MSD, and some don't. If your version of Windows 95 was installed from floppy diskettes, then you probably don't have it. To see, exit Windows 95 to the command prompt by selecting Start⇨Shut Down⇨Restart the computer in MS-DOS mode⇨Yes. When you get the DOS prompt, type **MSD** and press Enter. If MSD is present, it starts. If it's not available, you get the error message, Bad command or file name.

```
File  Utilities  Help

   Computer...      AST/Phoenix        Disk Drives...    A: C:
                    486SX

   Memory...        639K, 7168K Ext    LPT Ports...      1

   Video...         VGA, Phoenix       COM Ports...      2

   Network...       No Network         Windows...        3.11
                                                         Not Active

   OS Version...    MS-DOS Version 6.22 IRQ Status...

   Mouse...         Not Detected       TSR Programs...

   Other Adapters...                   Device Drivers...

Press ALT for menu, or press highlighted letter, or F3 to quit MSD.
```

Figure 1-3: The Microsoft Diagnostic (MSD).

You can double-check to see if MSD is available by looking for it in the C:\WINDOWS\ COMMAND directory by typing **DIR C:\WINDOWS\COMMAND\MSD.EXE** and pressing Enter. If you get the message File not found, then MSD is not available on your system. (*Note:* This assumes that the directory WINDOWS is your Window 95 directory. If your Windows 95 directory has a different name, substitute that name for WINDOWS.)

If you don't have MSD in your Windows 95 installation, you can obtain it from the Microsoft Download Service for the price of a long distance call (see Chapter 9), you can download it from the Internet from Microsoft's home page, or you can get it as part of the Windows 95 Resource Kit available through retail channels. Don't just copy MSD from a non-Windows 95 installation to a Windows 95 PC. It won't give you the information you want. If you need another tool, there are other ways to get information about your PC.

Your ROM BIOS and how to get into it

Not necessarily a diagnostic tool, your PC's *Basic Input/Output System* (BIOS) can be quite helpful in an upgrade. The BIOS is part of the *Read-Only Memory* (ROM) and is, hence, referred to by some as the *ROM BIOS* or just *ROM*. This utility, built into your system, determines to a large extent what components your system will support. Following is an explanation of what the BIOS is, why it is also called the *CMOS*, how you get to it, how to navigate it, and how to exit it when you're ready.

What is the BIOS?

The BIOS is software coded into an *integrated circuit* (IC) chip on your motherboard called the *BIOS chip.* (Some older systems have two BIOS chips.) The BIOS performs tasks or services to the operating system to make it work with the PC hardware. In order for the BIOS to know what PC hardware has been added to the system, it relies on the *Complementary Metal-Oxide Semiconductor Technology (CMOS)*. The advantage of the CMOS is that it requires low-voltage to store information. The BIOS determines what hardware can be added, and the CMOS stores that information. CMOS technology allows a small battery, such as a watch battery, to provide the needed power for years of information storage. In this way, information about the PC's components, as well as the time and date functions, are maintained even when power to the PC is off. The drawback to CMOS technology is that it tends to be slow.

Recent advances bring us the *Flash BIOS*. Flash chips have the ability to maintain information without any power source and have begun to replace the CMOS technology. The advantage to a Flash BIOS is as the BIOS manufacturer adds functionality to a new BIOS, you can obtain the new information in the form of a software update from the PC manufacturer and update the BIOS from a floppy disk. Whether it's Flash or actually based on CMOS chips, the place where you can make changes is still often called the CMOS setup or setup menu.

The bottom line is that if you install a new hard disk drive, more memory, or a new floppy disk drive, you must let the BIOS know via the CMOS so that the computer will talk to the new component. This form of communication is done by entering the PC's BIOS or CMOS settings.

The terms BIOS, CMOS, and ROM are often used interchangeably. The terms may be used in a sentence such as this: "Find out what hardware your BIOS will support, and then, after you install new hardware, enter the CMOS and make the appropriate changes." Someone may also say, "Look at your ROM" or "Look at your BIOS." These are different ways of referring to what I call entering the CMOS setup menu.

How to get to the CMOS settings

The CMOS can be accessed with special keystrokes. This access may be made during the boot process, but some newer PCs allow access anytime during a computing session. On older PCs, such as 286-based systems, you needed a diskette to make changes to the CMOS, but most PCs sold these days offer a message when they start-up to inform you what keystrokes will bring up the CMOS setup menu.

When your computer is starting, watch for a reference to the "setup," "setup menu," or "CMOS." The keystrokes to enter the CMOS setup menu can be anything, but there are industry conventions. These conventions include pressing the Delete key, pressing the F1 or F2 key, and pressing the Ctrl, Alt, and S keys. (See Figure 1-4.) Selecting "Standard CMOS Setup" brings you to the screen shown in Figure 1-5.

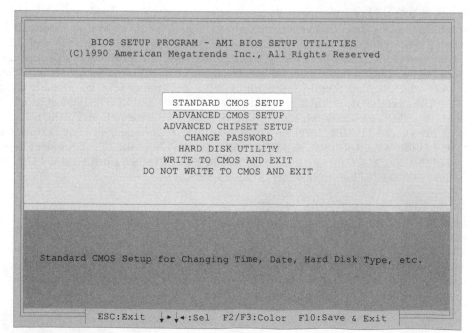

Figure 1-4: This American Megatrends Inc. (AMI) BIOS was entered by pressing the Delete key during the PC's startup sequence.

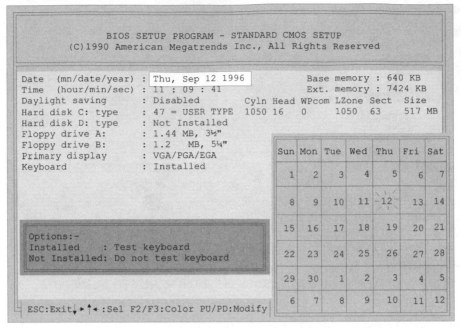

```
              BIOS SETUP PROGRAM - STANDARD CMOS SETUP
           (C)1990 American Megatrends Inc., All Rights Reserved

Date  (mn/date/year) : Thu, Sep 12 1996      Base memory : 640 KB
Time  (hour/min/sec) : 11 : 09 : 41          Ext. memory : 7424 KB
Daylight saving      : Disabled    Cyln Head WPcom LZone Sect  Size
Hard disk C: type    : 47 = USER TYPE 1050 16  0     1050  63   517 MB
Hard disk D: type    : Not Installed
Floppy drive A:      : 1.44 MB, 3½"
Floppy drive B:      : 1.2   MB, 5¼"
Primary display      : VGA/PGA/EGA
Keyboard             : Installed

                                      Sun Mon Tue Wed Thu Fri Sat
                                       1   2   3   4   5   6   7
                                       8   9  10  11  12  13  14
                                      15  16  17  18  19  20  21
  Options:-                           22  23  24  25  26  27  28
  Installed     : Test keyboard       29  30   1   2   3   4   5
  Not Installed: Do not test keyboard  6   7   8   9  10  11  12

ESC:Exit↓►↑◄:Sel F2/F3:Color PU/PD:Modify
```

Figure 1-5: The components on this PC can be seen and changed from this standard setup menu.

If your BIOS is one that you may access at any time, the system may need to reboot after you leave the CMOS setup menu. That means that if you're running a software program when you start the CMOS Setup, you could lose data or corrupt the software program that's running. It's safest to enter the BIOS from the C prompt after you exit all applications, including Windows.

Note: Some laptop computers are designed to let you enter the CMOS to activate and disable functions, such as the modem, while you're working in an application. This enables you to keep the modem turned off until you need it to save energy. In such a case, the computer brings you back to the program in which you were working instead of restarting the computer.

Navigating the CMOS setup screen

The industry convention is to place instructions at the bottom or the top of the CMOS screen explaining how to move from field to field and other instructions for navigating the CMOS screens. The tab key or arrow keys are often used to move the cursor from one field to the next, although some CMOS setup menus allow you to use your mouse. (See Figure 1-6.)

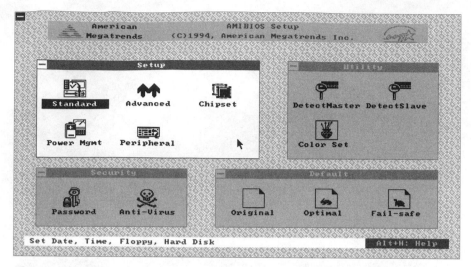

Figure 1-6: In this AMI BIOS, you can use your mouse or the arrow keys. Note at the bottom of the screen that the functions of the icon selected are explained.

You rarely type commands into a CMOS screen. Most of what you can enter is available for you to pick from, you just have to know how to see the selection list. Sometimes, pressing the Enter key brings you a pull-down list that you can scroll through, while other times you must use the minus (–) and plus (+) keys to select values in a field. You must experiment with moving through your CMOS and changing values in the fields. Watch the bottom or sides of the screen for instructions on how to navigate.

Most CMOS menus have more than one menu, with the more advanced settings on a second or third screen. You can use the Page Up and Page Down keys to move from one screen to another in some CMOS menus, while others have a listing of menu screens at the top from which to choose. Some CMOS menus even have icons that enable you to pick a menu to enter with your mouse.

When you learn how to move to these additional menus, print a copy of the CMOS screens by using the Print Screen key on your keyboard before you make any changes. If you have trouble doing this with your printer (especially if you have a laser printer), check the information in Chapter 15.

How to exit your CMOS

Each CMOS allows you to exit and either save or not save the changes you've made. If you're just in looking around, don't save the changes. Usually, you can bring up the menu to exit by pressing the Esc key or choosing Exit as an option by using the arrow keys, as shown in Figure 1-7. Be sure to select the option of exiting *without saving changes*. In this book, when an upgrade requires you to make CMOS changes, I explain to you what to look for to make the changes. When you've made those changes, be sure to exit and save your changes.

TIP

You can exit your CMOS without saving any of the changes you've made. Look for that option when you exit.

What You Should Do

I would be remiss in my responsibilities toward you if I didn't emphasize the need to have a rescue diskette for your PC. Making this diskette should be done before anything else, and it's easy to do. In fact, you should make one before and one after any major changes to your PC. Turn to Chapter 13 for complete instructions on how to make this diskette in DOS, Windows 3.*x*, and Windows 95.

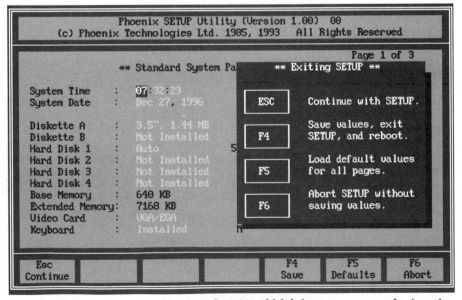

Figure 1-7: Press Esc to exit this Phoenix BIOS, which brings up a menu of exit options.

It's also a good idea to have a full backup of your system, meaning a copy of all the software and data. Your data is your responsibility. Although hardware and software vendors warrant their products, no one makes any guarantees when it comes to your data. If everything on your hard disk drive is lost, including your software and data, there isn't much you can do but start over, unless you have a full backup of your hard disk drive. Making a full backup copy of your hard disk can be difficult to do without a tape backup drive, so you may want to start by installing one (see Chapter 4).

When you've completed the steps in this chapter and have your rescue diskette, you're ready to choose an upgrade and get started. Have fun!

Summary

✦ Read the chapter on the upgrade you have in mind before you buy anything.

✦ You should learn the keystrokes to enter your CMOS setup menu.

✦ It's safe to look around in your CMOS menu as long as you exit without saving the changes.

✦ Print out your CMOS settings before you begin an upgrade.

✦ Make a rescue diskette before you begin an upgrade.

✦   ✦   ✦

The Shocking Truth about Protecting Your Upgrade

In This Chapter

✦ Learning how common static electricity can ruin your PC upgrade

✦ Discovering how static electricity works and when it can be expected

✦ Discovering how an earth ground works and how to connect to one

✦ Uncovering the tools the pros use to thwart static discharge

✦ Preventing ESD

Static electricity that you can't feel can cause permanent damage to your computer and the components you want to install. Yet static electricity is easy and inexpensive to prevent.

Static electricity, also known as *electrostatic discharge* (ESD), is the most deadly enemy to your computer in an upgrade situation. The average computer uses either 5 or 12 volts of electricity. The average static electricity charge, ESD, is somewhere in the neighborhood of 10,000 volts and can be as high as 50,000 volts. This means that the same electrical charges that you can produce by rubbing your feet against carpet or rubbing a piece of paper on a balloon can *fry* the circuits in your computer.

At 3,000 volts, a charge of static electricity is small enough to escape your notice but large enough to cause problems with your computer. This chapter shows you how to avoid disappointing, costly, and frustrating damage caused by ESD.

Question: Why can ESD be as high as 50,000 volts, and yet all I receive is an unpleasant shock?

Answer: The combination of *amperage* and *voltage* creates the power behind electricity. If the amperage (or power) is low, the voltage can be high and you will not be hurt. However, the circuits in the computer are sensitive to both voltage and amperage, so high-voltage, low-power ESD can still cause permanent damage.

What Happens when Components Are Damaged?

Say that you are wearing a wool sweater on a dry, cold day and you want to install more memory into your computer. You've purchased the memory and are getting ready to add it to your computer, but you don't know about the dangers of ESD. Your kids meet you at the front door, and you spend some time chasing each other around the house generating static electricity to shock each other before you go inside to install your memory.

When you install your memory (as explained in detail in Chapter 6), you don't notice any static electricity. But then the memory doesn't appear to work. Worse yet, each time you try to find out what's wrong, the computer becomes less responsive until it doesn't work at all. You return the memory to the computer store, only to discover that the store doesn't take back electronic components. You notice that your computer and the memory look the same as they did before — no burnt-looking places or obviously fried components — however, neither of them work.

Does this sound far fetched? It isn't. It happens every day. But don't let ESD frighten you from doing your own computer upgrades. ESD is easy to handle. The first thing you need is a grounding strap, which is explained in the next section.

Question: Why is ESD worse during cold weather?

Answer: In cold weather, the air is less humid. Your skin is continually building a static charge, but in warm weather or humid climates the moisture in the air drains off that charge. In cold weather, there is less water in the air to drain off the charge.

The Wrist Grounding Strap

For a minimal amount of money, usually less than $20, you can get a *wrist grounding strap.* This grounding strap discharges static electricity that has built up on you and transports it away from your computer or any component you handle. Figure 2-1 depicts the grounding strap worn on the wrist. Figure 2-2 shows how it connects via an alligator clip to the housing of your computer's power supply.

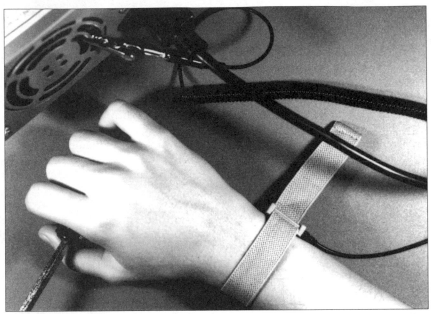

Figure 2-1: The wrist grounding strap discharges ESD through the power supply or the metal case of the computer.

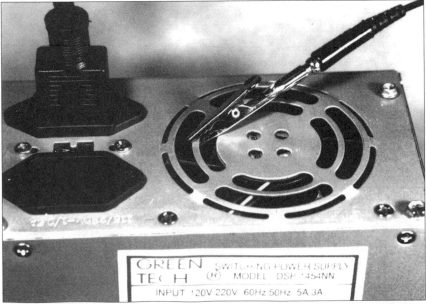

Figure 2-2: The easiest place to connect your wrist grounding strap is to the outside of the power supply housing.

You can be seriously injured if you leave your computer or power supply on while you're connected to your PC via a grounding strap. The computer should be plugged in but turned off. You can special order a wrist grounding strap that plugs directly into a power outlet so that you can unplug your PC while working on it and still be grounded. Check with electronics stores or call Jensen Tools for a free catalog at 800-426-1194.

Be sure to connect the grounding strap so that it has a secure connection. You can also connect the grounding strap to the case of your PC, if the PC has a metal housing, because the housing is also in contact with the power supply. Making sure that the metal portion of the wrist strap makes contact with your skin is important. In Figure 2-3, you can see the metal portion of the wrist strap on the inside of the strap. This discharges any accumulated ESD from your body.

If you wear the grounding strap too loosely or over your clothing, it won't be able to discharge ESD away from your body. Of course, you don't want to wear it too tightly, either — just tight enough to make contact with your skin, as shown in Figure 2-4.

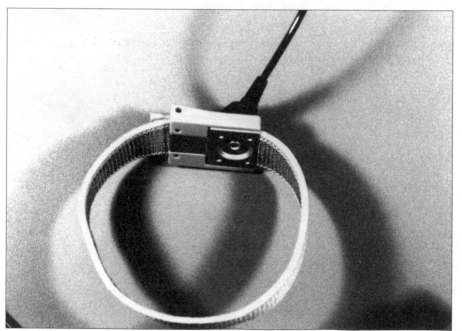

Figure 2-3: The grounding strap has a metal connection inside that must be in contact with your skin in order to discharge ESD.

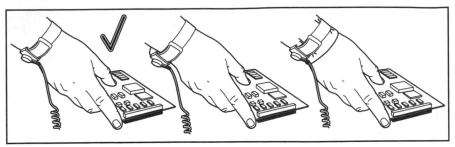

Figure 2-4: If you wear the grounding strap too loosely or over other clothing, it will not be able to do its job.

CASE STUDY

Wrist grounding strap horror story

As a new computer repair student at a local college, Mike was eager to get inside the new Pentium computer his parents had purchased for him. After only the first week of the semester he decided to get to know his PC better by taking out all the boards out and putting them back in. He did not use a wrist grounding strap.

The computer worked fine before he removed all the boards. Although Mike replaced the boards correctly, the computer refused to boot. The system beeped continuously, and no display appeared on the monitor. After some careful testing in the computer lab, I determined that the problem was the motherboard itself, though no physical damage was evident. When questioned, Mike said he thought it would be okay if he just touched the power supply when beginning the job, but he didn't wear a grounding wrist strap as advised in class.

The new motherboard cost $350, and Mike brought it to class, where I helped him reassemble the PC. Everything worked fine after the motherboard was replaced. After that experience, Mike became a believer in grounding wrist straps and now cannot be found working on his computer without one.

What Is an Earth Ground?

Think of electricity as favoring Mother Earth to any other place it could go. An electrical charge finds the quickest path to the earth. You can use this fact to your advantage. When you wear your grounding strap, you need to be sure it is connected to something, such as the power supply fan housing, which in turn is connected to the power supply. The power supply is connected via the electrical cord to a three-prong outlet, which in turn is connected to an *earth ground.*

The third plug of a three-prong outlet is supposed to be wired to a point in direct contact with the earth. Notice the words *supposed to be*. Earth grounds from outlets can be connected to copper plumbing that leads into the earth, but usually earth grounds are connected to a metal rod simply stuck into the earth. Static electricity, or ESD, then follows the wire into the earth and is discharged there.

The problem is that sometimes the outlet is no more than a three-prong outlet designed to accommodate three-prong plug appliances and, consequently, has no earth ground. You must test the outlet you plug your computer into to make sure that it has a ground.

How to Test for an Earth Ground

Fortunately, testing for an earth ground is easy and inexpensive. Figure 2-5 shows a simple, inexpensive circuit tester device available at almost any department store. This type of tester plugs into your outlet and the amber lights activate to indicate an earth ground. On this particular tester, the far left light is red and is lit only if a dangerous situation exists. If the red light is lit, do not plug your computer into that outlet and be sure to call an electrician for help.

ESD Protection in Review

When protecting your equipment from ESD, follow these steps:

1. Test for an earth ground.

2. Wear some type of grounding strap.

3. Be sure the metal inside part of the grounding strap makes contact with your skin.

4. Be sure the grounding strap is connected to something plugged into an earth ground, such as the power supply or metal chassis of the computer.

5. Check to make sure that the power supply is plugged into the outlet that you've tested for an earth ground.

6. *Important*: Be sure the computer (including the power supply) is turned off.

Other ESD Protection Devices

The wrist grounding strap isn't the only way to guard against ESD, but it is one of the most convenient and reliable ways to do so. In a pinch, you can touch the power supply each time before you touch a component, but this isn't a reliable way to protect against ESD. Some technicians prefer ankle grounding straps, but those straps are more difficult to find and more cumbersome to put on. However, department stores are beginning to carry items such as antistatic mats and antistatic sprays. These products and their uses are described in the following sections.

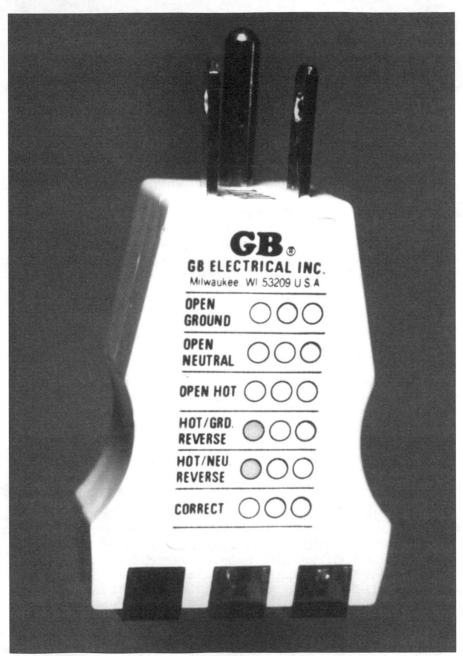

Figure 2-5: An inexpensive circuit tester available at almost any department store that you simply plug into an outlet to test for an earth ground.

Antistatic mat

You may want to consider taking other precautions against ESD, especially if you're planning to work on your computer on a regular basis. You can purchase an *antistatic mat* on which to set your computer and components. Antistatic mats can be connected to the power supply with an alligator clip, just like a wrist grounding strap. (Remember that the power supply must be plugged into an outlet with an earth ground or into a surge protector plugged into an outlet with an earth ground.)

Antistatic spray

Antistatic sprays are useful for general protection, whether or not you upgrade your computer. The spray used on clothing is as good as specialty sprays purchased in electronics stores and is also less expensive. Spraying the antistatic spray on a cloth and then wiping down the monitor, computer case, and keyboard is a good idea. The viewing area of the monitor tends to crackle with static electricity in as little as a month after the last application (if you run your hand across the glass, you can feel it), so regular antistatic spray treatments help reduce the amount of static electricity.

Power Surge Protectors

One other protective piece of equipment you should have is a *power surge protector*. A power surge protector is a device that you plug the computer, monitor, printer, and other peripherals into that, in turn, plugs into the wall outlet, enabling you to control the power to these devices from one convenient location. Surge protectors usually are placed beneath the monitor and offer a master switch that enables you to turn everything on and off with a flip of the switch.

A good surge protector will not allow a large upswing in voltage to enter your computer system. A voltage surge could be caused by any number of things, including an electrical storm or higher-than-normal fluctuation in the electricity delivered to your home or office.

Although I encourage you to invest in a surge protector, especially a UL-listed one, it won't do anything to protect your system from ESD. The outlet is what should be connected to the earth ground. If the outlet isn't connected this way, the surge protector won't help against ESD. However, there's no reason you cannot place your surge protector between your power supply and the outlet that has an earth ground. In fact, I would encourage you to do so to protect your equipment from power surges. You can expect to pay at least $20 for an adequate UL-listed power surge protector.

UL-listed means that the samples of the surge protector submitted to Underwriters Laboratories, Inc. have met the company's safety requirements. In essence, this designation means it's a better mouse trap.

ESD Transportation Protection for Components

When you purchase a new component, be it large or small, you should receive antistatic material in which to transport your purchase. Antistatic materials come in a variety of shapes and sizes, including, but not limited to, zip plastic bags in a gray/silver color; bubble wrap which is characteristically pink in color; and gray or pink foam for packing. (Be sure the foam or plastic is antistatic, as other types of foam and plastic that are not specially designed for electronic components tend to be static-loaded.) If you save these materials, they also can be used for storing hardware that you remove from your system but want to hang on to for future use.

You should always leave components in their original packaging until you're ready to use them and you should place components you remove into antistatic packaging so they can be re-used.

Summary

♦ A dangerous and often unseen enemy to your upgrade, *electrostatic discharge* (ESD) damage is preventable.

♦ ESD is so common that many computer parts retailers, electronics stores, and even automotive parts houses that sell electronic components for cars do not allow returns on electronic parts.

♦ Damage from ESD is difficult to impossible to detect. The component usually just stops working.

♦ Earth grounding is the key to preventing ESD, and wearing a grounding wrist strap is the easiest and surest way to prevent problems.

♦　　♦　　♦

Upgrading Your Keyboard or Pointing Device

In This Chapter

✦ Selecting the right keyboard upgrade for your PC

✦ Determining the type of pointing device upgrade to make

✦ Selecting the correct mouse connector

✦ Defining pointing device resolution and making it work for you

✦ Setting and testing your pointing device software

✦ Installing specialized keyboards and keyboard/pointer combination units

With new options in keyboards and pointing devices, upgrades of this type of hardware have become popular. Furthermore, many new keyboard and pointing device options are fun.

These upgrades can be painless, if you have the right information. You find that information here. A short amount of time spent reading this chapter can save you hours of frustration.

Keyboards and pointing devices are known as *input devices*. Input devices enable you to give the computer instructions and put information into the computer. Several new options for input devices make it attractive to upgrade an existing keyboard or pointing device. These options include keyboards with special ergonomic designs, pointing devices that allow you to use your finger on a pad to direct the on-screen pointer, wireless pointing devices, and others.

You may find yourself needing to upgrade because your current keyboard or pointing device stopped working. These mechanical devices can receive heavy use that causes them to get dirty and/or wear out. The price of these components can make cleaning or repair impractical (except in special situations) when sticking keys or other unresponsive behavior indicates the need for attention.

This chapter is divided into two sections. The first section covers keyboards and the second covers pointing devices. The most common reason why people struggle with keyboard or pointing device upgrades is because they get an upgrade with the wrong type of connector for their computer. With that in mind, I include preparation sections for both keyboards and pointing devices that lead you through the connectors and adapters and tell you what to look for.

Because keyboards are starting to include pointing devices, you may need both sections to make your upgrade successful. Under pointing devices, in addition to the preparation and installation sections, I include information on resolution issues, examples of pointing device software, the most common installation mistakes, and money-saving tips. Along the way, you find shortcuts for DOS, Windows 3.x, and Windows 95.

Keyboards

Until recently, you didn't have many keyboard choices. Now keyboards vary widely, and comfort and ergonomics are important considerations. Basic keyboard design has expanded into a vast variety of shapes, sizes, and even colors, with no end in sight.

Want a calculator on your keyboard? No problem. How about stereo speakers and volume control for your PC sound integrated into your keyboard? You can get that, too. As keyboards change, the manner in which they are installed changes as well, especially when you install a keyboard that integrates some other PC function, such as sound or a pointing device. You can expect to pay $25 to $50 for a basic keyboard, in the $100 to $150 range for a keyboard with a specialized pointing device built in, and upwards of $300 for keyboards that have specialized ergonomic functions or include built-in scanning devices.

Be sure to read the preparation information before you buy. The information on connectors and adapters will save you time and effort.

Preparation

You should always consider noise level, key placement, and ergonomic issues when you purchase a keyboard. Further preparation issues concern the manner in which the keyboard connects to your PC and what you can do to make the keyboard you want work with the PC you have. This section covers those key issues.

Noise level

You may want to note the click of the keyboard you have in mind. Some keyboards offer a clearly audible click when you press each key, while others have a soft feel and make no sound. The less expensive keyboards have a tendency to be softer and quieter because they are made using a different process than the more expensive brands. However, the gap between the two is rapidly closing, so the difference in price between a keyboard that feels and sounds the way you want it to and one that doesn't may be only a few dollars.

One other item to consider is the argument among persons studying ergonomics that keyboards with a click are better for you than those without. The idea is that you receive feedback when you make enough contact to produce the character you want, so you don't hit the keys with more force than necessary. Obviously, you get visual feedback in most cases, but one school of thought says that visual feedback is not quick enough and that we respond faster to sounds. Keyboards make varying degrees of clicking noise when in use. You may want to keep in mind that what you hear in a noisy store environment may seem much louder when fewer competing sounds exist, such as in a quiet office environment.

Key placement

Choosing a keyboard is a matter of individual taste. You should always try out the keyboard to see if it is comfortable. Most computer retail outlets have keyboards on display for you to try, as well as a number of PCs equipped with keyboards. If the keyboard of interest isn't already plugged into a PC for demonstration, you shouldn't have a problem getting a salesperson to help you plug in the keyboard for a test run. You may not need to plug in the keyboard. Many people can tell what they like simply by putting their hands on the keys and typing.

The placement of the keys also can have a profound effect on how you like working with a keyboard. Look at the placement of the function keys. If you're a touch typist, you may be distressed to find that you must take your hands off the keyboard to press function keys located on the far left side of the keyboard. However, if you're a southpaw, you may want the function keys on the left side.

If you work with spreadsheets or enter numbers on a regular basis, you want a 10-key numeric pad on your keyboard. The 10-key pad is usually located on the right side of the keyboard. You may also want a separate set of arrow keys located between the 10-key pad and the main keys on the keyboard.

Look at the location of special function keys, such as Esc, Alt, and Ctrl. If you're accustomed to reaching up in the left-hand corner for the Esc key and the keyboard has the Esc key down in the lower right corner, you may want to look at another keyboard.

You also want to have indicators that light when various functions are operative, such as the Caps Lock, Num Lock, and Scroll Lock. If you have lights for the function keys, you can tell at a glance if the Scroll Lock key is activated, which explains why your word-processing program suddenly starts scrolling text instead of moving the cursor when you try to move through the on-screen text. Some computers turn on the Num Lock key when the PC reboots, and some applications automatically turn on the Num Lock key when they start. If you like to use the 8, 6, 4, and 2 keys on the keypad as the directional arrow keys, you may be frustrated not to have a light indicator telling you when the number functions of these keys are locked in.

Types of keyboards

You can choose from a variety of keyboards, which are detailed in the following sections.

Ergonomic keyboards

Ergonomics in the computing arena involves making the human form work well with the computer. As people spend increasing amounts of time in front of a PC, the effects of this machinery on the human frame become more important. Significant issues include back support from the chair, the correct height for the desk the computer is on, how the hands and arms should be supported, the optimum height for the monitor, and avoiding electro-magnetic radiation from the monitor. Injury in the form of carpal tunnel syndrome is of paramount concern when evaluating keyboards.

There's also the contention that the natural way for hands to work is at angles parallel to the sides of the body and not flat in front of you. The nerves feeding the wrist are twisted slightly when the hand is held flat, and a common belief is that this twisting is at least partially the cause of carpal tunnel syndrome.

Evidence suggests that carpal tunnel syndrome may be caused by cervical spine injury due to improper placement of the monitor that causes the head to be pitched forward, placing strain on the neck. This strain on the neck, coupled with improper seating and support of the hands and wrists at the keyboard, is called the *double crush*, referring to stress placed on the nerves at the neck and at the wrists. Despite controversy over the neck issues, few people disagree that support for the wrists in the form of a rest in front of the keyboard is beneficial, if for nothing else than comfort.

Ergonomics is not a one-size-fits-all proposition. You need to use what is comfortable for you, hence the reason for ergonomic keyboards.

Widely available, ergonomic keyboards come in a variety of sizes, shapes, and price ranges. One of the most common additions to a keyboard to make it more comfortable is the *wrist rest*. It's also the cheapest investment you'll make in your own comfort. I spend a great deal of time in front of a PC and wouldn't work without one. However, a rolled up hand towel works just as well as a purchased wrist rest, and you can throw the towel in the washer when it gets dirty. (Using a towel is a particularly good idea if you happen to be stuck in a hotel room with a laptop computer and lots of typing to do.)

Keyboard shortcuts

DOS

Shortcut	*Description*
F3	Repeats the last line you typed, even if it's been executed. It's great for repetitive operations such as copying the same file to a number of floppy disks.
Crtl+C	Stops the execution of a DOS command. You can use this shortcut to stop the scrolling of long directory listings after you've already seen what you want to see.
F5	Clean boot. Press this key at the `Starting MS-DOS` prompt and the CONFIG.SYS and AUTOEXEC.BAT files are not executed.
F8	Press this key at the `Starting MS-DOS` prompt and you are asked whether to execute each line in the AUTOEXEC.BAT and CONFIG.SYS files.

Windows 3.x

Alt+Tab	Enables you to switch between running applications.
F1	Help.
Ctrl+F4	Closes the document window. This is a fast way to close the groups back down to icons in Program Manager.
Alt+F4	Closes the application window.

Windows 95

Crtl+Esc	Opens the Start menu.
Shift+Del	Allows you to delete without adding the file to the Recycle Bin.
Alt+Enter	Properties.
Shift	Hold down this key when inserting a CD to stop the CD from automatically running.
Alt+F4	Press these keys to exit Windows.

Probably the most widely publicized ergonomic keyboard is the Microsoft Natural Keyboard. The keys are arranged in the same manner as they are on a standard keyboard, but the design places the hands more at an angle parallel to the sides of the body, instead of flat in front of the body. In addition, support for the wrist is built in. See the next section for more details on the Microsoft Natural Keyboard.

Windows 95 keyboards

The Microsoft Natural Keyboard shown in Figure 3-1, combines an ergonomic design with new function keys for Windows 95 use. These keys provide for special keystrokes in Windows 95.

Third-party keyboards with the special Windows 95 function keys are also available.

Other specialized keyboards

Outside of ergonomic keyboards, most specialized keyboards are standard keyboards with something added. For example, adding a calculator to a keyboard makes sense and doesn't change the functionality of the keyboard. However, most specialized keyboards combine a couple of functions, such as stereo speakers or a pointing device. These keyboards must have some way to connect the special function to your PC. You need to know how this is done before you buy.

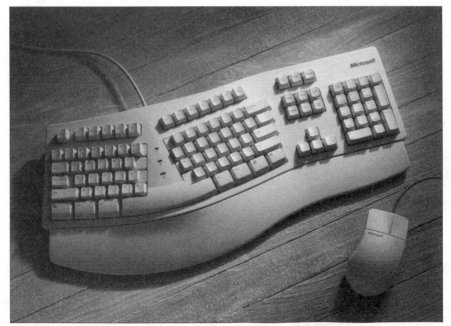

Figure 3-1: The Microsoft Natural Keyboard unifies ergonomic design and new Windows 95 function keys. (Photo courtesy of Microsoft Corporation.)

Shortcut keys for keyboards with the Windows 95 function key

Shortcut	Description
Win+F1	Help
Win+E	Starts Explorer
Win+F	Finds files or folders
Ctrl+Win+F	Finds computer (on a network)
Win+Tab	Taskbar options
Win+Break	PSS hot key (system properties)
Win+R	Runs dialog
Win+M	Minimizes all
Shift-Win+M	Undo the minimize all

For example, if you purchase a keyboard with stereo speakers, you can expect a stereo plug to plug into your sound card on the PC, as well as a keyboard connector. (You probably also need an extra outlet available to plug in the power for the amplified speakers built into the keyboard.) The stereo plug can also be plugged into your CD-ROM drive so you can listen to music CDs while you work. The stereo phone jack on your CD-ROM drive cannot, unfortunately, be used for sound from files and programs on your computer. It only plays audio CDs in much the same way a portable CD player does. If you don't have a sound card or a CD-ROM drive, then purchasing stereo speakers on your keyboard is a waste of your money. (For more information about sound and multimedia, see Chapter 11.)

If you're considering a keyboard with a built-in pointing device, such as a track ball or a touch sensitive pad, that built-in pointing device must communicate with the PC. Some keyboards have a connector that splits near the end into two connectors — a keyboard connector and a serial port connector. You're now facing the same issues as you would be installing any pointing device, along with the issues involved in a keyboard upgrade. I cover pointing devices in the second half of this chapter, so read that section.

Keyboard connectors

You find two types of connectors for keyboards: a 5-pin *DIN*, or standard connector, and the smaller 6-pin *PS/2* connector (see Figure 3-2). The PS/2 connector is also known as the mini-DIN connector. DIN stands for *Deutsche Industrie Norm* (translated German Industrial Norm) and is the name of the committee that sets German industrial standards.

Keyboards are attached to connectors fitted directly on the motherboard, as shown in Figure 3-3. Although the industry is moving to the smaller PS/2-type connector, you find both types available.

Keyboard adapters

Sometimes you need to connect a 5-pin DIN connector to a 6-pin PS/2 connection, or vice versa. Adapters are available that fit on the end of the PS/2 connector on your keyboard and allow you to plug that keyboard into the standard connection on your PC. You can also purchase adapters that make a standard DIN keyboard connector fit into a PS/2 connection. An example of these adapters is shown in Figure 3-4.

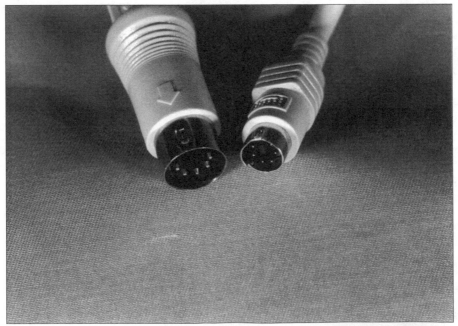

Figure 3-2: The 5-pin DIN keyboard connector is on the left, and the 6-pin mini-DIN, or PS/2, keyboard connector is on the right. The PS/2 connector is gaining in popularity.

Figure 3-3: Keyboard connectors are fitted on the motherboard, as shown by this DIN connector on a 486 motherboard.

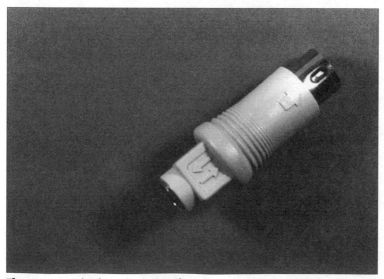

Figure 3-4: A keyboard adapter that allows a DIN connector to fit into a PS/2 connection.

Just because you can adapt a keyboard to fit a connection on your PC doesn't mean it will work. Whether it works depends mostly on the keyboard. Note that if you adapt a keyboard with a PS/2 connector to a standard 5-pin DIN connector on the PC, you lose one pin going from six to five pins. This may cause a problem with the keyboard. However, the keyboard may have been designed with the possibility it may be adapted to fit a standard DIN, in which case it will work if adapted from the 6-pin mini-DIN to a 5-pin DIN connector. The only way to tell is to look carefully at the documentation that comes with the keyboard. If the packaging says it comes with an adapter, then you can be fairly certain the keyboard will work.

Keyboard adapter saga

I wanted to use a full-size keyboard with my PS/2 Notebook computer while I worked at home. I have several keyboards, but they all have the larger standard connectors. I bought an adapter identified by the store as a "PS/2-to-PC Adapter F5/M6 Mini," which means it's a standard 5-pin female connector on one end (F5) and a PS/2 6-pin male connector on the other end (M6).

I brought the adapter home, plugged it into my PC, and plugged the keyboard into the adapter. It didn't work, and I ended up buying a keyboard with a PS/2 connector so that I could have a full-size keyboard to use with my laptop at home.

Installation

Keyboard installation is a straightforward task, if you've done the homework outlined in the "Preparation" section. As I mention earlier, the most common problem in keyboard upgrades is getting the right connector. The following steps serve as a reminder of what you need to do to make your keyboard installation successful. If you're having trouble, check the troubleshooting section that follows.

1. Check the connector on your current keyboard.

2. Shop for a comfortable keyboard with the correct connector. (For keyboard/pointing device combinations, see "Installation in review" later in this chapter.)

3. Power down the computer.

4. Plug in the new keyboard.

5. Power up the computer.

6. Try out your keyboard.

Troubleshooting

An error that keeps the computer from booting is known as a *fatal* error. If your PC won't boot and you hear beeps, it could be the keyboard. Many PCs issue two beeps to indicate a keyboard error, and some may display a keyboard error message on the monitor. Some computers issue six short beeps, and some issue a code of three beeps, followed by two beeps, followed by four beeps. The best way to determine if there's a fatal keyboard error is to watch the monitor for a message indicating that the keyboard is at fault. Most popular BIOS manufacturers have included messages to indicate the problem.

Things to look for

The most common time for a keyboard error message to occur is just after the keyboard has been removed and replaced, which occurs during an upgrade or after the PC has been relocated. If you receive a keyboard failure message, unplug the keyboard and plug it in again. Be sure to power down the PC and touch the power supply (or wear your antistatic wrist strap) to discharge any static electricity you may have picked up while you disconnected and reconnected the keyboard. Then restart the PC.

Other common causes for errors can be an object sitting on the keyboard that holds down one of the keys or a stuck key. Sticking keys occur gradually, unless something sticky has been spilled in the keyboard. As I've said, unless you have a specialty keyboard, it's easier and cheaper to upgrade than to repair. And speaking of specialty keyboards, the "Pointing Devices" section covers (as you may expect) pointing devices, which is something many new keyboards are beginning to include.

Common mistakes checklist

Here's a quick checklist of the most common mistakes made when installing a keyboard.

1. Wrong keyboard connector.

2. Keyboard unplugged or not plugged in all the way.

3. An object is on the keyboard or a key is stuck during boot up of the PC, causing an error message or boot failure. (If you're holding down a key sequence during boot, but started to late to get into the CMOS set up, you sometimes get this message.)

4. Mixing up the keyboard and mouse when both have PS/2 style connectors.

Pointing Devices

A *pointing device* is used to move the on-screen cursor. It is usually a mouse, but a wide variety of pointing devices is available. These devices range from track balls to wireless mice to touch pads you control with your finger. You'd be hard pressed to find a PC for sale these days that doesn't include a mouse, but a number of tempting upgrade options are available. You can expect to pay from $20 to $200 depending on the type of pointing device you choose. What pointing device you choose in your upgrade is a matter of individual taste, but installing one requires about the same steps, no matter what type of device it is.

Preparation

You may have constraints due to your system design that limit your choice of a pointing device. These constraints will affect your purchase. If you are installing a pointing device and your system has never had one, you may also want to look over the serial port section in Chapter 9.

You can save yourself time, effort, and frustration if you read through the installation procedure *before* you purchase a pointing device. You want to pay special attention to the connector section.

When you begin taking steps to upgrade your pointing device, you need to consider what type of pointing device you want to use, the resolution of the pointing device, and the connection the pointing device makes with your PC. (If you're connecting a pointing device to your system for the first time, you may want to look over the section on serial ports in Chapter 9.) I explain these points in the following sections.

Types of pointing devices

Pointing devices have two basic functions. The first function is to translate your movement into pointer movement on your computer screen. The second function is to enable you to select an object on the viewing screen for action. Pointing devices perform these two main functions in a number of ways.

Translation of your movement to the on-screen pointer can be accomplished using either a ball or using a touch-sensitive device. A ball that turns as you move is the most common method. This turning moves other devices inside the pointing device and is measured in increments. This incremental measure then is translated as direction and distance to the pointer on the computer screen. The ball itself can be underneath the pointing device, as it is with most mice, or above the pointing device, as it is with a track ball. Other variations of the ball include a pen-like device with a very small ball in the end. (See Figure 3-5.)

In order for the ball-oriented device to work, you have to get a certain amount of traction; otherwise, the ball simply slides against the surface and doesn't roll. When you use a track ball, your fingers provide the traction necessary to move the ball. But with mice and other similar devices, the traction problem is solved by moving the device on a special pad, called a *mouse pad*.

Figure 3-5: These pointing devices from left to right are: a trackball, a pen-mouse, and a mouse.

The other main way to translate your movement is by touching and moving your finger on a sensitive device. This device records and translates your touch to the pointer on the screen. The most common device is a special pad called a *touch pad*. Many find that using a touch pad is a more natural way to move the on-screen pointer.

The second function of the pointing device is to enable you to select an object on the computer screen. This is commonly accomplished using buttons on ball-oriented pointing devices. Once you get the pointer on the object in question, you click a button to perform an action, such as starting a program. Although touch devices can also be equipped with buttons, you have the additional ability to quickly tap your finger to perform the same action on a touch pad that you would with a button. This finger tapping takes some getting used to if you've been using a button pointing device, but again, some users find it a more natural way to work.

As with keyboards, you want to get a pointing device that's comfortable. Comfort for some users is more a matter of what meets the budget than what they'd like to have. Since there are so many options available, do yourself a favor and get a device with which you're comfortable. One point to consider is *resolution*, or the sensitivity of the mouse, which I discuss next.

Resolution (or sensitivity)

Upgrading your pointing device is a matter of preference, but most upgrades are performed because the user feels the need for better control of the pointing device. You get better control at least in part by increasing the sensitivity of the pointing device. The sensitivity of a pointing device is measured by its resolution, which is expressed in dots per inch. Most pointing devices vary in resolution from 200 dpi to 400 dpi.

Mouse shortcut for Windows 95

The second mouse button opens a list of commands that pertain to a highlighted object. For example, if you highlight a file in Windows Explorer by clicking on it once with your main mouse button, then you can click the second mouse button to open an options menu. You are able to rename or delete the file, look at the file properties, create a shortcut to the file, and more.

The menu that the second mouse button opens varies depending on the highlighted object. This button also opens a pop-up menu in some Windows 3.1 applications.

The resolution of the mouse is a measure of the relationship between your movement of the mouse and the corresponding movement of the on-screen pointer. For example, if your mouse is set at 400 dpi, the pointer moves half as far as the same move with a mouse set at 200 dpi. This works well for detailed work where you need more control, especially if you're using a high-resolution display card with a large monitor to perform computer-aided design (CAD) functions or for art. Some pointing devices advertise much higher resolutions of 1800 dpi, but those higher resolutions are usually a function of the software included with the pointing device.

Most pointing devices come with software that enables you to adjust the relationship between your movement of the pointing device and the cursor on the screen, which is called adjusting the sensitivity of the mouse. Before you can adjust the sensitivity of the mouse, you have to get it connected to your PC. The next section covers connecting your mouse to your PC.

Pointing device connectors

A pointing device, such as a mouse, tends to have either a serial connector or a mini-DIN (also known as the PS/2 mouse connector). Both are shown in Figure 3-6. The PS/2 connector offers attractive benefits but is only practical to use if your system already has the connection for one. The next two sections examine both types of connectors.

PS/2 mouse connector

The PS/2 mouse connector and the PS/2 keyboard connector look similar because they are similar, but the connectors on the back of the PC are not interchangeable. They are, in fact, the same type of mini-DIN connector, and these connectors are often in close proximity to one another, as shown in Figure 3-7. Most computers with similar connectors for the keyboard and the mouse offer a visual or written guide that indicates where each of these components should be plugged in, as shown in the figure, but it is easy to accidentally plug the keyboard into the PS/2 mouse connection, or vice versa.

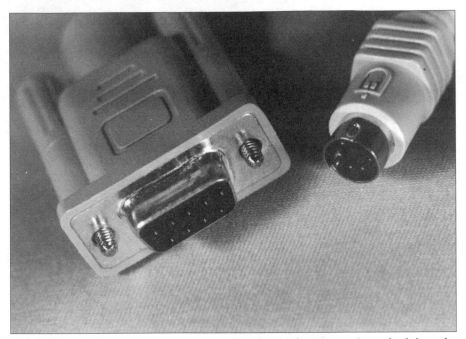

Figure 3-6: Pointing device connectors. The 9-pin serial connector is on the left, and the PS/2 is shown on the right.

If you have a PS/2 mouse and your PC has a PS/2 connector for the keyboard, it is important that you take care to get the keyboard and mouse plugged into the correct connectors. If not, serious and expensive damage can result that may require replacement of the system's motherboard.

Common practice is to refer to the PS/2 mouse connection as a bus mouse connection, though technically this is not correct. A bus mouse is different. It is connected to the PC via a special card that fits into one of the PC's expansion slots. True bus mice are just about nonexistent in newer PCs. The PS/2 mouse connection hardware is controlled by the system's BIOS and is recognized in much the same way as the keyboard is when the PC boots.

The PS/2 mouse connection also offers the advantage of leaving the PC's serial ports free for other devices. The connector on the motherboard or system board of the PC is mounted in a way similar to the mounting of the keyboard connector. Having the PS/2 mouse port on the motherboard can require a special opening in the case that coincides with the connection, just as there's a special opening for the keyboard connection in the case. Having the mouse port on the motherboard also requires a BIOS designed to handle the PS/2 mouse. This means that if you don't already have a PS/2 mouse connection on your PC and you want one, you need to replace the motherboard and probably the case as well. Rather than replace your motherboard, you should consider a serial mouse, which is easier to install than a new motherboard.

Figure 3-7: Note that the PS/2 connectors are identical. The drawing below each connector is the only indication of what goes where.

Mouse/keyboard connection mix-up

An employee in a large company moved his computer. As part of the move, he disconnected his mouse and keyboard. Upon reaching the new location, the employee plugged in the mouse and keyboard, but because both the mouse and keyboard used PS/2 connectors, he got them mixed up. Because everything appeared to fit, the employee assumed all was well and turned on the PC.

Neither the mouse nor keyboard would function, so the employee called the computer repair department. Upon inspection of the system, the repair technician discovered that the mouse and keyboard connectors were mixed up and plugged them in correctly. The mouse worked, but the keyboard still refused to operate. A new keyboard was substituted, but there was still no response.

The technician opened the system and noticed that the keyboard controller chip on the motherboard was burned on the top. This was the problem. Although the technician thought it might be possible to replace the keyboard controller chip, it was more cost-effective to replace the entire motherboard. In addition, with a visible burn on the chip, the technician couldn't be sure that other motherboard components were free from damage.

A simple mix-up of the mouse and keyboard connectors caused a problem serious and expensive enough to warrant replacement of the motherboard.

Serial port connector

Most users know that PCs have both serial and parallel ports. Serial ports are used mainly for communications devices, such as modems, and parallel ports are used mainly for printers. Four serial ports are widely available on PCs, although some PCs only have two. These serial ports are called *COM* ports (for communication), and each one is designated by a number: COM1, COM2, COM3, and COM4. If a PC only has two serial ports, it has COM1 and COM2.

You want to use COM1 or COM2 for your mouse and avoid using COM3 or COM4, especially if you're running any version of Windows. A pointing device is a basic piece of hardware in a graphical environment, and COM1 and COM2 are more stable places for a pointing device connection, as you'll see later in the book when I discuss serial ports. If you're adding a serial pointing device for the first time, or if you're interested in the details on serial ports, see the discussion of serial ports in Chapter 9.

If you don't know much about serial ports and you're replacing your serial pointing device with an upgraded model, don't be too concerned at this point. For the most part, you can simply note where your pointing device plugs in now and plug the new one into the same spot. Usually, this is a 9-pin male serial connection on the back of your PC (see Figure 3-8). Sometimes, you may be fortunate to have this port labeled COM1 or COM2, which makes things easy. But if not, the software that comes with your pointing device, when installed, tests each of the serial ports to find which COM port your pointing device is connected to and sets things up for you. The software should also inform you of the COM port where it found your pointing device.

Don't confuse the monitor port with the serial port. Some examples of serial and monitor port connections can be seen in Figure 3-9. Note that the monitor port is usually female and has its pins in three rows, while the serial port has nine pins in two rows.

Pointing device adapters

You can adapt a pointing device from a PS/2 mouse connector to a serial connector and vice versa by using an adapter designed for that purpose. The most common adapter for these situations has a female 6-pin PS/2 mouse connector on one side and a female 9-pin serial connector on the other (see Figure 3-10). However, some adapters don't work because they're not wired correctly. The product you're buying should indicate if the pointing device works with either a PS/2 or a serial connection, which will indicate it has an appropriately-wired adapter enclosed. Usually you'll find a PS/2 to serial adapter inside.

Check to see if the adapter you need is included in the pointing device package before you purchase a separate adapter.

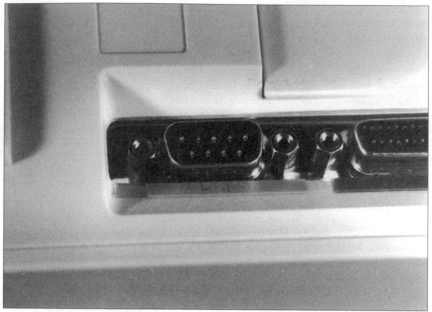

Figure 3-8: A 9-pin male serial port.

Figure 3-9: A 9-pin male serial port and a video port shown side by side. The video (VGA) port has three rows of pins and is female.

You may find that your available serial port on the PC is a 25-pin serial port (see Figure 3-11). Most PCs have both 9-pin and 25-pin serial ports, as the 25-pin port can be used for a modem or a printer. However, you may have another device attached to your 9-pin serial port or, on older PCs, you just may not have a 9-pin serial port. Don't worry. You can easily obtain a 25-pin to 9-pin adapter (also shown in Figure 3-11). Serial ports have become standardized, so serial adapters work without a hitch as long as you have the right male to female connections.

By the way, parallel ports are also 25-pin, following the 25-pin RS-232 standard. RS-232 is simply a standard for 25-pin ports designed to communicate with devices attached to the PC. Although the PC industry is moving toward 9-pin ports (or connections) for serial and 25-pin for parallel, you may find PCs with 25-pin serial and 25-pin parallel ports. How do you tell the difference? Serial ports tend to be male, whether they're 9-pin or 25-pin, and parallel ports tend to be female (see Figure 3-12). Also, look for labels or symbols on the ports that indicate a printer or a serial connection.

If you still have trouble determining your serial port or configuring your software to work with a serial port, see the "Troubleshooting" section in Chapter 9.

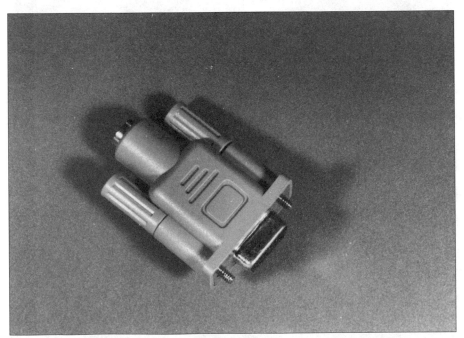

Figure 3-10: An adapter used to make a PS/2 mouse fit into a serial port.

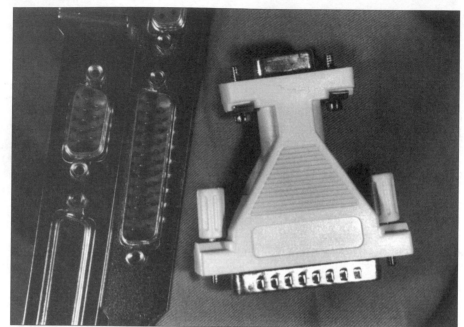

Figure 3-11: Examples of a 9-pin male serial port, a 25-pin male serial port, and an adapter used to make a 9-pin device fit a 25-pin port.

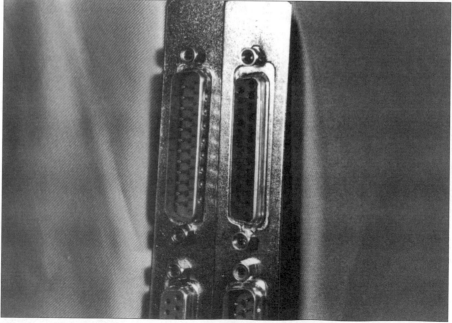

Figure 3-12: Examples of a 25-pin female parallel port and a 25-pin male serial port.

If you're replacing a keyboard or pointing device with a newer model, the easiest way to avoid confusion when connecting is to label the spot where your current keyboard or mouse connects with your PC. Then take your current keyboard or mouse when you shop for an upgrade to ensure that the connectors on the upgrade match the connectors on the old device.

Installation

Installation of a pointing device involves three basic steps: connecting the pointing device to your PC, installing the software, and testing. None of these need take long, but it's important to take precautionary measures first.

Precautionary measures

As you should before any software installation, you need to make a bootable system disk and copy your AUTOEXEC.BAT, CONFIG.SYS, WIN.INI, and SYSTEM.INI files to that disk. This is merely a precaution, but an important one. The boot disk with these important files on it allows you to go back to your original settings in case the software installation is unsuccssful, or worse, in case the installed software causes problems with your system.

If you're running Windows 95, you need to make a Startup Disk and copy to it your AUTOEXEC.BAT, CONFIG.SYS, WIN.INI, SYSTEM.INI, SYSTEM.CB, and SYSTEM.DAT files. These critical files in Windows 95 enable you to go back to your previous settings should the installation produce unexpected results.

When you have copies of these critical files, you can roll back to your previous system configuration should the installation create unexpected problems. (See Chapter 13 for more information about creating a recovery disk and recovering files.)

Connecting the pointing device

Connecting the pointing device should be straightforward, especially if you have an existing pointing device and have gone through the "Preparation" section. If the pointing device is serial, you need to tighten some screws to be sure that the device is making a secure connection. You need a small flat head or Phillips screwdriver, depending on the screws, to perform this step. After the pointing device is connected to your PC, you can proceed to the software portion of the process.

Installing the software

No matter what the pointing device, two characteristics remain the same. One is that the pointing device must have a physical connection to the PC, and the other is that a software driver, also known as the *device driver or driver,* must be present in order to make the device function properly. In addition to the software driver, there may also be software that enables you to adjust the resolution (sensitivity) and make other changes to the operation of the pointing device. This means that the installation of a pointing device is often a two-step process. You have to properly connect the device to the PC, and you may have to install software as well. The software usually installs the device driver (or mouse driver) for you and then allows you to make adjustments to the functions of the mouse.

Most mice (including a number of inexpensive, third-party versions) and other pointing devices are compatible with the Microsoft Mouse software. If you already have a mouse and are upgrading, you might check to see if the new pointing device you want will work with the mouse device driver and software that you already have installed. If you have a choice between the Microsoft Mouse software and generic third-party software, I'd stick with Microsoft unless you have a specialized pointing device such as a touch-type mouse or a pen mouse. You have a better chance of the software working the way you expect it to when it's from from a large, well-known vendor rather than a smaller, lesser-known vendor.

Device drivers included in Windows 3.x and Windows 95

As I mentioned earlier, *device drivers* are special programs designed to talk to the hardware. In the case of pointing devices, these drivers interpret the signals sent by the device to the computer. There's not a whole lot to know about device drivers, but what little there is to know can make the difference between success and failure in getting your pointing device to work.

Under normal circumstances, if you are installing an operating system, such as Windows 3.x or Windows 95, and are upgrading a mouse, the software driver needed for the mouse is included with Windows. Windows recognizes the mouse if it is properly installed before Windows is installed, and if it can't find the mouse, this is an indication the mouse is not installed correctly. If it can find the mouse, Windows then uses its own driver for controlling or "talking to" the mouse.

In most mouse upgrade situations under Windows, the mouse driver is already installed. This could mean all you need to do is connect, and perhaps adjust, the new mouse. For example, if you have the Microsoft Mouse Manager software loaded, you can use it with the Microsoft Ballpoint Mouse, the Intellipoint, and many mice from third-party manufacturers.

Making your pointing device work in DOS applications

The Windows mouse driver only works in Windows and Windows applications. If you exit Windows to work at the DOS prompt or use DOS-based software under Windows, you need to install a separate software driver for your pointing device. However, you don't need to worry. The manufacturers of pointing devices want you to be success-ful, and most provide you with software that sets up your pointing device to work in DOS applications and, if necessary, changes the driver in Windows. You'll find most of this software designed for easy installation and it will allow you to make adjustments to the sensitivity and other characteristics of the pointing device.

When the mouse software for DOS is installed, it adds a line (called a command line) to your AUTOEXEC.BAT file. To display your AUTOEXEC.BAT file, type **TYPE C:\AUTOEXEC.BAT** at the DOS prompt and press Enter. You should see a line that looks something like this:

```
C:\MOUSE\MOUSE.COM
```

The file, MOUSE.COM, is being executed from the MOUSE directory on the C drive. If you look at your AUTOEXEC.BAT file and notice that a mouse driver is not being loaded, check your CONFIG.SYS file. You may have a MOUSE.SYS driver being loaded by the CONFIG.SYS file. If you do, you'll see a line that looks very much like this:

```
DEVICE=C:\MOUSE\MOUSE.SYS
```

Both the MOUSE.COM and the MOUSE.SYS drivers accomplish the same goal: getting a mouse driver loaded to interpret the actions of the pointing device.

For Versions 8.*x* or earlier of its mouse software, Microsoft recommends using the MOUSE.COM driver in the AUTOEXEC.BAT rather than using the MOUSE.SYS driver, which must be loaded from CONFIG.SYS. Using MOUSE.COM provides you with additional flexibility; you can remove or "deallocate" the mouse driver from memory using the command **C:\MOUSE\MOUSE OFF**. You can also load the mouse driver by typing in the command line from the DOS prompt, just as you can any command in the AUTOEXEC.BAT. By the way, Versions 9.0 and higher of the Microsoft mouse software do not include a MOUSE.SYS file.

After the mouse driver is loaded and you've started the computer, you see a message generated by the Microsoft Mouse Manager software driver similar to the following:

```
Microsoft ® Mouse Manager Version 9.01
Copyright (c) Microsoft Corp 1986-1993. All rights reserved.
Mouse driver installed
Serial Mouse enabled on COM1:
```

Note that this message gives you the version of the software as well as notice that the mouse driver has been installed. You also know that the mouse is working because the software reports that it is a serial mouse working or "enabled" on the serial port COM1.

Almost all software drivers allow you to set *switches,* or optional parameters, in the command line itself. For example, if you want the mouse to be loaded without a message on the screen, add a space, a forward slash (/), and the letter Q for quiet. The resulting line looks like this:

```
C:\MOUSE\MOUSE.COM /Q
```

If your mouse driver is being loaded without a message on the screen, this /Q switch is probably present in the AUTOEXEC.BAT. To see all switches available for the mouse software, type the command line, but instead of using slash Q (/Q), use slash question mark (/?). The resulting command line looks like this: **C:\MOUSE\MOUSE.COM /?**. A list of available switches then appears on your screen.

If you install a driver for a pointing device, check your CONFIG.SYS to see if a mouse software driver from a previous pointing device is still being loaded there. These software drivers take up memory, so you don't want any more drivers loaded than you're actually going to use.

Software tools in DOS and Windows 3.1

During the software installation, you are asked to perform tests and make choices about how your pointing device works. This section contains an example of the Microsoft Mouse software in DOS and Windows 3.1.

Microsoft Mouse Manager Version 9.01 software in DOS and Windows 3.1

My Microsoft Mouse Manager software came with my Microsoft Ballpoint Mouse. The software gave me both DOS and Windows 3.1 software, and it loaded a driver into my AUTOEXEC.BAT. After the Microsoft Mouse Manager software was installed, I got the DOS Mouse Manager software started by typing MOUSEMGR and pressing enter at the DOS prompt.

Although the terms described in the Mouse Manager software can be difficult to interpret, they were obvious when I entered Windows and started the Windows version of the Mouse Manager software. After I installed the software, I got to the Windows 3.x Mouse Manager screen by clicking on Main⇨Control Panel⇨Mouse. I found that the Windows interface makes the mouse functions easier to understand and set. A tutorial that came with the software also describes how to set up and install the Microsoft Ballpoint Mouse.

In the Mouse Manger software, I can adjust the mouse sensitivity. Also, I can change the orientation to specify which way is up. That way, if up happens to be a little more to the right than straight up, the mouse still responds the way I want it to. I found that I can also change the buttons on the mouse. If I want to use the mouse with my left hand, I can designate the right mouse button as the primary button. Although this may sound like something a left-handed person may want to do, many right-handed users like to orient the mouse to their left hand. I've done it to spread out the work that my hands and arms do, especially because I answer the phone and write with my right hand.

Software tools in Windows 95

The Microsoft Mouse software included in Windows 95 offers a few nifty animations to make things interesting. To get to the mouse software, click on Start⟳Settings⟳ Control Panel and double-click on Mouse. If you're installing a mouse, click on the General tab, then on Change, as shown in Figure 3-13. If a disk came with the software, you want to click on Have Disk.

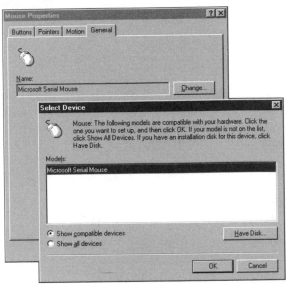

Figure 3-13: The Mouse Properties General menu from Windows 95.

The remaining three menus are shown in Figures 3-14, 3-15, and 3-16. One particularly helpful feature can be found under Button. You have the capability to select the double-click speed for the mouse and then test the setting right in the menu. You set the double-click speed using the slider, then double-click on the animated box in the lower left corner. When you've double-clicked on the correct speed for the setting you've chosen, the jack-in-the-box pops up. You can close the jack-in-the-box by double-clicking on it again.

The beauty of this menu is you can make adjustments, then try them out with the Apply button on the lower right. This means that you don't have to exit the menu to try the adjustment you made, then restart the Mouse Properties to make a change.

Under Pointers, another helpful option is to change the type and size of the Windows pointers. Although fun and interesting pointers are available, on a practical side, you can change to larger pointers. Larger pointers are especially good if you have a vision problem or if you have Windows 95 on a laptop computer. An Apply button enables you to test the settings you've chosen before you leave the menu.

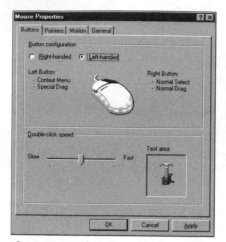

Figure 3-14: The menu for the Buttons tab under the Windows 95 Mouse Properties menu.

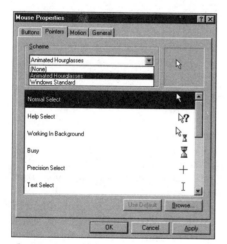

Figure 3-15: The menu for the Pointers tab under the Windows 95 Mouse Properties menu.

The motion tab allows you to set the characteristics of the mouse pointer movement. The sensitivity adjustment is called the *Pointer speed* on this menu, and a slider allows you to adjust how far the mouse pointer on screen moves in relationship to how far you move the pointing device with your hand. The *Show pointer trails* option helps you track with the mouse pointer on your screen as you move it. This helps prevent the "lost mouse" syndrome that happens when you move the mouse pointer and then spend the next few seconds trying to find it on your screen. Note the Apply button here as well.

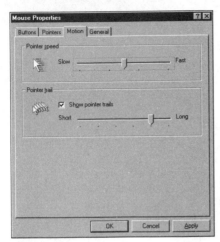

Figure 3-16: The menu for the Motion tab under the Windows 95 Mouse Properties menu.

Alps Glidepoint Keyboard installation under Windows 95

I decided to try a Glidepoint Keyboard from Alps, a specialized combination of a Windows 95 keyboard and a Glidepoint touch pad pointing device (see the following figure). The keyboard came with a cable that had a "Y" split into a PS/2 connector for the keyboard and a serial connector for the mouse. Two adapters were included. One adapter takes the keyboard to a standard 5-pin DIN connection, and the other adapted the serial connector to a PS/2 mouse connector.

I installed the keyboard on a Packard Bell Pentium mini-tower PC with a PS/2 keyboard and a PS/2 mouse connector, so I didn't need either adapter. I shut down the PC, plugged in the Glidepoint keyboard and mouse connectors, and restarted the PC to install the accompanying software.

The software warned me not to have any applications running during the installation. I followed the instructions, which said the software would be installed in Windows 95 and DOS. I had previously created a Startup Disk, so I made sure that I knew where that disk was. I then created a folder named LR (my initials) on the hard disk drive and copied to it my AUTOEXEC.BAT and CONFIG.SYS from the C directory. I then moved to the Windows directory and copied WIN.INI and all SYSTEM files. After the copying was complete, I knew I was covered in case something unexpectedly went wrong.

Following the instructions, I chose Start⇨Run, typed **A:\INSTALL**, and clicked on OK. The installation program opened a DOS window and, after finding the Glidepoint hardware, offered me a choice between express installation and a custom install. The program also informed me that I had backed up my critical system files and offered me an uninstall utility. I chose express install, and the installation was over in a flash. I restarted Windows 95 as instructed and found that the pointer responded to my finger without a hitch. Clicking is accomplished on the Glidepoint by tapping with your finger, or you can use the buttons below the touch pad for mouse button functions.

I exited Windows to a DOS prompt and changed to the GP_KYBD directory, where the DOS version of the software was installed. I ran the TEST program by typing **AMOUSE TEST** and pressing Enter. I typed AMOUSE /? and got a two-page listing of all switches I could set in the mouse software.

In Windows 95, I checked the Control Panel and noted that the installation changed my mouse icon to a paper airplane icon, though the icon still said *mouse*. Everything else was the same. I adjusted the double-click speed so that my index finger's double-tap on the touch pad worked better for me.

The documentation said I could install and uninstall the software as often as I wanted. So, just for grins, I tried the uninstall. I had to repeat the process for the install, but this time I instead chose the custom installation option, which included the uninstall option. The software informed me that it would place REM in front of the lines in the AUTOEXEC.BAT file that loaded the software, and a semicolon in front of the lines it had placed in the WIN.INI and SYSTEM.INI files.

In the AUTOEXEC.BAT and CONFIG.SYS files, REM at the beginning of a line means that the remainder of that line is a remark and is not to be executed by the computer. The semicolon in the .INI files serves the same purpose. I restarted the computer after the uninstall and had my old configuration back, but if I really wanted to uninstall, I would copy everything back from the directory I made with my initials before I started the installation.

One further note — I noticed that the Packard Bell PC on which I installed the Glidepoint software used the Microsoft Mouse driver version 8.02 and loaded the driver MOUSE.SYS in the CONFIG.SYS file. The Glidepoint installation didn't change that. Although the Glidepoint took over, the Microsoft Mouse driver was still loaded each time I restarted the computer. I deleted the DEVICE=C:\MOUSE\MOUSE.SYS line from my CONFIG.SYS to save memory, since deleting the line keeps the driver from being loaded.

Installation in review

Here are the steps for installing a mouse or other pointing device:

1. Make a visual inspection for a PS/2 mouse connector or free serial port. (If a pointing device is currently installed, use its port for the new pointing device, if possible.)

2. Shop for a pointing device. Be sure that the new device has a connector that fits your port.

3. Copy the environment files AUTOEXEC.BAT, CONFIG.SYS, WIN.INI, and SYSTEM.INI. Under Windows 95, copy the SYSTEM.DAT and SYSTEM.CB files, as well. Be sure to have a Rescue disk available.

4. Power down the computer.

5. Connect the new pointing device and disconnect the old pointing device, if you have not already done so.

6. Power up the computer.

7. Install the pointing device software.

8. Test the pointing device.

Troubleshooting

Unlike a keyboard, a working pointing device is not necessary for the computer to boot. However, you can get error messages during the boot up sequence if there's a problem with the pointing device after installation. Because such a wide variety of pointing devices is available, going through the possible error messages for each one is not possible. However, I can list the most common types of problems you're likely to encounter.

Pointing device error messages and possible causes

`Driver Not Installed`: The software driver was not installed, possibly because the pointing device hardware was not found where the software expected it to be located. In addition to this error message, some software drivers say that the hardware device was not found. Check the connections for your pointing device to make sure you correctly connected it to the computer.

This message also can be caused by a conflict with another hardware device. If you have both an internal modem and your mouse software set to COM1, you have a hardware device conflict. A software switch (a way to set parameters) may allow you to change the COM port for the device driver. For example, the Microsoft Mouse uses the /c1 parameter to set the mouse driver to look at COM1 and the /c2 parameter to set the mouse driver to look at COM2. Try the /? parameter to obtain a list of switches that work with your mouse driver. (This is explained earlier in this chapter in the section titled "Making your pointing device work in DOS applications.") More information on troubleshooting serial port conflicts is available in Chapter 9.

You may also look for a conflict between the pointing device driver and another driver loaded during the boot sequence, which can also cause a "device not found" message. You may be loading software in your AUTOEXEC.BAT file that remains in memory, waiting for a keystroke from you to start operation. This is known as a *terminate, but stay resident* (TSR) program. Calendar programs, pop-up address books, and programs that remind you of appointments at a certain time are all TSRs. The pointing device driver needs to load into the computer's memory, but if another program already occupies the location that the pointing device driver was going to use, then the pointing device driver won't work. Try changing the order of the lines in the AUTOEXEC.BAT file and loading the pointing device driver before other TSR software begins. For more information on troubleshooting TSRs and device drive conflicts, see Chapter 13.

`Existing Driver Enabled` or `Existing Driver Installed`: These messages indicate that the pointing device driver was already loaded into the computer's memory, but a second attempt was made to load the driver. When you install an upgrade to your existing mouse or pointing device, the installation software may not be smart enough to remove a previous driver from the AUTOEXEC.BAT or CONFIG.SYS files from the last installation. For information on how to edit your AUTOEXEC.BAT or CONFIG.SYS to get rid of duplicate drivers, see Chapter 13.

Common mistakes checklist

If you're experiencing trouble with your pointing device installation, go through this list of common mistakes.

1. Reversal of the keyboard and mouse when both have PS/2 style connectors.

2. Purchase of a serial mouse to upgrade/replace a PS/2 mouse or vice versa.

3. Attempting to add a serial mouse before checking to see if a serial port is available.

4. Conflicts between two serial devices (mouse and modem, for example). (See Chapter 9.)

5. Mouse software is not installed during boot up, so mouse doesn't work in DOS or in DOS applications.

6. Wrong software or no software for pointing device.

7. Serial pointing device installed to COM3 or COM4, instead of COM1 or COM2.

8. Incorrect software adjustment of the pointing device. (You can't seem to double-click fast enough to get action, or you lose the mouse on the screen.)

Wireless Pointing Devices

Wireless pointing devices (mostly mice) have a device with an infrared or radio frequency transmitter that connects to the serial port. The mouse sends signals to the transmitter, and the transmitter sends the signals through the serial port into the PC.

Preparation

In addition to the preparation you do for a serial mouse, you should keep in mind some issues concerning the placement of the wireless mouse on your work surface. Although some wireless mice require you to have the mouse in the line of sight of the receiver, others, such as the Logitech Cordless Mouse, only require the mouse to be on the same plane. This means that the mouse may not work if you set the receiver on the floor or on top of your monitor while the pointing device is on your desk. The receiver should be on your desk if the mouse is on your desk. If this arrangement won't work for you, then you should consider a corded mouse instead.

Installation

Installation of a wireless mouse should be much the same as the installation of a standard serial mouse. However, the wireless aspect adds a few wrinkles. For example, wireless mice have an operating range of usually 2 to 5 feet from the receiver. You need to keep the mouse in that range. Wireless mice also require battery power. Be sure the batteries are recharged according to the instructions accompanying the mouse.

In addition, the software may add a mode command line to your AUTOEXEC.BAT file that sets the baud rate for the serial port in DOS. The mode command looks something like this:

```
MODE COM1:96,N,8,1,P
```

This statement indicates that the serial port is COM1 and is to operate at 9600 baud. If Windows has a different baud rate set for that serial port, the wireless device may not work. To make sure COM1 is set to 9600 baud in Windows 3.x, go to Main⇨Control Panel⇨Ports⇨Settings.

To check the COM1 baud rate in Windows 95, click Start⇨Control Panel⇨System and click on the Device Manager tab. Scroll down to Ports and double-click to show the available ports. Click on COM1 to highlight it, click on Properties, and select the Port Settings tab to see or modify the baud rate.

After you have the wireless mouse and the software installed, you can test the mouse. This may be a good time to see what the range of the mouse is. Move the mouse to various locations where you think you may want to use it, and give it a try. If you have problems, check the next section for help.

Troubleshooting

The information here is specifically aimed at problems particular to wireless mice. If you have trouble with your wireless mouse, you should look over the troubleshooting sections for installation of a pointing device, in addition to checking the following information.

Wireless mice communicate with the PC in much the same way as modems do, so you may have communications issues to deal with. One of these issues has to do with the use of wireless mice under Windows. If Windows has a lower baud rate for the serial port than the pointing device is expecting, then the device won't work. For example, if Windows has COM2 set at 2400 baud and your wireless mouse is expecting a 9600 baud rate from COM2, you need to adjust Windows so that COM2 is at 9600 baud. Information on baud rates, serial ports, and making these adjustments in Windows is in the serial device troubleshooting section of Chapter 9.

Additional problems can come from other devices you have operating near or around your PC. Radio frequency mice, such as the Logitech Cordless Mouseman, can be hampered by transmitting devices, such as cordless phones, operating in the immediate area. You might try disabling any cordless phones or other radio devices to see if the mouse works, then go from there.

You can attempt to change the mouse's frequency, using the manufacturer's instructions, to see if you can get it to work. However, the receiver and the mouse need to be on the same frequency. If you're not sure that they are, you can reset the frequency to a factory default setting by removing the battery from the Mouseman for a few seconds and then replacing it.

Troubleshooting Practice: What's Wrong in this Photo?

Here's a photo of a common problem situation. See if you can tell what's wrong.

Figure 3-17: See answer.

Answer:

While both connectors are PS/2 type, the keyboard connector should be plugged into the connector with the keyboard symbol. The mouse should be connected to the port with the mouse symbol.

Summary

✦ Keyboards use either 5-pin standard (DIN) connectors or 6-pin PS/2 (mini-DIN) connectors.

✦ Pointing devices use PS/2 mouse connectors or serial connectors.

✦ PCs can be equipped with PS/2 connectors for both mice and keyboards, but these are not interchangeable. If not connected correctly, damage can result.

✦ Adapters are available to connect keyboards and mice with PS/2 connectors and vice versa.

✦ The system BIOS is set to test the keyboard. A keyboard problem can cause a fatal error in the boot cycle.

✦ Pointing devices, whether part of a keyboard combination or installed separately, require software drivers to work in DOS.

✦   ✦   ✦

CHAPTER 4

Installing a Second Floppy Disk Drive or Tape Backup Drive

In This Chapter

+ Installing a second floppy disk drive

+ Testing tips

+ Troubleshooting tips

+ Making your A drive the B drive or vice versa

+ Choosing and installing a tape backup drive

+ Windows 95 tips for tape drives

Tools Needed

+ Phillips screwdriver

+ Needlenose pliers

+ Wrist grounding strap

Nothing inspires bravery like success. I've seen timid souls whose successful floppy disk drive installation gives them lion-like courage to tackle other upgrade tasks on their PCs. After you've been inside and have accomplished something signifi-cant, you will never be the same.

Installing a second floppy disk drive is not only rewarding but also a popular activity, especially among users who like to share data with others. When you have only one type of floppy disk drive on your computer, you can be faced with situations in which you need the other type of drive. This is especially true if you only have a $5^1/4$-inch drive, because so much software is distributed now on $3^1/2$-inch diskettes.

Installing a second floppy disk drive is also a gentle introduction to working on the inside of your PC. Floppy disk drives are not fussy and work without a hitch if installed with relative care. Internal tape backup drives are very similar to floppy disk drives in their installation, but no discussion of internal tape backup drives is complete without including the increasingly popular portable external tape backup models.

Another popular activity is swapping your existing floppy disk drives to make your B drive the A drive, and vice versa. You can also add a tape backup drive as an inexpensive and easy way to ensure that the most difficult part of your PC to replace, your data, is protected.

This chapter introduces you to what to look for before you purchase a second floppy disk drive, how to get your system to accept the drive, how to make the A drive the B drive and vice versa, and installing internal and external tape backup drives and software. You find a "Troubleshooting Practice: What's Wrong in These Photos?" section at the end of the chapter to help you spot and correct common errors.

If you read this chapter before you purchase a floppy disk drive to install, you save yourself one, if not several, trips to the computer store for additional components. You may need small but necessary accessories, and you won't know until you open your PC and take a look inside.

Question: Why is installing an internal tape backup drive in the same chapter with installing a floppy disk drive?

Answer: Installing an internal tape backup drive is much like installing a $5^1/4$-inch floppy disk drive. In fact, many popular internal tape backup drives operate off of the floppy disk controller, with a special cable connecting them to the floppy drive cables. So, it makes sense to talk about installing floppy disk drives along with installing internal tape backup drives because both are so similar. Further, because I'm already talking about tape backup drives, I may as well discuss external and portable drives.

Adding a Second Floppy Disk Drive

The first thing you want to decide before adding a second floppy disk drive is the type of drive you want to add. After you make that decision, I walk you through the steps to install the drive. The next section provides you with the preparation steps necessary before buying and installing a drive.

Preparation

By doing your homework, you can save yourself aggravation, not to mention trips to the computer store. Plus, you get the added benefit of looking very thorough and like you know what you're doing. Following are the preinstallation steps used by the pros.

Determining the type of floppy disk drive to add

Five basic types of floppy disk drives exist, but only two are readily available for purchase. Floppy disk drives are known by their width and height, or *form factor*, and the maximum diskette size available to you.

You sometimes see the term *half-height*, which harkens back to the original full height of floppy disk drives (about $3^{1}/_{2}$ inches). Half-height (about $1^{7}/_{10}$ inches) drives were a big deal back when they were first released because you could fit two drives into the space where formerly only one drive could fit.

As for width, the two most popular widths are $5^{1}/_{4}$-inch (referred to as a *five-and-a-quarter inch)* and $3^{1}/_{2}$-inch (referred to as a *three-and-a-half inch).* Of the two, the $3^{1}/_{2}$-inch drive is the most popular.

Standard diskette sizes

Most standard $5^{1}/_{4}$-inch floppy disk drives use double-sided high-density (2HD) diskettes that have a 1.5MB capacity (see Figure 4-1). The process of formatting the disk so that data can be stored on it reduces the available capacity of each disk to about 1.2MB. The drive can also read and write to lower capacity diskettes, such as the $5^{1}/_{2}$-inch 0.5MB diskettes that, after formatting, provide 360K of available storage space.

Most standard $3^{1}/_{2}$-inch floppy disk drives use double-sided high-density (2HD) diskettes sometimes referred to as *microdisks* to distinguish them from the $5^{1}/_{4}$-inch variety. These microdisks are 2MB before formatting and offer 1.44MB of space after formatting (see Figure 4-1). The $3^{1}/_{2}$-inch drive can read and write smaller capacity diskettes, such as the 1MB $3^{1}/_{2}$-inch diskette, which offers 720MB of available data storage after formatting. A higher capacity diskette, the 4MB diskette (2.88MB after formatting), is also available, but reading it requires a special $3^{1}/_{2}$-inch floppy disk drive. You can expect to pay between $35 and $50 each for standard $5^{1}/_{4}$-inch and $3^{1}/_{2}$-inch floppy disk drive and several times more for a $3^{1}/_{2}$-inch drive that uses the 4MB diskettes.

Floppy disk drives are referred to by both their width and the maximum capacity of the diskettes to which they can read and write. The common vernacular in referring to a $5^{1}/_{4}$-inch form factor drive that can read and write 1.2MB diskettes is *five-and-a-quarter, one-point-two-meg drive.* This is commonly written as $5^{1}/_{4}$ 1.2MB. The $3^{1}/_{2}$-inch drive that can read and write 1.44MB diskettes is commonly referred to as a *three-and-a-half, one-point-four-four-meg drive* and is written $3^{1}/_{2}$ 1.44MB.

Figure 4-1: The 5¹/₄-inch 1.2MB diskette and the 3¹/₂-inch
1.44MB diskette.

TIP

It is common in the PC world to refer to diskettes by their size after formatting. This
can be confusing. For example, the same 3¹/₂-inch 2MB diskette works on both a PC
and a Macintosh. However, in the PC world it is called a 1.44MB double-sided high-
density (2HD) diskette, and in the Mac world it is known as the 1.4MB double-sided
high-density diskette. The difference is because the Mac uses more disk space in
formatting — 0.04MB more.

The five types of floppy disk drives and their capabilities include the following:

✦ 5¹/₄-inch 360K drive can read and write only 360K diskettes.

✦ 5¹/₄-inch 1.2MB drive can read and write 360K and 1.2MB diskettes.

✦ 3¹/₂-inch 720K drive can read and write only 720K diskettes.

✦ 3¹/₂-inch 1.44MB drive can read and write 720K and 1.44MB diskettes.

✦ 3¹/₂-inch 2.88MB drive can read and write 720K, 1.44MB, and 2.88MB diskettes.

Notice that the higher capacity drives can read and write to all diskettes of lower
capacities. Although the 2.88MB drive looked like it might catch on, it never took a
strong hold in the market, and you'd be hard-pressed to find a new one.

Combination diskette drives

An option you have with the two most popular drives is a *combination drive*. Combination units include both the 5¹/₄-inch and the 3¹/₂-inch drive in a single drive the size of
a standard 5¹/₄-inch drive (see Figure 4-2). This combination is especially helpful if you
have no room to add another standard drive. Other interesting combinations are
available as well, including a 3¹/₂-inch, 1.44MB drive combined with a tape backup unit.
There's also a CD-ROM and 3¹/₂-inch, 1.44MB drive combination, but I don't recommend this unit unless you're in dire straits. The CD-ROM drive in these units is slow
compared to a standard CD-ROM drive.

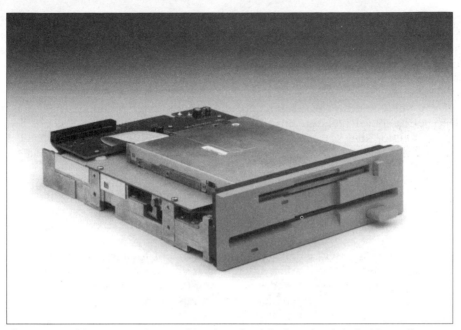

Figure 4-2: This space-saving combination of $5\frac{1}{4}$-inch and $3\frac{1}{2}$-inch drives allows you to add a second floppy drive when space is limited.
(Photo courtesy of Teac.)

When you install a combination unit, you use the same procedure as for installing an individual drive. For example, the instructions for installing a floppy drive and the instructions for installing a tape backup apply to a combination $3\frac{1}{2}$-inch, 1.44MB drive and tape backup drive. Although the economy is mostly in the space savings, you save time because you have to install only one unit.

There's not much monetary economy associated with these combination drives. They cost about the same as buying both units separately. You would purchase a combination drive because you're out of space and want to remove a single drive and replace it with the combination unit.

Checking the BIOS

Before installing a second floppy disk drive, check the computer's BIOS to make sure that your computer will support the floppy disk drive you want to add. I show you how to do that in Chapter 1. Most BIOSs support all floppy disk drives, so you shouldn't have a problem. However, you want to know how your current drive is configured in the CMOS menu where the BIOS settings are displayed, and how you will configure the new drive after you install it.

Entering the CMOS setup

As I explain in Chapter 1, the CMOS is the term used for that area of read-only memory (ROM) that is made up of Complementary Metal Oxide Semiconductor (CMOS) chips known for their low-power consumption characteristics. This is the area of the BIOS where you can make changes so that your PC knows about components you add.

The way you enter the CMOS setup depends on your computer and your BIOS. If you need help on how to get into the CMOS, you can look over the examples here. If you're still not comfortable, you can turn to Chapter 1 and read the information on entering the CMOS.

Be sure you have a copy of the information in your CMOS setup. This copy enables you to go back to your previous settings in case you accidentally change the setup in a detrimental way. If you haven't done so before, now would be a good time to obtain that information. Chapter 1 has the details on how to copy the CMOS setup.

After you enter the CMOS setup menu, you need to look for a menu item or text that says "floppy drive" or "floppy disk drive." This is where you find the option to change the CMOS to support the second drive you want to add. At this point in the installation process, you don't want to change the settings, but you do want to confirm that your CMOS supports the floppy disk drive that you have in mind.

Example CMOS setup menus

Here are two examples of floppy disk drive settings in CMOS setup menus so that you can see the type of thing you're looking for. The first is from an Award BIOS (see Figure 4-3) and shows that a 5¼-inch, 1.2MB drive is installed as Drive A, but no drive is installed as the Drive B drive. To change this CMOS, use the arrow keys to move the highlight down to the field in front of the Drive B field. After you highlight "none," press the minus or plus key on your keyboard to cycle through the list of available drives that the BIOS supports. When you reach the drive you want to install, in this case probably a 3½-inch, 1.44MB drive, you simply leave it in the field and exit the CMOS, saving your changes when you exit.

In this AMI graphical CMOS setup menu, you select the Standard Setup (shown darkened in the background) to get the menu shown in Figure 4-4. From here you select the drive you want to add, either A or B, which brings you a list of diskette drive types supported by the BIOS that you may pick from.

```
                    ROM PCI/ISA BIOS (2A59FT5G)
                       STANDARD CMOS SETUP
                      AWARD SOFTWARE, INC.

   Date (mm:dd:yy) : Mon, Jan 29 1996
   Time (hh:mm:ss) : 13 : 23 : 16

   HARD DISKS         TYPE   SIZE    CYLS HEAD PRECOMP LANDZ SECTOR   MODE

   Primary Master  : Auto     0       0    0      0      0     0     AUTO
   Primary Slave   : Auto     0       0    0      0      0     0     AUTO
   Secondary Master: Auto     0       0    0      0      0     0     AUTO
   Secondary Slave : Auto     0       0    0      0      0     0     AUTO

   Drive A : 1.2M , 5.25 in.
   Drive B : None
                                         Base Memory:     640K
   Video   : EGA/VGA                 Extended Memory: 19456K
   Halt On : All Errors                 Other Memory:    384K

                                      Total Memory: 20480K

   ESC : Quit             ↑ ↓ → ←  : Select Item    PU/PD/+/− : Modify
   F1  : Help          (Shift)F2 : Change Color
```

Figure 4-3: This Award Software CMOS setup menu has a $5^1/_4$-inch drive designated as Drive A and no B drive.

Figure 4-4: This AMI graphical CMOS setup menu presents you with icons that you can select to get a pick list of diskette drive types supported by the BIOS.

Checking the case

After you've looked at your CMOS setup, noted your current floppy drive settings, and determined that your system will support a second floppy disk drive, you should take a look at your case. You want to determine if there's room for this second drive, and inspecting the case helps you determine what accessories you may need to purchase.

Looking for free bay space on the outside

You first want to examine the outside of your case for unused drive bays. As you can see in Figure 4-5, the computer has covers over two $5^1/_4$-inch size drive bays and one $3^1/_2$-inch drive bay. This means that there's room on the front of the PC for a second drive of either form factor.

Looking for an open drive bay inside

Now that you've checked the outside of the case, remove the cover from the PC and take a look inside. Free drive openings on the outside don't necessarily mean that you have space on the inside. A hard disk drive could be taking up the drive bay behind the cover, as shown by the computer in Figure 4-6.

Figure 4-5: The covers over the drive bays indicate room for a second floppy disk drive.
(Photo courtesy of Micro Express)

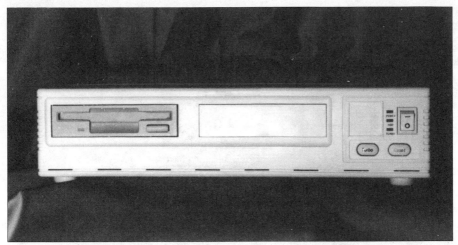

Figure 4-6: A hard disk drive is behind the plastic cover of an unused external opening in this computer's case.

Height is a factor here. You need at least a half-height (just under 1.7 inches) of open space to install a floppy disk drive. It doesn't matter if the fit is tight because drives can be stacked very closely, one on top of the other, but a minimum amount of space is needed. Designers of PC cases know how much space you need and have designed the openings to these industry-standard sizes.

The best possible scenario is when the unused opening on the outside of the case and the unused drive bay inside are both the size of the floppy disk drive you want to add. For example, if you're planning to add a $3^1/_2$-inch drive, you want a $3^1/_2$-inch opening on the outside and a $3^1/_2$-inch drive bay available inside. However, you may find that you have a $^1/_4$-inch opening and a $5^1/_4$-inch drive bay available for your $3^1/_2$-inch addition. This is not a problem, because you can buy an inexpensive kit to adapt the $3^1/_2$-inch drive to fit the $5^1/_4$-inch opening and a faceplate (or bezel) to cover the extra space around the drive on the outside of the case.

One more thing to look at is how your existing drive is mounted. Some cases require plastic or metal rails to be screwed to the sides of the drive, and then the drive is guided into the bay and held up by these mounting rails (see Figure 4-7). Other cases have holes in the sides of the drive bay that you can use for mounting the drive directly to the case using screws (see Figure 4-8). No screw holes is a lead-pipe cinch that you need those mounting rails. The rails are easy to come by and are inexpensive — ask for them when you purchase your floppy disk drive. Some drive mounting kits have both the adapters and the mounting rails needed to mount a $3^1/_2$-inch drive in a $5^1/_4$-inch bay.

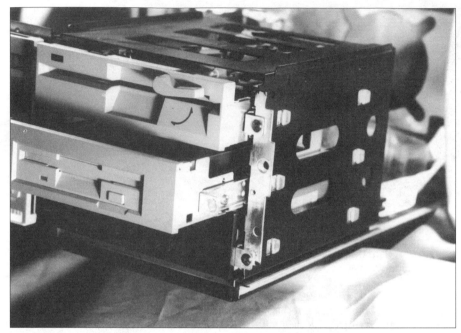

Figure 4-7: This $3^1/_2$-inch drive has been placed in an adapter to fit the larger $5^1/_4$-inch drive bay and is held in place by metal mounting rails on each side.

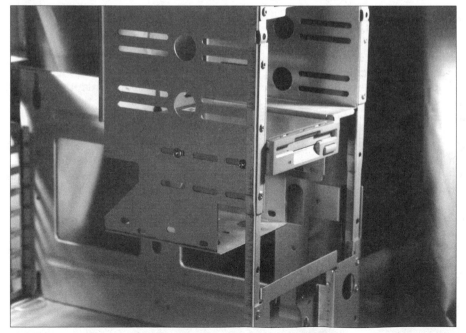

Figure 4-8: This $3^1/_2$-inch drive is held in the drive bay by screws.

Power tools and PCs generally don't mix. I know people who've drilled holes in the drive bay when all they needed were the plastic rails. Not only is a power drill inappropriate, but drilling holes may not work because the screws designed for mounting are so short. Nix the power tools, except maybe a cordless screwdriver, of course.

Checking the floppy drive cable

The next step in checking the case is to check the flat ribbon cable that goes from the controller card to your floppy disk drive. If your BIOS supports two floppy disk drives, they both are connected to the controller card by a single cable with three connectors — one that goes to the controller card and two on the other end for the two floppy disk drives (see Figure 4-9).

If you have a single floppy disk drive, chances are that you have a cable with just two connectors, one on either end, for the controller card and for the disk drive. If this is the case, you need to add a new floppy drive cable to your shopping list. The type of cable you get depends on the type of connector you have on your existing drive.

There has been a transition in floppy disk drives from a 34-pin edge connector to a 34-pin male connector (see Figure 4-10). These connectors perform the same function, but you need to look at your floppy disk drive to determine which one you have in order to purchase the correct cable. New floppy drives have gone exclusively to the 34-pin male connector, but your existing drive may have either one.

If you have a 34-pin male connector on your existing drive, you need to get a floppy drive cable with three 34-pin female connectors. One connector goes to the controller card, and the other two connectors are close together on the other end to be attached to the floppy disk drives.

If you have an edge connector, you have two ways to go. You can get a cable that has five connectors so that you can accommodate two drives with either type of connector, such as the one shown in Figure 4-9. (These cables are not meant to connect four floppy disk drives, however.) You may also purchase an edge-to-male adapter to adapt the drive so that it works with a 34-pin female connector, as shown in Figure 4-11. Be sure to get a floppy drive cable with a twist in it, as shown in the figure, so that you can correctly connect the drives. Either one works, so it's a matter of what is available when you purchase your drive.

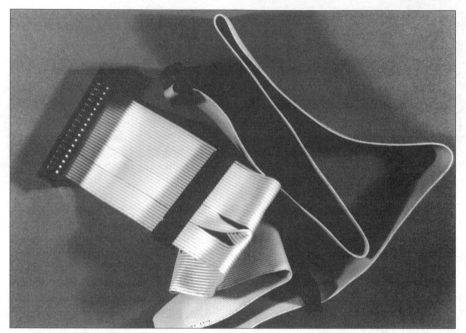

Figure 4-9: This floppy drive cable supports two floppy disk drives with either 34-pin or edge connectors. You want a cable with a twist in it, as shown.

Figure 4-10: Shown is a floppy disk drive with an edge connector.

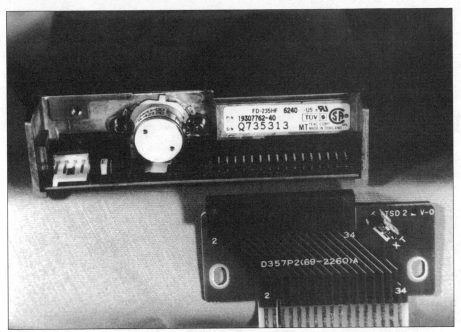

Figure 4-11: Shown is a floppy disk drive with a 34-pin male connector. An adapter to make a 34-pin male connector into an edge connector is also shown.

Checking for an unused power supply cable

You now need to check the power supply cable. Look for an unused power cable connection (called a *Molex connector*) from your power supply. Notice that there are large and small power supply connectors. The smaller type of connector is the more recent type, and you're most likely to find it on a new floppy disk drive. Your power supply may have both types of connectors available. If not, you can get an adapter (see Figure 4-12) that makes the larger connectors from your power supply fit the smaller connection on your floppy disk drive.

If all the power supply cables are in use, meaning each one is connected to a drive of some type, you can still add a second floppy disk drive. You can purchase an adapter that splits a single connector into two connectors.

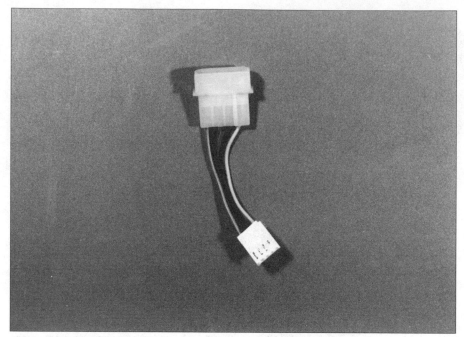

Figure 4-12: Power supply connectors come in large and small sizes. Shown is an adapter to take a large connector to the smaller-size connector.

Purchase checklist

After you look over your system, you can make your checklist of items to purchase, along with the floppy disk drive you want to add. Here's a checklist that helps you remember what you need. You definitely need

1. A floppy disk drive

2. A flat ribbon 34-pin cable with three connectors

You also may need

3. An adapter to convert a 34-pin edge connector to a 34-pin male connector

4. A faceplate

5. A mounting kit

6. An adapter to take a Molex power supply plug to smaller size

7. A splitter for power supply cable

8. A disk with data on it to test the new drive

If you're purchasing a floppy drive installation kit (especially if it's a $3^1/_2$-inch drive), the adapters, faceplate, and mounting kit that you need may already be included.

Installation

After you gather all your parts, it's time to mount your new drive into the case. Mounting the drive is a two-step process. First, you test the new drive outside the case to make sure it works. Second, you mount the drive in the case and test it again.

Pros always test any new floppy disk drive outside the case. If it works, they then mount it into the case. Components tend to be tested very little before they're sold because it's simply cheaper for manufacturers to replace a component than to pay someone to test it. Testing the drive is important because you don't want to go through the trouble of mounting the drive in the case, only to find that it doesn't work.

Testing also eliminates variables should you run into problems. If the drive works outside the case but doesn't work when you mount it, then you probably just forgot to connect something.

The first step is to open your computer case (be sure the power is off) and take a careful look inside. Note where the cable from the floppy disk drive connects to the controller card. If the current cable already has a second connector on it, you won't need to disconnect it from the controller card.

Connecting the cable to the floppy disk controller card

If you need to replace the cable, disconnect it from the controller card and from the floppy disk drive. Before you connect the new cable to the controller card, note the red stripe or other marking on one side of the cable. That marking indicates pin 1. If you look on the controller card to which the floppy disk drive is connected, you see *FDD* or the word *floppy* silk-screened on the card near the floppy drive connection. A small 1 is marked on one side of the pins jutting out from the card. This indicates pin 1. To connect the cable, make sure pin 1 on the cable (the side of the cable that's marked) lines up with pin 1 on the controller card connection.

As you can see in Figure 4-13, the controller card usually has other cables connected to it as well. (Note that each cable connection has the number 1, which indicates pin 1.) This card is called a *multi-I/O card* (multiple input/output) and saves space in the PC by allowing one expansion slot to control several devices.

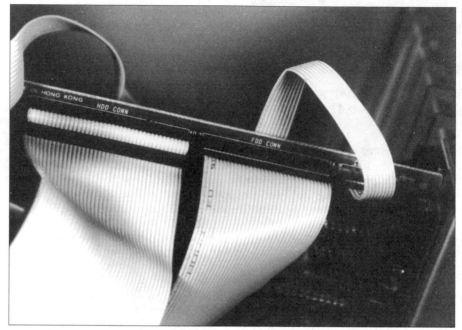

Figure 4-13: The floppy drive connection on a multi-I/O card.

 Avoid disconnecting and connecting any cable, except the one you're working with, which in this case is the floppy drive cable. If you haven't spent much time inside a PC, it's easy to disconnect stuff and then not remember where it all goes.

Connecting the cable to the floppy disk drives

For the floppy disk drive, you want the drive designated as drive B to be connected midway in the cable and the drive designated as drive A to be connected at the end of the cable. Look at Figure 4-14. The $3^1/_2$-inch drive connected at the bottom is the A drive, and the $5^1/_4$-inch drive on the top is the B drive.

 Even in well-lit rooms, it can be difficult seeing well enough to be sure you're connecting these cables correctly. Take a tip from the pros and keep a flashlight handy rather than fumble around when visibility is limited.

You may be wondering how you're going to connect the new drive without installing it in the case, especially if your cable is short. Consider setting the drive on top of the PC's drive bays for testing. You may also be able to set the drive into the bay without fastening it to the case, depending on the design of your computer case.

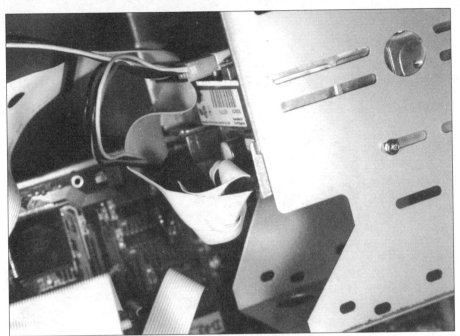

Figure 4-14: The floppy disk drive that's first in the cable from the controller card is the B drive, and the last drive on the cable is the A drive.

When you connect the ribbon cable to your floppy disk drive, be sure to connect the marked or striped side of the cable that indicates pin 1 to the pin 1 connection on the floppy disk drive. (If you're connecting to a 34-pin edge connector with a cable that supports it, this isn't a problem because the edge connector has a notch and can be connected only to the cable one way.) Pin 1 on the floppy disk drive is on the side of the 34-pin male connector nearest the power supply connection. However, you can verify the position of pin 1 on some drives. Turn the drive over and look for the silk-screened 1 on the circuit board on the bottom of the drive (see Figure 4-15).

Connecting the power supply to the new drive

Connecting the power supply to the drive is a straightforward operation because the power supply connector connects only one way. If you need to adapt the larger Molex connector to the smaller power supply connector, now is the time.

TIP

If you need to use a splitter to split a power supply cable, be sure to split the cable going to the other floppy drive and not the one going to your hard disk drive. Because you won't be using the two floppy drives at exactly the same time, you won't endanger the read or write data capability to the other floppy disk drive. However, your hard disk drive is a different story because it spins continuously while the computer is on, so splitting the power may make your hard disk drive lose power when it needs it. This could cause data loss.

Figure 4-15: Pin 1 is indicated on the floppy disk drive and is usually also indicated by the side the power supply connection is on.

Telling the BIOS about the new drive

After the drive is connected, you need to restart the PC, enter the CMOS setup, and tell the BIOS about the new drive. For example, if you're installing a 1.2MB 5¼-inch drive as drive B, you enter the BIOS setup, go to the floppy drives description, and change the floppy drive B setting to a 1.2MB 5¼-inch drive.

When you exit the BIOS, the computer starts the boot process again and attempts to find both your new drive and your existing drive. If you've watched your computer boot, as I recommend in Chapter 1, then you know that it attempts to access each drive before emitting a single beep to indicate that all is well. If you don't get the single beep, don't panic. It's easy to forget to connect something. Recheck your connections to the drive, power supply, and controller card. Photos of common errors that you can look for are found near the end of this chapter, so check them to see if you made one of those mistakes. If you did, then simply correct the mistake. A troubleshooting section can also be found at the end of this chapter.

Testing the floppy drives

If the computer boots and you don't get an error, you still need to test both floppy disk drives to make sure everything works. The easiest way to test is to try to access the drives. Place a disk that has data on it into each of the drives. (The data on the disk doesn't matter, just as long as something is there.) From a DOS prompt, type **DIR A:** to test the A drive, then **DIR B:** to test the B drive. If you receive a directory of the disk in each drive, then the drives are probably connected properly. Try to copy a file from the hard disk drive to the A drive using this command: **COPY C:\AUTOEXEC.BAT A:**. Then type **TYPE A:\AUTOEXEC.BAT** to display the file on the screen. Type the same commands for the B: drive, substituting B:\ for A:\ in each of the commands. If all these tests work, then you're ready to install the drive in the case.

If you get a drive seek error, the ribbon cable is probably incorrectly attached to either the controller card or the drive. Go back and check your cabling connections at each end. Make sure that you have pin 1 on the cable connected to pin 1 on both the controller card and the floppy disk drive. You sometimes have to press hard on the cable to get it to fit securely to the drive or controller card. If the pins weren't exactly straight to begin with, or if you're working in shadows where it's tough to see detail, you sometimes can accidentally bend one or more pins away from the connection so that they stick out where you can't see them. Look carefully at the connection. It should look like the one shown in Figure 4-16. You should not be able to see any part of the gold pins sticking out underneath or around the connection.

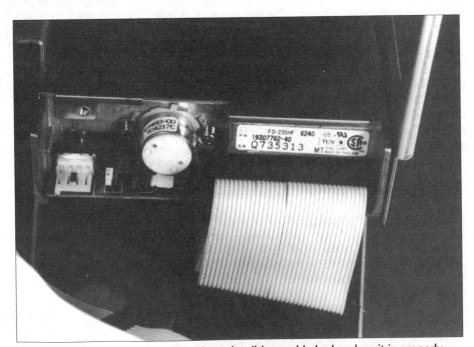

Figure 4-16: Here's an example of how the ribbon cable looks when it is properly connected to the floppy disk drive. Note that no pins are visible.

Sometimes, the only way to see if everything is connected correctly is to disconnect the cable, examine the pins, and then reconnect it. If pins are bent, carefully straighten them with needlenose pliers before you reconnect the cable. The common mistakes checklist and the "Troubleshooting Practice: What's Wrong in These Photos?" sections in this chapter are designed to help you see where the problem is.

Installing the new drive in the case

If the new drive works outside the computer case, and the existing drive works as well, then it's time to place the new drive into the case. Following the instructions earlier in the chapter, you've already checked the case and the drive bays to see where the new drive will go, so now you should be able to execute the plans you've made. You probably have to disconnect the cables to the drive to mount it in the case, so you want to note how you connected the cables so that you can reattach them after the drive is mounted.

There are several variations on drive bays, depending on the computer case. Three basic variations exist: drive bays in both $3^1/_2$-inch and $5^1/_4$-inch sizes, drive bays in only the $5^1/_4$-inch size, and drive bays that require mounting rails. You need to determine if the drive inserts from the front of the case or if it slides in from the back of the case. If the drive inserts from the front, you may have to take off the front of the case or remove the plastic cover over the drive bay, especially if you have a mini-tower case. If the drive already has mounting rails, you probably need to install the drive from the front of the case. You determine how the new drive should be inserted by looking at how the existing drive is inserted and by experimentation. You may have to try the drive a couple of different ways in the case before you get it right, especially if you're using drive rails to mount it. One thing to note is that the new drive should not stick out past the old drive.

If your case has drive bays that are the same size as the drive you're installing, then you have an easy installation on your hands. Slide the drive in, either from the back or from the front, depending on the design of your case. There are already holes in the sides of the bay and threaded screw holes in the sides of the drive, but there may be several sets of holes in both the drive and the bay. You need to experiment with the drive by holding it in the case and moving it forward and back until the drive is even with your existing drive in the front of the case and the screw holes line up. You then simply put the screws in place to hold the drive.

If you're attaching mounting rails or an adapter to adapt a $3^1/_2$-inch drive to fit in a $5^1/_4$-inch bay, you need to pay a little more attention. You probably have a couple choices of threaded screw slots on the drive, and the set you choose can effect how far forward or back the drive fits in the drive bay. You may need to experiment by attaching the adapter or drive mounting rails a couple different ways until the floppy disk drive lines up with the existing drive. You neither want the new drive too far in nor so far out that it juts past the front of the case. After you have the drive mounted in the drive bay, reattach the ribbon cable and the power cables.

If you're installing a 3¹/₂-inch drive into a 5¹/₄-inch bay, you also need a faceplate. The faceplate usually snaps onto the front of the drive after you mount the adapter kit, but before you slide it into the case.

After the cables are attached, you want to move the ribbon cable so that it doesn't block the air holes to the power supply and doesn't lie across the CPU. A ribbon cable lying across the CPU can pick up heat from the processor and eventually malfunction due to the heat. The cable can also block the air flow to the processor needed for cooling. In addition, you want to make sure that the cables are out of the way so that they don't pull loose when you put the top on the case. This is more of a problem in desktop cases where the case screws attach to tabs sticking down from the top of the case.

Before you close up the case, you want to restart the PC and test the drives. Be sure you haven't left any loose screws or tools inside the unit before you restart the PC.

When you restart your PC, see if the computer appears to recognize the drive during the boot sequence. If the drive's light goes on and it spins, this is a good sign. To confirm that the new drive works, you need to attempt to access a diskette placed in the drive. One way to do this is to place a diskette with data on it in the new drive, go to the DOS prompt, and execute the directory command by typing DIR, a space, the drive letter with a colon, and press Enter. For example, if you were testing the B drive, you'd type **DIR B:** and press Enter. If the drive is working, the files and/or directories on the diskette will be displayed on your screen. If you have problems, check the troubleshooting section.

You can get the computer to boot quickly to the DOS prompt by pressing F5 when the `Starting MS-DOS` message appears under DOS/Windows. To go directly to the DOS prompt under Windows 95, hold down the Shift key and press F5 (Shift + F5) when you see the `Starting Windows 95` message.

The final installation step may be removing the plastic cover over the drive bay opening on the outside of the case, depending on how your case is designed. (You may already have performed this step to get the drive into the case.) Some covers snap off when you apply pressure, while others require you to remove screws. You need to look at your cover. But, as I mention earlier, whether or not you need to perform this step at this stage depends on the design of your case.

Burning in the new drive

You're feeling good. You've installed your floppy drive and it works. But remember what I said earlier about components not being tested much by the manufacturers. If you want to be safe, you should perform a *burn-in* of the new drive. You don't want to wear out the drive testing it, but software is available that allows you to read and write to the drive for a time interval that you set. An hour or two with a floppy disk drive should be enough.

There are a couple of reasons for performing a burn-in as soon as possible after the installation. You probably received a 30-day warranty on the drive, so if it's going to fail, you want it to fail during that 30 day period. Also, finding failures within a day or two of installation is easier on you because the installation procedure is still fresh in your mind.

Most PC diagnostic software packages, such as Norton Utilities and Check It, offer burn-in utilities that enable you to select the component to burn in. There's also shareware available for performing a burn-in called *Burn-In* from OsoSoft of Los Osos, California. (See the Appendix for diagnostic software vendor contact information.) You can also use a backup program and work the drive doing an extensive backup and comparison. The beauty of a burn-in utility is that it can be used unattended, which means it works overnight or when you're away. If a problem occurs, the utility logs it, and you can look at the log when you return. The log gives you something to print out and take with you, should you feel you need it, when you return the drive.

Installation in review

To add a second floppy disk drive, follow these steps:

1. Check the BIOS.

2. Check the outside of the case for an open bay.

3. Check the inside of the case for free space.

4. Check the floppy drive cable to be sure it will connect two floppy drives. Get a new cable if necessary.

5. Check for free power supply cable. Get a splitter for the power cable, if necessary.

6. Obtain the drive and any adapters necessary for making the drive fit into the drive bay.

7. Connect the power supply and floppy drive cables. Make sure that the original floppy drive is correctly connected to the cable as well.

8. Start the computer, enter the setup (BIOS), and change the CMOS settings to reflect the presence of the new drive.

9. Test the drive.

10. Now that you know the drive works, power down the computer and place the drive into the drive bay. Connect any adapters and the screws, and reconnect the ribbon cable and the power supply cable.

11. Test the drive one more time to make sure everything works before closing up the computer case. Then power down the computer and close it up.

12. Burn in the new drive for a couple of hours (optional).

Troubleshooting

If you have a problem installing your floppy disk drive, it should show up during one of the testing phases in the installation. Some of these are error messages you may see from your PC. Here are the most common problems and how to fix them.

1. `Diskette Drive Failure`: This means the BIOS could not find one or both of the floppy disk drives during the boot sequence. This can happen if the drive either does not have power or is incorrectly cabled. Check the ribbon cable connection at the drive and at the controller card. Be sure the ribbon cable is connected so that you cannot see any pins and so the striped side is on the same side as pin 1 on the controller and on the floppy disk drive. (Remember that pin 1 on the floppy disk drive is usually on the same side as the power connection.) Also check to be sure the power cables are connected.

   You may need to disconnect the ribbon cable and look for bent pins. It's also easy, especially if the light is low, to connect the ribbon cable to only the upper half of the pins, so be sure all pins are going into the ribbon cable connection. If you find bent pins, straighten them gently with needlenose pliers.

2. `Diskette Drive A Failure`: This means that the BIOS is specifically listing the floppy drive with the problem. Look for the same problems as those listed under item 1, but you can limit your search to the drive that the BIOS specified.

3. `Seek Error Reading Drive A`: See the troubleshooting tips under item 1.

4. `Diskette Read Fail`: This message probably appears when you reboot the computer or when you execute the DIR command on a disk in the drive. This message occurs if the diskette in the floppy disk drive is not bootable. To eliminate the error message, remove the disk from the drive and reboot the computer. (Depending on the BIOS, you may be able to press a key to continue the boot sequence.)

   If the message appears when you attempt to read a diskette in the drive, then the diskette is not formatted. Format the disk or place a formatted diskette in the drive and try again.

5. `Non-bootable Disk in Drive`: See the troubleshooting information under item 4.

6. `Invalid Configuration Information`: The information about your configuration that the BIOS contains is not the same information it received during the boot sequence tests. This happens when the ribbon cable is installed backwards on either the floppy drive or the controller card. See also the troubleshooting information under item 1. You may also have entered the wrong drive type in the CMOS menu, so you'll want to check that as well.

7. `This Disk Cannot Be Formatted`: The information in the BIOS about the drive does not match the information that the drive is sending about itself. This usually means that you have the wrong drive type specified in the BIOS; for example, selecting a 3¹/₂-inch, 720K drive in the CMOS setup menu when you actually have a 3¹/₂-inch, 1.44MB drive installed. Check to be sure that the type of drive you selected in the CMOS is the same type you installed.

TIP If the message says to proceed with format and you enter **Y** for yes, you get a message saying at what capacity the diskette is being formatted. If the diskette is being formatted at 720K, that may be your tip that in the CMOS setup you have the drive set to 720K instead of 1.44MB.

8. `Parameters Not Supported By Drive`: This message, or one like it, indicates that your drives may be mixed up in the CMOS setup menu. If you set the A drive to be a 5$\frac{1}{2}$-inch, 1.2MB drive, and it is actually a 3$\frac{1}{2}$-inch, 1.44MB drive, you get this error message when you attempt to format a diskette. This type of error is common when switching drives, so the A is the B and the B is the A. To fix the problem, re-enter the CMOS setup and correct the settings.

Swapping Your Floppy Drives (So the B is the A)

If you're adding a second floppy disk drive, these days it's best to make the 3$\frac{1}{2}$inch drive the A drive. These diskettes are more durable due to their more rigid plastic housing, and they don't require sleeves. Most software now is distributed on 3$\frac{1}{2}$-inch diskettes as well, including software to bring your PC back from the brink of disaster.

But even if you have a reason to make the 5$\frac{1}{4}$-inch drive the A drive and the 3$\frac{1}{2}$-inch drive the B drive, how to swap the floppy drives is a question I'm frequently asked. Fortunately, swapping floppies so the B is the A and vice versa is easy.

Looking for swap floppies in the CMOS setup

Swapping floppies is such a common practice that some BIOS manufacturers have made it an option in their more recent CMOS setup menus. So, you want to find out if your BIOS has a swap floppies function. You may have to look through several menus in the CMOS setup menu to find it. Here's an example of a Phoenix BIOS and how the swap floppy function can be used.

On page three of this CMOS setup menu, you have the `Swap Floppies` option, as shown in Figure 4-17. The general setting for this field is `Normal`, but when you press the minus or plus sign key on the keyboard, you can change it to `Swapped`. For example, if your 5$\frac{1}{4}$-inch drive is the A drive and the 3$\frac{1}{2}$-inch drive is the B drive, setting this field to `Swapped` would make the 3$\frac{1}{2}$-inch drive the A and the 5$\frac{1}{4}$-inch drive the B. Be sure to save your settings when you exit the CMOS setup menu.

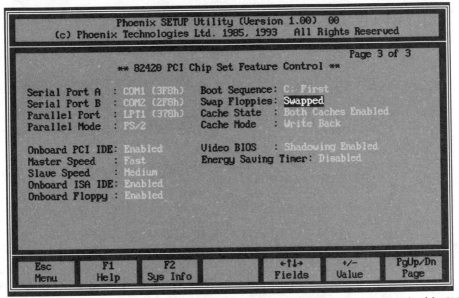

Figure 4-17: A press of the minus key changed this `Swap Floppies` setting in this CMOS setup menu from `Normal` to `Swapped`.

What to do if there's no CMOS swap function

If your BIOS doesn't have a swap floppies function in the CMOS setup, you can still swap them. It's just going to take an extra couple steps.

First, you need to enter the CMOS setup and change the floppy disk drives settings to the settings you want. For example, if I have a 5^1/$_4$-inch, 1.2 MB drive as A and a 3 ^{1}/$_2$-inch, 1.44MB drive as B, then enter the CMOS setup and switch the settings. So in the CMOS setup menu, I'd simply change the A to the 3^1/$_2$-inch, 1.44MB drive and the B to the 5^1/$_4$-inch, 1.2 MB drive. For examples of CMOS setup menus, take a look at the section entitled "Telling the BIOS about the new drive" under Installation earlier in this chapter.

Once the BIOS is changed, you need to disconnect and switch one end of the flat ribbon cable inside the case. Power down the PC and open the case. Note the position of the ribbon cable that goes to the floppy disk drives, particularly to which drive the end of the cable is connected. If the end of the cable is connected to the 5^1/$_4$-inch drive, disconnect the end and reconnect it to the 3^1/$_2$-inch drive. Now connect the 5^1/$_4$-inch drive to the connector midway through the cable. Don't disconnect the power cables to the drives, and don't disconnect the ribbon cable from the controller card. Concentrate just on switching the cabling on the floppy disk drives. When reconnecting the ribbon cable, be sure that the side of the cable with the stripe indicating pin 1 is on the side nearest the power supply connection.

Leave the computer case open and power up the PC. Test the drives. The B drive should now be the A drive, and the A drive should be the B drive. If you have a problem, check the troubleshooting steps in the previous section. To be doubly sure that you set up the drives correctly in the CMOS setup menu, format a disk in each drive. If you have problems formatting a disk, go to the "Troubleshooting" section under installing a second floppy disk drive and check items 7 and 8.

You may want to move the drives so that the A drive is above the B drive in the case, but this is not necessary. If you do decide to move the drives, follow the instructions for installing a floppy disk drive earlier in this chapter.

After you've tested the drives and are sure they're working, close up the case and give yourself a pat on the back.

Adding an Internal Tape Backup Drive

Adding a tape backup drive is even easier than adding a floppy disk drive. Most tape backup drives work off the floppy drive controller, and the internal models are installed in much the same way that floppy disk drives are. After you've installed the drive, install the accompanying software and you're off to the races.

Tape drives are relatively inexpensive. Depending on the capacity of the drive, you're looking at between $100 and $400.

Preparation

Internal tape backup drives come in both $5^1/_4$-inch and $3^1/_2$-inch form factors, so you need a free drive bay. As you remember from earlier in this chapter, you can adapt a $3^1/_2$-inch drive to a $^1/_4$-inch drive bay, and you find that many $3^1/_2$-inch tape drives already have the necessary adapter included in the package. The first step, then, is to check for an available drive bay. Next, determine if you need any components. Finally, install and test the drive.

Checking the case for a free drive bay

To examine your PC for an available drive bay, you want to go through the same physical inspection process of the drive bays both inside and outside your PC as you do for installing a floppy disk drive. Tape backup drives are available in both $3^1/_2$ inch and $5^1/_4$-inch sizes, but you can count on needing a half-height drive bay to install most of these drives.

TIP

Remember, an apparent free drive bay on the outside of the case doesn't mean that the corresponding space inside is free. You need to check inside to be sure that space isn't taken up by a hard disk drive.

Checking for an unused power supply cable

If you purchase the type of internal tape backup drive that uses the floppy disk drive controller, it should come with a cable to connect it and the floppy disk drive. This means that you don't have to worry about floppy disk drive cabling issues like you do when you add a second floppy disk drive. You want to make sure a power supply cable is free; if not, you can place a splitter off one of the floppy drives to supply power to the tape backup. You cannot use the floppy disk drives while your tape backup is working, but that's not usually a problem because most people want the tape backup to run while they're away from their computer (such as overnight). Just be sure that you do not split the power for the tape backup off the power cable that goes to the hard disk drive. The hard disk drive requires a constant power level because it spins continually while the computer is turned on.

Installation

Now that you've finished your preparation, you can install your internal tape backup drive. Installing these drives is similar to installing floppy drives. Like a floppy disk drive, you want to connect the backup drive to the floppy disk controller and to the power supply. Before you go through the time and effort of mounting the drive inside the case, test it outside to determine if it is working. In order to test tape backup drives, you need to install its accompanying software, which is covered in the next section.

Some tape backup drives work off their own controller card. The advantages of these drives are that they can be up to twice as fast at performing backups as their floppy controller-connected counterparts. In addition, the software that comes with the controller card configures it to your system.

However, the disadvantages to you are the extra time and expense involved in installing another card in the system, and the fact that you must have an unused place on the motherboard (known as a *free expansion slot*) inside the PC to plug in another card.

For most users, installing an internal tape backup drive that works off the floppy disk drive controller is simply easier and cheaper, so this is what I've covered in this chapter. If you decide that this is what you want to do, you can still get help here. Chapter 8 will help you with installation of the controller card, and you can get help with the actual installation of the tape drive here. If you decide to go this route, read on, paying special attention to how the drive is installed in the case. Then, turn to Chapter 8 for help with installing a separate controller card.

Connecting the tape drive

After you've purchased your tape drive, it's time to connect it to the PC. Tape drives designed to use the existing floppy drive controller come with a special ribbon cable. The ribbon cable connects directly to the floppy drive controller using a special connector, called a *pickoff*, that connects to the 34-pin floppy drive cable. Just like connecting a floppy disk drive, the ribbon cable has a stripe or other marking that indicates the side of the cable for pin 1. This side should line up with pin 1 on the controller card and with pin 1 on the tape drive. (See Figure 4-13 in the "Connecting the cable to the floppy disk controller card" section earlier in this chapter.) Instructions come with the tape drive, and you should look them over. Read the case study of a tape drive installation for an idea of what to expect.

Installation of a Colorado 350 internal tape backup drive

Jerry wanted to install a Colorado 350 internal tape backup drive into an Acer Pentium mini-tower with a side-opening case. The PC was running DOS 6.22 and Windows 3.11. He performed a visual inspection of the outside of the case and noted that two 5$\frac{1}{4}$-inch slots were available. He then opened up the PC to check the space inside. A 5$\frac{1}{4}$-inch drive bay corresponding to the outside opening was available, so Jerry checked the power cables to be sure that an extra cable was available to provide power to the tape drive. There was no extra power cable, so Jerry made a note to get a splitter to split the power from one of the floppy drives. He also made a note to check the type of power connector on the new tape drive.

Jerry purchased the tape drive, but he opened the package before he left the store and noticed that this particular model took power from the larger Molex power connector. A splitter was included in the box, but he had to split the power from the 5$\frac{1}{4}$-inch drive in his PC because his 3$\frac{1}{2}$-inch drive used a smaller power connector.

When he returned from purchasing the drive, Jerry noticed that he'd neglected to check for mounting rails on his other drives. He checked the drives to see how they were mounted and noticed no mounting rails; the drives mounted directly into the case using screws. Fortunately, this meant that he did not have to make another trip to the store for mounting rails.

Jerry read through the instructions for mounting the tape drive and put on his wrist grounding strap. The case was still open from his earlier check, and he reached in and disconnected the floppy drive cable from the controller card. He then connected the cable that came with the tape backup drive to the controller card, placing the stripe in the cable on the side where pin 1 was indicated on the controller card connection. He took the floppy drive cable that he detached from the controller card and connected it to the 34-pin connection in the tape drive cable, making sure that the stripes on the ribbons of both cables were on the same side. He then connected the ribbon cable to the tape drive, carefully making sure that the ribbon cable's stripe was on pin 1. Jerry set the tape drive on top of the case in a secure position so it could be tested.

He disconnected the power cable from the 5¼-inch drive, but he needed a pair of needlenose pliers because the cable was securely connected. He attached the splitter and ran one end to the tape drive and the other end back to the power connection on the 5¼-inch drive.

With the tape drive outside the case, Jerry prepared to test the drive. He checked for tools or other objects accidentally left inside the computer, and when satisfied that there were none, he turned on the power switch to the PC. Jerry watched the boot sequence to see if it checked the floppy drives as it normally did, and he noticed that the light on the front of the tape backup drive went on. When Windows came up, he installed the software by going to File⇨Run and typing **a:\setup** as instructed by the software installation instructions. The installation was automatic and, when complete, took him into the Colorado Backup for Windows software.

Jerry ran the configuration as recommended by the Colorado software, placing the tape that came with the drive into the drive and allowing the software to read and write to the drive. When the software informed Jerry that the drive was properly configured, he exited Windows, turned off the PC, and prepared to secure the tape backup drive into the computer.

To secure the drive in the case, the cover over the 5¼-inch opening needed to be removed from the front of the case. On the Acer case, the closures over the openings in the front were designed to be popped out, so Jerry took the back of a screwdriver and applied pressure to the opening cover from the inside. He slipped once with the screwdriver and almost took out the opening underneath the one he was trying to pop out. Because that opening had to be hot-glued back on if it was accidentally popped out, Jerry made a mental note to be more careful.

After he managed to remove the opening in the front of the case, Jerry realized that he needed to disconnect the tape drive and slide it in from the front, then connect the screws and reconnect the cables to the drive. He slid in the drive, put the screws in place to hold the drive in the bay, and connected the cables. He then restarted the computer, but the tape drive light did not go on. He placed a tape in the drive, but the drive did not respond to the insertion of the tape as it had in the past.

Taking a closer look at the power connections, Jerry discovered that he hadn't secured the power connector to the tape drive. He turned off the PC, pressed in the connector, and turned the computer back on. This time the tape drive light went on during the boot sequence, and the drive acted on the tape when it was inserted.

Now that the tape drive was working, Jerry took a couple of floppy disks and attempted to read the A and B floppy disk drives. The 3¹/₂-inch A drive read fine, but he received an error message each time he tried the B drive. He turned off the computer and checked the cables. When he pressed on the cable to the B drive, it moved into place more securely, and Jerry realized that he'd probably pulled on the ribbon cable to the B drive when he reconnected one of the cables to the tape drive. Jerry turned the power back on and retested the B drive, which now read the diskette.

As he was preparing to close the case, Jerry noticed inside the case that the cable from the tape drive required him to neatly fold the ribbon cables so they would all fit in the case. Being careful not to pull the ribbon cables lose from the drives, Jerry closed the case while positioning the ribbon cables out of the way. After the case was closed, Jerry powered up the PC to again test the floppy drives and the tape drive. This time, everything worked fine. The next thing Jerry did was make a full backup of the system with his newly installed tape backup drive.

Installing the software and testing the tape drive

To test the tape drive, you have to turn on the PC and install the accompanying software. You don't need to worry about installing software if you installed Windows 95 from a CD-ROM and an internal tape backup drive in 120MB, 250MB, 350MB, and 740MB capacities from one of the following manufacturers: Colorado Memory Systems (CMS), Conner (Archive brand), IOmega, or Wangtek. The tape backup drivers are part of the MS Backup included with Windows 95 distributed on CD-ROM.

If you installed Windows 95 from diskettes instead of a CD-ROM, you won't find MS Backup. To get it, contact Microsoft or purchase the Windows 95 Resource Kit, which includes several utilities not available in the diskette version. If you're unsure if you have MS Backup, look for the MS Backup program in your Windows 95 installation by going to Start⇨Programs⇨Accessories⇨System Tools. If you have the MS Backup utility, it should be listed in the System Tools menu (see Figure 4-18).

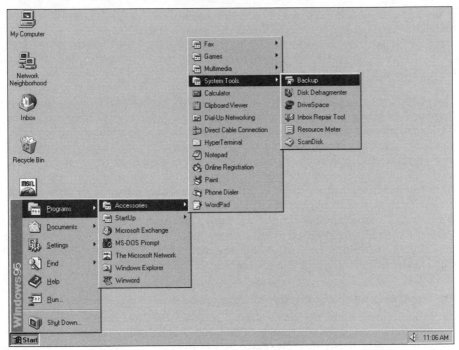

Figure 4-18: The Windows 95 System Tools menu with the Backup utility displayed.

During the software installation, you soon discover if the tape drive is working because the software attempts to talk to the drive. Most tape software installs itself to your hard disk drive and then asks you to allow it to configure itself, meaning it looks for the tape backup drive, writes data to the drive, and attempts to read back the data. So, during the configuration process, you are asked to insert a tape (which should have come with the tape backup drive). When you insert a tape, the drive may begin acting as though it's doing something, even though the software hasn't been started. This is because the drive automatically begins searching for the beginning of the tape, winding the tape back and forth. This means you have the power cable connected correctly, but does not mean that the software is correctly talking to the drive.

 The tape drive performs an automatic seek each time you insert a tape and each time you restart the computer with a tape still in the drive. This is nothing to worry about, but it is different behavior than the other drives on your PC and can be a cause for concern to those who have never used a tape backup drive before.

While some software packages allow you to skip the configuration portion, you don't want to because you need to know if data is being correctly recorded to the tape. This test reads and compares data from the tape to your hard disk drive, and it writes and compares the data as well. You don't have a backup if you can't restore the data, so you want to perform this configuration test.

If the software installs successfully and the configuration goes smoothly, you can install the tape backup drive into the case. If you have problems, such as receiving error messages from the software saying it cannot access the tape drive or concerning the floppy disk drives, then you need to follow the troubleshooting steps for installing a floppy disk drive.

The purpose of a tape backup is to restore the data in case of an emergency. In order to make this happen, you need to be prepared for the worst-case scenario, which is the loss of all your data. In that case, you need to boot your computer from a floppy disk, reload the operating system, and then reinstall the tape backup software. You then can have the tape backup software copy everything back to the hard disk drive.

What this means is that you need to have a rescue disk, a copy of your operating system (you may need both your DOS and Windows diskettes if you're running a Windows 3.x-based tape backup software program), and a copy of your tape backup software installation diskettes, in addition to the tape with your data on it, if you plan to restore in the event of a disaster. See the case study "Installing a Zip drive on a small network" at the end of this chapter for an example of the steps involved.

Placing the tape drive securely in the case

After the drive is tested, you can secure it into the case. You want to power down the PC, and you may have to disconnect some of the cables you've connected in order to install the tape backup drive. The drive may fit tightly inside your PC, so you want to be sure you haven't accidentally pulled any cables loose from your hard disk drive or from other floppy disk drives. I usually give each cable a quick visual check and push in on each one, just to be sure that the connections are secure.

Final testing the tape drive and floppy disk drives

Before you put the case back together, you want to restart the computer and test the tape drive and the floppy disk drives. This doesn't have to be complex testing, but it's easier to make sure everything's working before you put the case on than to open up your PC again because you simply forgot to reconnect a power cable. Put a diskette in each of the drives, go to the DOS prompt, and perform a **DIR A:** and **DIR B:** (if there's a B drive) to be sure you can still talk to the drives. Then start the tape software and run the configuration test again.

You can just read, compare, and write a single file or two, but it's usually easier to run the configuration test if you're new with the software. When you're sure everything works, close up the case and enjoy your accomplishment.

Special instructions for Windows 95

When Windows 95 starts, it checks the hardware and automatically installs software for devices it recognizes. You receive a message during the boot sequence that Windows 95 has found new hardware and is setting up drivers for it. If you install a tape backup, Windows 95 may recognize it and set up the correct driver you restart the computer (although Windows may ask you for the installation diskettes or CD to accomplish this). However, Windows 95 in the 4.00.950 version supports only internal drives that use the QIC-40 (120MB), the QIC-80 (250MB), and the QIC-3010 (740MB) tapes from the following manufacturers: Colorado Memory Systems, or CMS (a division of Hewlett-Packard); Conner (Archive brand); IOmega; and Wangtek.

These manufacturers all make tape backup drives in higher capacities, and you probably want a larger tape backup drive as well. The good news is that some of these manufacturers, such as CMS, offer free software upgrades for Windows 95 that support their larger tape backup drives. CMS's Colorado Backup for Windows 95 Version 1.51 (CBW95 1.51) looks very much like the MS Backup utility, as you can see in Figure 4-19, but it adds features such as the capability to perform selective restores from full system backups, an unerase feature, and a scheduling program for automating backups. You may get this software directly from the company for a nominal fee, or you can download it from the company's Internet site, CompuServe forum, or bulletin board service. Contact information for all previously named companies appears in the Appendix.

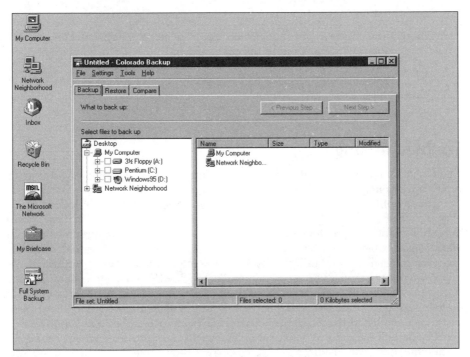

Figure 4-19: A screen shot of Colorado Backup for Windows 95.

One further wrinkle with Windows 95 is that several tape backup manufacturers have announced that they will not support backups made with their DOS-based or Windows 3.x-based software under Windows 95. The DOS or Windows 3.x software works, but it cannot handle the Windows 95 System Registry or the long filenames. Without the System Registry, you cannot accurately restore your software installed under Windows 95. (More information on the Windows 95 System Registry is in Chapter 13.) So, if you're planning to back up Windows 95 data, you need a Windows 95-based software program to do it.

Installation in review

To install an internal tape backup drive, follow these steps:

1. Check outside the case for an open bay.

2. Check inside the case for free space.

3. Check for a free power supply cable. Get a splitter for the power cable if necessary.

4. Obtain the tape drive.

5. Place the drive in the drive bay. Attach the screws.

6. Connect the power supply and the floppy drive cable. Be sure the original floppy drive is correctly connected to the cable as well.

7. Test the drive.

8. Test the tape drive and any floppy disk drives before you put the lid back on the case.

Troubleshooting

The installation problems that pertain to installing a second floppy disk drive are also common when installing an internal tape backup drive. If you're having problems, check the troubleshooting section under "Adding a Second Floppy Disk Drive."

One other problem is particular to tape backup drives, which I've already mentioned briefly. This problem occurs under Windows and involves the software drivers for the tape backup drive. Several utility software applications offer drivers for tape backup drives, including DOS 6.22, Norton Utilities, Fastback, PC Tools, and others. These drivers tend to conflict with one another and with drivers from the manufacturer. A prime example is the Colorado Backup for Windows software, which loads its own driver when you start the program to perform a backup. If a conflicting software driver is loaded, the Colorado software displays an error message saying that there's a conflicting driver and refuses to run. To correct the problem, you need to go into the Windows SYSTEM.INI file, look for the conflicting driver, and either delete the lines or add a semicolon in front of them so that they are not executed by Windows.

Most of the time, the Colorado Backup for Windows software and tape drive run fine when the software is first installed. However, when a new software utility is installed, it detects the tape backup drive and installs its own driver. The next time you try to run CBW, you get an error message saying that a conflicting driver is loaded. A classic case of this is the "DOS 6.22 upgrade halts Colorado Tape Backup for Windows 3.1" case study later in this chapter. Detailed information on how to correct this type of error is offered in the case study. You may prefer to use the utility software to make your backups instead of using the software that came with the tape backup drive, which is not a problem, but you need to be aware that you're making a choice. This isn't a problem with all tape backup drives, but it does tend to happen with popular drives, such as those from Colorado Memory Systems.

Here are some of the most frequently asked questions about using a tape backup, along with the answers.

Question: If I restore from tape, does the data on the tape automatically overwrite files with the same names on the hard disk drive?

Answer: You should be able to set the software to always overwrite, ask permission to overwrite, or never overwrite. You may even be able to get the software to compare the revision dates on files and restore only the newer files. When you restore, look for those options in the software program you're using.

Question: Can I run a program from the tape? I stored programs on the tape that I don't have room for on my hard drive, but I still need to run them occasionally.

Answer: You can't run a program from the tape with most popular tape backup drives. Tape backup is meant for archival purposes. You must copy the software back to your hard disk drive and run it from there.

Question: Does the backup I'm doing now overwrite an earlier backup I did on the same tape?

Answer: It doesn't have to. You can choose the options *multi-volume* backup or *append,* and the software adds this backup after the previous one. If you have too much data for one tape, the software asks for another.

Question: I have one file on the tape I'd like to erase. Can I do that?

Answer: Nope. You can erase the entire *volume*, or group, of data from a single backup session, but no one as yet has created a utility for erasing a single file from the tape. You can, however, perform a partial erase with some software that erases from a certain volume clear to the end of the tape.

Recovery from the brink of disaster

A small but successful construction company, owned by a husband-and-wife team, the Smiths, decided to upgrade its copy of Microsoft Works for Windows to the multimedia version. The Smiths had a Pentium computer running DOS 6.22, Windows 3.11, and an internal Colorado tape backup drive.

Mrs. Smith purchased the multimedia version of Microsoft Works. During installation, the software reported that it needed to modify the AUTOEXEC.BAT to add the device driver SHARE.EXE. SHARE is a device driver included with DOS to handle file sharing and drive access. It's historically been used with PCs on networks, and it is needed to run the multimedia version of Microsoft Works.

The Smiths didn't know much about SHARE, but they had experienced problems in the past when installing or upgrading software. Because of these problems, they made periodic backups, especially before an installation of any kind. In this particular case, they not only performed a backup but also placed a call to a computer consultant friend, who told them to check with the software company from which they purchased their accounting software program before they allowed the addition of SHARE to their environment files. SHARE has been known to conflict with other programs in the past.

The Smiths called the software company. The company said SHARE was fine, and a support technician talked them through installing SHARE in the AUTOEXEC.BAT file so that Microsoft Works would run. The multimedia version of Microsoft Works ran without a hitch. But a day later, when Mrs. Smith started the accounting software to do the payroll, the accounting software crashed and could not be recovered. The Smiths could boot the PC, but unusual things started happening. They started getting error messages when the PC booted. When they tried to go into Windows, the Program Manager started to come up, but then Windows crashed and they were back to a DOS prompt.

They called their computer consultant friend back, who asked them to start the computer but not Windows. The consultant had them run SCANDISK, which reported over one hundred cross-linked files in the accounting software directory. (Cross-linked means that two files have the same address in the DOS address book for files, the file allocation table.) The phrase *cross-linked files* strikes fear into the heart of any knowledgeable computer user, because the only way to recover the files is to delete them and sometimes reformat the entire disk.

With Windows acting up, there was no way of knowing how far-reaching the corruption was. Fortunately, the Smiths had their recently-made complete backup on tape, their bootable floppy disk with all the necessary DOS files, and a copy of the tape backup software. The consultant talked them through booting from the bootable floppy, formatting the disk using the /s switch, and restoring the tape backup software.

Because they were using Colorado Backup for Windows, the Smiths thought they would have to reload Windows, but the Colorado software includes a DOS version. All the Smiths had to do was reinstall the DOS version, which could read and restore not only Windows, but their accounting software and all their other Windows and DOS software applications as well.

Obviously, the Smiths were angry at the accounting software company. They called to complain and went up the chain of command in the technical support division, looking for someone to reimburse them for the expenses they'd incurred. The accounting software company pointed out that they could not be responsible for the error, and that factors other than loading SHARE could have caused the error, such as turning off the computer before exiting the accounting software. The software company agreed to reimburse the Smiths the annual fee for technical support, but it would no longer provide technical support for the accounting software. The Smiths considered changing accounting packages, but after all the time and effort they'd put into this package, they decided it would cost too much. Instead, the Smiths had their computer consultant friend create a multiple boot configuration so that they could run their accounting software and the multimedia version of Microsoft Works for Windows.

The moral of the story is have a good backup and be prepared for the worst.

Adding an External Tape Backup Drive

The main difference between an external tape backup drive and an internal tape backup drive is that the external drive has a housing of its own. There are a couple different types of external tape backup drives. The most popular type, because it can be used on more than one PC, is one that connects to the parallel port of the PC. There are also external tape backup drives that connect to the floppy disk controller or to a controller card especially for the tape drive. These types are less popular because you still have to open up the PC and perform an installation, and they cannot be moved from one PC to another. Because the installation of these drives is similar to internal drives, and because I'm concentrating on the most popular upgrades, I'm going to focus on the type of external tape backup drive that operates from the parallel port. These types of drives range in price from $150 to $400.

Preparation

The only real preparation for using a parallel port tape backup drive is to locate the parallel port on your PC. The parallel port is a female 25-pin connection, as shown in Figure 4-20. Serial ports can come in 9-pin and 25-pin varieties, and the 25-pin variety can look like it's a parallel port. However, the convention in the PC industry is to make the 25-pin parallel port female and the 25-pin serial port male. The PC world is moving away from 25-pin serial to 9-pin serial, so if your PC is relatively new, your only 25-pin port is probably the parallel port.

The easiest way to spot a parallel port is to note where your printer is connected, as this is usually the parallel port. Sometimes you see the symbol of a printer on the case.

Installation

Installing an external parallel port tape backup drive is a twofold process. First, you connect the drive to the parallel port, and then you install the software included with the drive.

If you plan to leave the tape backup drive connected to the PC, several tape backup drives provide a *pass-through* connector, such as the one on the IOmega Ditto tape backup drive shown in Figure 4-21. This connector enables you to connect your printer cable to the tape backup drive so that signals not meant for the tape drive pass through to the printer.

Figure 4-20: The parallel port on a PC — a 25-pin female connection.

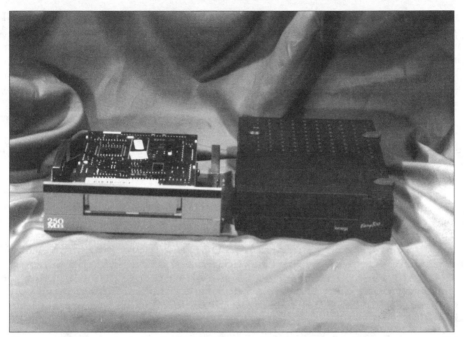

Figure 4-21: Shown are a Colorado internal tape backup drive and an IOmega parallel port tape backup unit.

Installing the software for parallel port tape backup drives

The most convenient software for parallel port tape backup drives is software you can run from a floppy diskette. Unfortunately, this type of software is hard to find. The next best software is licensed software. You can install licensed software on numerous PCs, which enables you to connect your tape drive and backup whenever you're ready.

In order to talk to the tape drive, the software uses a special program, called a *device driver*, that is designed to talk to the tape drive hardware. You have to be concerned about this device driver only under Windows, because it seems that every utility program these days has its own device driver for a tape backup drive. Unfortunately, these drivers don't always get along. Under Windows, device drivers are usually installed in the SYSTEM.INI file that's executed each time Windows starts. If you install a new software utility that supports tape backup drives, such as an upgrade of DOS or Norton Utilities, this new utility will probably clobber the device driver that's in the SYSTEM.INI and install its own.

However, some popular software packages, such as Colorado Backup for Windows, don't activate their device driver until the user actually starts the program. So, if SYSTEM.INI has already loaded a device driver, there may be a conflict. This is another reason for always backing up your system files, including the Windows .INI files, before installing new software. If you do back up, you can roll back to the previous settings, just in case the new program presents conflicts with an existing program.

DOS 6.22 upgrade halts Colorado Tape Backup for Windows 3.1

Sarah wanted to upgrade an older computer system that she kept for her kids from DOS 6.0 to DOS 6.22 because her newly pur-chased PC had DOS 6.22 and Windows 3.11. She heard from people who knew about PCs that it was much safer to have all her PCs using the same operating system because she could use the boot disk from one PC to restore another should it go down.

The PC she wanted to upgrade to DOS 6.22 was an Epson 386 with an external Colorado tape backup drive that ran off the floppy drive controller card. She had to use an external drive because she had two floppy disk drives and no more available drive bays to use for an internal tape backup drive. She also ran Windows 3.11 on this PC.

The upgrade went without a hitch until a week later when she decided to use the tape backup drive to back up the kids' reports and saved games. She double-clicked on the Colorado Tape Backup software icon. When the software started, she received an error message that said a conflicting driver was present, and the soft-ware refused to run.

The error message said that one of several drivers could be at fault, listed the drivers, and recommended a check of the Windows SYSTEM.INI file. Sarah knew a little bit about the Windows and DOS environment files, so she went to the Program Manager, accessed the File⇨Run menu, typed **sysedit,** and clicked on OK to start the Windows system editor.

After the system editor was on the screen, Sarah clicked on the SYSTEM.INI file to make it active. She then went to the Edit⇨Find menu and started searching for the names of the drivers the Colorado software had listed. These drivers had filenames that ended in .386, so Sarah searched for .386. In the SYSTEM.INI file, she found these lines in the [386Enh] section:

```
;======== MS-DOS 6 Setup Modification - Begin========
device=C:\DOS\VFINTD.386
;======== MS-DOS 6 Setup Modification - End ========
```

She looked in the Windows Resource Kit documentation and found that 386Enh stands for 386 Enhanced. This section of the SYSTEM.INI file is for drivers and settings specific to running Windows in 386 Enhanced mode. The 386 Enhanced mode of Windows allows the operating system to take advantage of the virtual memory capability of the 80386 Intel processor.

Obviously, the DOS 6.22 upgrade had made this change to her Windows SYSTEM.INI file. Before making changes, Sarah exited SYSEDIT, created a directory with her initials as the name, and saved the SYSTEM.INI and WIN.INI files to that directory. She then restarted SYSEDIT, deleted those three lines from SYSTEM.INI, and saved SYSTEM.INI (File⇨Save). She could have left the lines there, but she instructed Windows not to execute the driver by placing a semicolon in front of the device line, just as there is a semicolon in front of the lines of comments before and after the DOS device driver line. However, Sarah felt this may prove to be confusing later.

Sarah had to exit and then restart Windows to get the changes to take effect, but when she tried the Colorado software again, it worked. Curious as to why the DOS 6.22 upgrade would make this change, she went to the Colorado Memory Systems support services on the Internet and performed a search using the keyword *troubleshooting*. She found a file that answered her question.

As it turns out, the DOS backup software installs its own driver so that it can make use of the tape drive for backup. This driver conflicts with the Colorado Backup for Windows driver loaded when the Colorado software starts. But it's not just DOS that installs a driver that conflicts with the Colorado Backup for Windows software. The list of software programs that install their own drivers includes packages from Irwin, IOmega, Central Point, Arcada, My Backup, Fastback, and others.

The bottom line, Sarah learned, is that you can use only one backup program. You can also inadvertently create a conflict that you may not find for awhile, such as she did when she performed her DOS 6.22 upgrade.

Windows 95 software for parallel port tape drives

Software that recognizes the drive is required for a parallel port tape backup. The Windows 95 MS Backup comes with support for only the CMS Trakker parallel port tape backup drives in 120MB, 250MB, and 700MB capacities. However, the other drive manufacturers have jumped on the Windows 95 bandwagon and offer software that works with Windows 95, as well as with earlier versions of Windows and DOS.

If you're using the MS Backup program, and the drive is connected to the parallel port when you start the PC, Windows 95 should recognize the drive during its startup sequence. (Be sure to power down the computer when connecting or disconnecting any peripheral from the ports.) However, because the drive is portable and you can move it to another PC, Windows lets you know that you've disconnected the tape drive from the parallel port when it restarts. You can ask Windows to redetect the drive from within the MS Backup menu when you connect it again. Go to Start⇨ Programs⇨Accessories⇨System Tools⇨Backup. In the Backup menu, select Tools⇨Redetect Tape Drive. If you start the MS Backup software without the drive detected, Windows informs you that it cannot find the drive and suggests several options to troubleshoot the situation, as shown in Figure 4-22.

Installation in review

Here are the steps to adding a parallel port tape backup drive.

1. Locate your parallel port.

2. Purchase a parallel port tape backup drive.

3. Disconnect your printer and connect the drive to the parallel port.

4. Connect your printer to the pass-through port on the drive (optional).

5. Install the tape backup software.

6. Test the drive using the configuration utility in the software.

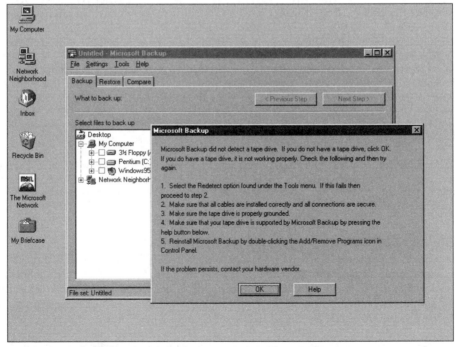

Figure 4-22: If Windows 95 cannot detect the parallel port tape drive, it gives you an error message and suggests several options.

Troubleshooting

After connecting your parallel port tape backup drive, what do you do if the accompanying software says that it cannot find the drive? The first thing to do is check the connections between the drive and the cable and between the parallel port and the cable to make sure they're secure.

Also, be sure the power cord is plugged into the tape drive and the power switch is in the *On* position. If you insert a tape, and the drive is getting power, you should see a light come on in the front of the drive and hear the tape "spin" in the drive.

If you have a problem running the software, especially if you're running it under DOS, you want to see if there's enough lower memory free for the software to run. You do this by typing **MEM** at the DOS prompt, and pressing Enter, and looking for the available memory figure. If the memory is less than 500K, you probably don't have enough memory to successfully run the software. To solve this problem, you need to free some lower memory or set up a multiple boot configuration. If you want to know more about memory issues, consult Chapter 6. For more information on setting up a multiple boot configuration, check Chapter 13.

Portable tape drives are sensitive to the electromagnetic field (EMF) produced by your monitor. Try moving the tape drive farther away from the monitor. Most manufacturers say that an external tape drive should be operated at least 18 inches from the monitor.

You might also check the PC to see if it has a sound card. Sound cards can interfere with parallel port tape backup drives because they can be set to share some of the computing resources that the parallel port uses. If you do have a sound card, and the parallel tape backup drive won't work, you may have a sound card that is sharing the same IRQ as the parallel port. Although you can check into Chapter 11 to adjust the sound card so that it doesn't use the same IRQ (assuming another IRQ is available), it may be less trouble to get a tape backup drive that runs from the floppy disk controller.

Peripheral devices and ports are assigned interrupt request lines (known as *IRQs* or *interrupts*) so they can get processing attention from the CPU. You can think of IRQs as interrupting the processor, just as a secretary may interrupt a conversation the boss is having to present something of a more critical nature. The average PC has 16 IRQs, and the parallel port is usually assigned either IRQ 5 or IRQ 7. However, several sound cards on the market now share an IRQ with the parallel port, especially if there are two parallel ports. In the case of two parallel ports, the sound card may be using the same IRQ as the second parallel port. This means that you may need to change either the IRQ that the sound card is using or the IRQ that the parallel port is using.

You need to educate yourself to determine if this is indeed the problem. If you want to tackle it now, turn to the troubleshooting section of Chapters 9 and 11. (Even though we're talking parallel ports here, the IRQ information in Chapters 9 and 11 applies.) If you're not ready for that level of detail yet, you may want to try either a tape backup drive that works off the floppy drive controller or one with its own controller card.

Remember, you bought a tape backup drive to save your data, so take an extra couple of steps to make sure you can recover that data. Be sure to have a bootable floppy disk, a copy of the operating system you're using, and a copy of the software you used to make the backup. It's also a good idea to store some of your backup tapes off-site, just in case of a fire or other disaster.

If the drive works but seems very slow, it may be *shoeshining*, which is spinning the tape back and forth for long periods of time. Shoeshining is caused by a mismatch between the speed of the computer's processor and the speed of the tape drive. What is a long period of time? I connected an IOmega Ditto Travan portable tape drive, capable of backing up 800MB of data, to a 486SX running at 25 MHz. It took two hours just to perform the configuration, which was to read, write, and compare a 0.5MB file, and it was shoeshining the entire time. I connected the same tape drive to a 75 MHz. Pentium, which took about a minute to perform the configuration and about 20 minutes to perform a partial backup of over 250MB of data. A Colorado Trakker capable of handling 350MB of data took nearly two hours to back up the same amount of data on the same Pentium-based PC.

The larger capacity tape backup drives are made to talk to faster computers. If you're using a newer tape drive with an older PC, you can attempt to slow down the tape drive using the software settings, but this option is not always available. The best thing to do is find a match between the tape drive and the computer you plan to use it on. You find a match by looking at the size of the hard disk drive and the capacity of the tape backup drive. For example, the 486 was sold originally with a 250MB hard disk drive, so the Colorado Trakker 350 is a good fit for that PC. I've since put a 1.2GB hard disk drive in that 486, so if I use the Trakker 350, I need to use multiple tapes to make a backup.

If you want to move large amounts of data between a number of different computers with different configurations, one workable option is to use a large capacity portable disk drive, such as the Zip drive from IOmega. However, the diskettes for the Zip drive only hold 100MB each. The case study about installing a Zip drive may help you decide if this type of drive is for you.

Installing a Zip drive on a small network

Shawn wanted to back up data on the small computer network for her business, which included four PCs. She'd had bad experiences with tape backup drives in the past, so she wanted something different. After visiting several computer stores, she decided on a Zip drive from IOmega. Even though the drive and the special diskettes were a little more expensive than tape, she felt more comfortable with the parallel port drive.

The Zip drive comes with a diskette, but Shawn decided to pick up more diskettes because she wanted to archive her business data. The computer store where she bought the drive was out of PC formatted diskettes for the Zip drive, but they did have a bundle of three Mac formatted diskettes at a substantial savings. The salesperson said the software that came with the Zip drive would allow her to reformat the Mac diskettes to a PC format.

Shawn got the drive to her office. The instructions were brief but simple. Still, Shawn was cautious, so she created a bootable disk on her PC and copied to it the AUTOEXEC.BAT, CONFIG.SYS, WIN.INI, and SYSTEM.INI files. She was running DOS 6.20 and Windows 3.1. She hoped she would be able to install the Zip drive on her PC, and then back up the important data from the other PCs on the network to the Zip drive on her PC. She noted that the Zip drive has a pass-through connector for her printer, so she figured she could reconnect her printer to the pass-through port and leave the Zip drive connected to the parallel port on her PC.

The 3^1/$_2$-inch, 1.44MB diskette that came with the Zip drive got the installation started, but when the PC recognized the Zip drive, the remainder of the installation was performed from the software on the Zip diskette included with the drive. Shawn realized that she couldn't reuse that Zip diskette without losing the data on it, and she was glad that she'd purchased additional Zip diskettes.

Shawn was also glad she'd backed up her configuration files, because the Zip drive installation remapped the drive letters of all the drives, including the CD-ROM drive, on her PC. Her original hard disk drive was C, the CD-ROM was D, and the network drives were E and F. After the installation, her hard disk drive was still C, but the Zip drive was D, the CD-ROM was E, and the network drives were F and G. This situation was unacceptable for Shawn. She would have to reconfigure the network and reinstall all her CD-ROM-based software because the network and the CD-ROM software were set to her previous drive letters. At this point, she was cut off from her network, but she remembered to reformat the three Mac diskettes while she had the Zip software loaded.

After the Mac diskettes were reformatted, Shawn looked through the documentation on the Zip utility diskette to see if she could make the Zip drive take the last drive letter instead of changing the letters of her other drives. There was a mention of drive letter changes, but when she got to it, she was disappointed to discover that Zip advised reinstalling the CD-ROM software and contacting the network administrator about remapping her network drive letters.

Shawn was about to give up, put everything back in the box, and take it all back to the store when she found information concerning the *Guest* utility, which came on the 3¹/₂-inch diskette. If executed from the 3¹/₂-inch drive, Guest finds the last drive letter and assigns it to the Zip drive. The Zip drive then could be treated just like another floppy disk drive. Shawn restored her original system settings by recopying the AUTOEXEC.BAT, CONFIG.SYS, WIN.INI, and SYSTEM.INI files over the ones the IOmega software installation modified and rebooted the PC. She then exited Windows, went to the DOS prompt, put the 3¹/₂-inch diskette in the A drive, and started the Guest utility.

The next message on her monitor said the Zip drive was now configured to drive G. To test the Zip drive, Shawn put the Zip utility diskette in the Zip drive and used the DOS command DIR (for directory) to view the files on the drive. The files on the Zip diskette displayed on screen just like any other diskette. Shawn was able to use DOS copy commands to move her data from her hard disk drive to the Zip drive. However, the network didn't recognize the Zip drive, so Shawn moved the Zip drive around the office from PC to PC and made complete backups of the data on each PC using the Guest utility. The Zip drive was just a touch slower than the 386-based PC in the office, but it performed quickly and reliably using the Guest utility. Shawn made several backup copies of the 3¹/₂-inch diskette that contained the Guest utility and, she stored the original and a copy with her system-wide backups for safe keeping.

Although the Zip drive wasn't as easy to use as Shawn had first thought it would be, she was willing to stay with the drive. She used the DOS COPY and XCOPY commands to make her backups, was comfortable with the speed of the drive, and knew that she could get her data back.

Troubleshooting Practice: What's Wrong in These Photos?

Here are some photos of common problems situations. See if you can find what's wrong.

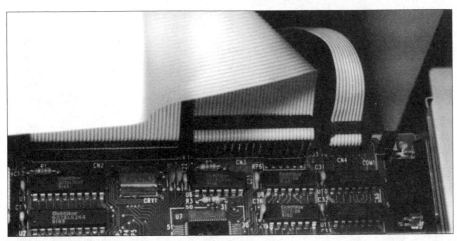

Figure 4-23: See answer 1.

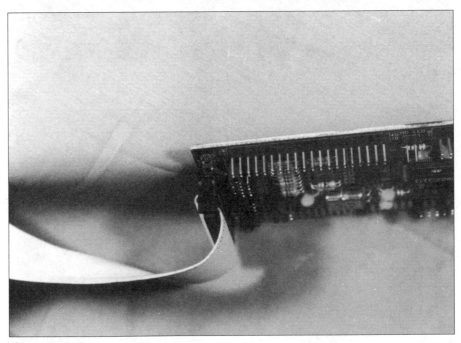

Figure 4-24: See answer 2.

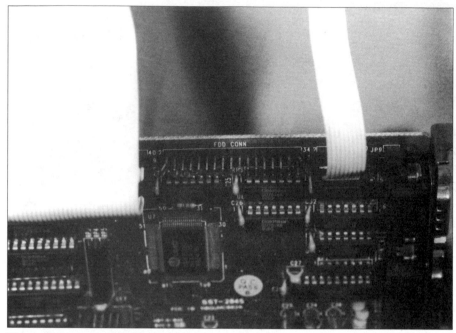

Figure 4-25: See answer 3.

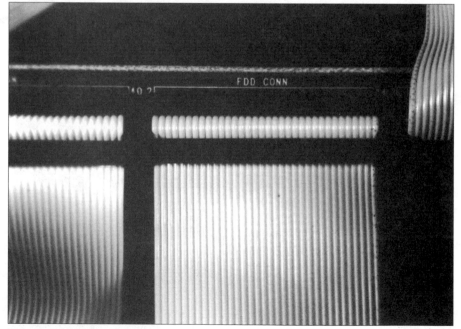

Figure 4-26: See answer 4.

Figure 4-27: See answer 5.

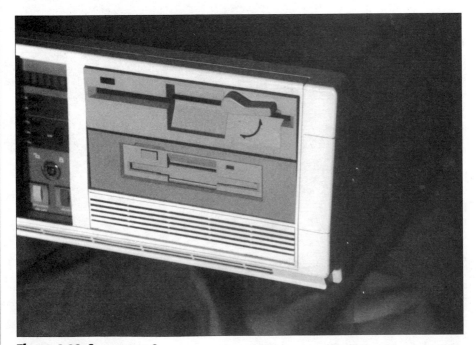

Figure 4-28: See answer 6.

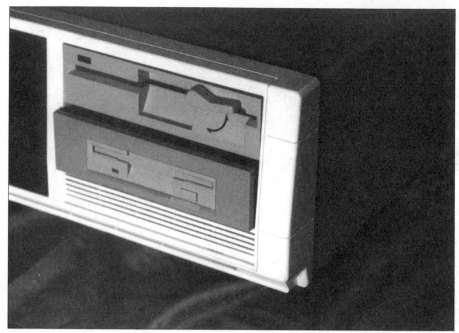

Figure 4-29: See answer 7.

Figure 4-30: See answer 8.

Answers:

1. Only the top half of the pins on this connector are connected to the cable.

2. One pin at the end of the connector is bent and sticking out.

3. The pins on this floppy disk drive controller connector are bent.

4. The cable is installed on the controller card backwards, so pin 1 on the cable is not at pin 1 on the connector.

5. The cable is installed on this floppy disk drive backwards, and there is no power to the drive.

6. The $3^1/_2$-inch floppy disk drive is installed upside down.

7. The drive adapter kit or sliders are installed incorrectly. The symptoms of this problem include the drive sticking out past the case or not fitting in the drive bay.

8. The face plate is missing from this $3^1/_2$-inch floppy disk drive.

Summary

✦ Be sure to check your computer case for unused space before you purchase a second floppy disk drive.

✦ You may need a new ribbon cable that supports two drives, a splitter for the power, and an adapter to make a $3^1/_2$-inch drive fit a $5^1/_4$-inch drive bay.

✦ When installing a second drive, test both drives before you go to the trouble of securing the drives in the drive bays and again after you secure the drives before closing the case.

✦ Higher capacity floppy disk drives and tape drives can usually read lower capacity diskettes and tapes.

✦ If you're short on drive bays, you should try a combination drive, such as a $3^1/_2$-inch and a $5^1/_4$-inch drive that fits in the $5^1/_4$-inch half-height drive bay (approximately $1^7/_{10}$ inches high by $5^1/_4$-inches wide).

✦ To make the B drive the A drive, look for the Swap Floppies option in the CMOS setup before you physically swap the cables and CMOS settings.

✦ The most popular tape backup drives are the internal tape drives that run off the PCs floppy drive controller and the portable tape backup drives that connect to the PC via the parallel port.

✦ Be sure to test the floppy drives as well as the tape backup drive when installing a tape drive that uses the floppy disk drive controller.

✦   ✦   ✦

Installing a Hard Disk Drive

In This Chapter

+ Installing a larger, faster hard disk drive in your PC

+ Getting your old hard disk drive to work with the new one

+ Using drive translation to get past the 500 MB barrier

+ Discovering tips for successful testing

+ Making the new hard disk drive the boot drive

Tools Needed

+ Phillips screwdriver

+ Needlenose pliers

+ Wrist grounding strap

I f you feel that your hard disk is shrinking, you're not alone. Software applications are becoming larger and larger, taking up more and more of your precious hard disk space. Windows is also a hard disk-hungry application, and a faster hard disk drive is key to making Windows perform faster on your PC. With hard disk space more affordable than ever, providing yourself with a larger hard disk drive makes sense, and you can install one yourself in a couple of hours by using the information in this chapter.

Upgrading Your Hard Disk Drive

So, you've decided that you want to install a larger and faster hard disk drive. For the purposes of this section, assume that you will upgrade (replace) the current hard disk drive in your PC. You may be able to keep your current hard disk drive and use it as a second drive. This chapter also contains a section on how to add a second drive to address this issue.

Whether or not you want to keep your current drive, you'll always have an easier and more successful upgrading experience if you first install the new hard disk drive as a stand-alone drive and then make the modifications to get it to work with your current hard drive. If you think that you want to keep your current hard disk drive, read over that material before you purchase your new drive so that you know which adapters you need to get.

First, I concentrate on the background information you need, what to look for in your BIOS, what to look for inside your PC, and how to determine what the maximum storage capacity of the hard disk drive is that you can install. Then I cover how to cable the drive, how to tell the computer that the new drive is there, and how to get the new drive working.

Hard disk drive prices vary depending on the capacity of the drive. You'll probably not spend less than $150 no matter what size drive you buy. But larger capacity drives cost less per MB than smaller capacity drives. For example, you may see a 540MB drive for $150, but a 1.2GB drive (or 1200MB drive) may go for $200, which means you get twice as much capacity for only $50 more.

Preparation

As with any upgrade, you can do some investigating beforehand that will save you time and money. You need some background information on hard disk drives. You want to create a backup of your data and a bootable floppy disk containing the key utility programs for installing the hard drive. You also want to peek inside your PC to see if you need an adapter for your new hard drive, and you should look at your BIOS to determine what capacity hard drive you can install.

You need to know some basic information about how hard disk drives work in order to make your installation successful, so I talk about that first. Then I talk about how to upgrade your current hard disk drive with a new one, including what to look for in your system to determine the size and type of hard disk drive that your PC can support. I finish the chapter by discussing how you can use your current hard disk drive as a second drive.

What you need to know about hard disk drives

If you understand a few key facts about how hard disk drives work, you'll find the installation process easier and you'll have more success. Following is the basic background information that you need.

How hard disk drives work

In an oversimplified view, a hard disk drive consists of one or more round, rust-coated ceramic platters (hard disks) spun by a motor. These disks spin at speeds of 3,600 rotations per minute (RPM) or greater. Hard disk drives are built in super-clean assembly facilities that surpass several times over the sanitary requirements of hospital operating rooms. Even the air is filtered for impurities in these high-tech assembly plants. After it is sealed at the factory, your hard disk drive should never be opened, because impurities in the air (even those as small as dust) can destroy your drive's capability to store and retrieve your data. (*Iron oxide,* also known as rust, has been replaced by materials with better magnetic qualities, but this is an oversimplified view, remember?)

Read/write heads, which resemble metallic arms, stretch out above and below these spinning platters and apply a positive or negative charge (represented as a 0 or a 1) to the rust particles on the platter whirling past. (Technically, instead of a magnetic *charge,* a magnetic *flux* is applied, and the transition in the flux creates the sequence of 0s and 1s, but you get the idea.) The read/write head moves back and forth across the platters, but it does not actually touch the surface of the platters while they are in motion. Instead, the heads float above the surface, at microscopic distances, on the cushion of air created by the rotation of the platters. If the read/write head hits the surface of the platter, it can destroy the data written there. Such an occurrence is called a *head crash*, and the portion of the platter where a crash occurs can never again be used to store data.

Your hard disk drive spins constantly from the time you turn on your computer until the time you turn off your computer. When you turn off the computer, the drive automatically parks the heads; that is, the drive senses the power loss and moves the heads to a place where data is never written. This head parking space is known as the *landing zone*.

I've described how hard disk drives work to help reinforce the fact that you should be gentle when handling your hard drive. Hard disk drives may look tough on the outside with their rigid metal cases, but they are still sensitive to sudden jolts or bumps that could knock the heads lose or harm the mechanisms inside the drive. You want to avoid any rough handling of the drive whether or not it is receiving power.

TIP Most likely, the heads of your hard disk drive will be floating over data you care about, so after your hard disk drive is installed, you want to make sure that your computer is placed on a solid surface out of the path of jars and jolts. One of the most common problems I see is a PC placed on a table near a door that swings open and hits the table. Watch out for this type of situation, and never move the computer while it is on.

Your hard disk drive requires a way to access the central processing unit and memory of your PC. This is done via a controller card that plugs into one of the expansion slots on your PC (see Figure 5-1). Recent advances in motherboard design have integrated the hard disk drive controller right onto the motherboard (see Figure 5-2). However, there must be a connection between the hard disk controller and the hard disk drive. That connection comes in the form of a ribbon cable that runs between the drive and the controller. In addition to the ribbon cable, hard disk drives require a power supply and a place where it can be mounted inside the PC.

Figure 5-1: An ISA hard disk controller card plugged into an expansion slot on the PC.

Figure 5-2: An IDE hard disk controller integrated into a motherboard.

When working with hard disk drives, you need to know something about the terminology for how data is stored on the drive. Heads write the data to the drive, and drives often have multiple heads to speed up the tasks of reading and writing to the disk. A *track* is the area that passes under the head during one rotation of the hard disk drive. *Sectors* divide the tracks into smaller parts. These sectors are bundled in groups called *clusters*. A concept that is rarely used except when in hard drive installation is that of *cylinders*. A cylinder on a hard disk drive is the space located under all drive heads at one time. (See Figure 5-3.)

For the purpose of hard disk drive installation, the information that you care about is the number of cylinders, heads, and sectors on a hard disk drive. This is information that you may need to enter in the CMOS setup menu in order to get your computer to recognize the new hard disk drive. These specifications should be provided for you when you purchase the drive. They may be printed on the drive along with the other settings and the name of the manufacturer.

Figure 5-3: The position of the four heads on this hard disk drive (one on the top and bottom of each of the two platters) makes up a single cylinder. The track first head is shown, and a blow-up view shows the track divided into the smaller units called sectors.

The most important information on the hard disk drive, which is the information that the computer needs to boot and access the hard disk drive, is written on the outermost track in the first sector, or to track 0, sector 0. This is where the *master boot record* (MBR), created when you install the hard disk drive, is stored. You learn how to create that information when I cover how to partition the drive later in this chapter.

When buying a hard disk drive, keep in mind that the size of the drive you purchase will not be the same as the size of the drive after you install it. If you purchase a 1GB hard disk drive, you could end up with a 900MB–1100MB drive, depending on how the BIOS calculates the drive geometry. Furthermore, formatting the hard disk drive also consumes usable space. This is true no matter what type of hard disk drive you purchase, so expect it when you purchase a hard drive. Speaking of drive types, I cover that next.

A good rule of thumb when you buy a hard disk drive is to expect to have 90 percent of the space available for use after you install it. If you buy a 1.2GB drive, expect to get 1.08GB of usable space after you install. If you need more than that, buy a bigger drive.

Types of drives

Hard disk drives come in two basic types: IDE (pronounced *eye-dee-e*) and SCSI (pronounced *scuzzy*). IDE stands for *Integrated Drive Electronics*. SCSI stands for *Small Computer Systems Interface*. If you have a SCSI hard disk drive, you'll know it, because it requires a special controller card and typically is available only when customers request it. IDE, or Enhanced IDE (EIDE — pronounced e-eye-dee-e), is standard equipment on PCs. Because IDE is the most widely used, that's what I focus on here.

If you look at your hard disk drive and see that it has two ribbon cables — a thin cable and a wider one — in addition to a power cable, it is not an IDE or SCSI drive. It is probably an MFM (Modified Frequency Modulation) or an RLL (Run Length Limited) drive, and those drives and controller cards are not made for the mass market anymore. You see these drives most often on 286-based PCs, although 386-based PCs occasionally have them.

The beauty of an IDE drive is that much of what is needed to make the hard disk drive operate is built right into the drive. Earlier drive standards, such as MFM and RLL, required large controller cards dedicated only to handling the hard disk drive. These drives also required you to go though a great deal of work to set them up to run properly in your PC. But because the electronics needed for the IDE drive are built into the drive, the controller card can be very small — just large enough to act as an interface to the PC. Because the intelligence for running the drive is built into the drive, the drive can provide information, such as its manufacturer and its settings, to a PC BIOS designed to ask it for that information. The capability of a BIOS to do this is sometimes called the *auto-configure* or *auto-detect* capability. You see how this feature works later in this chapter.

Also, much of what had to be done by the user in previous drive standards has been done at the factory during the manufacturing process for IDE drives. You may have heard about items, such as low-level formatting and a drive-defect table, but these should no longer concern you as they are part of the tasks already completed for you when you purchase an IDE drive. IDE drives also are self-parking, which means that the drive senses the power loss when you turn off the PC and moves the read/write heads to a resting place where data is never written.

Back up your current hard drive

The first step to any hard disk installation is to make a backup of the data stored on the current hard disk drive. The most valuable thing on your PC is your data, and you want to put that data onto the new hard disk drive after you install it. The easiest way to back up your data is with a tape backup drive, which is covered in Chapter 3. You could use floppy diskettes and a backup utility included with the operating system, but this type of backup can require several diskettes, depending on how much data you have on your hard disk drive.

You may be able to copy the data from your current hard disk drive to your new hard disk drive, a topic that I cover in the section on installing a second hard disk drive. *But you cannot count on being able to copy the data from your current drive to the new drive.* You'll see why as we get further into the preparation and installation instructions. The only way to ensure that you can copy the data to the new drive is to have a copy on another medium, such as floppy diskettes or tape.

Make a bootable floppy disk

Part of the installation process requires a bootable diskette that you can use to restart the computer and to prepare the hard disk drive for use. If you're running DOS or Windows 3.*x*, the instructions for making this diskette appear in the section that follows. If you're running Windows 95, skip down to that section for instructions on how to make a bootable floppy diskette for your computer.

Make a bootable floppy under DOS or Windows 3.*x*

You need a floppy disk that will work in drive A of your PC. Place the diskette in the drive and format it using the /s parameter, which transfers the DOS system files to the diskette and makes it bootable. To do this task, go to the DOS prompt, type **FORMAT A: /S**, and press Enter. The computer formats the diskette and transfers the essential operating system files to the diskette. Put a label on the diskette and write the following information on the label: the date, "boot disk," and the version of the operating system you used to create the disk. If you're not sure which version you have, type **VER** at the DOS prompt, press Enter, and then copy the version information to your floppy disk's label.

When you have a bootable floppy disk, you need to copy to it the software tools that you need to set up the hard disk drive. These utilities should be in the DOS directory on your hard disk drive. You want to copy the utilities FDISK.EXE, FORMAT.COM, and SYS.COM. To copy these files to your bootable floppy disk from the DOS prompt, use the copy command and type **COPY C:\FDISK.EXE A:**, and then press Enter. Repeat the copy command, substituting the name of the two files for FDISK.EXE.

You also should have a *rescue disk*, which is a bootable floppy disk containing the environment files and your software drivers. (More information on the rescue diskette is available in Chapter 13, which covers operating systems.) The preceding steps, however, place the tools that you need on a separate diskette and enable you to complete the installation without distracting error messages.

Make a bootable floppy under Windows 95

In Windows 95, you need to make a *Startup Disk*, which is a bootable floppy disk containing the software utilities needed to install the hard disk drive. Windows 95 writes all the utilities you need, such as FDISK.EXE and FORMAT.COM, to the diskette for you — all you have to do is tell it to make the Startup Disk.

To make the Startup Disk, have ready a high-density disk that will work in your A drive (either a 1.2MB, 5¼-inch or a 1.44MB, 3½-inch), and then click on Start⇨Settings⇨ Control Panel⇨Add/Remove Programs. Select the Startup disk tab and click on the Create Disk button (see Figure 5-4). This causes Windows 95 to create the Startup Disk. You may be asked for your original Windows 95 diskettes or CD-ROM. If you don't have either, you can still create the Startup Disk, but turn to Chapter 13 for details on how to do so.

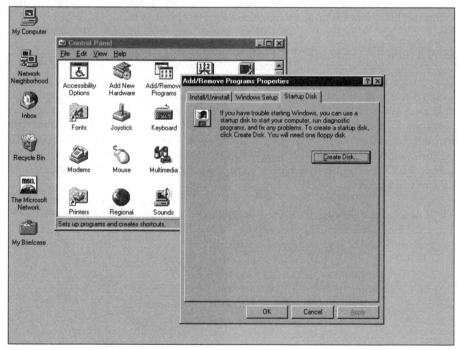

Figure 5-4: The Windows 95 Create Startup Disk function.

When the Startup Disk is complete, you can view the files on the diskette by clicking on My Computer and double-clicking on drive A. Then choose View⇨Options⇨View tab and select *Show all files* to see all the files on the diskette.

Check the BIOS

Check to see if the BIOS can support two drives, as well as what capacity hard disk drive the BIOS is capable of supporting. You also want a copy of the settings of your current hard disk drive. To get this information, you need to access the CMOS setup menu on your PC and check the settings. You also want to jot down the settings for your current hard disk drive. If you need to review what the CMOS setup menu is and how to get to it, turn back to the Chapter 1 section, "Your ROM BIOS and how to get into it."

An example of the CMOS settings for a 504MB Maxtor hard disk drive is shown in Figure 5-5. Although the CMOS doesn't record the brand of the drive, it does list information about the drive needed for operation. You can manually change these settings, but first you want to record them, just as they are, so that you can reproduce the settings if the installation of the new drive doesn't work or if you want to use the current drive along with the new drive.

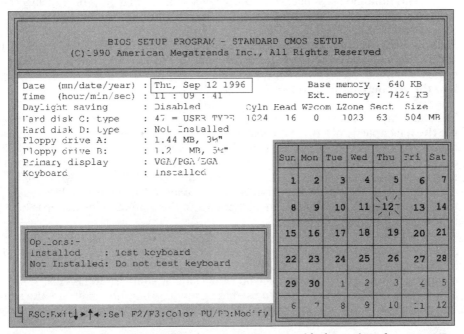

Figure 5-5: An American Megatrends, Inc., (AMI) BIOS with the settings for a 504MB Maxtor drive, model LXT535A.

Capacity and translation issues

It is possible that you will purchase a hard disk drive that can hold 1.2GB of data and only be able to use approximately 500MB of that available storage space. And just because you can't use the entire capacity of the drive after installing it doesn't mean that the store where you bought it will take it back. You may be stuck with capacity you paid for but can't use. There are ways around this problem, but first you need to determine whether your system has a means of getting around this bottleneck (some systems do). If not, you can look at your options to see if you want to purchase additional resources to resolve this problem or purchase a drive with a capacity of 500MB. First, I talk about the limitation and how it works.

A limitation inherent in some BIOSs, when coupled with a similar limitation in DOS, prevents you from having drives larger than 500MB in capacity. The actual numbers vary depending on how the BIOS and DOS calculate the size of the drive (an attribute known as the *drive geometry*). The geometry is calculated by multiplying the number of cylinders, the number of heads, the sectors per track (SPT), and the number of bytes per sector (which is usually 512).

The 500-plus MB limit is based on a limit of 1,024 cylinders, which in turn has to do with the space allotted to store the cylinders when the original design decisions were made. This limitation is similar to the odometer on a car that goes only to 99,999 miles before turning over to all zeros, except that the standard BIOS odometer that DOS can address can't go higher than 1,024 cylinders, 16 heads, and 63 SPT. To get 528, you'd multiply 1024 cylinders x 16 x 63 x 512 = 528,482,304 bytes, or 528MB. In practice, this varies, probably based on the bytes per sector, so you can end up with a number of capacity limits in the 500MB range, such as 504MB, 528MB, and 540MB, depending on how the geometry is interpreted.

The exact capacity isn't as important as your being aware that you may not be able to use the full capacity of a drive greater than 500MB without some help. Help comes in the form of *translation*. Translation enables the number of cylinders of the hard disk drive to be interpreted as a number below 1,024, simply by increasing one of the other factors, such as the number of heads. For example, a hard disk drive with 1,400 cylinders and 16 heads could be translated as having 700 cylinders and 32 heads. The numbers come out the same when multiplied, but the number of cylinders is kept below the 1,024 limit.

Another type of translation, known as *Logical Block Addressing* (LBA), gets around this 528MB barrier as well. LBA, if available, is usually incorporated into the BIOS of the computer. Western Digital has come up with a similar standard to LBA called *Enhanced IDE*. LBA and EIDE are often used as synonyms, but the results are the same — the ability to use drives larger than 528MB in size.

EIDE controller cards are available that come with their own BIOSs to handle the disk translation. Translation also can be done with software. The best way to accomplish drive translation is through the BIOS or the controller card, because software-based drive translation is memory-resident and therefore has the potential to cause conflicts with other software programs and operating systems.

Hard disk drive manufacturers are aware of this drive translation issue, so many of them have bundled drive-translation software with their drives. These software products are also available through retail software distribution channels. Some of the most popular titles include *Disk Manager* from Ontrack, *SpeedStor* from Storage Dimensions, and *Drive Pro* from Micro House.

If you want to install a hard disk drive larger than 500MB, you need to take a look at your BIOS first to see if translation is available. To do this, go into the CMOS setup menu on your PC and look specifically at the hard disk drive parameters. You may have to go to a submenu or to an "auto" setting to find it, but you're looking for the terms *drive translation, Logical Block Addressing, LBA, Enhanced CHS* (for Enhanced Cylinder/Head/Sector), *ECHS*, or some subset of those terms.

TIP

If the copyright date for your BIOS is earlier than 1994, most likely it does not offer the translation feature. You can see the BIOS copyright dates when the computer boots, or you can find them when you go into the CMOS setup menu. The date you want is the last date on the copyright if a range of dates is listed. For example, if the copyright dates are 1989–1993, then your BIOS is an unlikely candidate for translation.

Figures 5-6 and 5-7 show you examples from two BIOSs of drive translation in the CMOS setup menu. "Auto" means that the BIOS goes out and talks to the drive to get the drive geometry. It doesn't mean that the BIOS offers a mode that allows you to use a drive larger than 528MB in size. But, when in doubt, select "Auto" first.

```
                    ROM PCI/ISA BIOS (2A59FT5G)
                       STANDARD CMOS SETUP
                       AWARD SOFTWARE, INC.

   Date (mm:dd:yy) : Mon, Jan 29 1996
   Time (hh:mm:ss) : 13 : 23 : 16

   HARD DISKS          TYPE   SIZE    CYLS HEAD PRECOMP LANDZ SECTOR  MODE

   Primary Master   : Auto     0        0    0      0      0     0    AUTO
   Primary Slave    : Auto     0        0    0      0      0     0    AUTO
   Secondary Master : Auto     0        0    0      0      0     0    AUTO
   Secondary Slave  : Auto     0        0    0      0      0     0    AUTO

   Drive A : 1.2M , 5.25 in.
   Drive B : None                      ┌─────────────────────────────┐
                                       │  Base Memory:      640K      │
   Video   : EGA/VGA                   │  Extended Memory: 19456K     │
   Halt On : All Errors                │  Other Memory:     384K      │
                                       │                              │
                                       │  Total Memory: 20480K        │
                                       └─────────────────────────────┘

   ESC : Quit          ↑ ↓ → ←  : Select Item    PU/PD/+/-  : Modify
   F1  : Help          (Shift)F2 : Change Color
```

Figure 5-6: An Award BIOS with the auto-detect feature.

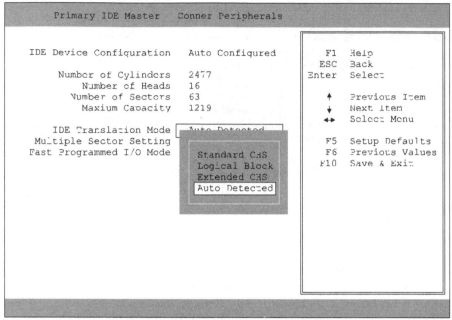

```
      Primary IDE Master   Conner Peripherals

  IDE Device Configuration   Auto Configured        F1    Help
                                                   ESC   Back
      Number of Cylinders   2477                   Enter  Select
        Number of Heads     16
        Number of Sectors   63                       ↑    Previous Item
        Maxium Capacity     1219                     ↓    Next Item
                                                     ↔    Select Menu
      IDE Translation Mode  Auto Detected
    Multiple Sector Setting                          F5    Setup Defaults
    Fast Programmed I/O Mode      Standard CHS       F6    Previous Values
                                  Logical Block      F10   Save & Exit
                                  Extended CHS
                                  Auto Detected
```

Figure 5-7: An AMI BIOS CMOS with several options for handling the drive translation. When in doubt, select Auto.

Western Digital translation example

Drive manufacturers tend to talk about translation from an engineering point of view. Take this text from drive maker Western Digital concerning the company's Caviar 540MB drive model AC2540.

"For example, on the AC2540 drive, a translate BIOS sets the parameters of the drive to the full 1,048 cylinders by 16 heads by 63 sectors per track, but presents a drive to DOS as 524 cylinders by 32 heads by 63 sectors per track."

What this means is that the BIOS capable of performing translation with the auto detect function sets the AC2540's CMOS menu settings at 1,048 cylinders, 16 heads, and 63 sectors, so those are the settings you would see in the CMOS menu. However, the BIOS would present (or translate) the drive to DOS as having 524 cylinders, 32 heads, and 63 sectors.

Your options if there is no BIOS translation

If you don't find any hint of translation, LBA, or ECHS addressing in your BIOS, then chances are your BIOS doesn't support it. You have several options at this point:

✦ You can stick with drives approximately 500MB in size. (If you have a larger drive, you can use it, but you'll only have access to about the first 500 MB — the rest of it will be unusable.)

✦ You can install a controller card that has its own BIOS translation built in, known as an EIDE card. This is an inexpensive fix, but it takes some work to do. These cards usually provide faster throughput than older varieties, so you may see significantly increased performance from your hard disk drive. Some EIDE cards also include software drivers that can introduce the same problems that you may encounter with software translation, especially if you're running Windows NT, OS/2, or Windows 95. Installation of a new hard disk controller card is covered in Chapter 8. It would be a good idea to read over the material in Chapter 8 about installing a new controller card before you decide to go this route.

✦ You can check into a BIOS upgrade to see if you can upgrade your BIOS to one that offers drive translation.

✦ You can use software to attempt to do the translation. I personally think that you should avoid using drive translation software if possible. It tends to slightly reduce the speed of your hard disk access. Also, as I mentioned earlier, this software is memory-resident. This means that you reduce the amount of lower memory available to your applications and thus could encounter conflicts between other operating systems or software applications.

After you use the software to install a large drive, removing the software is a painful process if you decide later that you need to. You have to back up your data, reinstall the drive (following the installation instructions provided later in this chapter), and restore your data to get the translation software out. The advantage of using the software is that it can make preparing the drive for use less intimidating. This fact only holds true after the drive is physically connected to the computer, however; after you see the steps for setting up the drive without the software, you'll wonder why anyone would find the task intimidating.

The software exists because it fills a need that often cannot be filled any other way, however. I cover the use of drive translation software and what you can expect from it in the installation section. I also cover some troubleshooting procedures, in case you run into problems with this type of software, in the troubleshooting section.

Check inside the PC

You know that you have a hard disk drive, so you know that you have the space to replace it inside the PC. But you may want to know whether you need an adapter kit to make a $3^{1}/_{2}$-inch hard disk drive fit into a $5^{1}/_{4}$-inch drive bay. The new hard disk drives are about $1^{7}/_{10}$ inches high (or half-height) by $3^{1}/_{2}$ inches wide and are designed to fit in the same space as a $3^{1}/_{2}$-inch floppy drive. If you have only $5^{1}/_{4}$-inch drive bays, you need an adapter kit.

Figure 5-8 shows a case with an opening for a single hard disk drive in a 5¼-inch drive bay, whereas Figure 5-9 shows a case that has room for two hard disk drives. (You don't need to concern yourself about an opening in the front of the case because you don't need one for your hard disk drive. Also, some cases are designed so that the hard disk drives have bays different than the floppy disk drives, so that distinction will be obvious when you open up the case.) If your case uses plastic rails to support the drives, you may need to pick up a set for your new drive, although you can use the rails of your old drive if you don't plan to keep it. Adapter kits for fitting 3½-inch drives into 5¼-inch slots and the plastic rails used to hold drives in place are the same, whether they are used for a hard disk drive or a floppy disk drive.

Installation

Hard disk drive installation is a three-step process. First, you make the physical connections to the drive, then you set up the drive so that the computer can talk to it, and finally, when you're sure it works, you install the drive into the computer case.

Figure 5-8: Only a single hard disk drive fits in this case, behind the floppy disk drive and on top of the cable.

Figure 5-9: Two hard disk drives, in addition to the 3¹/₂-inch floppy disk drive, fit in this case without adapters or drive rails.

Just as a reminder, you should have the following items before you begin this procedure:

✦ A bootable floppy diskette with the FDISK and FORMAT utilities on it

✦ The CMOS settings for your current drive

✦ The CMOS settings for your new drive

✦ A backup copy of the data on your current hard disk drive

If you skipped to this section but aren't sure how to get the materials listed here, the preparation section earlier in this chapter tells you how.

Physical connection of the hard disk drive

You need to turn off the computer, open the case, and remove the 40-pin ribbon cable from your existing hard disk drive. Do not remove the ribbon cable from the controller card. You want to avoid disconnecting anything you don't have to, especially if you are new at this.

Connect the ribbon cable you removed from your old hard disk drive to your new hard drive. Make sure that the stripe indicating pin 1 on the cable is on the same side as the power connector on the hard disk drive (see Figure 5-10). Then disconnect the power cable from the old hard disk drive and connect it to the new hard disk drive.

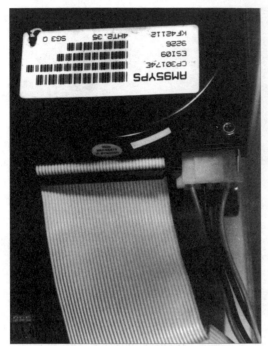

Figure 5-10: A properly cabled hard disk drive.
Note that the power connector is on the pin 1 side,
and so is the stripe on the ribbon cable.

Like all pros, you want to make sure that you set the new hard disk drive on a flat, stable, non-conductive surface — such as a desktop — for testing before you install it more permanently in the case. The ribbon cables for hard disk drives tend to be short, so be careful not to pull the ribbon cable away from the connection to the controller card while you're moving it from the old hard disk drive to the new hard disk drive.

You may need an adapter to convert the larger, 4-pin Molex connector to the newer, smaller power connectors, or vice versa. You can easily obtain these adapters, which are shown in Chapter 4, from your local computer store.

Be sure to note the parameters of the drive, which are usually recorded on top of the drive, as shown on the Seagate drive in Figure 5-11. You need these parameters for the next step.

Configure the new drive in the CMOS

After you connect the ribbon cable and the power cable to the new hard disk drive, you need to turn on the PC and display the CMOS setup menu to configure the drive as drive C. Saving your old drive C settings is important, so be sure to write them down before you begin this section.

Figure 5-11: This Seagate drive has the parameters recorded right on the cable on the top of the drive.

To enter the new drive settings, you need the drive parameters. These parameters include the number of cylinders, number of heads, the precomp or WPC (I explain this later), the number of sectors per track, the landing zone, and the size of the drive.

If the BIOS has an auto-detect or similar function, make use of it now. (A BIOS with translation probably provides auto-detection as well.) You may have to invoke the function, which has the BIOS ask the drive for its settings, and then brings back the settings to place them into the CMOS for you. You then need to follow the instructions in your CMOS setup menu.

If an automatic detection function is not available, you want to look for the *User Defined* setting for the hard disk drive. The most important values are the cylinder (abbreviated *cyl*), head (sometimes abbreviated *HD* or *hd*), and sector (sometimes abbreviated *sect* or *spt* for sectors per track). You can scroll through the list of possible parameter settings to look for the exact settings for your hard disk drive, but going to the User Defined option and entering the settings yourself is easier. Most BIOSs have a list of drive parameters that you can choose from, with *User Defined* typically appearing as the last one on the list. (Figure 5-12 shows a typical user-defined setting.)

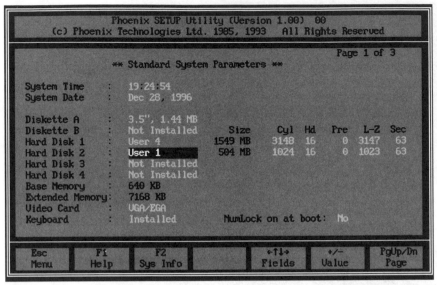

Figure 5-12: The user-defined option is often the last one on the list of drive parameters. This Phoenix BIOS enables you to set up four user-defined drive types.

Next, you want to enter the parameter information in the User Defined settings area. Two additional fields of the hard disk drive parameters that you may not have found in the settings provided with your hard disk are the *write precompensation* (also known as *read/write precompensation, precomp, RPC/WPC, or WPC)* and the *landing zone* (LZ).

Write precompensation is a way of compensating for the *drift* of the magnetic information written on the disk. Put simply, it enables the read/write head to space the magnetic charges that would repel each other closer together, while spacing the charges that would attract each other farther apart. The value requested by the BIOS in the precomp setting is the cylinder where this compensation should begin.

The landing zone is where the hard disk drive parks the read/write heads when the drive shuts down. You may not find the precomp or the landing zone information anywhere on the drive, but that is because these functions are controlled by the IDE drive. That means whatever you enter will probably be overridden by the drive. The CMOS may require you to enter something in those locations, however; in such a case, the precomp and landing zone settings have conventions that you can follow.

Traditionally, the precomp setting is either 0 (zero) or 65535. If you don't know what to enter, enter **0** for the precomp.

The landing zone is the last cylinder on the drive. One convention is simply to enter the number of cylinders here — for example, if the number of cylinders is 1,024, you enter 1,024. However, one school of thought says that the number entered for the landing zone should be the number of cylinders minus one. This is because the number of the first cylinder is 0, so if there are 1,024 cylinders, then the last cylinder would be number 1023. As I mentioned earlier, the IDE drive controls parking the heads, but, more than likely, the CMOS will make you enter a value, and entering settings that make sense is an industry convention. Personally, I enter the number of cylinders minus one; if the drive has 1,024 cylinders, I enter **1023** for the landing zone setting.

After you enter the parameters, the CMOS calculates the size of the drive, so you don't have to enter it. The drive size may be different than the size you expect, depending on how the BIOS calculates the drive geometry, but it should be in the same size range. For example, a drive advertised at 540MB may come out to be 528MB, but it should not be 212MB.

After the new drive's parameters are entered into the CMOS, you want to save and exit the CMOS menu and proceed with the next step, which is to boot from the floppy disk you created earlier.

Boot from the bootable floppy

Now is the time to use that bootable floppy diskette you created earlier. When you exit the CMOS menu, the computer restarts, so you want to put the bootable floppy diskette in drive A. You may get an error message concerning an invalid setup, but you can ignore that message. If the message requires you to take action, such as `press F1 to continue or F2 to enter setup`, then press the key required to continue (F1 in this case). You'll be asked for the time and date, and then you'll get the A:> prompt.

In Windows 95, if you boot from the Windows 95 Startup disk, a DOS prompt appears that looks like the following.

```
[Windows 95] A:>
```

MS-DOS version 7.0 is part of Windows 95 and is not available independently of Windows 95.

Partition the drive using FDISK

At this point, you're ready to partition the drive. All drives must have a partition so that the BIOS knows where to find the operating system files. With hard disk drives, you have the option of making several partitions, but it's easier to make just one. To do this, you need to use the DOS utility FDISK, which you should have copied to your new drive from the bootable diskette created from the previous hard disk drive.

When you reach the A:> prompt, type **FDISK** and press Enter. You see the following menu on your screen:

```
Choose one of the following:
     1. Create DOS Partition
     2. Set Active Partition
     3. Delete Partition
     4. Display Partition
```

You want to choose the first option to create a DOS partition. DOS then presents you with the following menu:

```
     1. Create Primary DOS Partition
     2. Create Extended DOS Partition
     3. Create Logical DOS Drive
```

Again, you want to choose number one to create the primary DOS partition that your computer will use to boot. DOS then shows you the maximum space available for that partition and asks if you want to use that space for the partition. You can create several logical partitions, which look like separate drives with separate drive letters (C, D, E, and so on) to your programs, but most people create a single large partition because one partition is easier to deal with. To accept the maximum size, press **Y** for yes.

If you create several partitions and later decide that you want to repartition the hard disk drive so that you have only one large partition, you need to know that you'll lose all your data if you delete the partition. So, you need to make a good backup of the drive(s) involved.

To change a partition size or eliminate a partition, you should boot from your bootable floppy diskette, start FDISK, and delete the current partitions. You do this by choosing Delete Partition from the main FDISK menu and following the menu instructions. After the existing partitions are deleted, you can create a new partition or partitions.

When FDISK has created the partition, the computer restarts. You need to leave the bootable floppy diskette in the drive until you complete the next step, which is formatting. You may also receive the same error message you got earlier when you booted from the floppy diskette, so, like before, bypass the message and continue with the boot process until you get to the A:> prompt.

Format the hard disk drive as a system disk

After the disk is partitioned, you need to prepare partitions for use by formatting them. You format the hard disk drive by typing **FORMAT C: /S** and then pressing Enter. The */S* parameter tells DOS to copy the system files for the boot process from the floppy disk to the boot sector of the hard disk drive. The format command then issues the following statement: All data will be lost on hard drive, do you wish to proceed? When you see this statement, press **Y** for yes. As the formatting proceeds, DOS gives you feedback on its progress. After the formatting is complete, DOS also gives you an opportunity to label the hard drive. You can choose an 11-character description of the drive. Stick with standard characters such as alphabet letters and numbers and avoid spaces and special characters such as ?, @, #, $, or %.

After the volume label, you should see the message System transferred and the A:> prompt again. Your hard disk drive should be ready for use, and you now should be able to boot from the new drive. After the drive is bootable, it is time to perform a few quick tests to make sure that it is operational.

By the way, if you created any logical drives when you created the partition, then you need to format each one before you can use them to store data. Only drive C can be made bootable, so there is no point in adding the /S parameter when you partition any logical drives that you created using FDISK. During the partitioning process, DOS assigns drive letter designations to the drives that you must use during formatting. As a result, the first partition would be the C drive, the second partition would be the D drive, the third would be the E drive, and so on. You're asked for a volume label at the end of the formatting process for each logical drive, as well.

Test the new hard disk drive

At this point, you want to attempt a boot from your newly installed hard disk drive. To accomplish this task, you should turn off the computer for at least ten seconds. This is a *cold boot,* which allows the PC's electronic circuits to clear. Make sure that you removed the bootable diskette from drive A, and then turn the computer back on. You need to reenter the time and date, and then you should see a C:> prompt. Type **DIR** and press Enter. If you installed a 540MB drive, you see something like this:

```
Volume in Drive C: is unlabeled
Volume Serial Number is 3950-1201
Directory of C:/



COMMAND    COM       54,645 05-31-94      6:22A
      1 FILES(S)                          54,645 bytes
                    502,827,264 bytes free
```

Notice where I underlined the numbers in the preceding code listing — of that 9-digit number, these first three digits represent the available capacity of the disk measured in MB. A drive that is bigger than 1GB will have a ten-digit number, and the first of the 10 digits will be the size of the drive in gigabytes. For example, a 1.6GB drive may show 1,247,674,264 bytes free, which would equal approximately 1.2GB of free space.

If you experience problems, go to the troubleshooting section that follows this installation section for help.

Mount the drive into the case

Because you are replacing your current drive, placing the new drive into the case shouldn't be very difficult. You simply need to look at how the old drive is currently mounted, take the old drive out, and mount the new drive in its place. Be sure to power down the computer and wait a few seconds to let the drive park the heads before you move the hard disk drive. You have already looked at how the current drive is mounted, so you should have any rails or adapters that you need.

This is not the time for using drilling or power tools (other than a cordless screw-driver). If you are tempted to drill holes at this stage, you don't have the proper adapters, so you need to go to your computer store and secure the correct rails and adapters.

After the new drive is mounted, you should turn on the PC and retest it before you put the lid back on your computer case. Sometimes you have to disconnect a cable or two while mounting the drive to get it into place, especially with smaller cases, so you want to retest the drive to make sure that your connections are secure and working before you close up. Follow the test instructions listed earlier. Also, make sure that you didn't leave any screws or tools in the case before you power up the computer for testing.

Be sure to test the floppy disk drives before you close up the case. You may have pulled a cable loose accidentally, or forgotten to reconnect a cable, and these problems are easier to fix now than later. Put a diskette in each of the floppy disk drives, and then create a directory on the diskette by using the DIR command, just to make sure that each drive is properly connected and works. After you are sure that everything is working, you can close up the computer case and restore the data from your old hard disk drive.

Restore your data

After you've determined that the drive is working, you need to restore your data. Typically, this means you have to restore the software you used to create the backup, particularly if you are using a tape backup. If you are running DOS, first restore the DOS backup software, and then start the software and restore the data to the new hard disk drive. If you are using software that runs in Windows 3.x, you can check for the availability of a DOS version of the Windows software that you can use to restore the backup you made in Windows. That way, you don't have to reinstall Windows 3.x — all you have to do is install the DOS-based version of the backup software, and you can get Windows 3.x back during the restore process.

If the software that you are using to make backups requires Windows 95, you need to reinstall Windows 95, reinstall the backup software (if it is separate from the backup software available in Windows 95), and then restore your Windows 95 backup. Despite the fact that the Startup disk created by Windows 95 displays a DOS prompt, and the fact that you can get a DOS-version of tape backup software that works with that DOS version (which is DOS 7.0, by the way), the DOS tape software does not support long filenames or the registry that Windows 95 uses. As a result, you cannot count on getting a true restore unless you use the Windows 95 software with which you created the backup, and that happens only if you restore Windows 95 and then the backup software.

Burn-in your hard drive

A burn-in is a test period where you put the new hardware through its paces to find problems. This step is optional for some people, but I think it's an important one, especially considering how much you depend on your hard disk drive. Although some hard disk drives come with warranties that cover as many as three years against failure, finding a serious fault early in a drive's life (as opposed to later) is easier on you.

You can accomplish an adequate burn-in by leaving your computer on for 24 hours. The hard disk drive spins continuously while the PC is on, so you can at least be assured that the motor in the drive is working by performing this test.

I prefer a more rigorous burn-in test that involves writing to and reading from the hard disk drive over a 24-hour period (or longer — but 48 hours is the longest burn-in I'd recommend). To do this test, I use software designed to do the job and report back errors. I use the PC during the day, and then start the burn-in software so that it runs overnight for two or three nights. Burn-in capability is included in most diagnostic software packages, such as Norton Utilities and Check It. A shareware program called *Burn-In* also is available from OsoSoft of Los Osos, California, for performing a burn-in. (See Appendix A for diagnostic software vendor contact information.)

Installation in review

To install a new hard disk drive, follow these steps:

1. Make a bootable floppy diskette and copy the FDISK and FORMAT utilities to the diskette.

2. Back up the data on the existing hard disk drive.

3. Record the current CMOS settings for the existing hard disk drive.

4. With the computer off, attach the ribbon cable from the old hard disk drive to the new hard disk drive. Attach a power cable to the new drive.

5. Turn on the computer, enter the CMOS setup, and configure drive C with the parameters of the new hard disk drive.

6. Reboot the computer with the bootable diskette in the drive A so that the computer boots from the diskette.

7. Run FDISK from drive A to partition the hard disk drive.

8. Format the new hard drive using the /S parameter (FORMAT C: /S) to transfer the system files from drive A to the new hard disk drive.

9. Take the floppy disk out of drive A and reboot the computer. The computer should boot from the new hard disk drive.

10. Briefly test the new drive.

11. Install the new hard disk drive into the computer case.

12. Briefly test the drive once more before placing the lid back on the computer case. Test the floppy disk drives also.

13. Close the computer case.

14. Burn-in the new hard disk drive.

15. Restore your data.

Troubleshooting

If you have a problem during the installation of your hard disk drive, you should find it during one of the testing phases. Here are the most common problems and how to fix them:

1. Fixed Disk Configuration Error. This means that the BIOS could not find the hard disk drive during the bootup sequence. You may encounter this error if the drive does not have power or if it is cabled incorrectly. Check the ribbon cable connection at the drive and at the controller card. Make sure that the ribbon cable is connected so that you cannot see any pins and so that the stripped side appears on the same side as pin 1 of the controller and of the hard disk drive. (Remember that pin 1 of the hard disk drive usually is on the same side as the power connection.) Also make sure that the power cables are securely connected. If you want examples of what to look for when you're searching for bent pins, read the "Troubleshooting Practice" section at the end of Chapter 4. Though that chapter deals mainly with floppy disk drive installation, the connections for hard disk drives and floppy disk drives are similar, so they share similar problems.

   You may need to disconnect the ribbon cable and look for bent pins. Another common mistake, especially if the light is low, is to connect the ribbon cable only to the upper half of the pins. Make sure that all pins are going into the ribbon cable connection. If you find bent pins, straighten them gently with needlenose pliers, then reconnect the cable and try again.

   You can also go to the CMOS setup menu and check the CMOS settings you entered against the settings for your new hard drive. Make sure that you entered the settings correctly in the appropriate fields.

2. Invalid configuration information. You will probably see this message (along with information on how to enter the CMOS setup menu) before you partition and format the drive, but you should not see it afterward. You may get this message if the BIOS cannot find the hard disk drive, or if the ribbon cable is

installed backwards on either the hard disk drive or the controller card. Check the ribbon cables and the other connections by following the troubleshooting procedures listed in the preceding error message description.

3. `HDD Controller Failure`. You may get this message if everything is connected correctly but you haven't yet partitioned (FDISK) or formatted the drive. This error message may also appear, however, if the cabling is incorrect between the controller card and the hard disk drive. Check the ribbon cable and make sure that the stripe appears at pin 1 on both the controller card and the hard disk drive. In addition, check the connections using the guidelines in Step 1 of this section. If everything looks all right, then you can try to partition the drive using FDISK. If you cannot partition the drive, then you need to go back and recheck the connections.

Also, make sure that the controller card is correctly seated in the slot if you have a controller card that uses a slot rather than being integrated into the motherboard. If the controller card is integrated into the motherboard, check the BIOS settings in the CMOS setup menu. Some motherboards have more than one controller for hard disk drives, and you can turn these controllers on and off in the BIOS.

If that doesn't work, check the jumper settings of the hard disk drive. These jumpers determine the *master* and *slave* settings needed to use two hard disk drives together. The jumpers may have come loose and fallen off or are set incorrectly. Make sure the jumpers are set to the master setting. Recently, drive manufacturers have started printing the jumper settings on the top of the drive. If these settings did not come on the drive or in the accompanying documentation, you may have to get information from the drive manufacturer to determine the correct settings. If you need more information on this topic, check the section on jumper settings under installing a second hard disk drive.

4. `No Fixed Disks Present`. FDISK provides this error message, which tells you that it cannot find the hard disk drive. This means that the drive either is not receiving power or is not cabled correctly.

5. `Cannot create partition`. FDISK tells you that it cannot create a partition if one already exists. Go to the main FDISK menu and select 4, "Display partition information." Make sure that the ribbon cable is connected to the new hard disk drive so that you do not end up looking at partition information from your old hard disk drive.

If you created a partition incorrectly or are installing a drive from another computer, you should delete the current partition and then create a new partition. Deleting the partition destroys all data on the hard disk drive, so be sure you want to do this.

You delete the partition by selecting option 3, Delete Partition, from the opening FDISK menu and then following the instructions provided on-screen. After the old partition is deleted, you can create a new one.

6. `No boot device available`. This message means that the hard disk drive does not have the required operating system files, nor do you have a bootable floppy disk in drive A. You need to boot up from the bootable disk, and then type **DIR C:** and press Enter to see if the file COMMAND.COM exists on the hard disk drive. If there are no files listed, or if COMMAND.COM is not listed, you need to reformat the hard disk drive according to the directions listed in the "Format the hard disk drive as a system disk" section earlier in this chapter. Make sure that you use the /S parameter to get the system files transferred to the hard disk drive.

Question: I understand that low-level formatting used to be done by the installers but is now done by manufacturers at the factory. Why aren't hard disk drives pre-partitioned and pre-formatted as well?

Answer: The partitioning and formatting process prepares the drive for the interaction of the operating system with the hardware. Low-level formatting, however, was done as a function of the hard disk controller and was independent of the operating system. Low-level formatting was standardized, so it can now be performed at the factory. The operating system that *you* choose to use on the PC, however, must be used to partition and format the hard disk drive. Even a different version of an operating system from the same manufacturer can make a big difference in the partitioning and formatting — so much so, that if you formatted a PC's hard disk with one version of DOS and booted from a floppy diskette with another version of DOS, the hard disk controller could be damaged. The manufacturer of the hard disk drive has no way to know what version of DOS (or even what operating system) you'll choose to place on that hard disk drive. So, if you choose to do the installation, you have to do the partitioning and formatting as well.

By the way, if you have multiple PCs, that reason is also why it is a good idea to have them all running the same version of DOS. If you need information on how to upgrade a PC to a newer version of an operating system, see Chapter 13.

Question: I've installed the hard disk drive, but my system doesn't see it. Why is that?

Answer: The system won't recognize the hard disk drive until you have correctly entered its parameters into the CMOS, partitioned the drive, and formatted the drive.

Question: If I decide to use the drive translation software that came with my hard disk drive to set it up, how does that change the installation procedure?

Answer: You still need your bootable floppy disk, but just follow the instructions for physically installing the drive. When you restart the system after physically installing the drive, most drive translation software programs have you first boot from a floppy disk, then replace the floppy disk with the disk containing the drive translation software, and then type **setup** or **install**. At that point, the drive translation software takes over and may ask you a few questions regarding the particulars of the hard disk drive. The translation software handles the partitioning and the formatting, although it may ask you to reinsert the bootable floppy into drive A so that it can place the correct version of DOS on the hard disk drive.

Question: Why do I have to repartition and reformat my hard disk drive if I want to remove the drive translation software?

Answer: The drive translation software writes itself into the master boot record (MBR) of the hard disk drive, which is where the partition information is stored. Every time the computer boots, the software for the translation is loaded. To remove the translation software, you have to delete the partition, which means you lose all formatting information for the drive and must repartition and reformat the drive to make it usable again.

Question: I have a drive translation option in my CMOS setup, and I also have the drive translation software. Which should I use?

Answer: The drive translation in your BIOS is always better than the drive translation software. The CMOS menu enables you to change the options you have for your BIOS. Drive translation software can cause conflicts with operating systems such as Windows NT, OS/2, and Windows 95, as well as memory conflicts with applications software. Given a choice, I recommend that you use the drive translation in the BIOS.

Question: I installed a large drive, but when I used the DIR command to see the space available on the drive, I found that it was less than half of what I expected. Why is that?

Answer: You can install a drive that has more than 1,024 cylinders into the CMOS setup, use FDISK on it, format the drive, and it appears to work. However, when the BIOS doesn't have translation functionality, DOS doesn't know how to properly handle the drive. If you don't have any translation software or hardware and want to use the drive, set the cylinders in the CMOS to 1,024. At least you get the maximum capacity available, which is in the neighborhood of 500-plus MB.

Question: Can I use FDISK and partition the hard disk drive into several drives if I have a drive greater than 500MB in size and no translation available?

Answer: Nope, it doesn't work that way. You can partition a hard disk drive into smaller drives, but only if DOS will address the drive space. Anything past the 1,024 cylinder limit without translation in place is just dead space.

Question: What are the master and slave settings on my hard disk drive? Do I need to worry about them?

Answer: The master setting is for the drive from which you want to boot. Most BIOSs can support a second hard disk drive, which has to be set to the slave setting in order for the two drives to work from the same controller. This means you can use a single cable with two connectors in it and operate two physical drives in your system. If you have only one hard disk drive, that drive should be set to the master setting, which is the way most drives are set when they come from the factory. The only time you set a drive to its slave settings is when you want to use it as a second drive in your computer. If you have only one hard disk drive, then no, you typically do not have to concern yourself with the master/slave settings.

Installing a Second Hard Disk Drive

Most people prefer to keep their current hard disk drive, when they install a new hard disk drive. The reasons are obvious — it is easier to transfer data between the two drives, and the storage space on the old drive is already paid for.

If the new hard disk drive can be the bootable drive, or drive C, all the better. The new drive is probably faster than your old drive, and with Windows and other disk-intensive operating systems, you want all the hard disk speed you can get. Also, you can simply copy the software applications you have from the old drive to the new one. This eliminates the need to reinstall your application software if you set the new drive as drive C and the old drive as drive D.

IDE drives are notorious for presenting sticky problems when you attempt to get two of them to work together, however, even if both drives are from the same manufacturer. Professionals use a three-step process to install two hard disk drives. The first step is to get the new drive to work independently of the old drive. I covered that step earlier in this chapter. The second step is to get the new drive to work as a slave to the old drive, which I cover next. The third and optional step is to make the old drive the slave (drive D) and the new drive the master (drive C), with the goal of copying the data from the old drive to the new drive. I show you how to tackle these two steps in the following sections, starting with getting the new drive to work as drive D.

Preparation

To do this step, you need to follow the same preparation process as that for installing a new hard disk drive, as well as a take into account a couple of special considerations for installing a second drive. Those considerations are next.

Look for room in the case

Make sure that you have room in your computer case for both the new drive and the old drive. You need to open up your PC and look inside the case for room in which to install the new hard disk drive. The standard size for hard disk drives is $3^1/_2$ inches wide by $1^7/_{10}$-inches tall, so you want to look for that size of space. In addition, you can mount hard disk drives close together, although some air space is desirable to help manage the heat inside the case. You also can mount hard disk drives sideways, and some cases are designed to allow you to do just that.

See if you need adapters or mounting rails

Another consideration is getting the proper materials to mount the drive into your case. This is the time to look over your case, see how the other drives are mounted, and make note if you need an adapter to fit a $3^1/_2$-inch drive into a $5^1/_4$-inch drive bay, or if you need mounting rails to hold the drive in the bay.

After you have determined that you have the necessary space and supplies for mounting the drive, you are ready for the next step.

Obtain a two-drive 40-pin ribbon cable

You need a special ribbon cable that can support two hard disk drives. Hard disk drive cables are 40-pin cables (as opposed to the 34-pin ribbon cables that connect floppy disk drives). Figure 5-13 shows such a cable. If you buy the drive in retail packaging, the cable may be included, but be sure to check. If not, be sure to ask for one of these cables when you purchase your new hard disk drive.

Check to see if you need a splitter or power cable adapter

Some power supplies have fewer power cable connectors than others. You can obtain splitters that can split a single power cable from the power supply into two connectors, as well as adapters that change a large Molex connector to the newer, smaller

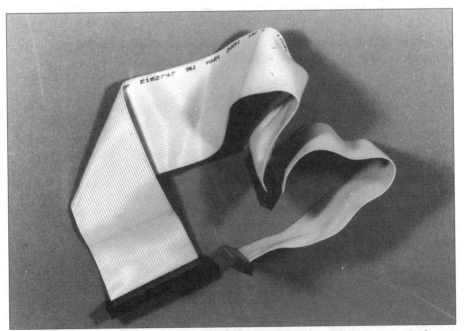

Figure 5-13: A 40-pin ribbon cable for connecting two hard disk drives to a single controller.

type of power adapter. Although I don't advocate splitting the power from a single power supply cable to run two hard disk drives, you can split a single power cable to serve two of the floppy disk drives, leaving a power cable free for connection to your new hard disk drive.

Check to see whether or not you require a splitter to free up a power cable for your new hard disk drive. In addition, you want to note whether you have large or small power connectors available, and then note the type of power connection on the hard disk drive when you purchase it to determine if you need an adapter there as well. If you need to see this type of an adapter, turn to Chapter 4.

Installation

As I've mentioned, the only reliable way to install a second hard disk drive is to install it as if you were going to replace your current hard disk drive. That means you follow the same steps outlined earlier in this chapter for replacing the drive, up to and including the first test after the new drive has been partitioned and formatted. After you have completed the initial test, you can confidently proceed with getting the two drives to work together. Now you need to set the new drive to slave mode, cable the two drives, and test again. (An "Installation in Review" section for installing a second hard disk drive is provided for your convenience at the end of this section.)

Set your new hard disk drive to slave mode

Before you can get two hard disk drives to work together, the master and slave modes need to be set correctly on each drive. This section introduces what master and slave modes are and how to set these modes.

What are the master and slave modes?

As I mentioned earlier in this chapter, the default settings (or the factory settings) for hard disk drives are set to the master drive mode. The master drive is the drive from which the computer boots, whereas slave drives hand over boot control to the master drive. To get two drives to work together, one must be set to master mode and the other must be set to slave mode.

Because your current hard disk drive is set to master mode (you know that because the drive boots and previously was the only drive in your PC), you need to set the new drive to slave mode to get both drives to work together. This involves setting jumpers on the new drive.

Slave settings are not the same for all drives and vary from model to model, even if the drives are from the same manufacturer. The constant here is that both drives have jumpers, which you need to change for the two drives to operate together.

You need to set the jumpers to slave mode on the new drive, and then try to operate the drives together. After you set the jumpers to slave mode, you're ready to cable the drives.

How jumpers set master and slave modes

Jumpers are small, plastic-coated connectors that connect pins on the drive to change the functionality of the hard disk drive (see Figure 5-14). These connectors also can be referred to as *shunts*, whereas the actual pins to which they connect are called jumpers. In any case, jumpers on a hard disk drive enable you to change the master and slave settings of the drive.

Some drives have stand-alone master settings, for when the drive is the only drive on the system, and slave settings, meaning the drive can be used as the D drive on the system with another drive as the C drive. If you don't know the jumper settings for a drive you have, you can often get these settings from the manufacturer via the Internet, a bulletin board system, or a faxback system. (A faxback system enables you to call an automated menu, from which you can make choices using a Touch-Tone phone, and then have the information you selected faxed back to you.) Figure 5-15 shows the jumpers on a Conner 1.2GB drive set to stand-alone master mode. These settings are similar to the Conner CFS540A drive featured in the "The second hard drive dilemma" case study later in this chapter. The documentation for the jumper settings from the Conner faxback system is shown in the case study.

Figure 5-14: On the lower left are the jumpers on the underside of the Seagate drive.

Figure 5-15: The jumpers on the Conner drive set to master mode.

Connect the cables to the drives

As I mentioned in the preparation section, you want each drive to receive power directly from the power supply. If you need a splitter to supply power, you should split the power to the floppy disk drives, freeing a power cable for your new hard disk drive.

Some new hard disk drives have the new, smaller power connection. You should check your hard disk drive and have that adapter ready if you need it. After you have power supplied to both drives, you can connect the 40-pin ribbon cable.

The cable has a female connector on each end and another female connector near one of the ends. The cable end with the two female connectors is for the hard disk drives, whereas the other end goes to the hard disk drive controller. You should already have a ribbon cable connected to the controller card, so you want to remove that ribbon cable and replace it with the new ribbon cable. Because the other cable worked, all you have to do is make sure that the stripe indicating pin 1 on the new ribbon cable is on the same side as the stripe on the old ribbon cable. The controller should have a small 1 printed on one end of the connection pins, and the stripe should be on the same side as the 1 (see Figure 5-16).

Don't disconnect too many things at once. If you are new at this, figuring out where the cable goes may become confusing, especially if you disconnect all the cables at once.

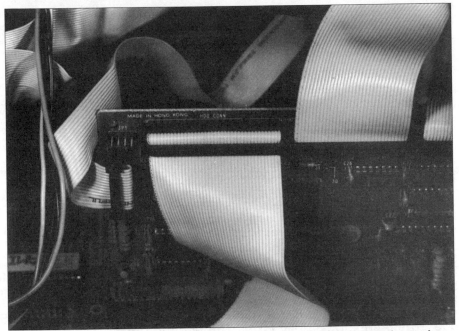

Figure 5-16: Pin 1 on the controller card should be on the same side as the marks or stripe on the ribbon cable.

Change the CMOS settings to reflect both drives

At this point, you need to restart the computer and access the CMOS menu to enter the parameters of both drives. If you have followed my instructions so far, you should have the parameters for the new drive entered as drive C in the CMOS. You also should have recorded the parameters for your old hard disk as part of your preparation for installing the new hard disk drive.

Now you need to reenter the parameters you recorded for your old drive into the settings for drive C. Then enter the parameters for your new drive as drive D. You should have the parameters for the two drives entered, as shown back in Figure 5-13. If you want (and your CMOS is able to do so), you can have the CMOS auto-detect each drive and enter the settings for you. Whichever way you opt to do this task, you need to have the settings for the drives entered and then save and exit the CMOS menu. The computer should restart at this point and boot from your old drive C.

Test the drives

If you did what you were supposed to do and have already partitioned and formatted the new drive, you now should be able to go straight into testing both drives. The old drive stays as drive C, and the new drive will be drive D. Start your tests by using the DOS directory command on each drive to see if the computer recognizes each one. The next paragraph explains how.

You automatically start at drive C, so type **DIR** and press Enter to see the contents of your C drive. The contents of the drive should be the same as what they were before you started this installation process. Then switch to drive D by typing **D:** and pressing Enter, and then perform the same directory command there. Only COMMAND.COM should appear for this drive, but this test lets you know that the drive is working.

Turn off the computer, wait ten seconds, then restart the PC. Perform the same tests again. If you don't have any problems, then your job is just about finished. If you do have problems, see the troubleshooting tips provided at the end of this section.

The second hard drive dilemma

What first appeared to be a straightforward addition of a second hard disk drive turned into an all-day project for one user. The culprit was an undocumented jumper switch.

Susan wanted to upgrade her PC in steps. Because she already had a 386 multimedia clone, she decided to expand her hard disk storage capacity with a second hard disk drive. This setup offered several benefits. The first benefit was that the larger drive not only could be used now, but it would be available for use in the 486 PC she was planning to build later. The second benefit was that adding the faster and larger drive would provide Susan with needed storage space. And finally, the faster speed of the new drive would speed up the overall performance of disk-intensive Microsoft Windows. Susan's 386 was a true clone with an ISA/AT/Classic Bus and an American Megatrends BIOS dated 05/05/91, and it could easily support a second hard disk drive.

Susan purchased another Conner hard disk: the CFS540A drive with a 540MB capacity, dimensions of 3½ inches wide by 1 inch tall, and a 15-ms access time. When she purchased the new drive, she asked for documentation on the master and slave jumper switch settings. The dealer pointed out that the master and slave switch settings were printed on the label on top of the drive, along with the settings for the heads, cylinders, tracks per sector, and the precomps. She also purchased a set of brackets to enable the 3½-inch drive to fit in the 5¼-inch drive bay of her computer.

Susan was careful to ask about the switch settings because she planned to move all the data on her old hard disk to her new one. This convoluted process involved first installing the new drive as a stand-alone, bootable master drive. That step would enable Susan to partition (or FDISK) and format the drive with her current version of DOS — version 6.22. She planned to then set the new drive to slave mode by changing the jumper switches (which makes the drive no longer bootable) and recabling the existing IDE drive (a

170MB Conner CP-30174E) as the master, or boot drive. After finishing that process, she planned to use the Windows File Manager to quickly copy all data and directories, intact, from her old drive C to the new drive D. If that operation was successful, she then could change the switch settings on both drives so that the faster 540MB drive would be the master, and the slower 170MB drive would be the slave. Such a setup adds disk space, but it produces no significant differences in her working environment.

After backing up the entire system with her previously installed Colorado Tape Backup drive, Susan created a bootable floppy disk by using the FORMAT /S command. She copied EDIT.COM from the DOS directory of the current hard disk drive to the bootable floppy disk drive so that she could use the file to edit the environment files, if necessary.

After completing the precautionary steps, Susan put on her grounding strap, opened up the computer's case, and used compressed air to blow out the dust and other debris that had accumulated inside the PC. With the case still open, she connected the CSF540A Conner drive to the existing cable and used a spare power connection from the hard disk drive to power the new hard drive. Susan didn't put the brackets on the drive to hold it in the drive bay yet — she knew she should verify that the drive worked correctly before going through all the work of making it fit into the case. She connected the new hard disk drive and disconnected the old drive.

She restarted the computer and pressed Delete, as the boot-up procedure instructed, to get to the setup menu. She then went to the Standard setup menu to change the hard disk drive settings to reflect those of the new drive. The Conner CFS540A drive had 16 heads, 63 tracks per sector, and 1050 cylinders, as well as a precomp of 0. Susan set the landing zone for the last cylinder (cylinder 1050) and then exited the setup menu and saved her changes.

With her bootable floppy disk ready in drive A, she waited for over a minute while the computer's BIOS determined that the hard disk wasn't yet ready for use. When she saw the hard disk failure message, the computer booted from the floppy and gave her the A:\> prompt. She started FDISK and partitioned the new drive C as a single, large drive, using the default settings presented by the utility. She didn't need to reconfigure the drive for master mode because she bought the drive already configured that way. She set up the drive with a single 517MB partition, although she knew that Windows sometimes conflicts with drives larger than 1024 cylinders.

After completing that step, she exited FDISK and typed **FORMAT C: /S/V** to format the hard disk and transfer the system files. She added the /V switch to indicate that she wanted to give the drive a volume label to distinguish it from the other drive.

Everything was going smoothly. The formatting went quickly, the system files were added, and she assigned the volume label when prompted to do so. Now it was time to change the new drive to slave mode, and then connect it and the old hard disk drive to the new, 40-pin, hard disk drive cable by using the two connectors she had purchased just for this purpose.

She turned off the PC and disconnected the new drive from the drive cable. She then looked at the switch settings for slave mode printed on top of the drive and moved the jumper from the master setting to the slave setting. Susan noticed an extra jumper positioned between the master and slave pins. The pins for this jumper were shown in the diagram but not documented, so she didn't think much about it.

She connected the new drive to the connection in the middle of the cable, then connected the old drive to the last free connection at the end of the cable. She also made sure that both drives were connected to the power supply. Susan then booted the computer, re-entered the BIOS setup menu, and configured the BIOS for both drives, entering the cylinders, heads, sectors per track, precomp, and landing zone settings for each. The precomp setting wasn't listed on the top of the drive with the other information, so she set it to zero as instructed by the BIOS help. She set the landing zone to a value equal to the last sector of the hard disk drive. She saved her changes and rebooted the PC.

The computer booted, but after a long wait, the monitor displayed a hard disk drive failure message. Susan started FDISK, and it displayed flashing letters at the bottom of the screen saying that it could not talk to drive D. Confused, Susan turned off the PC and tried again, with the same result. She checked the cable, the jumper switches on each drive, and even pulled out the documentation she'd saved on the IDE controller card.

The IDE controller was integrated into a multi-input/output (I/O) board that also had connectors for the floppy disk drive, two parallel ports, two serial ports, and a game port. She checked the documentation to see if it was necessary to change a jumper setting on the card in order for it to support two hard disk drives, but the documentation revealed that only one jumper setting existed for IDE support. She compared the documentation to the IDE card itself and noted the jumpers on the card were configured correctly.

Confused, she disconnected the 170MB drive, connected the 540MB drive to the end of the cable, changed the CMOS settings so that the larger drive was drive C and no drive D was installed, jumpered the new drive to master mode, and tried again. This time, the new drive booted. She tried to set the 170MB drive as the slave drive by changing the CMOS settings to the correct values, but in this case, the computer wouldn't talk to either drive. It was obvious that the problem had something to do with the two drives working in master and slave mode together. The 170MB drive had some additional pins that looked as though they could be undocumented jumpers, so she decided to find detailed information on the drives.

The first place she looked was in the *Pocket PCRef,* a small reference manual from Sequoia Publishing, but it had neither of the Conner drives. Susan then decided to look for a faxback or BBS number for Conner Peripherals in the *Pocket PCRef,* which has a listing of computer industry companies and their phone numbers. Both a faxback and a BBS number were listed for Conner Peripherals. Susan choose the faxback number. From there, she was able to obtain the documentation for both the CP-30174E and the CFS540A drives. The documents she received contained the clues to solving the problem. Figures 5-17 and 5-18 are the diagrams of the hard disk drives that accompanied the specifications and explained the switch settings.

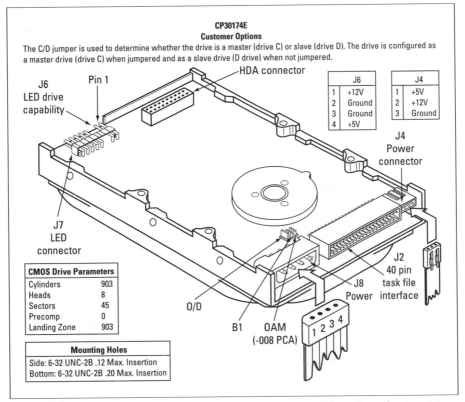

Figure 5-17: The documentation for the 170MB CP-30174E drive from the Conner faxback system.

(This drive is no longer being manufactured.)

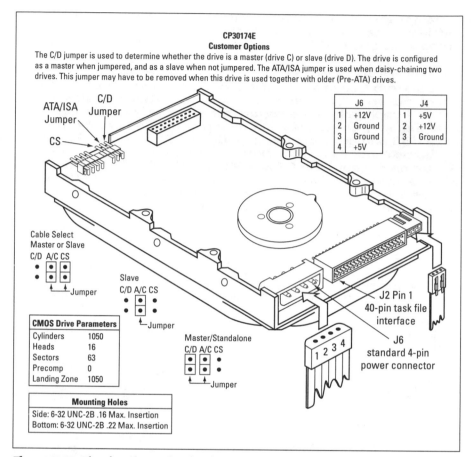

Figure 5-18: The documentation for the 540MB CFS540A drive from the Conner faxback system.

(This drive is no longer being manufactured.)

If you look at the master and slave jumper settings in Figure 5-17, you see that there are only two jumpers. In Figure 5-18, there are three jumpers, and the jumper in the middle is labeled ATA/ISA. Susan looked up the acronym and discovered that ATA is an interface specification used for IDE drives, as well as PCMCIA, credit-card-sized, solid-state disk drives. ISA stands for Industry Standard Architecture.

After reading the "Customer Options" heading in Figure 5-18, Susan realized that the 170MB drive did not have such a jumper, so she decided to remove it and try to use the drives together again. She removed the jumper, set the 540MB drive back in slave mode according to Figure 5-26, reset the CMOS settings to reflect both drives, and tried again. It worked! It was the ATA/ISA switch, which had not been documented on the drive, that caused the problem between the two drives.

Now that the drives were both running, Susan started Windows and used File Manager to drag and drop the C drive onto the D drive. This action instructed Windows to reproduce everything, including the existing subdirectories, on the new, 540MB hard disk drive. (She could have used the XCOPY command with the /S switch to do the same thing from the DOS prompt.)

After the copy operation was completed, Susan switched the jumper settings on the drives so that the 170MB drive was the slave and the 540MB drive was the master, changed the cabling so the 540MB drive was connected last, and reset the CMOS settings so that drive C was the 540MB drive and drive D was the 170MB drive. She rebooted the computer and checked the drives, noting that both drives worked fine and that the new, faster drive was now the boot drive.

Susan's job now was to decide which programs and data should reside on which drive. Note that if some of the software left on drive D was set to look for critical files on drive C (where it was originally installed), she would have to reinstall the software. However, the hard work of installing this second drive was finished.

Install the new drive in the case

TIP

If you want to make the new drive the master and the old drive the slave, wait to install the hard drive in the case until after you perform the instructions in the section "Swap the drives so that the new hard drive is the drive C," later in this chapter. If you want the new drive to be the master, you need to check to see if the drives work together and also make sure that you have the jumper settings for your old drive before you mount the drive.

Now that you know the new drive is working with the old drive, you can install it in the computer case. You should have the old drive already installed, so turn off the power, attach any drive rails or adapters, and then secure the drive into the case. You may end up disconnecting cables, especially if the drive is a tight fit. Try to disconnect as few cables as possible, and pay special attention to how the cables were connected so that you can get them reconnected correctly.

Test again before you close the case

After the new hard drive is securely mounted in the case and any disconnected cables are reconnected, you need to turn on the computer and rerun the brief tests mentioned in the preceding section. In addition, you should test the floppy disk drives by placing a diskette in each drive and executing the DIR command for each, just to make sure that they are working. After you complete the tests and verify that everything is working, you can close the case.

If you encounter problems, you should get an error message that you can look up in the troubleshooting sections earlier in the chapter. However, there are a few problems particular to getting two drives to work together, which I address next.

Installation in review

The following list provides an overview of the steps for installing a second hard disk drive:

1. Make a bootable floppy diskette and copy the FDISK and FORMAT utilities to the diskette.

2. Back up the data on the existing hard disk drive.

3. Record the current CMOS settings for the existing hard disk drive.

4. With the computer off, attach the ribbon cable from the old hard disk drive to the new hard disk drive. Attach a power cable to the new drive.

5. Turn on the computer, enter the CMOS setup, and configure drive C with the parameters of the new hard disk drive.

6. Reboot the computer with the bootable diskette in drive A so that the computer boots from the diskette.

7. Run FDISK from drive A to partition the hard disk drive.

8. Format the new hard drive using the /S parameter (**FORMAT C: /S**) to transfer the system files from the A drive to the new hard disk drive.

9. Take the floppy diskette out of drive A and reboot the computer. The computer should boot from the new hard disk drive.

10. Briefly test the new drive.

11. With the power off, set the new drive's jumpers to the slave setting.

12. With the power off, connect power cables to each drive. Connect the 40-pin ribbon cable so the old drive (the master) is closest to the controller and the new drive (the slave) is at the end of the ribbon cable.

13. Turn on the PC and test both drives.

14. (Optional.) Turn off the PC and set the jumpers on the new drive to master mode and the jumpers on the old drive to slave mode. Recable the drives so the drive currently set to master (the new drive) is closest to the controller and the slave drive (the old drive) is located at the end of the cable.

15. (If you perform Step 14, be sure you perform this step.) Turn on the PC and test both drives. Also test the floppy drives.

16. Close the computer case.

17. Burn-in the new hard disk drive.

Troubleshooting

The most common problem in getting two IDE drives to work together is that the computer will recognize one drive but not the other. If you have already checked the other troubleshooting sections, here are some additional things to check.

Check the jumper settings

Make sure that one drive is set to master and the other is jumpered to slave mode. This means you have to double-check the jumper settings. You may have to change jumpers on the old drive because some drives have a *dual master* mode as well as a *single master,* or *standard master,* mode. Look at the number of jumpers on the old drive. If there are more than two jumpers, you may be dealing with a dual master setting, and you'll need to look at the documentation on the drive to tell how the jumpers should be set.

You can start by looking for the jumper settings on the outside of the case of your old hard disk drive. If these settings are not available, you need to get them from the manufacturer of your old drive. Check the troubleshooting section and the information on how to get the jumper settings from a drive manufacturer later in this chapter.

Also, make sure that the model number of the new hard drive you have fits the model number of the documentation given to you for the drive. If the computer store purchased the drive they sold you in a bulk shipment, they may be photocopying the documentation and could have accidentally given you the wrong documentation.

If the jumper settings are printed on top of the new drive, make sure that you double-check those settings against the jumper settings on the drive.

Look for undocumented jumpers

Does one or both of the drives have an undocumented jumper or jumpers? Some drives have a jumper that sets the drive to an enhanced mode known as ATA/IDE (Advanced Technology Attachment, or AT Attachment/Integrated Drive Electronics). Another, more recent version of the ATA/IDE is the ATA-2/EIDE (Advanced Technology Attachment-2/Enhanced Integrated Drive Electronics). This jumper (or jumpers) may not be documented on the drive or in the documentation that comes with the drive, even if other jumpers are documented. You can try to disable this function by unjumpering the additional jumper(s) to see if the drives work together, but such an action is like shooting in the dark. It's also difficult to remember the jumper settings prior to making changes if you don't draw a picture or write them down first. You're better off contacting the manufacturers of the drives to find out the jumper settings so you get them right.

Although contacting the manufacturer for jumper settings may sound intimidating, it is not as difficult as you may think. The next section on swapping the hard disk drives so that the new drive is drive C outlines how to do this task. The case study earlier in this chapter also provided an example of how one person retrieved this information from a drive manufacturer.

There a couple of drive combinations that you can have. For example, you may have a combination in which both drives have ATA jumper settings, but only one is jumpered for this mode. You also may have a combination where one drive initially offers this setting (or a similar setting) and the other drive does not, but to get them to work together, you have to disable the setting on the drive that offers it.

When it still doesn't work

If none of these troubleshooting tips works, one other possibility exists — the two drives simply may not be able to work together. This reason is why it is so important to establish that each drive works individually by installing the new drive as though it was a stand-alone drive. This way, you can firmly establish that the drives work and rule out the possibility that one of the drives is faulty. Don't give up until you contact the technical support at the manufacturer of each drive and talk to a person, though. You should get a technical support number when you get the documentation for the drives from the available automated support. Contacting that automated support is included in the next section on swapping the hard drives.

Swap the drives so that the new hard drive is drive C

If you can establish that the new drive and the old drive work together, then you can swap the drives so that the new drive is the boot drive (or master drive) and the old drive is the slave. Getting the two drives to work together with the new drive set as the slave *before* you proceed to this step is important. If you haven't done so, you may be wasting your time and energy on a setup that isn't going to work; you need to go back and perform that step before moving ahead here.

If you were able to get the drives to work together and are wondering why you'd want to bother swapping the drives, here's the reason: The advantages to doing this hinge on the fact that your new hard disk drive probably has a significantly faster access speed and data transfer rate than your old drive. The biggest advantage has to do with performance. The faster your main or boot hard disk drive, the faster your system will boot, and the faster your programs will be loaded in and out of memory.

Another advantage deals with operating disk-intensive programs, such as Microsoft Windows (in any version). I've seen cases where a computer user spent big bucks upgrading his or her processor to a faster one, but did not receive a significant increase in the speed of Windows. A faster hard disk drive, however, will make a significant difference in Windows performance, because Windows depends heavily on the hard disk drive for its functionality. In fact, Windows uses a portion of the hard disk space as a substitute for memory (known as *virtual memory*).

You have to do a little homework to swap your drives, however, because you need to get the jumper settings for the old drive as well as the new drive. (You may have to get the jumper settings for the old drive anyway if you couldn't get both drives to work with the new drive set to slave mode.) After you have the documentation for your old drive, you can change the jumper settings on the old and new drives and copy the data from the old drive to the new drive.

If you are feeling guilty because you don't have the jumper settings for your old drive, don't. Few people have the documentation for the hard disk drive that came in their system. Most computer retailers and manufacturers don't provide that information because they want the option of providing a drive from whatever manufacturer suits them at a particular point in time, and they don't want to go through the hassle of reprinting the documentation for your computer when they change the type of drive they put in your computer.

Fortunately, getting the necessary documentation for your hard disk drive isn't difficult. The next section tells you how to get your hands on this information.

Get the jumper settings for your old hard disk drive

Hard disk drive manufacturers have tried to make obtaining the documentation for their hard disk drives as painless and automated a process as possible. But first you have to obtain some information. You must know the manufacturer and the model number of the hard disk drive for which you want documentation. This information can be found on top of your drive. You may have to remove the drive from the drive bay in order to see the model number and manufacturer information, so be prepared to do so.

When you have the manufacturer and model number, look in Appendix B for the contact information for your particular manufacturer. You'll need either a modem or access to a fax machine.

If you have a modem and access to the Internet, you often can obtain the drive information from the manufacturer's home page. The home pages for manufacturers are listed with other contact information in Appendix B. If you have a modem and software for telecommunications, you also can dial into the bulletin board service (BBS) maintained by the manufacturer to get the documentation you need.

You also can use the faxback service provided by the drive manufacturers. These services provide an automated menu, from which you typically have to order a catalog. When this catalog is faxed back to you, find your drive in the catalog and its accompanying number, call back with the accompanying number, and the manufacturer will fax you the documentation that you need. Don't expect to speak to a person when you use faxback services, but usually you can get a support number where you can speak to a person from a faxback service.

Change the jumpers and the cabling

After you have the jumper settings, you need to set the new drive to master (or dual master) mode and the old drive to slave (or dual slave) mode. You also want to swap the cables so that the new drive in master mode is closest to the controller and the old drive in slave mode is located at the end of the cable.

TIP Some manufacturers say their hard disk drives are not particular about where they're located on the cabling, as long as the jumpers settings are correct. To be safe, however, change the cabling rather than risk having a problem.

After you cable the drives, you can complete the steps listed in the installation section of "Install a Second Hard Disk Drive," starting with the step where you update the CMOS settings to reflect the new drives. Remember, you want to enter the new drive parameters as drive C and the old drive parameters as drive D. Again, if your CMOS has an auto-detect mode for the drives, you may find that easier to use, but using it typically takes more time than just typing in the parameters yourself (unless you need to use the auto-detect mode to get the LBA mode).

After the CMOS setup is complete, you can finish the rest of the steps, including testing the drives, installing the drives into the case, retesting the drives, and performing the burn-in of the new drive. If you get an error message during the testing process or the computer doesn't recognize the drives, look through the troubleshooting sections earlier in this chapter.

Common Mistakes Checklist

Here are the five most common mistakes people tend to make while installing a hard disk drive:

1. **Taking a bootable floppy disk from another computer and using it to boot the computer during the hard disk drive installation.** The bootable disk must use the same version of the operating system as the hard disk drive that you are upgrading, or you may damage your controller card. In addition, when you restore from your backup copy, you could end up with two different versions of DOS on the computer, which is a potentially dangerous situation for your data. Don't take the risk! Make a bootable floppy diskette from the computer you're working on before you install the new hard disk drive, and use only that bootable floppy diskette.

2. **Incorrect installation of the ribbon cable to the hard disk drive or to the controller card.** Make sure that you check pin 1 on the hard disk drive (it should be on the side nearest the power connector) and on the controller card to ensure that the stripe on the ribbon cable lines up with these pins.

3. **Forgetting to add the /S parameter to the hard disk drive so the new hard disk drive is formatted, but not bootable.** Reformat the drive using the /S parameter.

4. **Forgetting to reconnect the cables to one of the floppy disk drives.** The B floppy disk drive is especially prone to this mistake. If you follow the testing procedures outlined in the chapter and test the floppy disk drives before you close the case, you should catch this error.

5. **Neglecting to secure the proper adapters and rails to place the drive into the computer case.** This oversight often leads the user to mistakenly think he or she needs to drill holes in the case to secure the hard disk drive. If you've read the preparation section and looked at how the other drives are secured in your computer, then you will not make this common mistake.

6. **Neglecting to record the current parameters for the old hard disk drive before installing the new one.** Although this mistake does not completely burn your bridges, it makes it difficult to use both drives (if that's what you have in mind) or to roll back to the old hard disk drive.

Troubleshooting Practice: What's Wrong in These Photos

Here are some photos of common problem situations. See if you can tell what's wrong.

Figure 5-19: See answer 1.

Figure 5-20: See answer 2.

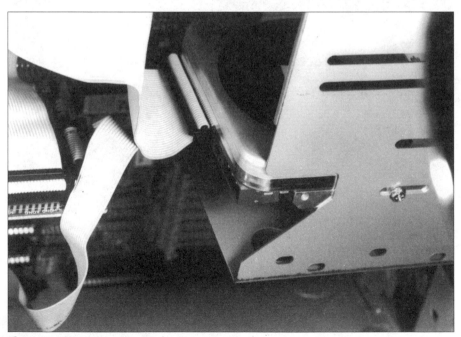

Figure 5-21: See answer 3.

Figure 5-22: See answer 4.

Answers:

1. The ribbon cables are connected backwards, so pin 1 on the cable is at pin 40 on the connector.

2. The hard disk drive connector cable is not securely attached to the controller card — pins are showing. This connector needs to be gently pushed into place so no pins are showing.

3. No power cable is connected to the hard disk drive.

4. The hard disk drive is installed upside down. Although most newer hard disk drives work this way, this is the mark of an amateur.

Summary

✦ You may need a new ribbon cable that supports two hard disk drives, a splitter for the power (split the power from the floppy disk drives to free a power cable for the new hard disk drive), and an adapter to make a 3^1/$_2$-inch drive fit a 5^1/$_4$-inch drive bay.

✦ You should get documentation on a new hard disk drive that shows the parameters of the drive. You'll rarely have documentation for a drive in an existing system, but the drive manufacturers provide automated, 24-hour support in various forms so you can obtain the information you need. Appendix B lists where you can get this information, by manufacturer.

✦ You must have a free drive bay to install a second hard disk drive. If you do not have a free drive bay, you must replace your current hard disk drive.

✦ Hard disk drives are installed by cabling the drive, setting the drive parameters in the CMOS setup menu, partitioning, and then formatting the drive using the /S parameter.

✦ Without some type of translation (either BIOS-based, hardware, or software) you cannot use more than about 500MB of your hard disk space, no matter how much capacity the drive has. Partitioning (using FDISK) will not get you around this barrier.

✦ In order for two hard disk drives to work together, their master and slave modes must be set correctly. Master drives are bootable; slave drives are not. Hard disk drives have jumpers that enable you to set which drive is master and which drive is the slave.

✦ When installing a second drive, test both drives before you go to the trouble of securing the drives in the drive bays. Then retest the hard disk drives after you secure the drives. Be sure to test the floppy disk drives as well before closing the case.

✦ There may be undocumented jumper settings that, when set incorrectly, can prevent two hard disk drives from working together. If you have problems, you need to contact the automated services provided by the manufacturers. Be sure to have drive model numbers handy.

✦   ✦   ✦

Memory Upgrades

CHAPTER 6

In This Chapter

+ Adding memory to your system

+ Uncovering the secrets to reusing your old memory with the new memory

+ Uncovering memory buying tips the pros use

+ Finding out how easy it is to install memory

+ Discovering memory troubleshooting tips

Tools Needed

+ Wrist grounding strap

+ Small, flathead screwdrivers (recommended)

Almost all computer users will tell you they wish they had more memory. Memory is where the work takes place in your PC. Without enough memory, your PC can be sluggish and unresponsive in performing its tasks. Worse yet, you can't run certain applications or perform certain tasks if you don't have enough memory.

The trick with memory is knowing when more memory will help you and when you need to look elsewhere for the solution to your problem. This chapter helps you determine if more memory will help you, if you can add more memory, how much memory you can add, how to get the most bang for your memory buck, and how to install your new memory. I focus on the most popular memory types and offer you tips that the pros use. Most of the time spent installing memory is spent on the preparation, so this chapter is heavy on the preparation. However, time spent preparing will save you time and money later.

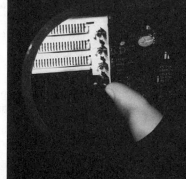

Preparation

You don't need to know much about memory to install it, but it is helpful to know how it works. The next section covers the definition of memory and the pertinent points concerning the DOS memory barrier, the physical forms that memory comes in, and the logical formats of memory and how they can speed up your computer. I also discuss how to determine what memory you can add and how to buy memory.

What is memory?

A computer, any computer, is made up of two basic components: a central processing unit (CPU) and memory. Memory, most of which is also known as random access memory (RAM), is where everything happens on your PC. When you start the computer, the operating system is loaded from the hard disk drive (or floppy disk drive if you boot from a floppy diskette) into memory. When you start an application, the program is copied from the hard disk drive into memory. When you save something, that material is written from memory onto the hard disk drive.

Every component in your PC has its own unique memory address so that it can access the CPU and vice versa. The video card, the hard disk drive controller, the floppy disk drive controller, the parallel and serial ports, the mouse, the keyboard, and so on all have a memory address.

Every time you start the computer, each component has to re-establish its communication with the CPU through the memory in the computer, and every time you start an application, it has to load into memory. When you create data, such as writing a letter in your word processor, that data is stored in memory until you perform a save to copy the data to the hard disk drive. The copy written to the hard disk drive must have a filename. Some applications save for you automatically, generating a filename such as DOC1 or DEFAULT.

This leads me to another important point concerning memory. When the power to the PC is cut, you lose the contents of the memory. The only way to keep the data you are working on is to save a copy of it to the hard disk drive. Frequent saves are obviously important, as anyone who has had a sudden power loss can tell you.

The kitchen analogy

If you are confused about memory, this analogy may help. Think about cooking in your kitchen at home. The CPU is the person cooking. Memory, or RAM, is the counter space the CPU uses to prepare the food. The cupboards, where the food, pots, pans, and dishes are stored, represent the hard disk drive space. Having a shortage of memory is like having too little counter space, which makes preparing meals difficult and time-consuming. In the same way, too little memory makes performing computing tasks difficult and time-consuming.

Virtual memory

If you have too little counter space for food preparation, you can clear some of the easy-to-reach cupboard space, leave the cupboard doors wide open, and use that space to set things you would normally place on the counter. That's what virtual memory is. The computer sets aside a portion of hard disk space for use as memory. Virtual memory is slower than conventional memory, but makes it possible to perform tasks that couldn't be done otherwise.

Virtual memory is used by operating systems such as Windows to enable you to run several applications simultaneously in less memory than is normally needed for such tasks. A *swap file* stores the screens and data from one or more applications while you're working in another application. This is why a faster hard disk drive can significantly increase the performance of Windows. If you're interested in improving your Windows performance, you can make a couple decisions concerning your Windows swap file. Tips to help you make these decisions are offered in the operating system information in Chapter 13.

The memory barrier

This section is included to help you understand the current memory limitations for PCs. I don't want you to get the mistaken idea that packing your PC with memory solves your memory problems. It can, but in certain situations, it may not. In order to explain why, I need to give you some background into the history of decisions made concerning PC design.

PCs were originally designed to have a maximum of 1MB of memory. (In the PC world, one megabyte of memory is actually 1,024 kilobytes, not 1,000 kilobytes.) That memory was divided into two portions. The lower two-thirds, or 640K, was reserved for the operating system and software applications. This lower memory is called *base memory,* or *conventional memory.* The upper 384 kilobytes (1024K-640K=384K) were reserved for functions of the PC, such as space for different types of video cards, and so on.

The lower 640K of memory is still important today. Although most PCs allow you to add more than 1MB of memory, some applications software, especially DOS-based applications and games, depend heavily or exclusively on that lower memory. Every time you load a driver, such as a mouse driver or a CD-ROM driver, it reduces the amount of lower memory available to applications that need it. The bottom line is that you can add several megabytes of memory to your PC and still have an application refuse to run because it can't get enough of the memory it needs.

Ways around this memory crunch are available, and I discuss them in more detail in Chapter 13. For now, I briefly mention a couple answers to this problem. You can try optimizing your memory by using utilities available with the operating system. You can also set up a multiple boot configuration. The information on performing these tasks is found in Chapter 13. The following case study may shed some light on the situation.

CASE STUDY

Memory addition doesn't turn out as planned

Li wanted more memory for his accounting software that ran under Windows 3.x but was still DOS-based. He had an Epson 386SX with 4MB of RAM and an 80MB hard disk drive. The problem began when Li installed the DoubleSpace hard disk compression utility that came with his DOS 6.0 upgrade in order to increase his hard disk space. He then hired a computer consultant to look into increasing the RAM in the Epson. The consultant reported that Li could add only 4MB of memory and that the memory would be difficult to obtain.

Rather than pour more money into a PC that he felt was losing its usefulness to him, Li decided to purchase a new Pentium PC. He purchased an early Pentium, but one that used standard memory, a 60 MHz multimedia machine that came with a 500MB hard disk drive and 8MB of RAM in the form of two 4MB SIMMs. (SIMMs are small circuit boards that fit into specially designed slots on the PC.) After looking over the documentation that came with the system, he determined (with the help of a computer store staff) that the motherboard design enabled him to add another 32MB in the form of two 16MB SIMMs with parity for a total of 40MB. (Parity is a way for the SIMM to check the data it is processing — a sort of self-checking feature.) Li paid a premium for the memory, but he was determined to get plenty of memory. He transferred his data from the 386 to the Pentium as well.

Li was also hoping to run a flight simulator game he'd purchased on CD-ROM, but he didn't mention that to the computer consultant or the computer store employees.

The flight simulator game didn't run due to a memory conflict with Windows, but the accounting software ran fine for a month. When the accounting software company sent Li an update, he installed the update and the accounting software slowed to a crawl. Sometimes it wouldn't work at all, dumping Li out of the software and back into Windows.

Li sought technical support from the software company and discovered that he had barely enough RAM to run the updated version of the software. The update had essential information that Li needed for the tax year at hand, however, so he needed to find a solution to his lack of memory problem.

Li upgraded to DOS 6.22, hoping that would help, and attempted to optimize the computer's lower memory. He used the MEMMAKER utility included in DOS 6.0 and higher. MEMMAKER is a utility that directs the way device drivers and environment variables are loaded into memory with the goal of providing the maximum amount of lower memory space. Using MEMMAKER, Li was able to get a little more lower memory, which made the accounting software run slightly faster. However, the real solution came in the form of a multiple boot configuration.

DOS 6.0 and higher has a feature that enables users to configure the AUTOEXEC.BAT and CONFIG.SYS files so that they can choose which commands are executed. This is accomplished by selecting a boot configuration from a menu that appears on-screen when the PC boots. Li learned to set up a boot configuration that loaded only the mouse driver and the high memory managers for the accounting software, freeing a significant portion of lower memory. (Instructions on how to set up a multiple boot configuration are available in Chapter 13.)

He then set up one boot configuration that loaded Windows 3.11 and his CD-ROM driver and another configuration that loaded only the mouse driver and the CD-ROM driver so that he could run the flight simulator program. Although he had to reboot the PC every time he wanted to run one of the three configurations, he was able to get the full use of his memory (and his software) for the various tasks he'd purchased it for.

Windows 95 has solved some of these lower memory problems, but it requires more memory overall than Windows 3.*x*. Windows 95 runs, though very slowly, in 4MB of RAM, but 8MB is more realistic, and 16MB is recommended.

As far as lower memory goes, Windows 95 doesn't remove the 640K barrier, but it does allow more lower memory for applications that depend heavily on that memory space. It also allows more freedom for those applications, so software that wouldn't run under Windows 3.*x* will run under Windows 95. This fact is true of all DOS applications but especially games.

Now that you know more about how memory works and the bottlenecks involved in dealing with software applications and memory, it's time to look into the actual memory components and how they work with your PC.

Types of memory and other memory issues

The kind of memory used in your PC for RAM comes in the form of integrated circuit chips known as *dynamic random access memory,* or *DRAM* (pronounced "dee-ram"). DRAM comes in several forms, the most popular being SIMMs, about which I spend most of the chapter talking. You need to look at the motherboard in your PC, but if you do not have slots for SIMMs, you're better off purchasing a new computer than attempting to upgrade your memory. The information here will help you take stock so you can find out what's best for you.

Physical formats

Memory in the form of DRAM was originally placed on motherboards in sets of nine chips that worked together to make a portion of memory. For example, nine chips could work together to represent 256K of RAM or 1MB of RAM, depending on how the manufacturer designed the capacity of the chips. Most motherboards used four rows of nine chips, for a total of 36 chips. (Remember that number — it's one you see again when configuring memory.)

DIPs, SIPs, SIMMs, and DIMMs

Later, these DRAM chips, known as *Dual In-line Package,* or *DIPs,* were integrated into small circuit boards that could be added and removed more easily. Special slots also were developed for motherboard design to accommodate these new memory circuit boards.

At first, two types of memory circuit boards were available, the *Single In-line Package,* or SIP (pronounced "sips"), and the *Single In-line Memory Module,* or *SIMM* (pronounced "sim"). SIPs have comb-like projections on the bottom that plug into specially designed sockets that look like rows of pin-holes on the motherboard. The problem with SIPs is that one or more of the comb-like contacts is easily broken off when inserting or removing the memory, which ruins not only the SIP, but the motherboard as well. SIMMs, which are more sturdy, eventually took over the memory market. SIPs are hard to find, and you probably won't see one.

SIMMs come in two formats, 30-pin and 72-pin, as shown earlier in Figure 6-2. Of the two formats, the 72-pin is capable of greater capacity. The majority of 30-pin SIMMs come in capacities of 256K, 1MB, 2MB, and 4MB. However, 72-pin SIMMs tend to have larger capacities, such as 1MB, 2MB, 4MB, 8MB, 16MB, and 32MB. Therefore, if you see a SIMM that is 8MB or larger in size (capacity), then you know it is probably a 72-pin SIMM.

Another type of memory called the *Dual In-Line Memory Module* (DIMM, pronounced *dim)* is available. This is a 168-pin circuit board that looks very much like a SIMM. It offers a wider data path for improved performance, and motherboards that support Pentium chips are available with DIMM sockets, as you see later in the chapter.

Figure 6-1 shows the more commonly available DIPs and SIMMs. Not pictured is the 168-pin DIMM.

As you can see, each type of memory is made up of chips that look similar. Essentially, the DIP has been made smaller, better, and has been placed on circuit boards called SIMMs.

The manufacture of DRAM chips is an expensive and time-consuming process. Building a DRAM manufacturing plant can cost upward of one billion dollars and take two years. Few companies have the resources to manufacture DRAM chips. However, a plethora of companies sell SIMMs. SIMM manufacturers buy DRAM chips from the companies that manufacture them and then design and produce SIMM circuit boards onto which they mount the DRAM.

Figure 6-1: A DIP, a 30-pin SIMM, and a 72-pin SIMM.

TIP

The popular terminology is to call DIP chips DRAM chips. You see advertising that says *DRAM, SIPs, and SIMMs*. What these ads call DRAM are really DIP chips.

SIMM sockets and banks

SIMMs fit into specially designed slots on the motherboard known as SIMM sockets. Sometimes the single sockets are referred to as a *bank,* but these sockets can also be paired or grouped by the system board designer so they work together. When configured this way, the sockets are also known as a bank. SIMM banks are designated by numbers starting at either 0 or 1 and going up to the total number of banks (usually no more than 4). The bank numbers are usually designated on the system boards, as shown in the example in Figure 6-2, as well as in the system documentation.

SIMM connectors

On the bottom of each SIMM is a row of connectors usually referred to as *contacts* or *tips.* Traditionally, the contacts or tips on SIMMs are either tin-lead (silver in color) or gold. PC manufacturers often express preferences for the type of contacts your SIMMs should have, and following the manufacturer's recommendations is a good idea, but you don't have to.

Speed

You must consider not only the capacity of the memory you're looking at, but also its speed. Memory speed is measured in nanoseconds (ns), which is a billionth of a second. The lower the number for the speed, the faster the memory. What you find for sale is mostly 70ns or 60ns SIMMs. Faster speeds cost more but deliver better perfor-mance. However, certain logical formats deliver faster performance, which I cover later in this chapter.

Figure 6-2: The banks are usually labeled on the motherboard itself, as well as in the system documentation.

Parity

I mention that nine DIPs make up an original unit of memory. Of those nine DIP chips, eight are for the actually memory storage and the ninth is known as the *parity chip*. Its job is to check the integrity of the data stored in the other eight chips. If an error is detected, the computer halts and displays an error message.

Some PC manufacturers have designed their motherboards so that you must have parity, but the growing trend is toward dropping the parity checking altogether. This means that eight chips make up a unit of memory instead of nine.

There is some controversy over dropping the parity. Those who are dropping parity checking say the DRAM chips are reliable enough that parity isn't needed. Besides, parity errors are few and widely spaced, even if they should occur. The other school of thought says data integrity is paramount and that no risks should be taken, even if the risks are small. The driving force behind the move to drop parity is the fact that parity costs more.

From an upgrade point of view, the bottom line on parity is this: DRAM with parity works in systems that do not require memory with parity. But if your system requires parity, non-parity DRAM doesn't work.

Instead of saying that memory is parity or non-parity, some references are more cryptic, referring to the number and capacity of the chips and allowing you to infer from these numbers whether there is a parity chip. Knowing that there are nine chips for parity and eight for non-parity helps you read memory configuration information.

Memory configuration

When purchasing SIMMs, identification numbers tell you how the DRAM is configured and whether or not it has parity. For example, you may see something like *1MB x 9, 1 x 9*, or *1M*9*. This reads as *one by nine* and refers to a 1MB SIMM with parity. The first number refers to the capacity of each group of chips, and the second number refers to the total number of chips. The chips are 1MB in capacity and there are nine of them (which tells us that a parity chip is present), so the total of the SIMM is 1MB.

Here's another example. You see a SIMM referred to as a *1MB x 36,* or *1 x 36.* This is a 4MB SIMM with parity. The 1 refers to the capacity of one group of chips, and because you know that nine chips make up a group of chips with parity, you divide 36 by 9 and get 4. Therefore, the SIMM is a 4MB SIMM with parity *organized* as 1 x 36.

If the previous SIMM did not have parity, it would be organized as a *1MB x 32,* or *1 x 32.* Because you know that a unit of chips without parity equals eight chips, then 32 as a multiple of eight indicates four sets of chips with no parity. In this case, the SIMM would be 4MB in size.

Table 6-1 contains typical organization listings for SIMMs and their values. This table is not all inclusive, but it does give you an idea of how to interpret the most common nomenclature for SIMMs.

Table 6-1		
Typical organization for SIMMs with parity and non-parity		
SIMM size	*Parity organization*	*Non-parity organization*
1MB	1 x 9	1 x 8
2MB	2 x 9	2 x 8
4MB	1 x 36	1 x 32
8MB	2 x 36	2 x 32
16MB	4 x 36	4 x 32
32MB	8 x 36	8 x 32

Integration has played a role in the configuration of SIMMs. Just because you see a 16MB SIMM advertised as 4 x 36 doesn't mean you find 36 chips on the SIMM board. The chips have been integrated into smaller and smaller designs, and some SIMMs have only two or three chips on a SIMM. It's not the number of chips on the SIMM but the capacity of the SIMM that matters.

How to read the capacity of SIMMs

The only surefire way to know the capacity of the SIMM is to test it. However, the DRAM industry has followed a few conventions that serve as standards for how DRAM chips are labeled to indicate their capacity. You cannot count on reading the capacity of every SIMM you find just by looking at the chip numbers, but following are the industry conventions that should help you read the capacity of SIMMs.

As I said, SIMMs come with DIP chips on board. Traditionally, DIP chips have been labeled by the manufacturer with the manufacturer's trademark and a number that often gives you the capacity and the speed of the chip.

To find the capacity or size of the SIMM, look for a long number that resembles a part number. The digits to the right of this part number will likely tell you about the capacity of the SIMM. If you're looking at a 30-pin SIMM, then you know the capacity has to be 256K, 1MB, 2MB, or 4MB. You want to look at the part number for combinations of digits to the right (usually between three to five digits followed by the letter *A*) that indicate the capacity. The digits 256, followed by the letter *A,* indicate that the chip is part of a unit of DIPs that make up 256K. The digits 1000 or 1024, followed by *A,* indicate a chip that is part of a 1MB set. The number 4000 or 4400 indicates 4MB, and the number 8000 or 8192 indicates an 8MB set, and so on.

If the chips in a set make up 4MB and you have two sets of chips on the SIMM, you have an 8MB SIMM, such as the one shown in Figure 6-3. You sometimes can spot the parity chip because it looks different (smaller than the others) and it's the ninth chip, but with integration, the parity chips aren't always that obvious. If you have eight chips, a multiple of eight, or an even number of chips on the SIMM, you probably don't have parity. If you have nine chips, a multiple of nine, or an odd number of chips, you probably have a SIMM with parity.

The speed of the SIMM is easier to find, if it is present on the chip. The speed usually is indicated by a one- or two-digit number preceded by a dash. Slower SIMMs are in the 120ns and 100ns range, so you may see a *-12* or a *-10*, which is not 12ns and 10ns but 120ns and 100ns, respectively. Most of the SIMMs you see have a dash followed by a 6, 7, or 8, though some have 60, 70, and 80. This represents 60ns, 70ns, or 80ns, respectively. Figures 6-4 and 6-5 show SIMMs of various speeds.

It's important to remember the information I've given you on reading the chip markings is meant as a guideline. Manufacturers can and do change the chip numbers, so no guarantee exists that the numbers on SIMMs you find will match these guidelines.

Figure 6-3: This 8MB, 70ns SIMM has parity, as indicated by the smaller parity chips.

Figure 6-4: These 30-pin SIMMs are of varying speeds. The two on the left are slow 120ns SIMMs, the one in the middle is a 100ns SIMM, and the two on the right are 80ns SIMMs.

Figure 6-5: These 72-pin SIMMs are of varying speeds. The top two are 70ns whereas the bottom one is a 60ns SIMM.

Logical formats: Fast Paging Mode versus EDO

Besides speed and capacity, the way data is handled internally in the chip design affects the performance of the memory chip. The way data is handled is what I call the *logical format* of the chip design. A couple of popular logical formats for memory are called *Fast Paging Mode* and *Extended Data Output,* or EDO (pronounced "e-dee-oh"). Both types of memory provide faster performance, but EDO memory enables the computer's processor to access memory up to 15 percent faster for chips rated at the same speed. This means that the processor can access 60ns EDO memory faster than it can access 60ns Fast Paging Mode memory chips. Consequently, you can expect to pay more for EDO.

To get the performance boost of EDO, your computer motherboard should use the Intel Triton chipset. I talk about chipsets in more detail when I talk about motherboards. The documentation that comes with your system should tell you if you have the Triton chipset, or you can flip to the chipset discussion in Chapter 12. Although you can use EDO memory on a motherboard that doesn't use the Triton chipset, you may not see the performance increase associated with EDO, so paying more money makes no sense if you're not going to get more performance.

Finding the amount of memory you can add to your system

Now that you know something about the various memory formats, it's time to decide what your system can use. You need to determine how much memory you have now and what type of memory you should add. You want to take a look at your system documentation or contact the manufacturer for available information. Then you want to look inside your system to determine the configuration of your current memory, determine how much memory you can add, and purchase and install the new memory.

Determining how much memory you have now

Determining how much memory you currently have is easy. Watch your system boot up and it tells you. Most BIOSs test the memory during boot up, so the final figure is the one you want. The number should be some multiple of 1024. For example, if you have 2MB of RAM, the number you get for memory should be 2048. 4MB is 4096, 8MB is 8192, 16MB is 16384, and so on. Your BIOS may be set to skip the memory test or to only test the first 1MB, but it should still display the amount of memory you have.

If you look at the memory settings in the BIOS, you may find that the memory you have is registered differently. You find 640K for the base memory and another figure for the extended memory. For example, if you have 8MB of RAM, your BIOS may register 640K base memory and 7168K extended memory. What's left out here is the 384K reserved by the computer for special hardware functions. If you do the math, 640K plus 7168K plus 384K equals 8192K, or 8MB.

Looking at your system documentation

Your computer system should come with some documentation concerning the type of memory and capacity you can add to your system. You want to look over this documentation. This is not the end of your research, however, because manufacturers often use a variety of motherboards and design changes, so your system documentation may be general or incomplete with regard to adding memory. However, this is the place to start.

Pentium processors require 8MB of RAM, so you can expect Pentium-based PCs to have a minimum of 8MB of memory.

In your system documentation, you need to look for a reference to memory, RAM, SIMMs, or some other similar term. For example, in the documentation booklet that comes with the Micronics M4Pi system board (motherboard) that uses the 486 processor is an entire chapter on installing add-on peripherals and system memory. Under that chapter is a section on SIMMs themselves, a section on installing SIMMs, and one on removing SIMMs.

TIP

A common practice for system manufacturers is to require you to add SIMMs in pairs. Some systems require all SIMMs on the motherboard to be the same capacity. Other systems require paired SIMMs to be the same capacity. These are not hard-and-fast rules, but you can expect to see these types of requirements.

Understanding your system requirements for memory configuration

The documentation for most computers is written with the PC technician in mind. This means that you need to know the implications of the information you're provided with. In order to help you, I've provided actual examples of system board documentation concerning memory configuration. After each one, I've pointed out the deductions you need to make in order to add memory to the system. First, I show you an example of the memory configuration information from the Micronics system board I introduced earlier, then I show you an example from an AST computer.

Under the SIMMs heading, the Micronics system board documentation says:

> The M4Pi has four, 36-bit (72-pin) SIMM sockets on-board. RAM memory can increase from 8MB up to 128MB using the following SIMM sizes:
>
> > 4 MB — organized as 1MB × 36
> >
> > 8MB — organized as 2MB × 36
> >
> > 16MB — organized as 4MB × 36
> >
> > 32MB — organized as 8MB × 36
>
> Memory requires at least two SIMM banks to be filled. Start with Bank 0, then work your way up. The SIMMs must be rated at 70ns or better, and the SIMM-type recommended is tin-lead contacts.
>
> Bank 0 and Bank 1 of the SIMM sockets must always be filled and contain the same size SIMMs.
>
> Bank 2 and Bank 3 of the SIMM sockets, if filled, must contain the same size SIMMs.

The number 36 in the reference to the organization indicates that the SIMMs added to this system board must have parity. This documentation also tells you that the first two SIMM banks, Bank 0 and Bank 1, must have SIMMs inserted in order for the system to boot, and those SIMMs must be the same size or capacity. This means you could insert two 1MB SIMMs, two 4MB SIMMs, two 8MB SIMMs, two 16MB SIMMs, or two 32MB SIMMs in those first two slots. However, you cannot insert a 2MB SIMM in Bank 0 and a 4MB SIMM in Bank 1.

Without opening the computer case, you can infer on a working system using this motherboard that the first two banks of memory are filled. For example, during the boot cycle, if the system says it has 4MB of RAM, then you know you have either two 2MB, 72-pin SIMMs in Banks 0 and 1 or four 1MB SIMMs that fill all available SIMM slots. The best scenario, from the standpoint of adding memory, is if only the first two banks have SIMMs because that leaves two banks to which you can add SIMMs. The only way to know how the memory inside is configured, however, is to open up the case and look.

Here's another example of the memory requirements you may find in typical system documentation of a Pentium motherboard:

> The mainboard lets you add up to 128MB of system memory via SIMM & DIMM sockets on the mainboard. Four SIMM sockets on the mainboard are divided into two banks, Bank 0 and Bank 1. Each bank consists of two 72-pin SIMM modules that must be filled with the same size and configuration SIMMs. There is one 168-pin DIMM module.

> All SIMM and DIMM module speeds must be faster than 70ns. Bank 0 cannot be used when the DIMM socket is used. SIMM sockets require DRAM type be either Fast Page Mode or Extended Data Out (EDO). 8MB RAM minimum.

In this system board example, notice that parity is not mentioned because parity is not required. Also note that if you want to use the DIMM socket, you cannot use Bank 0. In addition, a minimum of 8MB of RAM is required.

Memory requirements often come in the form of written documentation, as seen earlier, or as tables, as you see next. In the case of the Aspire board, AST uses both written text and a memory configuration table.

How to read memory configuration tables

System manufacturers usually show all possible combinations of memory configuration in the form of a table. Micronics has chosen the table form to show all possible combinations of memory starting at 8MB and going to the maximum of 128MB. The table lists the memory banks indicating the various possible combinations that work for placing memory on the motherboard. Figure 6-6 shows the table from the Micronics documentation.

There are a couple of items to note concerning this table. One is that the SIMMs must be added in pairs of the same capacity that fill a bank. Traditionally, most manufacturers require Bank 0 to be filled first, as is the case here. The other item to note is that the table tells how the memory is configured before you open the case. For example, if you purchased a PC that used this board that had 8MB of memory, then you must have two 4MB SIMMs in Bank 0. However, if you purchased the system with 16MB of memory, you could have two 8MB SIMMs in Bank 0 or four 4MB SIMMs that fill all available SIMM slots.

Figure 6-7 shows a configuration table from the Amptron International DX8000 486 system board. This board has eight 30-pin SIMM slots divided into two banks. This table indicates that you must fill Bank 0, meaning that you must have a minimum of four 256K SIMMs totaling 1MB of RAM installed in order for the motherboard to work. In addition, the SIMMs must be added in groups of four.

DRAM Memory Configuration

Bank 0	Bank 1	Bank 2	Bank 3	Total
4MB	4MB			8MB
4MB	4MB	4MB	4MB	16MB
8MB	8MB			16MB
4MB	4MB	8MB	8MB	24MB
8MB	8MB	4MB	4MB	24MB
8MB	8MB	8MB	8MB	32MB
16MB	16MB			32MB
4MB	4MB	16MB	16MB	40MB
16MB	16MB	4MB	4MB	40MB
8MB	8MB	16MB	16MB	48MB
16MB	16MB	8MB	8MB	48MB
16MB	16MB	16MB	16MB	64MB
32MB	32MB			64MB
4MB	4MB	32MB	32MB	72MB
32MB	32MB	4MB	4MB	72MB
8MB	8MB	32MB	32MB	80MB
32MB	32MB	8MB	8MB	80MB
16MB	16MB	32MB	32MB	96MB
32MB	32MB	16MB	16MB	96MB
32MB	32MB	32MB	32MB	128MB

Figure 6-6: The memory configuration table from a Micronics M4Pi motherboard.

DRAM Configuration

Size	Bank 0	Bank 1
1MB	(4) 256K x 9	None
2MB	(4) 256K x 9	(4) 256Kx9
4MB	(4)1M x 9	None
5MB	(4) 256K x 9	(4)1M x 9
8MB	(4)1M x 9	(4)1M x 9
16MB	(4) 4M x 9	None
17MB	(4) 256K x 9	(4) 4M x 9
20MB	(4) 1M x 9	(4) 4M x 9
32MB	(4) 4M x 9	(4) 4M x 9
64MB	(4) 16M x 9	None
65MB	(4) 256K x 9	(4) 16M x 9
68MB	(4) 1M x 9	(4) 16M x 9
80MB	(4) 4M x 9	(4) 16M x 9
128MB	(4) 16M x 9	(4) 16M x 9

Figure 6-7: The memory configuration table from the Amptron International DX8000 motherboard.

The documentation also enables you to draw some conclusions. For example, if your system uses this board and has 2MB of RAM, then by looking at this documentation, you know before you open the case that the RAM is in the form of eight 256K SIMMs. If you want to increase the amount of RAM in the system, you have to replace some or all of those SIMMs.

As you can see from these examples, you may need to replace the memory you already have in order to add more. The only way to know for sure what you have, however, is to take a look inside.

Some PCs require you to change jumper settings on the motherboard in order to add or change the amount of memory in the system. A jumper is made up of either two or three prongs called *pins*. When a pair of the prongs are covered with a plug or *shunt*, they become a connected circuit that activates the options on the motherboard. Setting jumpers to change the amount of memory in a system is not a common occurrence, but it does exist. If you want to learn more about jumper settings or to see what jumpers look like, refer to Chapter 7.

What to do if you don't have documentation

You may find yourself in situations in which you do not have the system documenta-tion, which includes the information I've shown you so far. Some manufacturers don't provide this documentation to the consumer, and you have to get it from their technical support or from their authorized repair facilities. You may also have a used system or one with lost documentation.

If you don't have the documentation, you should attempt to get it. You may be able to use a faxback, bulletin board service (BBS) or Internet location provided by the PC manufacturer to get the information you need. You may be able to get the technical support staff of the manufacturer to give you the documentation or provide it for a fee. You also may be able to go back to the seller of the PC and ask for the necessary materials. Third-party products are available that specialize in the documentation for system boards, but these products are aimed at the PC repair technician market and they're expensive. One such product is the MicroHouse Technical Library. Although you probably aren't able to justify the several hundred dollars such a reference manual costs, you may be able to locate an independent PC repair facility that has one of these products and pay them to supply you with the information.

Looking inside your PC

Although having the system documentation definitely makes life easier, you still must take a look inside the PC. You need the information on how much memory you have, as well as the system documentation, before you look inside in order to determine what memory you can add and how you can add it.

When you do look inside the case, you can expect to see something that looks like the examples in Figure 6-8 and Figure 6-9. Figure 6-8 is a system board that uses 30-pin SIMMs, and Figure 6-9 is a system board that requires 72-pin SIMMs. Some system boards have both 30-pin and 72-pin SIMMs, and your board may be one of those.

Figure 6-8: A system board using 30-pin SIMMs.

Figure 6-9: A system board using 72-pin SIMMs and a 168-pin DIMM.

When looking inside your PC, you first need to determine if all the SIMM or DIMM slots are filled. If so, then you probably have to replace all or some of the current SIMMs or DIMMs to add more memory.

The next task is to determine what capacity memory is currently in the slots. This helps you determine if you need to remove the SIMMs or DIMMs to reach your memory goal or if you can successfully add to what's there.

Comparing what the system says the total memory is to the documentation for installing SIMMs to reach the total memory gives you a pretty good idea of the capacity of the SIMMs you currently have.

You also can attempt to read the chip numbers on the SIMMs to determine the capacity of the SIMMs you have. You may need a flashlight to read the numbers and you may need to remove the SIMMs from the slots in order to read them. Removing (and installing) SIMMs is described in the installation section later in this chapter.

Some motherboards have memory in the form of DIPs that are added to the SIMMs installed in the system. You see this referred to as memory *on board,* or as *on board memory.*

Proprietary memory

Proprietary memory means the computer uses specially designed memory modules. Sometimes these modules look very much like standard SIMMs, and other times they have special connections and are obviously different in appearance. Notebook and laptop computers are especially prone to proprietary memory, but you're also likely to find proprietary memory in name-brand computers from large manufacturers. However, it's not uncommon to find a manufacturer that uses proprietary memory in one model yet uses standard memory in another model of PC. You simply have to check your system to see.

If you have a system that uses proprietary memory, you may have to buy that memory from the manufacturer. Third-party sources may carry the memory as well, depending on how popular the computer is that uses this particular memory. You may find that you cannot obtain the memory at all or that the price for the memory upgrade is much higher than standard market prices for PC memory.

Compaq Presario 900 disables on board memory when 32MB is added

The Compaq Presario 900 series of PCs comes with 4MB of memory on the system board and can handle up to 64MB of RAM. If you add two 32MB SIMMs, you reach more than 64MB of memory, and the 4MB of memory on the system board is disabled.

AST 68-pin SIMMs versus standard 72-pin SIMMs

Some proprietary memory looks very much like standard SIMMs. For example, Figure 6-10 shows a 68-pin SIMM from an AST computer compared to a standard 72-pin SIMM. AST hasn't used these SIMMs in all of its computers, but it has used them in some models.

Compaq also has a proprietary format for memory used in some models of its product line and laptop computers are well known for requiring proprietary memory formats. The only way to know for sure is to look carefully inside your case and at your documentation.

SIMM adapter boards

If all your SIMM slots full, but you'd like to add more memory, you may want to look into SIMM adapter boards. Sometimes referred to as SIMM converters, these boards enable you to reuse your old memory by converting it to a new capacity.

Here's how it works. You plug the SIMMs you have into a SIMM adapter board, which then plugs into the SIMM slot. For example, if you have eight 1MB SIMMs, which make up 8MB of RAM, taking up all your SIMM slots, you can plug all eight SIMMs into a SIMM converter board, which makes the board an 8MB SIMM. You then plug the SIMM converter board into a single one of your SIMM slots.

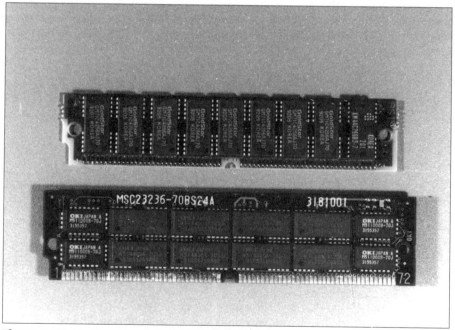

Figure 6-10: Here's a proprietary AST 68-pin SIMM next to a standard 72-pin SIMM.

You can get SIMM adapter boards that convert 30-pin SIMMs to 72-pin SIMMs, as well as boards that accept almost any combination of SIMMs. Figure 6-11 shows examples of SIMM adapters. These products are available directly from companies such as Autotime and MCP, and you can find them in computer retail outlets. (Contact information for the companies mentioned is found in Appendix A.)

There are three details to watch for with SIMM adapter boards. The first is that some boards make your memory take a performance hit in the speed arena. If you plug a group of 70ns SIMMs into some adapters, the SIMMs perform at 80ns. Others have special designs to compensate, so you don't lose any of the original speed of your SIMMs. You want to look for and purchase SIMM adapters that compensate for this performance loss so that your memory performs at the same speed as it did before.

The second detail to watch for is adapter boards that come in different heights and different orientations. Make sure you don't get adapters for your SIMMs that either are too high for your case or will interfere with other SIMMs installed on your motherboard. Adapters in various orientations are available, so you need to look at your case to see what you can use.

Figure 6-11: Examples of various SIMM adapter boards. The one on the left allows you to add four 30-pin and an optional 72-pin SIMM to make a single 72-pin SIMM. The one on the right converts four 30-pin SIMMs to a single 72-pin SIMM.

The third detail involves capacity. Some adapter boards won't use certain capacity memory. For example, the board may accept 1MB, 4MB, and 8MB SIMMs, but not 2MB or 16MB SIMMs. You need to read the small print so that you know the adapter board you have in mind can convert the SIMMs you need converted.

Buying tips

After you know how much RAM you have, how it's configured, and what you can add, it's time to go shopping. You want to consider the manufacturer of the DRAM you're about to buy, and whether or not the SIMMs have been tested, to be sure you're getting what you're paying for.

In the memory game, smaller capacity SIMMs and DIMMs cost less than those with a larger capacity. For example, you may pay more per MB for a 32MB SIMM than you would for two 16MB SIMMs. This is because there's more demand for the large capacity single SIMMs. You can expect to pay about $10 to $15 per MB, although DRAM prices tend to be very much like gold prices in that they vary from one day to the next.

What to look for in good quality DRAM

One consideration is the quality of the RAM you're buying. Like any other business, some DRAM and SIMM manufacturers have a reputation for producing good quality products, and others have a more tainted reputation. The brand-name manufacturers in DRAM production are companies such as Toshiba, Okidata, IBM, Fujitsu, Hitachi, Micron, Mitsubishi, Motorola, NEC, and Samsung. These companies have their names or their logos on the DRAM chips themselves. DRAM from these manufacturers often test faster speed-wise than the rating on the chip markings, which leads to the importance of testing.

Testing the memory

You can purchase DRAM *loose,* meaning it won't come in any shrink-wrapped packaging, or you can purchase DRAM in regular retail packaging. You pay more for DRAM that you buy in a retail package, but you may get more installation instructions, better documentation on the DRAM itself (the packaging may even state what make and model computers the DRAM works with), and a more liberal return policy. One important drawback here is that you won't be able to have the DRAM tested before you purchase it.

If you buy DRAM from most smaller computer stores, you'll probably buy it by the *stick* (a stick of RAM is a single SIMM or DIMM), with nothing more than an antistatic bag to carry it home in. (Be sure to get an antistatic bag to carry your DRAM in.) You pay less for stick DRAM, sometimes much less, but you probably won't be able to return it easily, or at all. However, most computer stores have a SIMM tester, which you want to take advantage of. Have the DRAM tested before you buy it, and ask to watch the testing process. You should never see the word *error* at any time during the testing of a SIMM or DIMM. If you do, you know that particular stick is bad, and you can insist on another. By testing the SIMM or DIMM, you also can find out if the DRAM tests at a higher speed rating than what is labeled.

TIP

You can also have the SIMMs you already own tested for a dollar or so at most computer stores. Some stores will test your SIMMs without charge. This is a particularly good idea if you can't figure out the capacity of the SIMMs or if you'd like to verify that the SIMMs are working correctly. Be sure to transport your SIMMs in an anti-static bag and protect them from ESD (as outlined in Chapter 2) while handling them.

Installation

After you've purchased your new SIMMs, you're ready for installation. This is the easy part. Make sure the computer is turned off, and make sure that you're grounded by using your wrist grounding strap.

Removing SIMMs (optional step)

If you have SIMMs that you need to remove, you must complete this step first. SIMMs are held in place by tabs on each side. If you put pressure on these tabs, pushing them away from the SIMM, the SIMM simply falls forward and can easily be removed. Putting pressure on the tabs is the important part.

If your tabs are plastic, you need to put gentle pressure on the tabs so that you don't break them. A couple of small, flathead screwdrivers work well for this purpose. With a screwdriver in each hand, press on the tabs and gently push them outward until the SIMM is released, as shown in Figure 6-12.

Figure 6-12: Plastic tabs for holding SIMMs need careful handling. Here's how to place gentle pressure on one to remove a SIMM.

You'll have an easier time with metal tabs. Simply take your fingernails or thumbnails of each hand and press on the tabs on each side of the SIMM. SIMMs usually fall forward when released, although they may need a gentle nudge with a free finger (see Figure 6-13).

Placing the SIMM in the slot correctly

When placing the SIMM into the slot, be sure pin 1 on the SIMM lines up with pin 1 of the slot. You should see the number 1 on the motherboard near the SIMM slots, which indicates the pin 1 position (see Figure 6-5). A notch on the bottom of the SIMM indicates the pin 1 side, which makes inserting the SIMM incorrectly almost impossible.

Take care not to touch the contacts on the bottom of the SIMM. You don't want to transfer skin oils or other contaminants to the connectors. As shown in Figure 6-14, tilt the SIMM to a 45-degree angle, press gently until it goes into the slot and then rotate the SIMM back into an upright position. Sometimes you can hear the SIMM click as it goes into place, and you see the round pegs of the SIMM slot fit into the corresponding round holes on each side of the SIMM. Do not force the SIMM into the slot if it is unwilling to go easily; instead, check the pin 1 orientation to make sure you're inserting the SIMM correctly. When the SIMM is in place, you're ready to test your new memory.

Figure 6-13: You can release the metal tabs for holding SIMMs with gentle downward pressure.

Figure 6-14: Insert the SIMM into the slot at a 45 degree angle and then push the SIMM backward and upright until it snaps into place.

Packard Bell Pentium memory upgrade scenario

Sheila wanted to upgrade the memory in her Packard Bell Pentium PC from the 8MB of RAM that came with the PC to 32MB of RAM. Despite the Packard Bell literature that suggested she take the PC to an authorized repair center for an upgrade, she decided to attempt the upgrade herself. Sheila purchased the Legend 106CDT Supreme model that was multimedia ready.

The first thing Sheila did was look through the materials that came with her PC to find an indication of how the memory inside was currently configured. When she didn't find anything, she opened the case and took a look inside. There were two 72-pin slots inside the Packard Bell unit. One slot had a SIMM, and the other was empty. Because she had 8MB of RAM, Sheila knew that the SIMM in the Packard Bell PC was probably an 8MB SIMM. She got a flashlight, looked more carefully at the chip numbers, and discovered that the SIMM was indeed an 8MB SIMM with a speed of 70ns. She also noticed that a number of the chips on the motherboard had the Intel logo, along with the word *Triton*.

To find out what she could add, Sheila called Packard Bell's technical support line. After a long wait on hold, she got a technical support representative, who asked her for the model number of her unit. The technical support representative, asked Sheila for the numbers on the motherboard of her PC and then asked how many SIMM slots Sheila had seen. A couple different motherboard configurations had been used for this model, and the support representative needed to identify the motherboard.

Sheila had noted the number of SIMM slots and that the motherboard had Intel chips that said Triton on them. The technical support representative was able to identify the motherboard and told Sheila that it had the Intel Triton chipset. That fact allowed Sheila to use either EDO SIMMs or Fast Paging Mode SIMMs on the motherboard.

The technical support representative explained to Sheila that to increase to 32MB, she needed to remove the 8MB SIMM and add two 16MB SIMMs. The support technician also recommended that she purchase SIMMs with tin-lead contacts. After Sheila got off the phone, she did some checking and discovered she could use a SIMM converter to make use of the SIMM she had. A friend advised Sheila to get a *SIMM doubler*, which is a type of SIMM converter that takes two 72-pin SIMMs and makes them into a single, higher capacity 72-pin SIMM. Sheila figured she could buy the SIMM doubler, one 8MB SIMM, and one 16MB SIMM to get her 32MB of RAM.

When Sheila got to the computer store, she read the fine print on the SIMM doubler package. She discovered that she could use 1MB, 2MB, 4MB, and 16MB SIMMs, but not 8MB SIMMs as she'd planned. Sheila then decided she had two choices. She could buy two 16MB SIMMs and take out her 8 MB SIMM, or she could buy one 8MB SIMM and settle for 16MB of memory instead of 32MB as she'd planned.

Sheila had decided to buy two 16MB SIMMs when another customer standing in line at the computer store offered to purchase the 8MB SIMM from her if she agreed to have the SIMM tested. Because Sheila knew the SIMM worked, she agreed. The computer store agreed to test the SIMM for free. Sheila got an anti-static bag from the store, went home, removed the SIMM and placed it in the antistatic bag, and returned to the computer store. She had her old SIMM tested, sold it, and bought her new SIMMs. She decided to spring for 60ns EDO SIMMs. These SIMMs cost more, but she hoped they would pay off in better performance from her PC.

When she got home, she inserted the two new SIMMs into the slots. The first SIMM did not want to go in, and when Sheila looked at it more carefully, she realized she had it backwards. Sheila turned it around so that pin 1 on the SIMM lined up with pin 1 on the motherboard, and it went in fine. After the SIMMs were inserted, Sheila powered up the PC. The computer counted up to the full 32MB of memory she had inserted, and then a message appeared on-screen saying that there was incorrect information in the CMOS and advising her to enter the CMOS setup menu. Sheila pressed the reset button to restart the PC, and the computer came up without a hitch the next time.

Sheila noticed immediately that the computer booted faster and Windows 95 came up more quickly as well. Sheila also noticed that her applications came up faster and performed tasks faster. She later learned that some businesses specialize in buying and selling used SIMMs. However, she also learned that she got more money for her SIMM from the individual she sold it to than she would have if she had sold it to one of those businesses.

Testing

Testing is the easy part. Make sure you have removed any tools or objects from inside the PC, and leave the case open. Turn on the computer and watch the boot process. You should see the memory count up to the total amount of memory you've added. Most BIOSs automatically recognize the new memory, but you can expect an error message (and two or more beeps to indicate a problem) that says the Setup is incorrect. This is because the amount of memory in the CMOS Setup menu doesn't match the amount of memory now in the computer.

You should enter the CMOS Setup menu, but you won't find a way to get to the memory settings. The CMOS should automatically update the memory capacity. All you need to do is save the changes made for you. Exit the CMOS by pressing the Esc key. Upon pressing this key, you should be presented with several ways to exit the CMOS. You want to choose the Save And Exit option. When you exit the setup, the computer reboots, and you shouldn't see any further error messages.

Installation in Review

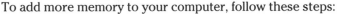

To add more memory to your computer, follow these steps:

1. Determine how much memory you have now.

2. Look at your system documentation for the memory requirements, or contact the manufacturer of your system.

3. Look inside your system to determine the configuration of your current memory.

4. Determine the amount and configuration of the memory you can add.

5. Purchase the new memory you need, based on the information you now have.

6. Remove old memory, if necessary.

7. Install the new memory.

8. Test the memory.

Question: Can I accidentally bend pins on a SIMM when I insert it?

Answer: Although SIMMs have pins, you can think of them more as electrical contacts than cylinder-shaped projections. Therefore, bending pins is not likely. The SIMM is a circuit board designed to take the pressure necessary to gently, but firmly, push it into the SIMM slot on the motherboard.

Question: What if I add memory that is faster or slower than the memory that's already in my computer? Will it work?

Answer: Yes, it will work. If you're mixing speeds, you want to put the faster memory in the first bank of the computer so it can help speed the boot process. However, mixing memory speeds is usually a waste of money, especially if you're paying extra for the faster memory. The best thing to do is match the speed of the memory that's already in your PC.

Question: Every time I boot my PC, I get the message *SMRAM good.* What does that mean?

Answer: Some PCs have a reserved block of memory that performs special functions. For example, some energy-saving PCs with the Acer BIOS have a block of special static memory where the energy-saving status and information (the *green* features) are stored. This memory is tested each time the PC boots, and this message lets you know that the memory is working correctly.

Troubleshooting

Most of the mistakes users make in upgrading memory happen before the installation and involve buying memory that doesn't fit into the PC. If you do your preparation work, you shouldn't have problems. However, there are a few things that can cause problems.

If the SIMM seems unwilling to go into the SIMM slot, check to make sure you have pin 1 on the SIMM lined up with pin 1 on the slot. There's a notch in the SIMM on the pin 1 side near the bottom that needs to be on the notched side of the SIMM slot. If you have the SIMM faced correctly, it should go into the slot without difficulty. Don't force it — you can damage the SIMM slot.

You can expect one error message and two or more beeps when you install new memory, but that message should go away after you enter the CMOS Setup. If it recurs, enter the CMOS Setup menu again, check the memory totals, and be sure to save your changes when you exit. If you don't save the changes, you get the same error message each time you reboot.

If you get an error message more than once during boot up, or if the amount of memory the computer counts isn't correct, you need to check the following:

1. Make sure you pushed the SIMMs into the slot firmly and that the SIMM sits level in the slot.

2. Check the motherboard to see if you have to set jumpers to reflect the new memory settings. Most system boards don't require this, but some do, so it's worth checking your system documentation. If you're not sure what jumpers are, how to find them, or how to set jumpers, read through the jumper setting information in Chapter 7.

3. Make sure that the SIMMs you added are the correct capacity and are in the correct banks. If a bank is four SIMM slots, and you add two SIMMs to that bank, you can expect an error message. You need either to add two more SIMMs of the same capacity or remove the two SIMMs from the bank.

If you get the error message, `Ram Parity Error`, you have a BIOS that allows you to choose whether or not parity checking is enabled. To correct this, enter the CMOS Setup. This type of fine tuning is usually in an advanced CMOS menu, so go to that menu. Look for *Memory Parity Checking* or *System Memory Parity* and check to see if this is enabled. If it is, look for a way to turn this checking off or *disable* this setting. Then save and exit the CMOS menu so the change can take effect.

If the amount of memory the BIOS counts during the boot sequence does not match the amount of memory you've added, then you may not have inserted the SIMMs correctly. If you have inserted the SIMMs correctly, then either the SIMMs you added were bad or you have bad (nonfunctioning) SIMM slots on the motherboard. Have the SIMMs tested. If the SIMMs test okay, then you could have bad SIMM slots on the motherboard, and you need to contact the manufacturer of the system.

Troubleshooting Practice: What's Wrong in This Photo?

Here is a photo of a common memory installation problem. See if you can tell what's wrong.

Figure 6-15: See answer.

Answer:

SIMM placed incorrectly in the slot. The SIMM should be level with the motherboard across the bottom when it is correctly inserted. To correct, remove the SIMM and re-insert it.

Summary

✦ Most of your time spent installing memory involves determining the type of memory that works in your system. You can often obtain the documentation for your system from the manufacturer using a faxback or BBS.

✦ For the most part, you can use SIMMs with parity in a system that doesn't require parity, but you cannot use non-parity SIMMs in a system that requires parity.

✦ An even number of chips on a SIMM, or a $\times 32$ or $\times 8$ notation for SIMMs, indicates non-parity SIMMs. An odd number of chips on a SIMM, or a $\times 35$ or $\times 9$, indicates the presence of parity. Non-parity SIMMs cost less than parity SIMMs.

✦ You are required to install SIMMs in pairs of the same capacity. Although you can mix the speed of SIMMs, it probably costs less to match the speed of the SIMMs in your system.

✦ If you're buying memory that doesn't have retail packaging around it, be sure to have the memory tested, and be sure to transport memory in antistatic packaging.

✦ When installing SIMMs, do not force them into place. If the SIMM is difficult to install, check to see that the SIMMs are oriented correctly so that pin 1 on the SIMM lines up with pin 1 on the SIMM socket.

✦ The BIOS picks up the fact that the memory on the system has changed. All you have to do is save the changes that the BIOS places in the CMOS setup menu.

✦　✦　✦

Nonremovable
brand ULSI
SX/SLC 33MHz
US 83587

Processor Upgrades

In This Chapter

✦ Locating and identifying your processor

✦ Decoding processor terminology and reading processor markings

✦ Understanding clock speed and system bottlenecks

✦ Discovering how to get the right processor for your upgrade

✦ Learning how to avoid voltage problems

Tools Needed

✦ Wrist grounding strap

✦ CPU extraction tool (optional)

One innovation in recent PC history has been removable, and thus upgradeable, central processing units, or CPUs. Also known as the microprocessor and by a variety of numerical names, the processor has changed from a chip soldered carefully into the system board by the board manufacturer to a chip that you can easily remove and replace.

CPU upgrades are popular, and they're an easy way to get increased performance out of a PC. You can expect a performance boost of as much as 50 percent or more if you replace your current processor with a faster model. The performance you get from an upgrade depends mostly on the design of your PC.

This chapter's focus is to introduce you to the benefits of upgrading your CPU, show what to look for when upgrading your processor, and explain how to accomplish a successful upgrade. Because most of the work is in preparing for the upgrade, that's where this chapter begins.

Preparation

You can upgrade a CPU quickly, if you know what CPU you should upgrade to and how to install it. To understand what you're looking for, you must have some background on what the CPU is, you must know how to recognize what CPU you have now, and you must know how to choose the right upgrade processor for your PC.

What is a CPU?

The *central processing unit (CPU)* is the brain of your PC. The CPU works by taking data out of memory, processing it, and placing it back into memory. It is through memory that the other devices that make up the PC interact with the CPU. It may be helpful if you think of the CPU as an agent, spending its time going from one device to another, asking if its help is needed. If the processing job the CPU is asked to do is lengthy, it may not be available to the other devices connected to the PC until that job is completed. This process explains why sometimes you can type a command and it seems to take a while for the computer to respond. The CPU was processing another instruction, and it took a moment for it to get to the keyboard's memory location, retrieve your keystroke, determine what the keystroke meant, and execute that instruction.

A processor's performance is measured in terms of the amount of data it can process at one time and the speed at which it can process that data. The data is measured in bits, the processing speed in megahertz (MHz). Megahertz is a million cycles per second. A system clock, based on a quartz crystal very much like those found in watches, keeps the processor in synchronization. This synchronization is why the speed of the processor is sometimes referred to as the *clock speed* or *clock cycles*.

The leader by far in the PC market for CPU manufacturing is Intel. However, Intel does have competitors, such as Cyrix, Advanced Micro Devices, and Texas Instruments. Because the Intel processor is the leader and other processors tend to define themselves in terms of the Intel processor family, this chapter uses Intel's terminology and chip numbers to explain what you must know about processors for the PC.

Because they were developed in the engineering community, the original processors were known by their numerical designations. One of the most confusing things to new computer users is the many names used to refer to the same processor. For example, an Intel 80486 processor is probably best known as the "486," but it is also known as a "32-bit processor." It wasn't until the 80586 processor was released in 1994 that Intel changed its long-time habit of numerical designations, calling this processor the *Pentium*.

The math coprocessor

For a long time, the processor for PCs had an optional companion chip called the *math coprocessor*. The math coprocessor was designed to perform arithmetic calculations quickly and off-loaded that work from the main processor. Because computer graphics tend to be mathematically based, help with that portion of the load could boost the performance of a PC doing graphics intensive operations such as computer-aided design (CAD) and drafting work. However, as PCs have become more graphics intensive, math coprocessors became increasingly in demand.

In the beginning, the math coprocessor took the next number in progression following the number of the processor it was designed to accompany. For example, an 80386 processor could be accompanied by an 80387 math coprocessor. Not all PCs were designed so that a math coprocessor could be added, but some high-end PCs came with a math coprocessor. After a while, a 7 at the end of the numerical name for a processor simply meant that it was a math coprocessor.

With the advent of the 486, one of Intel's major design changes was to build the math coprocessor into the CPU. To broaden its product offerings, Intel decided to offer 486 processors that did not have an enabled math coprocessor function, charging less for these chips and calling them *486SX* chips. The processors with this working math coprocessor function were the *486DX*. However, since the Pentium came along, Intel decided not to make the math coprocessor an option and has included a working math coprocessor in every CPU from the Pentium on. Hence, the 486 processor was the last one with an optional math coprocessor.

However, processors have and continue to vary in processing speed, measured in MHz. From the first 8086 processors that zipped along at a whopping 6 MHz, to Pentiums that zing at speeds well over 100 MHz, the speed options are wide and varied. To explain the relationship between speed and processing power, I use the wheelbarrow analogy.

The wheelbarrow analogy

The overall processing power of a CPU is a combination of the amount of data it can process and the speed at which it can process that data. In order for you to gain a better understanding of how this works, I liken the CPU to a wheelbarrow and the data to be processed to a pile of dirt to be moved. The amount of data that the CPU can process in bits is like the amount of dirt the wheelbarrow can hold. The speed of the CPU is how fast the wheelbarrow can make trips to and from the dirt pile.

If you want to move the dirt pile from one location to another quickly, you can do that one of two ways. You can either get a larger wheelbarrow or make more trips in the same amount of time with the wheelbarrow you have. Increasing the MHz of your processor is like making more trips with the wheelbarrow. However, you can sometimes increase both the capacity of the processor and the speed with a processor upgrade.

Low-voltage processors

One of the biggest problems with the new, faster processors is that they tend to generate heat. Electricity, when run through conduits such as circuits or transistors, can perform work, but some electrons are often lost in the form of heat. Heat is the enemy of computer components, so Intel needed to find a way to minimize the heat put out by the millions of transistors in the faster 486 and Pentium processors. Intel decided that the best way to reduce the heat output of its faster processors was to lower the amount of electricity the processor needed to operate.

Traditionally, the circuits and chips of the computer have used 5 volts, while the mechanical devices, such as hard disk drive and floppy disk drive motors, have been 12-volt systems. Laptop makers were the first to reduce the voltage in the circuits to 3.3 volts (some publications say 3.45 volts) in order to extend the battery life of the laptop. Running at 60 MHz and then at 66 MHz, the first Pentium processors stayed with that 5-volt tradition, but Intel reduced the voltage requirements of the 75 MHz and higher speed processors to 3.3 volts (including the 486DX4 100 MHz processor) to reduce the heat output.

Table 7-1 shows a simplified view of the most popular of the Intel processors, their capacity in bits, whether they have a math coprocessor, and their speed ranges. This is not intended to be an all-encompassing list, but it is intended to give you an idea of the performance progression in the Intel processor family.

Table 7-1 The Intel processor family			
Processor	*Data bus capacity in bits*	*Math coprocessor*	*Speed in MHz*
8088, 8086	8-bit	no	5 Mhz, 8 Mhz
80286 (also known as the 286) Mhz,	16-bit	no	6 Mhz, 8 Mhz, 10 Mhz, 12 16 Mhz, 20 Mhz
80386SX (also known as the 386SX)	in at 32-bit, but out at 16-bit	no	12 Mhz, 16 Mhz, 20 Mhz, 33 Mhz
80386DX (also known as 386DX)	32-bit	no	12 Mhz, 16 Mhz, 20 Mhz, 33 Mhz
80486SX (also known as 486SX)	32-bit	no	20 Mhz, 25 Mhz, 33 Mhz
80486DX (also known as the 486DX)	32-bit	yes	20 Mhz, 25 Mhz, 33 Mhz, 40 Mhz, 66 Mhz
486DX2 (also known as an OverDrive or speed doubling processor)	32-bit	yes	50 Mhz, 66 Mhz

Processor	Data bus capacity in bits	Math coprocessor	Speed in MHz
486DX4 (also known as an OverDrive or speed tripling processor)	32-bit	yes	75 Mhz*, 100 Mhz*
Pentium	32-bit	yes	60 Mhz, 66 Mhz, 75 Mhz*, 100 Mhz*, 120 Mhz*, 150 Mhz*, 200 Mhz* **
Pentium OverDrive	32-bit	yes	63 Mhz, 83 Mhz, 120 Mhz*, 133 Mhz* **
Pentium Pro	32-bit	yes	150 Mhz*, 200 Mhz* **

*Denotes a 3.3 volt processor.

** The Pentium is made up of 486 chips linked together inside the processor that divide the computing tasks. This is where it gets its speed.

The heat sink

A heat sink is a passive device that acts like a radiator to conduct heat away from the CPU. It's usually made of aluminum and is often silver or black. It sits on top of the CPU and has rises into spines or rows, between which air can pass. The heat sink is better than nothing, but it relies heavily on good air flow in the case of the computer, which is not always available.

CPU cooling fans

To handle the heat from the faster CPUs, a cooling fan has become standard equipment for most CPUs. This cooling unit is usually a combination of a heat sink with a fan on top that mounts on the processor to pull the heat off the CPU. The power for this cooling unit comes from one of the cables from the power supply. Many CPU cooling units come with splitters; if no power cables are available, it can split the power connection with one of the floppy disk drives. A CPU cooling unit is always a good idea, although Intel and other manufacturers are beginning to require the use of one of these inexpensive units.

Interposers

In the CPU world, an *interposer* is a circuit board that goes between the processor and the motherboard to solve a specific problem. See Figure 7-1. For example, there are interposers available from third-party manufacturers that allow you to run the 3.3-volt, 486DX4 100 MHz processors on a PC designed for a 5-volt 486DX2 50 MHz processor. Although the 486DX4 processor fits into the slot on the motherboard designed for a 486 upgradeable 5-volt processor, if you were to install it without an interposer, the higher voltage would fry the chip. This type of interposer is sometimes referred to as a *voltage-regulator daughterboard*.

Figure 7-1: This Intel Pentium OverDrive processor has a built-in interposer and a built-in heat sink with a cooling fan.

Another type of interposer offered by Intel is designed to mitigate a problem with the write-back cache design of some motherboards. *Cache* is a small amount of memory storage that the CPU can get to quickly that helps speed processing. Some 486 motherboard designs offer write-back cache designed differently enough so that the Pentium OverDrive processor doesn't work correctly on these boards. As a result, Intel offers an interposer that simply disables the write-back cache so that its Pentium OverDrive processors work on the 486 motherboards where this is a problem.

Upgradeable CPUs

In the early days, you could not choose what processor came on your motherboard. The processor was soldered on. Some processors are still soldered onto the motherboard. However, most PCs' motherboards are designed so that you can remove one processor and insert another, as shown on the 486 motherboard in Figure 7-2.

The problem is determining what upgrade processor will work in your system. The determining factor is the speed of the processor that's currently in your system. Upgrade processors typically double or quadruple the speed of the processor you have. For example, if you have a 25 MHz, 486 processor, you can replace it with a 50 MHz, 486 processor. In the 486 world, these "doubler" upgrade chips are often designated as DX2, while the triple speed chips are designated as DX4. Even though these DX4 chips are triple the speed, they're called "quadrupled" chips. The Pentium OverDrive processor also works in 486 motherboards designed to accept the larger OverDrive chip, as shown in Figure 7-3.

Figure 7-2: A motherboard with a LIF socket designed to accept an upgradeable 167- or 168-pin 486 processor.

Figure 7-3: This is a removable 486 processor in a ZIF socket that also accommodates a 237- or 238-pin Pentium OverDrive processor.

TIP

You can do a quick pin-hole count on a socket and tell if a Pentium processor will fit. Count the number of pin holes along the outside row of the side with the most pins. If you come up with 17 pin holes, that socket will fit a 486 processor. However, sockets that can accept Pentium chips have 19 pin holes on the side with the most holes, such as the socket in Figure 7-5.

The PC bus and the processor

The speed of the bus, which is the channel through which data moves back and forth between the CPU, memory, and other devices on the PC, has much to do with how fast the computer can process data. You can put a very fast processor on a PC, but if the bus cannot move data at the same speed the processor can, then you still have a performance bottleneck. For example, if you put a 486DX2 50 MHz processor on a motherboard designed with a 25 MHz bus, you may get 50 MHz processing speed, but the processed data will have to queue up until the bus can move it.

However, because so many different speed processors are out there, motherboard manufacturers have designed their systems to accommodate a variety of CPU speeds. These manufacturers use jumpers to enable you to set the motherboard for the type and speed of processor. The capability to change motherboard settings to accommodate processors of different speeds means that the bus of the motherboard probably operates at the highest speed processor it can accommodate, but it can be set to accommodate lower speed processors.

The IH4077C system board accommodates 486SX to Pentium OverDrive Processors

System designers have made motherboards to accommodate the various upgrade chips Intel has released. The IH4077C board in this example allows the use of an Intel 486SX, 486DX, 486DX2, and Pentium OverDrive chips P23N and P23T. This motherboard has a Zero-Insertion Force (ZIF) socket like the one shown in Figure 7-3.

Jumpers enable you to set the type of processor to be used on the board and the speed of the processor. The jumper settings are described in the documentation, but Figure 7-4 shows that the jumper settings are also documented on the system board itself. The board's jumpers are set to accept a Pentium OverDrive processor, and Figure 7-5 shows the actual jumpers.

Some motherboards also print in the socket the types of processors the board accepts, including chips from manufacturers such as Cyrix or AMD. The motherboard shown in Figure 7-2 accepts the Intel 486, the Intel Pentium OverDrive processors, and the Cyrix 486S processor, which is designated by "CX."

Figure 7-4: The jumper settings for the IH4077C are printed on the motherboard. This printing is not true of all motherboards, but it is certainly worth looking for.

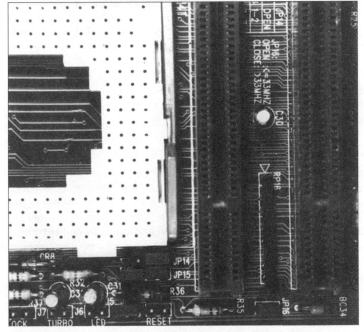

Figure 7-5: A close-up of the jumpers on the IH4077C set to select the Pentium OverDrive processor.

Determining what CPU you have now

The first step in preparing for a CPU upgrade is to determine what CPU you have now. You can often do this step by watching for messages during the boot cycle, but eventually, you have to take a look inside.

You're looking for the following three pieces of information about your current processor:

1. The manufacturer of the processor

2. The number or name of the processor

3. The speed of the processor in MHz

Looking for information during the boot process

You should get some information about the processor during the boot cycle when you start the PC. BIOSs are designed to support a particular processor or processors, so sometimes you can get a hint of what processor is inside from the BIOS. Look for key words or phrases, such as "main processor" or "processor speed," in the messages generated by the BIOS when you start your PC. For example, the Phoenix BIOS A486 Version 1.03 has 486 in its version number, so you can expect a 486 processor inside. In addition, this particular BIOS puts the following line on-screen during boot up: 486 SX processor detected operating at 33 MHz.

With Pentium-based PCs, you may find a label on the outside of the PC case that says "Intel Inside" and "Pentium Processor." Then it's a matter of finding out what speed the Pentium processor is. For example, if a PC with this sticker outside offers the message Processor Speed......75 MHz during the boot sequence, then you can assume that the processor is a Pentium running at 75 MHz.

Your PC may have a processor from another manufacturer, such as Cyrix or AMD, and that's important to note as well. When you've found out as much as you can by observation from the outside, you must take a look inside.

How to find the CPU inside your PC

When you open up the case, you must look for a square chip, usually larger than the other chips. Figure 7-6 shows examples of four removable Intel processors: a 386DX, a 486SX, a 486DX, and a Pentium processor. Figure 7-7 shows an Intel processor that is nonremovable or soldered into the motherboard. Figure 7-8 shows processors from Advanced Micro Devices (AMD) in both the removable and nonremovable types, while Figure 7-9 shows processors from Cyrix in both removable and nonremovable types. Note that the removable processors tend to be larger and more square than the nonremovable types. If you're still having trouble finding your processor, the photos in the section concerning sockets should help.

Figure 7-6: Four removable processors. Note how each family of processor is larger than its predecessor. The 486 processors are the same size but larger than the 386. The Pentium is larger than both previous processors.

Figure 7-7: A nonremovable Intel processor on a motherboard.

Figure 7-8: An example of Cyrix processors
in both the removable and nonremovable forms.

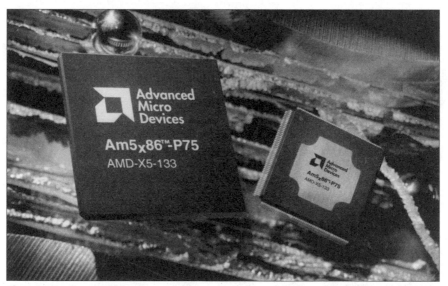

Figure 7-9: An example of processors from Advanced Micro Devices processors
in both the removable and nonremovable forms.

If you open up your PC, you may see something that looks like Figure 7-10; that's your CPU with a cooling fan on top. You can attempt to remove the cooling fan, following the instructions given under CPU installation later in this chapter. In isolated instances, you may find a cooling fan or heat sink glued to the top of the processor, hiding the identity of the chip. In that case, you must look for a CPU identification utility to help you determine the identity of your processor. Norton Utilities, PC Tools, and several shareware programs can help in this circumstance. You can also ask the store where you purchased the computer and hope that it has kept records of the type of CPU placed in PCs sold when you purchased yours. If not, the store should have a software utility that can aid you in discovering the identity of your processor.

How to read CPU chip numbers

When you've located your processor, you can read the information you need off the top of the processor. If you look back to Figure 7-6, notice that these processors have numbers printed on them. You're looking for a combination of the chip name or number and the speed of the chip, such as A80486DX-33. This combination indicates an 80486 (or 486) processor with an operational math coprocessor (the DX tells us that) that runs at 33 MHz. A lowercase letter *i* indicates Intel, although you may find the name Intel on the processor.

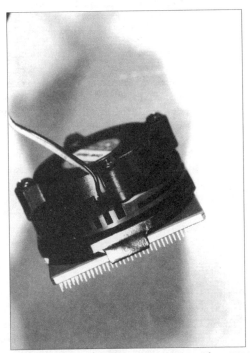

Figure 7-10: A Pentium processor with a CPU cooling fan on top.

Looking at your CPU socket

You've already seen processors, but now you need to see the type of socket your processor fits into. You'll find that you either have a soldered CPU, a low insertion force (LIF) socket, or a zero insertion force (ZIF) socket. You require a special type of upgrade processor if you have a soldered CPU, but you can use the same type of upgrade processor if you have a LIF or ZIF socket.

Soldered CPU

As shown in Figure 7-7, processors can be soldered onto the motherboard so that they are not removable. This type of socket is known as the *leaded chip carrier (LCC)*, or sometimes, if in a plastic case, it's known as the *plastic leaded chip carrier (PLCC)*. This inability to remove the processor doesn't mean that you can't upgrade the processor, but it does mean you cannot upgrade this processor with another Intel processor. Upgrades that work in these situations are offered from third-party manufacturers. These upgrades require a special circuit board that fits over the chip you have now that intercepts the signals to your current processor and directs them to the new processor. A software driver is also often a required component.

You may find upgrade products for nonremovable processors at retail outlets or via catalogs, such as those from Computer Discount Warehouse, Global Computer Supplies, or The PC Zone. The contact information for free catalogs from each of these sources is in Appendix A. Installation of this type of CPU is covered under the installation section of this chapter.

Low insertion force (LIF) socket

The second kind of socket you're likely to find is the *low insertion force* (LIF) socket, shown in Figure 7-2. Also known as a *pin grid array* (PGA) socket, this type of socket is known for its ability to put a large number of pin connectors in a small space. Chips that fit into this socket look like a bed of nails underneath.

This socket accepts the large number of pins on the removable CPUs, but requires that you press the CPU into the socket. Upgrades for CPUs using this type of socket are more plentiful from all the manufacturers, including Intel, Cyrix, AMD, Texas Instruments, and NexGen. It's much easier to get your processor out of this type of socket with a CPU extraction tool. This tool looks like a small rake and fits under the pins of the processor to gently lift it out. However, the easiest type of socket to work with is the zero insertion force (ZIF) socket.

Zero insertion force (ZIF) socket

The *zero insertion force* (ZIF) socket is easiest to work with because it has a lever or handle that you raise to release the chip and lower to secure the chip into place. This mechanism means that the chip should practically fall into the socket when placed correctly on top, so no force is required. You may find that your CPU doesn't take up all of the socket, especially if you have a 486 CPU, as shown in Figure 7-5. If your processor doesn't take up the entire socket, it is because the socket has been designed to accept the larger Pentium OverDrive processor, as well as the 486 processor.

OverDrive socket

Some PCs included a second PGA socket in the motherboard design so that you could insert an upgrade processor. Insertion of the upgrade processor into the socket in many cases can automatically disable the current processor, although sometimes a jumper needs to be changed as well. You will not see this design very much because users like the idea of having a second processor they can sell or use in another system, rather than simply disabling it. Plus, a second socket added unnecessary expense to the design of system boards. However, you may find that you have an OverDrive socket with a soldered 486 processor, and if so, you don't have any choice but to place the upgrade processor into the OverDrive socket.

Discovering what CPU upgrade you can add

Now that you know the manufacturer, type, speed, and socket your processor fits, you can start investigating your upgrade options. Your options depend heavily on the type of processor you have now, whether it's a 386 or earlier model, a 486, or a Pentium. Expect to spend between $50 to $350 or more for a new processor.

Upgrades for 286 or 386 processors

If you have a processor in the 286 or 386 family, you're looking at third-party CPU upgrade products. These products replace your current processor with a 486 processor. Although there are claims among the technical community that the 486 processor isn't really a 486 but a 386, the fact remains you can get some increase in performance from this replacement. The increase you get depends on the other components in your system.

The type of processor you get depends on the socket you have and the processor you're replacing. Your best bet is to talk to the technical support department of the catalog outlet or computer reseller who carries the processor so that you can be sure to get something that fits your particular PC.

CPU upgrade from 286 to 486

Ron owns a small business with a support staff that takes phone orders and inputs sales records. The staff was running DOS applications on a Novell network that used a variety of PCs that Ron picked up one at a time while his business was growing. The slowest one was a proprietary Zeos 286 with a proprietary motherboard and power supply design, as well as a small and crowded case. The employee using that machine was constantly complaining about the 286's slow performance, but when Ron checked into upgrading, he discovered that the proprietary components for the Zeos were simply too expensive.

One day, Ron was reading through a catalog and saw an advertisement for a CPU upgrade processor that could turn a 286 into a 486. Ron called the technical support and was instructed by the make and model number of his PC which upgrade processor to purchase. It was the Make-It 486 processor from Cyrix.

When Ron received the processor, he opened up the PC to install it, but he couldn't find for sure the 286 chip, and the number of chips and cables pressed inside made him change his mind. He talked with friends that made him even more nervous. Finally, he signed up for a computer repair course at a local college. During the class time when students could bring in repair problems, Ron brought in the 286 and the Make-It processor.

The instructor had Ron make a boot disk first, then make copies of the PC's AUTOEXEC.BAT and CONFIG.SYS files on the bootable floppy. The instructor then had Ron put on a grounding strap and open up the PC. The instructor showed Ron how to fit the new processor, which was a small circuit board with several chips on it, on top of the 286 processor soldered into the motherboard. The hard disk drive and floppy drive cables had been covering the 286 chip, and the instructor helped Ron gently move these cables to the side so he could get to the processor.

The old processor had several indicators for pin 1, including a dot in one corner of the 286 chip and a *1* silk-screened in that same corner on the motherboard. The new processor also had a pin 1 indicator, so Ron oriented the processor to line up the pin 1 indicators and pressed it down gently over the old processor, according to the instructions that came with the new chip.

When he was sure that the processor was secure, the instructor had Ron start the PC. Then Ron put the diskette that came with the processor into the A drive and followed the instructions to execute the installation program. Then Ron rebooted the PC and noticed right away a performance jump in the boot cycle. The instructor showed Ron how to look at the AUTOEXEC.BAT file, where he found a new driver to handle the cache for the new processor that had been added. The instructor cautioned Ron that the PC was not connected to the network, so there was no way to test it and be sure that it would work on the network. Until that testing was complete, the instructor advised Ron to hang on to the boot disk and be prepared to remove the processor and go back to the previous AUTOEXEC.BAT and CONFIG.SYS files if there were problems.

However, the only difference the processor upgrade made on the network was a little less lower memory in the PC, and it ran much faster. The employee who was complaining about the PC's performance was happy. Ron was happy because this meant he had the potential to get more service out of a proprietary PC that was still in good working order.

Upgrades for 486 processors

Although you can upgrade soldered 486 processors, you must use third-party products to do so, and these upgrades are not usually based on the speed of the processor. Instead, third-party products upgrade the entire processor to a 586 or beyond.

The majority of upgrade processors, however, are aimed at processors that fit LIF or ZIF sockets, because that's the most common type of desktop PC processor. If you have a 486 processor in this type of socket, you can expect to be able to upgrade to a double- or triple-speed processor.

Intel products for 486 processor upgrades tend to be either double or triple the speed of the processor being replaced. For example, if you have a 486SX running at 25 MHz, you can upgrade to a 486DX2 running at 50 MHz. The DX2 processors, however, double (internally) the external clock speed of the system, while the DX4 processors work internally at triple the external clock speed.

For example, you may be able to replace a 486DX 33 MHz processor with a 486DX4, 100 MHz chip. If, however, you attempt to use a DX4 processor, then you may need an interposer that contains a voltage regulator to run this 3.3-volt chip in a 5-volt socket. Interposers are available from AMP as well as other suppliers. (Suppliers are listed in the Appendix.) Some motherboards already have the voltage regulators built in.

The most common upgrades are double the clock speed of the processor currently in the system because those upgrades tend to have fewer complications. The most likely scenario for a 486DX4 100 MHz processor to be used in an upgrade is if the user already has a 486DX2 66 MHz processor.

You can also take the next step up to an Intel Pentium OverDrive processor or a 586-based processor from a third-party manufacturer. This procedure is not as straightforward as simply doubling the processing speed. Intel says that the Pentium OverDrive at 63 MHz can replace the 486 25 MHz, the 486SX2 50 MHz, and the 486DX2 50 MHz processors. The 83 MHz version can be used in systems with the 486 33 MHz and 486DX2 66 MHz CPUs.

Pentium OverDrive processors intended as replacements for the 486 processor family are often designated as the *P23N*, *P23T*, *P24N*, or *P24T*. For example, the P24T-63 is the Pentium OverDrive in the 63 MHz speed, while the P24T-83 is the 83 MHz model.

The companies that make processors offer much information as to what PCs their processors work in. Much of this information is available via the Internet. The Internet site addresses and other contact information for the manufacturers listed here are in the Appendix.

Upgrades for Pentium processors

If you have a Pentium processor, you can add a faster Pentium processor, depending on the speed of the CPU in your system now. Intel Corporation announced the availability of Pentium OverDrive processors for upgradeable Pentium processor-based systems. In the Pentium OverDrive processor family, upgrades double or less than double clock speed. For example, Intel has two processors aimed at the 5-volt Pentium processors. The Pentium OverDrive 120 MHz is designed to replace the 60 MHz Pentium processor, and the Pentium OverDrive 133 MHz is aimed at the Pentium 66 MHz processor.

In addition, upgrade processors from Intel exist for the 3.3-volt family of processors. A 125 MHz Pentium OverDrive processor is available to replace the first 3.3-volt 75 MHz Pentium, a 150 MHz OverDrive Pentium can upgrade the 90 MHz Pentium processor, and a 166 MHz Pentium OverDrive processor, is aimed as an upgrade for the 100 MHz Pentium.

If you decide to upgrade a Pentium processor, be sure to avoid placing a low-voltage processor directly into a high-voltage socket. This caution applies when upgrading the 60 and 66 MHz Pentium processors, because those chips are designed for 5-volt system board designs.

OverDrive processors from Intel designed as upgrades on existing systems have the letter *R* in their model numbers printed on top of the chip. This *R* stands for *replacement.*

Jumper settings

You can simply take out one processor and insert the compatible upgrade processor into the same slot, without changing jumpers or switches on the motherboard. If, however, you have the documentation for your motherboard, you may be able to get more bang for your buck.

Remember hearing about the bus? Well, if you can change your motherboard settings to accept a faster processor, you're probably allowing for a faster bus speed as well. This probability means that if you have the documentation, you should be able to get even more speed from your system by upgrading to a faster processor than you may have considered otherwise.

In addition, you may be able to add an even faster upgrade processor than you would expect from the speed of the original processor alone. For example, if you have a 486SX 25 MHz processor in your PC now, you could consider upgrading to a 486DX2 50 MHz processor without any jumper changes. If, however, your motherboard can also be set to accept a 486DX processor at 33 MHz, then you could upgrade to a 66 MHz processor instead of a 50 MHz processor. If you set the jumpers or switches on the motherboard to the settings for the 486DX 33 MHz processor, then you could install a faster 486DX2 66 MHz chip.

As shown in Figure 7-2, some motherboards have the jumper or switch settings for processors that the board will accept silk-screened on the board. So you want to look on the system board itself before you give up on finding the jumper or switch settings.

The CPU cooling fan

Some processors require a cooling fan, while others say that you don't need one. I recommend putting one on any processor that's going into a PGA socket, even if you don't feel you need it. Who knows when the air conditioning will break down or the fan on your power supply will go out, and that cooling fan may be the only thing that saves your processor from disaster. When processors overheat, they begin to produce errors in computations, and eventually the system simply stops working or locks up.

Get a cooling fan that fits your processor, because different families of processors come in different sizes. You may already have a cooling fan on the processor in your system, and you may want to continue to use it.

If you decide to replace a 486 processor with a Pentium OverDrive processor, you need a larger cooling fan because the Pentium processor chip is bigger than a 486 processor. Should you buy a new cooling fan, be sure to avoid the kind that sticks to processors or are glued on; get the one you can remove. It's inexpensive, so there's no reason to compromise.

Installation

When you select a new processor, installation is relatively simple. Be sure that you're wearing your grounding strap and that you leave the CPU in the protective antistatic packaging it came in until you actually install it. Put the old CPU back into the protective packaging when you remove it as well. To begin the installation, turn off the computer, open the case, and locate your old processor.

Removing the old CPU

If your CPU is soldered into the socket, then you can skip this step. Remember to have antistatic material to set your old CPU on after you remove it. If your old CPU has a cooling fan attached, you must unplug the fan from its power source.

 In some cases, especially with Pentium OverDrive processors, Intel says that you do not need the cooling fan with the new processor. I recommend that you install the cooling fan that you have on the new processor or even get a new cooling fan for your new processor, just as a precautionary measure.

Removing a CPU from a LIF socket

Removing a CPU from a LIF socket is best done with a CPU removal tool such as the one shown in Figure 7-11. The idea here is to place even, gentle pressure on each side of the processor until you get it far enough out of the socket that you can simply lift it out. Use the extraction tool, or something flat, and gently pry up on each of the sides of the CPU, raising it a little at a time out of the socket. This is a golden opportunity to bend the pins on your processor, so resist the urge to move too fast or pull up more on one side than on another. When you have the CPU up out of the socket far enough, it should begin to feel loose, and at that point you can go ahead and lift it out of the socket with your hand. If you feel resistance, then gently pry on each side once more and try lifting it again.

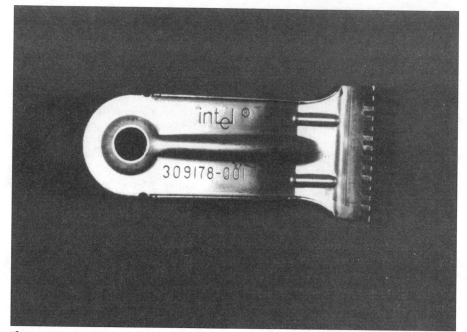

Figure 7-11: A CPU Extraction tool for use in removing a processor from a LIF socket.

Removing a CPU from a ZIF socket

The ZIF socket has a lever on the side that releases the CPU. A piece of plastic holds the lever in place, so you must gently push the lever away from the socket and then pull up, as shown in Figure 7-12. After the lever is free, lift it up, and then lift out the CPU.

Installing the new CPU

After you've removed the old CPU, you can place the cooling fan on the new CPU and install it. I cover installing the cooling fan first, and then installing of the new CPU.

Installing the cooling fan on the new processor

Although you are not required to put a cooling fan on most processors, some faster processors have a label stating that a cooling fan is required. Most cooling fans require that you remove the bottom portion, put the processor into the bottom piece, and then snap on the fan/heat sink combination.

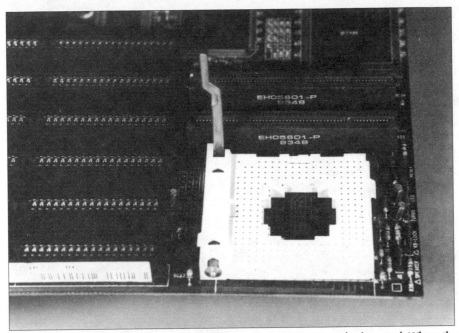

Figure 7-12: The lever is up on a ZIF socket so that the CPU can be inserted. When the CPU is in, the lever should be pushed back down into place.

Installing the new processor in the socket

The most important part of the installation is orienting the CPU so that pin 1 on the processor matches up with pin 1 in the socket. The processor makers don't want you to miss pin 1 on the processor, so they've put about four different indicators on the chip that are obvious to engineers, but not so obvious to users.

The easiest for newcomers to find is the notched corner. Although the other corners of the chip are squared, one corner is notched. This corner often contains a dot that's either black or white. You can see both of these indicators on the processors shown in Figure 7-6. Underneath the chip, a line points from the center of the processor to pin 1, and pin 1 has a square solder point at its base instead of a circle. Both of these indicators are shown in Figure 7-13.

On the motherboard, pin 1 is often indicated by a *1* on the motherboard near one corner of the socket. On a ZIF socket, pin 1 is the corner with no pin holes, as shown in Figure 7-14. When you're dealing with a LIF socket, or other sockets, you'll often see a square drawn around the processor socket with a notch in one of the corners to indicate pin 1, as you can see in Figure 7-10. Also, the socket may be missing connectors in the pin holes in the pin 1 corner, also shown in Figure 7-10.

Figure 7-13: The line and the square solder point indicate pin 1 on the underside of this processor.

Figure 7-14: Pin 1 on a ZIF socket is the corner with no pin holes, as shown in this Pentium ZIF socket.

If you're installing the CPU in a LIF socket or over another CPU, you need to put pressure behind the new processor in order for it to make contact and stay in place. With a LIF socket, your biggest concern should be bending or breaking off one of the pins on the processor. To install the processor, make sure that you have it oriented correctly to pin 1 in the socket, and then place gentle, even pressure on the chip starting in the middle, and then on each of the four corners, until the chip moves down into the socket. If you're working with a LIF socket, you'll know you have the processor properly inserted when you no longer can see the pins from the side.

If you're installing the CPU in a ZIF socket, you need to be sure that the lever is up, and then set the processor in the socket lining up the pins. Be sure that you have it oriented toward pin 1. The processor should practically drop into the socket with no force on your part. Be sure that you cannot see any of the pins from the side, and then lower the lever on the ZIF socket until you hear it snap into place.

Connecting the power to the cooling fan

When the processor is in the slot, connect the power to the new cooling fan. If you are reinstalling your existing cooling fan, you probably want to connect it back the same way it was before you started. Most cooling fans have a splitter arrangement so that you can pull power from one of the floppy disk drives to supply power to the cooling fan, as shown in Figure 7-15.

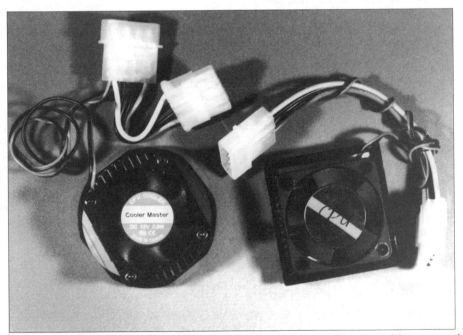

Figure 7-15: The CPU cooler often has a splitter so that it can be powered from one of the power connectors in use for one of the floppy disk drives, if necessary. Two typical examples of CPU coolers are shown.

TIP

Be sure that you do not split off the power for your cooling fan from the power going to your hard disk drive. The hard disk drive spins continually while the power is on, and so does the cooling fan. The floppy disk drives, however, face occasional use so they're better candidates for splitting power resources.

CASE STUDY

Processor upgrade stalled by wrong size cooling fan

Wilma wanted to upgrade her processor. She had a 486 SX running at 33 MHz in a LIF socket on her computer, and she wanted to upgrade to a 486DX2 66 MHz processor. She purchased the new processor and a new cooling fan and proceeded with her upgrade.

She wore her grounding strap, used her CPU extraction tool to gently remove the old processor, placed the cooling fan on the new processor, and inserted the processor into the LIF socket. The cooling fan seemed a little loose on the processor, but it was a close fit, so Wilma went ahead with the installation.

To her surprise, the computer refused to boot when she turned on the power. Wilma checked the jumpers to see if a change was needed, checked the orientation of the processor, and restarted the PC. It still didn't boot.

Wilma took out the new processor and put the old processor into the PC. When she restarted the PC, the computer booted. Now she knew that the new processor had a problem. Wilma tried the new processor again and received the same result. She called the computer store where she bought the new processor, and she was advised to bring in the new processor.

At the computer store, one of the technicians took the processor with the CPU cooling fan on it to test it. The technician noticed right away that the CPU cooling unit was the wrong size. The cooling unit Wilma had been sold was for a Pentium chip, and it was keeping the 486 from making proper contact with the socket. Wilma didn't notice that the pins on the 486 were not all the way in because the cooling fan was in the way. Wilma got the correct size cooling fan on her new processor and took it back to her computer. She installed the new CPU, and the machine booted without a problem.

Setting the jumper settings (optional)

As previously discussed, you may need to set jumpers or switches on your motherboard to accommodate your new processor. This need is especially true if you expect to increase the performance of the processor, or if you've upgraded the processor, on a motherboard capable of supporting a Pentium OverDrive or third-party processors, such as those from Cyrix.

The actual settings depend on your specific motherboard. Hopefully, you've followed my advice and have investigated which processors your board will support and looked at your motherboard for jumper settings.

Look for settings for both the type of CPU and the speed. The CPU and speed settings may be included in a single set of jumpers. Some boards, however, have a set of jumpers for the type of processor (such as a 486DX2 or 486DX4) and another set of jumpers for the clock speed. You may find a simple on or off setting for the clock speed that indicates a range to be used. The on/off setting can be indicated by instructions that look something like the following example for a jumper setting: `JP16 Open:<=33 MHz Closed: > 33 Mhz`. *Open* means that the jumper should not be connecting the pins if the processor operates at under or equal to 33 MHz. If the processor is faster than 33 MHz, then the jumper should be closed.

The pros never take the jumper connectors (called *shunts*) entirely off a board, and you don't need to, either. To open a jumper so that there's no connection, simply move the shunt so that it's over only one pin. This way, you keep the shunt in a safe place, ready for use. (See Figure 7-16.)

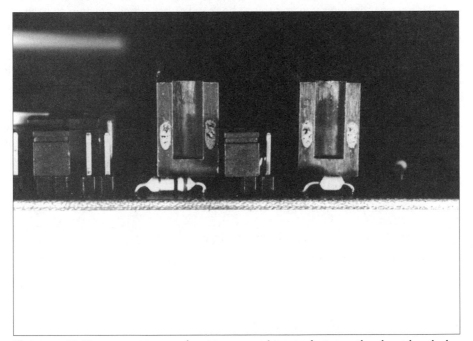

Figure 7-16: You can remove a shunt to open a jumper, but save the shunt by placing it over just one of the pins so that it doesn't get lost.

Testing

Don't close up the case, but make sure that you haven't left any tools inside the PC, and then turn on the power. If you have the right processor, and it's installed properly, the system should boot normally. In fact, the system should boot faster. If you've changed the jumper settings on the motherboard, the display during the boot process should reflect those changes.

Turn off the PC, leave it off for ten seconds, and turn it on again. If everything works, then you completed a successful upgrade. If you installed an upgrade product that came with a diskette to install, see the next section. Most upgrade processors come with benchmark testing software, but some, especially those from vendors other than Intel, have a software driver that you need to install.

Installing a third-party CPU upgrade

If you purchased a CPU upgrade from a vendor other than Intel, and the instructions say that you need to install a software driver, then you have a couple extra steps. Before you open up your PC to install the processor, the first thing you should do is make a bootable floppy diskette and copy your AUTOEXEC.BAT and CONFIG.SYS files to it. This precaution enables you to roll-back to your previous settings in case the new driver displays conflicts with your system, or it simply doesn't work. Chapter 13 covers making a bootable floppy disk drive under DOS/Windows 3.*x* and Windows 95.

When you have a bootable diskette, you can proceed with the preceding installation steps. When the new processor is installed, you must restart the PC and install the software. Follow the installation instructions for the software, and restart your computer. Run the software and applications that you normally run. The drivers that come with upgrade chips take memory, so your applications could balk. If you have problems, call the maker of the upgrade processor to see if it can resolve the problem.

Installation in review

To upgrade your processor, follow these steps:

1. Determine the type of processor you have.

2. Determine the type of processor socket you have.

3. Look at your system documentation for the type of processor you can use for an upgrade.

4. Determine the upgrade processor to use.

5. Purchase the upgrade processor, cooling fan, and a processor extraction tool or interposer, if necessary.

6. Remove your current processor by using the extraction tool or ZIF socket lever.

7. Disconnect the power from the CPU cooling fan, if one is present, and remove the CPU cooling unit.

8. Install the interposer on the new processor (optional).

9. Install the cooling fan on the new processor.

10. Install the new processor into the processor socket.

11. Connect the CPU cooler to a power cable.

12. Test the new CPU.

Question: Will a processor that fits in a ZIF socket fit into a LIF socket?

Answer: Yes. The main difference between these two sockets is the amount of force necessary to put the processor into the socket. As long as the socket accepts the number of pins your processor has, it will work.

Question: I understand Intel has released the 686 processor, named the Pentium Pro. Is there an OverDrive or upgrade from Intel available so that I can upgrade my Pentium to a Pentium Pro processor?

Answer: No. The Pentium Pro is a larger, rectangular-shaped chip with more pins. It will not fit a Pentium socket.

Question: Can I fry my motherboard if I insert the wrong processor?

Answer: No. You can only fry your motherboard if you insert a processor incorrectly. If you have the wrong processor, it simply will not work.

Question: What is an SL or SLC processor?

Answer: An SL or SLC label denotes that the processor supports special energy savings features, such as power management. These processors have been popular in notebook computers, but you may also see them in desktop PCs.

Troubleshooting

Processor upgrades either work or they don't. If you're having trouble with your upgrade, this troubleshooting section should help.

The system won't boot.

1. Make sure that the CPU is inserted correctly in the slot so that pin 1 on the processor lines up with pin 1 on the socket.

2. Check the jumper (and/or switch) settings on the motherboard.

3. Make sure that you cannot see any pins under the CPU, as this indicates that the CPU is not inserted correctly into the slot.

4. Make sure that the cooling fan is properly attached and is the right size so that the CPU is making proper contact with the socket. The cooling fan should not be in the way of the processor's contact with the socket.

5. Remove the CPU and check for broken or bent pins.

6. Check with the manufacturer for known conflicts with the CPU and other hardware on your system (such as video cards), especially if you're using a CPU from a third-party manufacturer or are replacing a CPU from a third-party manufacturer.

7. Replace the old CPU and see if the system still works. (Be sure to copy your old AUTOEXEC.BAT and CONFIG.SYS files if you installed a software driver with your new CPU.) If it works, then you know there's a problem with the new CPU. Reinstall the new CPU and check this list, especially items 2 and 6.

The system boots, but it locks up after a while.

1. This could be a heat problem. Did you install a CPU cooling fan?

2. Check to see if your BIOS or motherboard supports "Green" or energy saving settings. These settings sometimes need to be disabled for an upgrade CPU to work properly.

The system seems to work, but the BIOS is reporting a processor different than the one I installed.

1. Check your motherboard jumper (and/or switch) settings.

2. Contact the vendor of the upgrade processor with your BIOS manufacturer, version, and date to see if there are any known conflicts.

Some of my programs that worked with my old CPU don't work now or don't work the way I expect them to.

Some third-party processors have compatibility problems with certain application software. Contact the vendor of the software with the information on the processor you installed and ask if they know of other users who have had problems with this processor.

Troubleshooting Practice: What's Wrong in These Photos?

Here are photos illustrating common memory installation problems. See if you can tell what's wrong.

Figure 7-17: See answer 1.

Figure 7-18: See answer 2.

Answers:

1. The CPU has bent and broken pins.
2. The CPU is mounted incorrectly.

Summary

✦ You must know the type of processor you have before you can determine what processor you can upgrade to. You can get information about your processor during the boot sequence and by opening your PC and looking inside.

✦ Investigation into what upgrade processor will work in your system is necessary.

✦ Upgrade products for processors that can be removed and for those soldered on the motherboard are available. Many third-party processor upgrades require you to install a software driver as well.

✦ You don't necessarily need the system documentation to perform a processor upgrade, but it helps. You may find some jumper setting information on the motherboard itself.

✦ To properly install the new processor, be sure it's oriented correctly to pin 1 in the socket. Gently insert the processor so that no pins are bent and the processor do not show from the side.

✦   ✦   ✦

Low-Budget Upgrades

In This Chapter

✦ Speeding up Windows inexpensively

✦ Decoding the terminology behind video displays and hard disk controllers

✦ Recognizing the type of expansion slots you have

✦ Determining what you have now and what you can upgrade to

✦ Discovering secrets the pros use for success in upgrade situations

Tools Needed

✦ Wrist grounding strap

✦ Phillips screwdriver

There are two ways to make your PC run as if it's had a dose of steroids. One is to upgrade your video controller board with a faster version; the other is to get a faster hard disk controller board. These upgrades have two points in common: they can be inexpensive, and they can require you to replace a circuit board, also known as a *card*.

The performance difference that you experience after either upgrade depends on the hardware you have now and what you use to replace it. This chapter is divided into two sections. The first section deals with replacing a video card, and it introduces the various types of expansion slots for adding cards available in systems on the market today. The second section deals with hard disk controller card upgrades, including how to tell if your hard disk controller is on the motherboard and how to disable it if necessary.

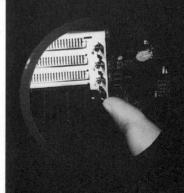

Although it may seem as if you can get economy of scale by performing both upgrades at the same time, this is a bad idea. If you change both cards at the same time, troubleshooting a problem becomes much more difficult — that is, of course, if you have a problem. You should perform these upgrades one at a time. If you can, perform the upgrades at least a week apart so that any latent problems have time to show up.

Section I — Video Card Upgrades

This section focuses on upgrading the video card, including background information you need to determine if you can upgrade. This section is divided into preparation, installation, and troubleshooting.

Preparation

Like any upgrade, the time you spend in preparation for a video card upgrade is well spent. This section covers how a video card works, the terminology surrounding video displays, various types of video cards, the various types of expansion slots, and what to look for when purchasing a video card.

What is a video card?

The video converts digital data into signals that can be sent across a connector to your monitor, which interprets the signal into an image on-screen. A good video card makes images on your monitor seem to just appear, while a slow or inadequate card causes images to slowly draw across your screen. Of course, in a Windows environment, the sooner the next menu or next choice appears on-screen, the sooner you can act. This is why a good video card can speed up the performance of Windows.

Video cards have their own processors, and they can have added memory as well. The processor on the video card can offload a portion of the video processing from the CPU, which is why it can speed up the screen displays. The more memory the better, but more memory means more money; the card costs more. In addition, software drivers are required so that your PC can take advantage of the video card functions. Usually, the software driver you need comes on a diskette bundled with the card, although software drivers for popular video cards come bundled with the Windows operating system.

You can expect to pay from $50 to $200 or more for a video card to upgrade your current video card. The price of the card depends on its features and the amount of memory it has.

Video terminology

When you look into replacing a video card, you run into terms that you must understand in order to upgrade. Here's an overview of the terminology used to describe video displays.

Resolution

The individual dots that are lit to display an image on the monitor screen are known as *picture elements* or *pixels*. In addition, the number of colors used to make up a color image can vary from 16 colors to 16 million colors or more. The number of pixels used to create a display, along with the number of colors, is the *resolution* of the display.

The majority of available video cards meets the *video graphics array* (VGA) standard that begins at 640 x 480 pixels and goes up to about 1280 x 1024 pixels (or higher). Figure 8-1 is a table of video display acronyms and the accompanying resolutions. This book assumes that you have a color VGA display.

If your monitor is not capable of VGA resolution, you're facing the purchase of a new monitor as well as a new video card. Although purchasing a new monitor no longer qualifies as a low-budget upgrade, it is probably a worthwhile upgrade.

You can tell if you have a VGA display by looking at the type of connector your monitor has and the type of connection into which it plugs. VGA display adapters have a 15-pin female connector, and VGA monitors have a male adapter with pins that fit the 15-pin female VGA connector. As shown in Figure 8-2, the monitor connector doesn't always have 15 pins to fit into the VGA display adapter, but the pins that are there are aligned in the three-rows-of-five-pins pattern. Lower resolution display adapters often have two rows of pin holes, and monitors designed for these displays have the corresponding two rows of male pins.

Video resolution standards

Adapter	Resolution	Colors
Monochrome Display Adapter	720 x 350 pixels	single color: amber, green, or white*
Hercules Graphics	720 x 350 pixels	white*
Computer Graphics Array (CGA)	320 x 200	4 colors*
Extended Graphics Array (EGA)	640 x 350	16 colors*
Video Graphics Array (VGA)	640 x 480	256 colors*
Super Video Graphics Array (SVGA)	800 x 600	65,536 colors*
Extended Graphics Array (XGA)	1024 x 768	16.8 million*

*These are not hard and fast rules, but are intended as guidelines only. These standards can and frequently do overlap. For example, you may find an SVGA card that boasts resolutions of 1024 x 768 or even 1280 x 1024, or VGA card that displays 800 x 600 in 256 colors. If you count black and gray scales as colors, the number of colors each standard can support increases. Also, you'll be hard-pressed to find a new CGA or EGA video adapters or monitors.

Figure 8-1: The various video resolution standards.

Figure 8-2: A 15-pin female VGA port and a typical 15-pin male connector from a VGA monitor.

If you don't have VGA and want to upgrade to VGA, you must set switches or jumpers on your motherboard to accommodate the higher resolution. To get the new settings, refer to the documentation for your PC's motherboard, or look in your CMOS setup menu.

Scan rates

The current design of most video and television screens includes a picture tube that is refreshed by a gun that excites the phosphor on the tube. Refreshing the screen is done both vertically and horizontally. For example, vertical scanning means that the gun starts at the top and "shoots" the width of the screen back and forth until it reaches the bottom, over and over again. This process is known as *scanning*. The rate at which scanning is done affects how much "flicker" appears in the image you see, especially when you're looking at detailed images such as on-screen text.

Scan rates, or *refresh rates,* are measured in hertz (Hz) for the horizontal rate and in kilohertz (kHz) for the vertical rate. Your biggest concern is the vertical scan rate, and usually, when scan rates are mentioned, it is assumed that what is meant is the vertical scan rate.

To give you an idea how scan rates work, most televisions scan at the rate of about 60 Hz, or 60 times a second interlaced. Most good VGA monitors are capable of a scan rate of 60 to 72 Hz. You should care about all this because when you set your video card software to a higher resolution, you may also need to set the scan rate up as well. If your monitor is not capable of the scan rate demanded by the resolution, you could have trouble with your display.

You can tell what scan rate your monitor is capable of by looking at the information printed on the back of your monitor. Some monitors give you a range, such as 50 – 72 Hz or 50 – 60 Hz, while others give you a single number. Remember, higher resolutions require higher refresh or scan rates. Usually, 640 x 480 pixels requires 60 Hz, 800 x 600 pixels requires 70 Hz, and any higher resolution displays require 72 Hz or higher. The normal range you run across is between 50 and 80 Hz.

TIP

Do not set your video card to a scan rate higher than your monitor is capable of displaying because you can damage your monitor. Most VGA monitors can handle 60 Hz, but if you want to go to 70 Hz or 72 Hz, you must check your monitor's labeling or documentation to be sure that it can handle that scan rate.

Vertical scan rates come into play at higher resolutions. Most of the time, it's not a concern, but occasionally you have the option of choosing a vertical scan rate. Usually it's a yes or no type of choice, such as whether to set the scan rate at 48.7 kHz or not. Unless you know your monitor is capable of such a scan rate, you're better off saying no.

Interlaced and non-interlaced monitors

To save money on video display designs, most televisions and some monitors only scan every other line each pass. This scanning method allows you to use a less-expensive component, making the video display less expensive to produce. This process is called an *interlaced* display. Interlacing is done so quickly that the human eye doesn't pick up the difference, except in an overall perception that the display's quality is not as good. However, you can see the effect of interlacing when a television or monitor is video taped because the video camera will pick it up. You can see the wide bands that have been scanned and the blank bands. Non-interlaced monitors scan every line every time, which produces a better quality display. However, these monitors cost more.

Reserved memory

As mentioned in earlier chapters, everything connected to a PC must have a spot in memory in order to be accessed by the CPU. Video cards are no exception. However, during the initial design of the IBM PC, the various types of resolution were antici-pated, and IBM planned memory addresses in the PC's upper memory between 640K and the 1MB level for each video type that was expected. Consequently, memory space has been reserved for Monochrome, Hercules (which is a monochrome graph-ics display), CGA, EGA, and VGA video cards. The convention in the computer indus-try is to reference this memory in hexadecimal, as shown in the display properties of a Cirrus Logic video card in Figure 8-3.

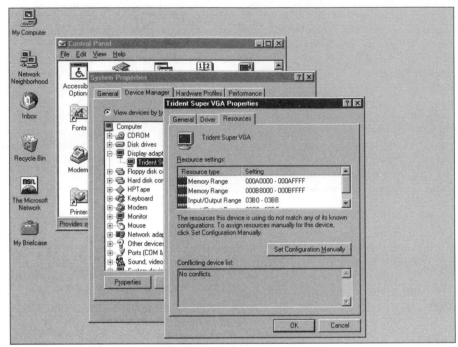

Figure 8-3: Windows 95 lets you see the memory address for your video card in the standard hexadecimal format.

Obviously, most people don't operate more than one monitor or video card, so usually the memory set aside for these various resolutions sits idle. Some video card makers have noticed this, and because high-resolution color displays need more reserved memory, these card makers have designed their video cards to allocate not only the reserved memory for VGA, but the monochrome memory space as well. This practice is relatively safe, because someone running a high-resolution graphics display is probably not going to be using a monochrome monitor.

Those who design other software programs, however, including terminate and stay resident (TSR) programs and memory management software, have also figured out that most people will not use the memory reserved for other types of displays and want to allocate that memory back to the computer user. This means that memory management software and TSRs can cause conflicts with your video card that can produce problems, especially at high resolution displays.

Why video cards need their own memory

The majority of video cards meets the *video graphics array* (VGA) standard that begins at 640 x 480 pixels and includes 800 x 600 pixels and 1024 x 768 pixels. You also have the Super VGA standard that starts at 640 x 480 pixels but has 256 colors. Sometimes you see the Super VGA referred to as the *VESA* or the *VESA VBE* standard.

What you care about from an upgrade point of view is that each higher standard means more work for the video card. Higher resolutions require faster scan rates and more processing power. For example, a single screen at 640 x 480 pixels in 256 colors can take 307K. If you go to 1024 x 768 pixels in 256 colors, you more than double the data displayed to 786K. At 1024 x 768 pixels, the refresh rate must be 70 Hz or 70 times a second, so you can see that there's some demand for processing power.

If the video card has its own processor and memory, it can better handle the increased demands of higher resolution video displays. The bottom line for you is that memory on the video card speeds up your video display.

Types of video cards

The most popular type of video card is the *graphics accelerator card*. This type of card takes over some of the processing work for drawing screens from the CPU to application-specific chips on the video card itself.

Memory on the card also accelerates video performance. Most graphics accelerator cards either have *dynamic random access memory* (DRAM) or a costlier version called *video random access memory* (VRAM). Although VRAM is faster, DRAM is usually adequate for most applications.

Vendors such as Orchid Technology, Diamond Multimedia, and ATI Technologies manufacture name-brand video cards, but generic versions are available as well. Most video cards come with between 1 and 4MB of memory on board. If your PC is a couple years old, chances are that even a generic video card will give you a performance boost if you get one with 1 or 2MB of memory. But before you buy a video card, you must take a look at what kind you have now and at the expansion slots inside your system.

How to find out what you have now

You must know what type of video card you have now to make a good decision on an upgrade. If you're running MS-DOS or Windows 3.*x*, follow these instructions for using MSD to look at your system. If you're running Windows 95, skip to the Windows 95 instructions.

How to use MSD to see your current video setup

If you're running Windows 3.*x*, exit to a DOS prompt. From the DOS prompt, type **C:\DOS\MSD** and press Enter. After you start MSD, select the Display option to see your current display driver. You should see something similar to the display shown in Figure 8-4. MSD tells you what graphics standard the card is (such as VGA or SVGA), and it may also offer information about the manufacturer of the card.

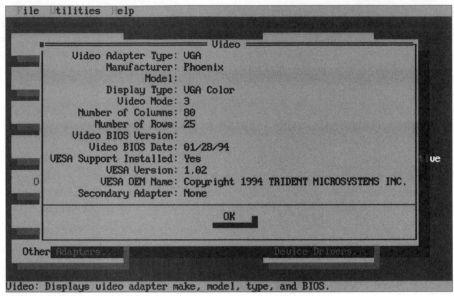

Figure 8-4: MSD running on a PC with a VGA display card.

How to use Windows 95 to see your current video setup

Because Windows 95 requires a VGA display, you know you have a VGA video card and monitor if you're running Windows 95. However, you need specific information about the video card you have now so that you can be sure that when you add a new video card, you're actually upgrading.

To see your current video hardware set up in Windows 95, select My Computer⇨ Control Panel⇨System⇨Device Manager. Make sure that View Devices by Type is selected, and then double-click on the Display Adapters icon. You should see the specific display adapter hardware for your system listed under Display Adapters. Highlight your display adapter hardware and select Properties to see the specifics concerning your display adapter. Write down this information.

Seeing what expansion slots you have

You must look inside your PC to see what type of expansion slots you have to deter-mine what type of video card you can add. Here is some information on what expan-sion slots are and what to look for in your system.

What is an expansion slot?

Expansion slots offer a way for you to add to the functionality of your PC. You plug cards into the slots, which allows you to perform various functions. The slots allow the card access to the system bus and the CPU. The newer expansion slots offer faster data throughput, but the cards for these slots cost a little more. You often can find the same card available to fit several different types of expansion slots on your PC.

Types of expansion slots

Six types of expansion slots are on PCs:

+ PC/XT

+ *Industry Standard Architecture* (ISA)

+ *Extended Industry Standard Architecture* (EISA)

+ Micro Channel

+ *Video Electronics Standards Association* (VESA — also known as Video Local Bus, VL-Bus, or local bus)

+ *Peripheral Component Interconnect* (PCI)

Micro Channel is an IBM standard and is characterized by boards that have blue tabs marked IBM. The majority of the systems in the market have ISA, EISA, VL-bus, or PCI expansion slots.

PC/XT slots, also known as 8-bit slots, are shown in Figure 8-5. An 8-bit slot refers to the amount of data that you can move to and from a board in that slot at one time. The more data that you can move, the faster the slot.

Figure 8-5: An 8-bit PC/XT expansion slot.

ISA and EISA slots look very much alike, although the VL-bus is a longer slot, as shown in Figure 8-6. ISA is a 16-bit slot, and EISA is a 32-bit slot. Figure 8-7 shows a motherboard with ISA and PCI expansion slots.

TIP

EISA slots are deeper, with two tiers of pins so that the 16-bit ISA cards can be plugged into an EISA slot, or deeper 32-bit EISA cards can be used. EISA hasn't really caught on, however, because the two-tier slot approach is expensive. So, if you have EISA slots, you can simply use ISA cards in them, but you probably will not find true EISA cards.

The most recent expansion slots are the VL-bus and PCI, which offer faster data transfer rates than ISA or EISA. VL-bus slots are 32-bit slots, and PCI slots can be 32-bit in a 486-based system and 64-bit in a Pentium-based system. Obviously, if you have a choice and are looking for speed, you should use the slot that delivers the most speed. So, if you're thinking of purchasing a video card to speed up your system, and you have a free VL-bus or PCI slot, you may want to consider a card that fits into one of those faster slots.

A look at cards that fit different expansion slots

Figures 8-8 and 8-9 show four cards: a PC/XT, an ISA, a VL-bus card, and a PCI card. The ISA card fits into either the ISA, EISA, or VL-bus expansion slots. However, the VL-bus card only fits into a VL-bus slot, and a PCI card works only in a PCI slot.

Figure 8-6: This motherboard has ISA and EISA expansion slots as well as a VL-bus slot.

Figure 8-7: This motherboard has ISA and PCI expansion slots. The PCI slots are white in color.

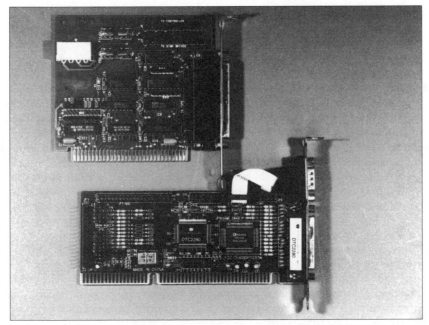

Figure 8-8: Here are two types of cards. The shorter card is a PC/XT, or 8-bit card, and the longer one is an ISA, or 16-bit card.

Figure 8-9: Here are two more types of cards. The card on the top is a VL-bus card, and the one on the bottom is a PCI card.

Taking a look inside your PC

Now that you know what you're looking for, take a look inside your PC. Look for the card that the monitor is plugged into and note the type of slot the card is in. Also look to see if there are other, faster expansion slots available for you to plug a card into.

You may run into a situation where the video controller is integrated into the motherboard, as shown in Figure 8-10. You can recognize this because the port the monitor plugs into is on the motherboard, as shown. When the video is integrated, you can disable the on-board video. In the documentation, the on-board video is sometimes referred to as a co-resident graphics adapter built into the motherboard. Usually, jumpers (or switches) on the motherboard enable you to disable the on-board video. You may be able to disable the on-board video in the BIOS by entering the CMOS setup. Look at the documentation for your system or contact your system manufacturer to be sure.

When two different types of expansion slots are next to each other, it's not uncommon for you to be able to use either slot, but not both. The motherboard shown in Figure 8-10 has a setting in the BIOS that lets you choose the expansion slot of those two that you want to use and disables the other one. The two slots are considered a "shared" slot and may be documented. In the case of the motherboard in the figure, the slots are documented as a "shared PCI/ISA slot." Look at your motherboard documentation (and perhaps your BIOS) to be sure.

Figure 8-10: This motherboard has the video adapter on board.

Buying tips

When you're purchasing a video card, be sure you know the type of processor you have, the kind of expansion slots you have, and the type of monitor you plan to use. Like the rest of the PC industry, these cards change fast, offering new speed and new features. Although computer periodicals are a good source for video card product reviews, the less expensive cards are probably not going to be reviewed, although reading through the reviews provides helpful information anyway.

Your best bet is to talk to the technicians in one or more computer stores. Ask them what card they would recommend for your system, and if they've seen any problems with the card they're recommending. It's not unusual to discover that certain video cards do not work well in systems from certain vendors, or even with CPUs made by manufacturers other than Intel. Also, compare prices, not only between cards, but also between the same cards for different expansion slots. Although you want to take advantage of the faster PCI slots if you have them, you may find that the additional cost of a card that fits a faster slot may not warrant purchasing the card.

TIP

Find out the store's return policy concerning the video card you're getting ready to purchase. If the card doesn't work in your system, you want to be able to return it.

Backing up your system

For insurance, before you get down to installing your video card, it's best to have a current complete backup of your system. Also, you should have a bootable floppy diskette so that you can recover your system in the case of a problem. You can find the information for creating a bootable floppy diskette for DOS, Windows 3.x, and Windows 95 in Chapter 13.

You also need to note the type of video driver you have now. If the new video card doesn't work, go back to the old card and the old software driver. If you're running DOS, load the video driver in either the AUTOEXEC.BAT or CONFIG.SYS file, and if you made a bootable floppy diskette as instructed in Chapter 13, then you can simply copy those files back and be up and running again. However, Windows 3.x and Windows 95 are a different story. Here's how to find and record what driver you're currently using.

Documenting your current Windows 3.x software driver

In Windows 3.x, you find your current software driver by selecting Windows Setup from the Main group. The Windows Setup menu lists your current video display driver to the right of Display, as shown in Figure 8-11. Write this information down. If you need to go back to your previous video card, you can go through the installation instructions that follow to reinstall your old video card, and when it comes to installing a driver, simply use this driver.

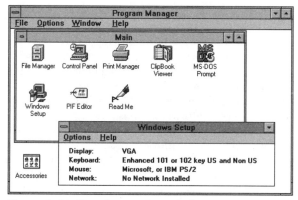

Figure 8-11: If you're running Windows 3.1, you must write down your current display driver settings found in this Windows Setup menu.

Documenting your current Windows 95 software driver

You can find your current video driver by selecting My Computer⇨Control Panel⇨ Display⇨Settings⇨Change Display Type. What you see is similar to Figure 8-12, except that your current adapter and monitor are shown. Write down the adapter type, manufacturer, version, current files, monitor type, and whether or not the Monitor is Energy Star Compliant box is checked. When you have this information, you can use it to go back through the installation instructions to restore what you have now in case the installation of the new video card doesn't work.

Installation

Install your video card as soon as you purchase it. Although it may seem as easy as taking out the old card and inserting the new one, here are a couple of hints that can help ensure a successful installation.

Selecting a vanilla video driver under Windows 3.x

The safest way to perform the installation of a video card under Windows 3.x is to be sure a *vanilla* display driver that comes with Windows is running before you install the new card. The Windows drivers are designed to work with the widest possible variety of video cards, so they're the safest ones with which to start.

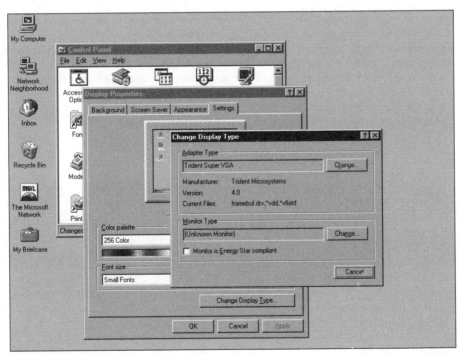

Figure 8-12: If you're running Windows 95, you must write down your current display driver settings found in this Change Display Type menu.

TIP

Don't worry about changing the driver to a vanilla one under Windows 95, because you can start this version of Windows in safe mode, which uses a vanilla VGA video driver and is designed for troubleshooting problems. You start Windows 95 in safe mode by pressing F5 when you see Starting Windows 95. More information is available in the "Testing the new video card" section later in this chapter.

If you don't change the display driver, then you're adding another variable to the situation that makes it difficult to tell what's wrong if your new installation doesn't work. For example, suppose that you have a display driver running now that works with your current video card. If you install another video display card without changing the driver specific to the old card first, then when you restart your PC, the software written specifically for features in your old video card will be attempting to talk to your new video card. If you have a problem, you will not know if it's the software driver or the video card.

So, it's best to use the standard Windows drivers, which are designed to work with the widest possible variety of video cards. To change the driver to a Windows driver, you need the original set of Windows installation disks.

Make sure that you have the original Windows installation diskettes. (Also, before you change your driver, write down what it is in case you have to go back to it.) You may not need the diskettes if the driver is already there. Select Windows Setup from the Main group. Select Options⇨Change System Settings⇨Display. From the list of display drivers available, choose the VGA driver, as shown in Figure 8-11, and click on OK.

If this driver is already present on your system, Windows says that it needs to restart for the change you've made to take effect. If the driver is not present, Windows asks for the appropriate diskette from the installation set and installs the driver, and then requests that you restart Windows. Restart Windows to be sure that the new driver is running correctly.

When you complete this step, you can open up your PC and install your new video card.

Removing your old video card

You've already located your video card, so now you need to open your PC and remove this card. (If your video controller is integrated into the motherboard, as discussed in the preparation section, see the section on disabling on-board video.) Be sure that you're grounded, and then disconnect the monitor cable and unscrew the screw holding the video card in place (see Figure 8-13). Using the bracket on the end, gently rock the card, lifting it out of the slot. After you remove the old card, you can install the new card.

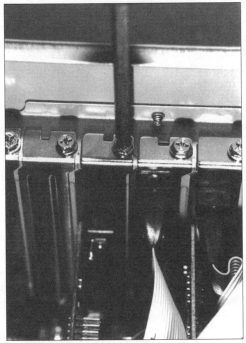

Figure 8-13: To remove the video card, remove the bracket screw and then gently lift out the card.

Installing the new video card

If your new video card can work in the same expansion slot that your old video card was in, then install the new card in the same slot. This way, you do not have to remove one of the brackets that cover the openings on the back of the PC. If your new card cannot work in the same expansion slot, remove the covering bracket from the slot you want to use by removing the screw and lifting out the bracket. Save this bracket and screw to place over the opening you created when you removed the previous video card.

Avoid touching the connectors along the bottom of the card with your hands because your skin oils and other deposits can interfere with the operation of the card. Try to handle the card by the edges as much as possible. Place the card over the slot with the connectors down and, with your open hand across the top of the card, press firmly straight down, without bending the card, until the card settles into the slot.

When the card is correctly placed into the slot, it will be even all the way across. You may be able to see some of the connectors over the top of the slot, but the card should be firmly down in the slot. The next step is to connect the monitor cable to the port on the card, but don't close up the PC yet.

Installing PCI cards

PCI cards are physically installed the same way other cards are installed, but you may find that you need to go into your BIOS setup menu and enable the PCI slot for your PCI video card. If you get a message during the boot cycle that says the CMOS settings don't match and invites you to enter the CMOS setup menu, that's a clue that you need to enable your PCI slot. Here's an example.

To enable the PCI slot in this particular Phoenix BIOS, you first have to go to the Advanced menu, which leads to the screen shown in Figure 8-14. Here you can enable the PCI slot, in this case Slot 0, by going to the Enable Device field and pressing the "+" key to change the field from "disabled" to "enabled," as shown in the figure. You can select another slot by going up to the Device Select field and pressing the + key. Be sure to save your changes when you exit the BIOS, and the boot process should proceed normally.

Testing the new video card

After installing the card, but before you close the PC case, you should test the card. Turn on the PC and the monitor, and watch the boot process. If the card is working, you should see boot messages similar to the ones you saw previously. You may see a few different messages (but not error messages) concerning the video display, but that's to be expected with a new video card.

Windows 3.x testing

If you're running Windows 3.x, you should have already loaded the vanilla VGA driver. Try to run Windows and see if it works. If so, install the video drivers for the card. If not, see the upcoming troubleshooting section.

```
              ROM PCI/ISA BIOS (2A59FT5G)
                  CHIPSET FEATURES SETUP
                  AWARD SOFTWARE, INC.

  DRAM RAS# Precharge Time : 4      PCI Slot IDE 2nd Channel : Enabled
  DRAM R/W Leadoff Timing  : 7/6    Peer Concurrency         : Disabled
  Fast RAS# To CAS# Delay  : 3      Chipset Special Features : Disabled
  DRAM Read Burst Timing   : x4444  DRAM ECC/PARITY Select   : Parity
  DRAM Write Burst Timing  : x4444
  DRAM Speculative Leadoff : Disabled  Onboard FDC Controller : Enabled
  Turn-Around Insertion    : Disabled  Onboard Serial Port 1  : COM1/3F8
                                       Onboard Serial Port 2  : COM2/2F8
  System BIOS Cacheable    : Disabled  Onboard Parallel Port  : 378/IRQ7
  Video  BIOS Cacheable    : Disabled  Parallel Port Mode     : Normal
  8 Bit I/O Recovery Time  : 1
  16 Bit I/O Recovery Time : 1
  Memory Hole At 15M-16M   : Disabled
  IDE HDD Block Mode       : Enabled
  IDE Primary Master PIO   : Auto
  IDE Primary Slave  PIO   : Auto   ESC : Quit         ↑↓→← : Select Item
  IDE Secondary Master PIO : Auto   F1  : Help      PU/PD/+/- : Modify
  IDE Secondary Slave  PIO : Auto   F5  : Old Values (Shift)F2 : Color
  On-Chip Primary   PCI IDE: Enabled  F6 : Load BIOS  Defaults
  On-Chip Secondary PCI IDE: Enabled  F7 : Load Setup Defaults
```

Figure 8-14: Here's an example of enabling a PCI slot from the advanced settings of an Award BIOS.

Windows 95 safe mode

If you're running Windows 95, you must start in *safe mode*. Safe mode is a special mode for Windows 95 especially designed for troubleshooting problems and testing installation. Safe mode automatically loads a vanilla VGA driver; it does not load any other special drivers, such as those for CD-ROM drives, network devices, or sound cards. So in safe mode, none of those devices works.

To start in safe mode, wait for the `Starting Windows 95` message. When you see that message, press F5. Windows 95 takes longer to boot than usual, and it gives you a message saying it is starting in safe mode. If all goes well, the Windows 95 desktop follows on your screen with the label Safe mode in each corner, as shown in Figure 8-15. The next step is to load the software drivers for the new video card.

Installing the drivers for the new video card

If everything works at this point, you can forgo installation of the video drivers that came with the new card. However, you will probably get faster performance from the card if you install the video drivers designed to work with it. Here's what you need to do for DOS, Windows 3.*x*, and Windows 95.

Figure 8-15: You're in safe mode when you start Windows 95 by using the F5 key.

DOS

If you're running DOS applications, you may have to go into the setup for each application and change the video display driver information. In some cases, you may need to reinstall your DOS application. Be sure that you've backed up any data you may need. In each instance, look at the documentation for each particular application to see what changes, if any, need to be made.

Windows 3.x

If you're running Windows 3.x, your video card software driver probably has an installation program for you to use, so look for that first and follow the instructions. If you cannot find an install or setup program, look for a README file on the diskette. This file may include instructions for installation and usually offers helpful advice and troubleshooting tips.

You can attempt to install the drivers yourself, which may be helpful if the software driver didn't come with an installation program. Windows is designed to look for a file called OEMSETUP.INF for third-party drivers. In addition, a convention in the computer industry is to have video drivers named with the extension .DRV. You may want to look at the diskette that came with the video card using File Manager or the DOS directory command to see if these files are present.

If you see a series of files whose last character is the underline (_), then those files are compressed, which makes the file unusable in its present form, but saves disk space. A utility supplied by the vendor, or one available under DOS, should decompress the files while copying them to an appropriate place on your hard disk drive. However, if you don't find an .INF file, and all the files have the underline character as the last character, then there's no way for you to know what was used to compress the files, and you must contact the vendor of the video card for technical support.

If you find a driver file on the diskette or otherwise obtained one, you can install the new video driver from the System Setup menu. To get there, from the Main group, select Control Panel⇨Windows Step⇨Options⇨Change System Settings⇨Display. Scroll through the list of drivers to the one that says Other driver (Requires disk from OEM). When you select that driver and click on OK, the Windows Setup screen appears, asking you for the location of the driver you want to install (see Figure 8-16).

Windows assumes that the driver is on a disk in the A drive, but you can change that location if the driver is on another disk or if you downloaded a driver from a hardware vendor. When you tell Windows where the driver is, it installs the driver and lets you restart Windows so that the new driver can begin working.

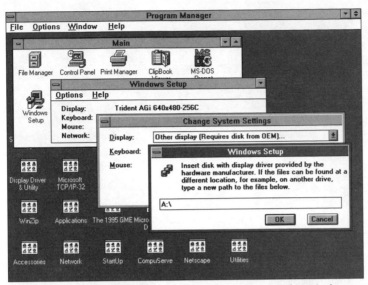

Figure 8-16: If you're installing a new video driver under Windows 3.1, you'll see this screen asking for the location of the new video driver.

Windows 95

If the video card has installation instructions for Windows 95, you should follow those instructions. Windows 95 is designed to check the hardware devices installed, and it may notice that you have a new video driver installed and will want to install a driver of its own. You may need your original Windows 95 diskettes or CD-ROM, so have these resources handy.

If the video card has no instructions, then you can install the software yourself. Select My Computer➪Control Panel➪System Setup➪Device Manager. Be sure that View Devices by Type is selected. Select the plus sign (+) in front of Display Adapters, select the hardware adapter for the video card you installed (see Figure 8-17), and then select Properties➪Driver➪Change Driver➪Have Disk. The convention in the industry is to provide a file on the diskette called OEMSETUP.INF, but Windows 95 looks for any file with the extension .INF.

When Windows finds the proper .INF file, it presents the drivers that are available and ask you to pick one. If there's only one driver, as shown in Figure 8-18, then it is highlighted, and you can click on OK. The files then are copied from the diskette to your Windows 95 system subdirectory on your hard drive.

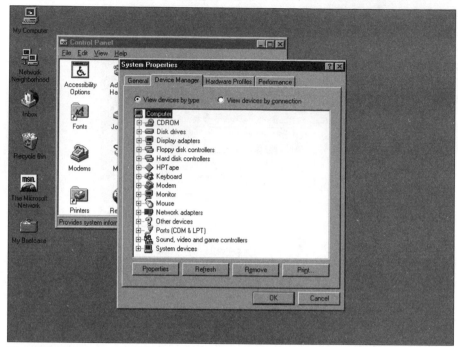

Figure 8-17: Under Windows 95, select the plus sign in front of Display Adapters in this Device Manager menu, highlight the display adapter, and then select Properties to change the video driver.

After Windows 95 finishes copying, it doesn't bring you back to the desktop, as you may expect. Instead, you must click on Close or Cancel where appropriate to close each window until Windows displays the System Restart menu. Click on Yes to restart the system.

When Windows comes back up and you see that the video is working, you may want to try different resolutions. To make adjustments to the resolution, select My Computer⇨Control Panel⇨Display⇨Settings to get the screen shown in Figure 8-22. After the adjustment, select Apply. Windows attempts to apply the settings you have selected, usually without restarting Windows. If you have problems after you've applied a resolution setting, see the troubleshooting section.

Identifying your monitor to Windows 95

If you haven't already done so, tell Windows 95 what type of monitor you have. This way you can avoid damaging the monitor by attempting scan rates that the monitor is not capable of displaying. You can identify your monitor at the Display Properties menu, shown in Figure 8-19. Select Change Display Type, and then look at the monitor currently defined under Monitor Type, as shown in Figure 8-12. If that's not your monitor, select Change and Show all Devices and choose the brand of your monitor first, and then the model from the menu shown in Figure 8-20. Windows may ask for

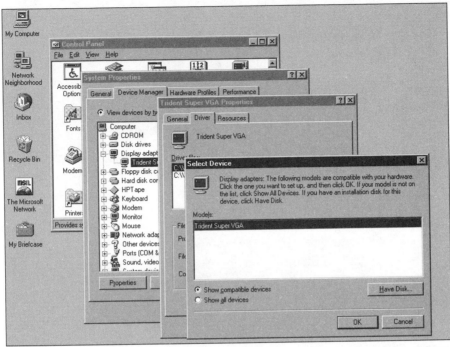

Figure 8-18: Windows 95 looks for the available drivers in the .INF file on the diskette when you click on the Have Disk button.

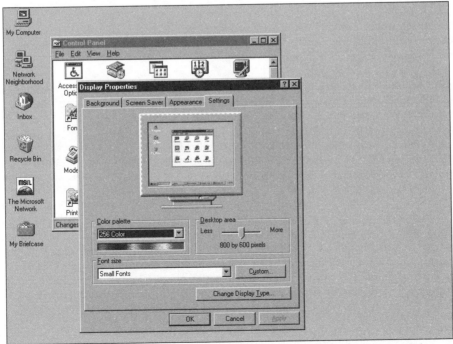

Figure 8-19: Windows 95 lets you adjust the display resolution by using the slider.

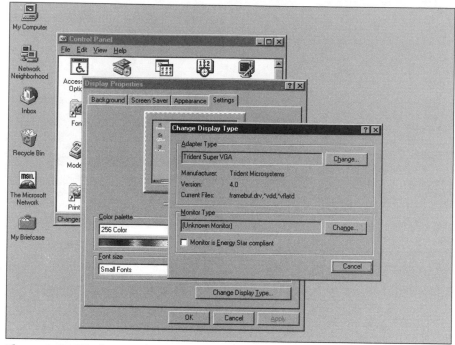

Figure 8-20: Windows 95 lets you select your monitor by choosing the manufacturer, and then the model.

the original Windows 95 installation diskettes, so have them handy. If your monitor comes with a diskette, now is the time to insert the diskette into the A drive and select Have Disk.

After you've correctly defined the monitor, Windows 95 knows what scan rates your monitor supports. Therefore, it does not let you select a resolution at a higher scan rate than your monitor is capable of displaying.

TIP

Some video cards come with software programs that let you set the scan rate and the resolution. Others simply chose a standard scan rate for a given resolution. The software usually installs itself under Windows and is often set to start automatically whenever you start Windows.

You may not want the software to start each time Windows starts, especially if you don't plan to change your video resolution much. Most of these programs create a group, but also install a copy of the software in the Startup group so that it starts automatically. If you don't want the software to start automatically, check the Startup group and delete the software icon, if one is there. If the icon is not there, but the software is still starting automatically, look at the troubleshooting section for instructions on how to check the Windows environment files for programs that automatically load.

Installation in review

To upgrade your video card, follow these steps:

1. Back up your system.

2. Write down the current video display settings.

3. Look inside your PC to see what type of display card you have now and what expansion slots are available.

4. Purchase your new video card.

5. Change the Windows display driver to a "vanilla" driver and test.

6. Remove the old video card or disable the on-board video on the motherboard.

7. Install the new video card.

8. Test the new video card.

9. Install the accompanying software driver appropriate for your system (optional).

10. Test the new driver.

Question: What's an OEM?

Answer: An OEM is the hardware vendor. It stands for *Original Equipment Manufacturer.*

Question: I see the term *dot pitch* used in reference to monitors. What does that mean?

Answer: The display on a color monitor is made up of picture elements or pixels. The size of these pixels is the dot pitch. Typical dot pitch sizes range from .39 mm to .26 mm. The smaller the number, the sharper and clearer the display, but it also costs more.

Question: In my BIOS, I see an option for *bus master* for each of my PCI slots. What does that mean?

Answer: Bus master allows the PCI slot to gain the use of the PC's data highway (the bus) on demand, taking precedence over other devices in other expansion slots. It can also allow the device plugged into the slot to bypass the CPU to talk directly to other peripherals. This method is used mainly for disk drives, CD-ROM drives, and SCSI devices. You are, however, limited to the number of bus masters you can have on a system; usually that limit is one.

Question: Under Windows 95, when I select My Computer⇔Control Panel, it looks like the same group I get when I select Start⇔Settings⇔Control Panel. Is it the same Control Panel in both cases?

Answer: Yes. You've just found two ways of getting there.

Question: Why are memory addresses in that cryptic hexadecimal format?

Answer: Memory is allocated in blocks, and hexadecimal is the most efficient way for the memory designers to reflect those allocation units.

New video card boosts performance

Laura wanted to speed up her Windows 95 display. She checked inside her 486-based PC and discovered that she had an ISA Oak VGA card. Laura wrote down the current settings for her video under Windows, which happened to be the standard Windows VGA driver at 640 x 480 pixels with 256 colors. She then visited a local computer store and purchased an inexpensive ISA high-resolution Super VGA card with IMB of RAM for under $80.

Reviewing the user manual prior to installation, Laura realized the card came with several options that she could select by changing the jumper switches. These options included enabling a zero-wait state, enabling a 48.7 kHz scan rate, enabling a BIOS autodetect, and allowing the card to work in either an 8-bit PC/XT slot or a 16-bit ISA slot. Laura decided to leave the card set at the factory defaults (which were a disabled zero-wait state, disabled 48.7 kHz scan rate, and enabled BIOS autodetect), enabling the card for the 16-bit ISA slot.

Laura then turned off her PC, grounded herself, removed the monitor connector from the card, removed the screw that held the card in the slot, and then removed the card from the PC. She placed the new card in the same slot and connected the monitor cable. With the PC open, Laura restarted her computer and then turned on the monitor's power switch and waited.

Immediately, Laura saw a difference in the video display while the BIOS messages were coming up. The messages seemed just to appear, and the boot sequence went faster. When Windows 95 started, Laura realized that some small spots that she assumed were a problem with the monitor were suddenly gone, and the screen image was much sharper. Windows 95 came up faster as well. Laura tried opening the Windows 95 menus and found that the menus seemed to pop onto the screen for her.

Laura decided to install the software drivers to see if she could get even better performance from the new video card. She followed the installation instructions in the documentation, which had her select File⇨Run, type **A:\INSTALL**, and click on OK for the new software to install itself. Laura was running at 640 x 480 pixels but decided that she wanted to try a higher resolution pixels such as 1024 x 768 pixels. The program said it would need to restart Windows for the changes to take effect.

When Windows came back up, the logo screen was fine, but then the screen shrank vertically, and what appeared to be several copies of Program Manager were displayed crosswise on-screen. Laura thought she could hear a high-pitched sound coming from the monitor as well.

Laura pressed Alt-F4 and Enter to exit Windows, even though she couldn't see the screen well enough to tell if the keystrokes were working. But they worked, and when she was back at the DOS prompt, she called the customer support number for the video card manufacturer.

She was on hold for a long time and then got a message that there was automated support. She switched to the automated support, selected her problem using her touch-tone phone, and discovered that her monitor could not support the scan rate at the resolution she had chosen. She looked at the back of her monitor and found a place where it said "60 Hz." The scan rate for the 1024 x 768 pixel resolution was a minimum of 70 Hz. Laura realized that in order to run at the higher resolution, she would need a new monitor.

She decided that a new monitor was not what she wanted to invest in right now. But she had to get back to the previous video settings. She restarted her PC, and from the DOS prompt typed **CD WINDOWS** and pressed Enter to change to her Windows directory. Then she typed **SETUP** and pressed Enter. The current hardware setup for her PC appeared on-screen. Laura used the up arrow key to choose the display setting and pressed Enter for a list of available displays. She chose the 640 x 480 pixel setting that she'd had previously and pressed Enter. Then she pressed Enter again to accept the new setting and exit the Setup menu.

Back at the DOS prompt, Laura restarted Windows, and everything was back to normal. Laura exited Windows, turned off her PC, and put the screw in the card to hold it in the case. She checked the monitor connection to be sure that it was secure and closed up the PC case. She then wrote the date on which she installed the card on the documentation, which she filed away for future reference, and congratulated herself on a successful installation.

Troubleshooting

It sometimes takes a little finesse to get a video card working. Plus, your card may work fine at one resolution, yet produce unexpected results at another resolution. Here's how to troubleshoot those problems and get your video working.

Computer beeps upon startup or the monitor screen lights up, but there's no display.

The beep codes vary from one computer to another, but two short beeps and one long beep is the most common code for a problem with the video display. You also may see the monitor screen light up, but no display.

1. Make sure that the video card is seated correctly in the expansion slot.

2. Make sure that the monitor cable is securely fastened to the card.

3. Make sure that your monitor cable is the 15-pin male VGA type (shown earlier in this chapter), and be sure that you're connecting that cable to the 15-pin female connector on the video card.

4. Try moving the card to a different slot, if you can. If all the slots of the type you want to use are full, trade the card with another card in the same type of slot.

5. Make sure that you've installed the card in the correct type of expansion slot.

6. Check your CMOS to see if video read-only memory (ROM) shadowing is enabled. You may have to check in the Advanced CMOS Setup. Shadowing means a copy of the information held in video ROM is placed in the faster RAM to enhance the performance of the system. If this shadowing is enabled, try setting it to disabled, and then try again.

7. Try a clean boot by pressing F5 when the Starting MS-DOS or Starting Windows 95 message appears. If the video works now, then there's a conflict with a program or driver that's being loaded during the startup sequence.

8. Be sure that you removed your old video card or disabled the on-board video on the motherboard if you have it.

9. If you're upgrading your video from another resolution to VGA, be sure that you've changed the switches or jumpers on the motherboard to VGA resolution. You should also check the BIOS video settings to see if you need to make a change, although often the BIOS picks up the changes in the motherboard settings.

10. If you've already checked items 1 through 9, then reinstall the old video card to see if it works. If it does, the new video card could be bad, or there could be a conflict between another card, such as a modem or network card installed on the system.

11. Try removing the modem or network card(s) one at a time and see each time if the system works. If it does, it could be that the video card and the card you removed are attempting to use the same memory address. Check your documentation for both cards to see if you can change the memory address used on the video card or the other card.

There is no monitor display.

1. Check the monitor to see if it is plugged in and turned on, and be sure that the monitor's power light comes on.

2. Check the outlet the monitor is plugged into by plugging something that you know works into that same location.

An error message appears during the boot process.

1. The CMOS setup menu settings may not reflect the type of video card you've installed. Check the CMOS settings for the type of display.

2. If you're using a PCI or VL-bus card, check the CMOS setup menu to be sure that the PCI or VL-bus expansion slot is enabled.

The video image shows several duplicate images, doesn't fill the screen, and is difficult or impossible to view.

TIP

This is a scan rate problem. The most important consideration is to get the monitor out of this display mode. Do not leave it this way because you can damage the monitor. Exit Windows if you can, but if not, restart the computer. If you're restarting the computer under Windows 95, be sure to follow the instructions for starting in safe mode presented under the Windows 95 portion of the "Installing the drivers for the new video card" section earlier in this chapter.

The only solution to this problem is to change the video driver to a lower scan rate. Some software drivers let you choose from available scan rates at each resolution. However, you usually have to change the video driver to a lower resolution.

Here's how to change the resolution to a lower setting under DOS, Windows, and Windows 95: If you're running a DOS-based video driver or have changed the video settings in a DOS-based application, you must check the documentation for the driver or application to see how to change the video settings.

Here's how to change the video resolution under Windows 3.*x:* If you're running Windows 3.*x*, you can change the resolution by using the Windows Setup program under DOS. To get to the Windows Setup type from the DOS prompt, type **CD WINDOWS** (or **CD**, a space, and whatever directory your Windows installation uses), and then type **SETUP** and press Enter.

Select the display setting and press Enter. You get a list of various display drivers available in Windows. If you choose a display driver other than one you've already had installed, you'll need the original Windows installation diskettes, because Windows does not install all the drivers but installs only the ones you use. If you've been experimenting with video drivers, you may find the drivers bundled with the video card you installed on this list. If you're unsure, the safest course of action is to use the vanilla Windows VGA driver mentioned earlier in this chapter.

Don't try to skip a step by typing **C:\WINDOWS\SETUP**, because that starts another version of SETUP to completely reinstall Windows on your system.

The Windows Setup starts, and your current system settings for Windows are displayed, as shown in Figure 8-21. Select the display setting and press Enter to get to the menu shown in Figure 8-22. You are presented with a list of available display drivers at various resolutions. Chances are that the display drivers you've installed are available there. Choose a driver with a lower resolution than the one you had that caused the problem. If you're unsure, use the vanilla Windows VGA driver mentioned earlier by starting Windows 95 in safe mode using the F5 key. This procedure is described next.

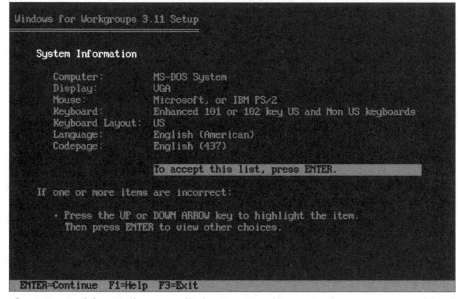

Figure 8-21: If the Windows 3.1 display is not working correctly, you can enter this Windows Setup menu from the DOS prompt to change the video driver.

```
Windows for Workgroups 3.11 Setup

  To change your display, select from the following list:

    • Press the UP or DOWN ARROW key to highlight the item.
      Then press ENTER.
    • To continue Setup without changing your display,
      press ESC.

  ┌─────────────────────────────────────────────────────────────┐
  │ 8514/a                                                        │
  │ 8514/a (small fonts)                                         │
  │ Stealth 64 Series                                           │
  │ Super VGA (1024x768, 256 colors, large fonts)              │
  │ Super VGA (1024x768, 256 colors, small fonts)              │
  │ Super VGA (640x480, 256 colors)                            │
  │ Super VGA (800x600, 16 colors)                             │
  │ Super VGA (800x600, 256 colors, large fonts)              │
  │ Super VGA (800x600, 256 colors, small fonts)              │
  └─────────────────────────────────────────────────────────────┘

  (To see more of the list, press the (↓) arrow key)

ENTER=Continue   F1=Help   F3=Exit   ESC=Cancel
```

Figure 8-22: You can choose a driver from this list for Windows 3.*x* to use when it restarts.

Here's how to change the video resolution under Windows 95: Restart Windows 95 in safe mode, which uses a vanilla VGA video driver. When you restart your computer and see the statement Starting Windows 95..., press F5 to start in safe mode. When you are in safe mode, you change either the resolution or the driver. Change the driver by following the instructions under the Windows 95 section of the "Install the drivers for the new video card" section.

To change the resolution by using the same driver, select My Computer⇨Control Panel⇨Display⇨Settings. You can adjust the resolution by using the slider, but be sure that you avoid any settings at the same resolution or higher that created the scan rate problem.

After you've changed the resolution, restart Windows 95. If you have the same problem, exit Windows 95 and restart again in safe mode. Try a lower setting. If none of the settings work, switch to the Windows 95 drivers instead of the ones that came with your video card.

A more permanent fix is to correctly identify your monitor to Windows 95 so that you cannot select a scan rate that the monitor cannot handle. For instructions on how to do this, check the section "Identifying your monitor to Windows 95" earlier in this chapter.

You may want to check the scan rate for the resolution you've chosen. Some video drivers allow you to set the scan rate as well as the resolution, while others default to a given scan rate for a given resolution. If you can set the scan rate separate from the resolution, it will be in a software program that comes with the video card, and it will be obvious.

Also, check your monitor scan rates, found on the back of the monitor, to see if your monitor supports the scan rate you've chosen. (Hint: It probably does not, or you wouldn't have this problem.)

The screen display is significantly smaller than the available display space.

The refresh rate may be too high, and the monitor is attempting to compensate for the higher rate by reducing the screen size. Prolonged exposure to this refresh rate can damage your monitor. You need to set the refresh rate down, but if the software doesn't allow you control over the vertical refresh rate, then go to a lower resolution. See the steps for changing the resolution for DOS, Windows 3.*x*, and Windows 95 previously listed.

Windows looks like it's going to start, but after the opening logo screen, I end up back at the DOS prompt.

This is a memory conflict between the video driver in Windows and some other program. The video driver and another program or utility are attempting to use the same portion of memory. Here's where to look for the conflicting program:

1. Check the README file for information. (If you need to know how to do this, check the instructions in Chapter 1.)

2. Check your video card documentation for troubleshooting information.

3. Check the WIN.INI file for programs that start automatically when Windows starts. If you don't know how to do this, check the section in Chapter 13 that covers editing environment files. Look for the line that starts with Load= and remove the programs loaded there, and then try starting Windows again. If Windows starts and loads, then one of the programs being loaded by the WIN.INI is conflicting with the video driver. To find out which program is causing the problem, add the programs back to the WIN.INI file one at a time until Windows will not start.

   Try starting the program in question after Windows is running, and see if you get an error message or another problem. If not, you can probably run this program successfully with the video driver as long as it is not loaded at startup. If you do have a problem, then you must choose between the video driver and the program. If you're running Windows 95, you can attempt to set up a multiple boot configuration, as outlined in Chapter 13, so that you can choose what gets loaded at startup, but this may be more trouble than it's worth.

4. Check the DOS environment files — the AUTOEXEC.BAT and the CONFIG.SYS. If you don't know how to bring up these files, read the instructions in Chapter 13. You're looking for portions of memory that have been allocated by memory management device drivers, such as EMM386, QEMM386, or 386MAX. (See the case study, "The Case of the Problem Display," later in this chapter.) Look for a line that contains something like `I=` or `Include=`, and a memory address in hexadecimal that looks like `B000-B7FF` or `A000-C7FF`. These commands are instructing a device driver to include certain portions of memory for use by other programs that the video card may need.

If you find such a statement, be sure that you have a copy of the file, and then remove only the statement concerning the memory address from the `Device=` line. For example, if the line were `DEVICE=C:\DOS\EMM386.SYS I=B000-B7FF /d=20`, then you would delete the `I=B000-B7FF` so that the resulting line would be `DEVICE=C:\DOS\EMM386 /d=20`. Then try starting Windows again and see if the problem recurs.

TIP

Sometimes you have to add special instructions to the memory manager device drivers to "block out" portions of memory needed for the video card. For example, if your video card uses the memory from A000 to C7FF, and you were using QEMM as your memory manager, you may need to add a line to the line that loads the QEMM memory manager that would keep QEMM from allocating the memory space needed by the video card. The terms `Exclude=` or `X=` and a memory address range are often added to the line where the memory manager is loaded in the CONFIG.SYS.

As an example, you might change the line in the CONFIG.SYS that says `DEVICE=C:\QEMM\QEMM386.SYS` to `DEVICE=C:\QEMM\QEMM386.SYS X=A000-C7FF`. The `X=A000-C7FF` excludes the memory in that range from use. You may also need to make modifications to the Windows SYSTEM.INI file that change the way memory space is allocated.

How do you know if you need to do this and what memory addresses you should exclude? Usually, your video card documentation or the README file give you specific information about what modifications you need to make based on the memory manager you're using. The memory address range used by the video card is usually given as well.

5. Contact the manufacturer of the video card software. Be sure to have specific information concerning your PC, such as the make and model, processor, operating system, amount of RAM, applications loaded, and so on. If you have access to the Internet or a modem, you might look to see if there's a Web site or a BBS with troubleshooting information. If you're having this problem, there may already be an updated version of the software available to solve it.

6. You can give up on the OEM software and set Windows to a safer vanilla driver or another driver included with Windows. Be sure to test again to make sure that the new driver works.

An annoying flicker is present in the screen images.

This is a sign that the refresh rate, or scan rate, is too low. Check the back of the monitor and the documentation for your video card to see if you can boost the scan rate. Do not exceed the scan rate your monitor is capable of, because you may damage your monitor.

The case of the problem display

Ben added a Diamond Stealth card with 1MB of RAM to a Pentium system running Windows 3.11. He removed his old card, installed the new card into a PCI slot, enabled the PCI slot in the BIOS, set the video card to 640 x 480 pixels at 256 colors, tested the video, and everything was great. At least everything was great until he got a larger monitor and wanted to set the display to a higher resolution.

When Ben set the Diamond Stealth software drivers to resolutions above 640 x 480 pixels, the Windows opening screen would come up, and then he'd get dumped back to a DOS prompt. The only way he could get the system going again was to go into the Windows 3.11 Setup from the DOS prompt and reset the video back to 640 x 480.

One of Ben's clues to the problem was that after setting the drivers to a higher resolution and restarting Windows so that the changes could take effect, Windows would start to display its opening logo screen before it dumped him back to the DOS prompt. Ben was advised by a colleague that this problem had the ear-marks of a memory conflict, so he looked for a possible conflict between the Diamond Stealth driver and some other piece of software.

Ben looked at the Windows .INI files and made sure that there were no software programs being automatically loaded by Windows in the StartUp Group or in the WIN.INI. He then tried to run at 800 x 600 again, but the problem persisted.

Next, Ben decided to look at the system environment files. He started looking for a terminate and stay resident (TSR) program that might be causing a conflict. There were none. However, a statement in the CONFIG.SYS file caught his eye. The line was:

```
DEVICE=EMM386 I=B000-B7FF /d=20
```

Ben knew that EMM386 was a high memory device driver, but he didn't know what I=B000-B7FF meant. He looked it up in a Windows reference book and discovered that the meaning of the I= statement was to include as usable memory the memory space designated by the hexadecimal address that followed. Ben decided to eliminate the `I=` statement from the line and tried the higher resolution settings again. He made sure that he copied the CONFIG.SYS file first, and he also wrote down the individual line before he made the modification.

This time, the video card worked at every available resolution. In addition, the flicker went away from the initial Windows screen at the 640 x 480 resolution.

The problem was solved, but Ben wanted to know why it occurred. After further investigation, Ben discovered that some video cards allocate the unused, yet reserved, monochrome memory space in upper memory for their own use, especially at higher resolutions.

He thought back to when, before he'd purchased the new monitor, he had optimized his memory by running the DOS MEMMAKER utility. After that, he noticed a new "flicker" in the Windows logo screen that hadn't been there before, but he hadn't seen any other problems until he decided to run the card at 800 x 600 resolution.

But he remembered that when he ran MEMMAKER, he was given a Yes or No choice as to whether or not to allow Windows to use the memory space reserved for monochrome memory. Ben answered Yes, because he didn't have a monochrome monitor, and MEMMAKER had allocated the monochrome memory space for use by the system.

Had the video card not worked at all, the problem may have been easier to trace. However, Ben was persistent in his approach and was able to find and correct the problem.

Section II — Hard Disk Controller Upgrades

You often can inexpensively increase the performance of your PC if you add a faster hard disk drive controller. This is especially true if your PC is two to three years old. In addition, you may want to add a hard disk drive larger than 540MB; one way to accomplish this is to add a hard disk controller with its own BIOS to do drive translation. (More information on this topic is available in Chapter 5.)

As explained in Chapter 6, many software programs and operating systems use virtual memory, which is the practice of setting aside a portion of the hard disk drive for use as memory. If you can speed up the data transfer rate between the PC and the hard disk drive, then you can often improve the performance of operating systems such as Windows.

As with many upgrades on a PC, the actual installation of a new hard disk controller can be accomplished in a matter of minutes. However, the preparation usually takes time and makes or breaks a successful upgrade, especially in this area.

A new hard disk controller can range from under $25 to over $200, depending on the features the card has.

TIP If you're not familiar with hard disk drives, serial ports/modems, and parallel ports, read Chapters 5, 9, and 15. Although the subject of ports may seem out of place in a discussion of hard disk controllers, the continual trend toward integration has brought controller cards that have everything but the kitchen sink. To avoid conflicts between two similar devices attempting to use the same memory space, it's helpful to understand something about how to identify the ports on a PC.

Preparation

Part of the preparation process includes deciding the type of controller you want to add, determining what you have now, making a backup, making a bootable floppy diskette, and collecting the information you need about your current hard disk drive so that it works with the new controller. Following is background information on hard disk controllers, and then preparation steps to make your upgrade a successful one.

What is a hard disk controller?

The hard disk controller is the card that allows data transfer between the hard disk drive and the PC. Since the advent of IDE type hard disk drives, the hard disk controller has shrunk in size because most of the intelligence needed for the hard disk drive is now integrated into IDE drives. This integration has allowed innovation in hard disk controller cards. I cover these innovations next, including controllers that have multiple functions, such as integrated floppy disk controllers, ports, and even their own BIOS for drive translation. This information will help you determine what kind of hard disk controller you should buy.

Integration

One innovation in the computer industry is the integration of the hard disk controller onto the system board or motherboard. This innovation makes sense because most of the intelligence needed for the hard disk drive is in the drive, and it's a space-saving feature that allows most motherboards to have fewer expansion slots. Figure 8-23 shows a motherboard with two integrated hard disk controllers on-board. Notice that several other functions are integrated onto this particular board as well, including the floppy disk drive controller and the serial and parallel ports.

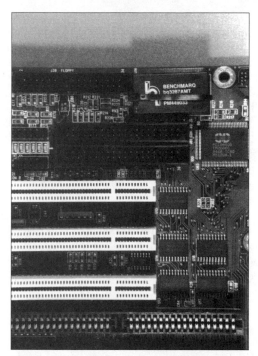

Figure 8-23: This motherboard has two integrated hard disk controllers, one that's standard IDE and one that's PCI IDE. Note that the floppy disk drive and ports are also integrated onto this motherboard.

Most PC makers realize that controllers occasionally fail, or the user may want to upgrade to a newer controller with more functionality, so they've built most motherboards with a way to disable the integrated, or "on-board," hard disk drive controller. So, if you're planning to add a new hard disk controller to a system with a hard disk controller built in, you need the documentation for the system board to determine what switches or jumpers must be changed to disable the integrated or *on-board* controller. Some BIOSs allow you to disable the controller from within the BIOS menu, so you may have to look there.

Integrated hard disk and floppy controllers

Although you can purchase some hard disk controllers that are only a hard disk controller, most controllers include the floppy disk controller. Although floppy disk controllers used to be separate, it is now common practice to include a floppy disk controller on a hard disk controller card.

Multi I/O Controllers

Many hard disk controllers are multi-input/output, or multi-I/O, controllers. These multi-I/O cards can include a hard disk controller, a floppy disk controller, parallel ports, serial ports, game ports, and even a network card such as Ethernet, all on the same card. What you get varies from card to card, but the most typical arrangement is a hard disk controller capable of supporting two hard disk drives, a floppy disk controller capable of supporting two floppy drives, one parallel port, two serial ports, and one game port (see Figure 8-24). The card itself occupies only a single slot, but the serial and parallel connectors may require a second opening to the outside of the PC. This means, in effect, that the card takes up two slots, even though it occupies only one.

Controllers with a BIOS for drive translation

As explained in Chapter 5, hard disk controller cards are available that have their own BIOS that offers a feature called *drive translation*. Drive translation, in a nutshell, allows you to install and use a hard disk drive larger than 540MB. Some PCs have drive translation built into the BIOS, but many do not. Adding a hard disk controller with a drive translation BIOS is one way to upgrade your PC so that it can use the widely available large hard disk drives.

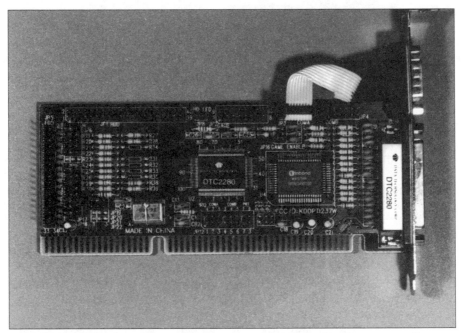

Figure 8-24: A typical multi-I/O card with a hard disk controller, floppy controller, one parallel port, two serial ports, and a game port.

Taking a look inside your PC

You must take a look inside your PC to determine what type of hard disk controller you have now and what expansion slots you have for a new hard disk controller. Types of expansion slots are covered in the preparation section of Section I on upgrading your video card earlier in this chapter. If you have a VL-bus or PCI expansion slot, you get faster performance out of your new controller if it uses one of these faster slots.

If your hard disk drive has a ribbon cable connected directly to the motherboard and not to a card in an expansion slot, then you have a hard disk controller integrated into the motherboard. You need your system documentation to determine how to disable this controller before you can upgrade to a new controller. There are probably jumpers or switches on the motherboard to disable this controller, although you should look in the CMOS setup menu because some BIOSs allow you to disable the on-board devices from there.

If your hard disk controller is integrated on your motherboard, chances are that your floppy disk drive controller and your serial, parallel, and game ports are integrated onto the motherboard as well. Check to see if the ribbon cable goes from the floppy disk drive to connect directly to the motherboard. Also, the port connectors will have cables that connect to the motherboard if the ports are integrated, or the ports may be integrated on to the motherboard directly, as shown in Figure 8-23.

If the ribbon cable connected to your hard disk drive goes to a card that is in an expansion slot, then you have a hard disk controller on a card. Look carefully at the card to determine if it also has a floppy disk drive controller and serial, parallel, and game ports like the one shown previously in Figure 8-24.

Looking for show stoppers

Now that you know what a hard drive is, what to look for in terms of expansion slots, and how to determine what type of hard disk controller card you have, you can determine if this upgrade is for you. Here's a list of circumstances that make your upgrade difficult. (I call these circumstances *show stoppers*.)

If you have an on-board hard disk controller, you may think twice about this upgrade. The success rate is lower on these types of upgrades because it's more difficult to disable the existing hard disk controller. If you don't have the documentation for your system, then you should definitely consider waiting until you do have the necessary information. You may be able to obtain the information from a bulletin board, Internet site, or fax back service provided by the OEM.

If you have an on-board controller and no free expansion slots for a hard disk controller card, you probably cannot add a new hard disk controller. The only way you can get around this problem is if you can remove a card from an expansion slot, meaning you have hardware in your system that you don't plan to use any longer, which doesn't happen very often.

If you have a proprietary connector to your hard disk drive that doesn't use standard hard disk cables and connectors, you may also find it difficult to upgrade. This may not be a show stopper if you can get another controller from the system manufacturer or an adapter for the connector, but these types of fixes can cost substantially more than they're worth. So carefully watch the costs.

Buying tips

If you have a multi-I/O card now, you must get a new multi-I/O card to replace it with. But if you don't have a multi-I/O card, you can still purchase a multi-I/O card as an upgrade because you can disable anything on the card that you don't want to use. This is important because, for example, you cannot have two ports set to use the same memory address. Also, you'll have the advantage of having a card that has the documentation needed to make those adjustments, and you may not have that information for hardware that is currently in your system.

You can expect to pay more for hard disk controller cards that have their own BIOS for drive translation or that fit into the faster type of expansion slots. You may find, however, that a card for a PCI expansion slot costs more than twice as much as a card for an ISA slot. Only you can determine what will benefit your situation the most, but these are considerations to keep in mind.

This type of upgrade works best if you replace the card you have with a similar card. If you have a multi-I/O card, then you should buy a multi-I/O card to upgrade. If you have a hard disk and floppy drive controller, then you should buy a hard disk and floppy drive controller.

Backing up your system

If you've determined that a hard disk controller upgrade is for you, you must follow one important step. Before you make any major changes to your system, especially changes that involve the hard disk drive, you should always make a complete backup of the contents of your hard disk drive. This way, you can recover in case you lose all the data on your hard disk drive. If you don't know how or need to install a tape backup drive, see Chapter 4.

Making a bootable floppy diskette

This is a precautionary step, and one you should do any time you add or remove hardware from your PC. You probably will not need this diskette, if everything goes well, but if there's a problem, you will definitely need it. Check the instructions in Chapter 13 for how to make a bootable diskette for DOS, Windows 3.x, and Windows 95.

Avoid using a diskette with a different version of the operating system than the one you have on your PC. It's always best to make a bootable floppy just before you proceed to an upgrade, because then you know that you have the most current information on the diskette.

Recording your hard disk drive parameters

The last preparation step is to record the parameters of your hard disk drive or drives as found in your CMOS setup. This is because when you install a new hard disk controller, the BIOS settings for the hard disk drive are often wiped clean in the CMOS setup menu. But, most of the time you can simply re-enter the previous settings and have access to the contents of the drive just as you did before, without having to repartition or reformat the drive. (If you need more information on partitioning or formatting a hard disk drive, see Chapter 5.)

All you need to do is write down the information concerning the hard disk drives found in the CMOS menu so that you can copy that same information in again after you install the new hard disk drive controller. Check Chapter 5 for examples of the CMOS menu information and the hard disk drive parameters you need to write down so that you can re-enter the information later.

Multi-I/O card preparation

If you're installing or replacing a multi-I/O card, it's important to know what ports were working on the card so that you can configure the new card so that the same ports are working. Also, if you have an internal modem, it acts very much like a serial port, and if the multi-I/O card's serial port and the modem are set to the same COM port address, neither the serial port nor the modem will work. So, you must determine if there's an internal modem or fax/modem and what COM port that modem is using. This means that you must know something about serial and parallel ports and port addressing. That information is provided in Chapter 15 where parallel port addressing is discussed and in Chapter 9 where serial ports and modems are discussed.

PCI multi-I/O cards

If you decide that you want to use your PCI slot, be aware that many PCI multi-I/O cards require the use of an ISA slot in addition to the PCI slot. PCI cards often come with a daughter card or "paddle" board that is to be installed in an ISA slot and connected via a cable to the main controller card installed in an adjacent PCI slot (see Figure 8-25). Many PCI cards recommend installation in a shared slot. If you remember, the shared slot is physically two slots, a PCI and an ISA slot next to each other.

Installation

Now that you've done your preparation, including making a backup, making a bootable diskette, determining what expansion slot you're going to use, and purchasing your hard disk controller, it's time for installation.

Figure 8-25: Here is a PCI multi-I/O card installed in a shared PCI/ISA slot. Note how the daughter card or *paddle board* in the ISA slot is connected to the PCI card.

Removing your old controller card

Be sure that you're grounded, and then open up your PC and remove your old hard disk controller card. (If you have a motherboard with a hard disk controller on board, disable the on-board controller.) Unless you're very sure of what you're doing, you might go ahead and leave the cables connected to the card. Sometimes you can lay a static bag on top of the power supply and place the card on that, or you can simply let the card lean on other cables near where you removed it so that it's out of the way enough to insert the new card.

Setting the ports and controllers on the new card

If the old card was a multi-I/O card, and the new card is a multi-I/O card, be sure that the same ports that functioned on the old card are functioning on the new card.

The trickiest situation is when there's an internal modem and a multi-I/O card installed on the system, because both serial ports and internal modems use a COM port. If a serial port and a modem are set to use the same COM port, neither one will work. If you've done your preparation work, then you know what COM port the serial port is using so that you can disable that port on the new multi-I/O card.

If you have the ports or other controllers on the motherboard, then the wisest course of action is to disable those ports and controllers on the multi-I/O card. The only reason you may not want to do this is if the multi-I/O card has a faster serial, parallel, or floppy drive controller than what you have on your system now. If the serial ports on the new card have the faster 16550 UART chips and/or a faster parallel port mode, and your current serial and parallel ports are slower, then you may want to go with these functions on the multi-I/O card.

The best course of action is to disable the ports on the multi-I/O card until you get the hard disk drive working. When your hard drive works, then you can go back and enable the ports on the card and disable the ports on the motherboard. Presumably, you've determined how to disable the hard disk controller on the motherboard, so you probably have the information on how to disable those other ports and controllers as well. This is a judgment call, but it's tough to pass up faster performance, especially if you've already paid for it.

Connecting the ribbon cable(s)

Although you may think that you should connect the cables to the new card *after* it's in the slot, the cables are easier to connect to the card *before* you place the card in the slot because the card is easier to get to. But be sure to handle the card by the edges, and avoid touching the contacts along the lower edge of each side because your skin oils and other deposits can interfere with the operation of the card. If you've followed this advice, you should still have the cables connected to the old card and be able to simply take them off the old card and place them in the appropriate spots on the new card, helping you correctly identify the cables.

The documentation that came with the card should give you a diagram indicating what cables go to what connections. The diagram looks something like the one shown in Figure 8-26. The widest cable, a 40-pin cable, is to the hard disk drive and its cable will go into the 40-pin hard disk connector on your new card. Be sure that the stripe on the cable (indicating pin 1) and pin 1 on the connector are on the same side of the connector. The floppy drive cable is the next widest cable at 34-pins. If you have cables for the other ports, be sure to connect them as indicated on the instructions that came with the card. (Chapter 5 shows detailed photos and instructions on connecting ribbon cables to the controller card.)

You may need to make one other connection, to the hard disk drive indicator light. A twin wire lead is sometimes attached to a light emitting diode (LED) on the front of the PC to the hard disk controller card. Whenever the hard disk drive is accessed by your PC, this connection causes this indicator to light. Figure 8-27 shows a wire attached to a hard disk controller card from an IDE LED output light. If your previous hard disk controller had this wire attached, you must attach the wire to the connector provided on the new card. The hard disk drive works whether this connector is attached or not, and some PCs don't provide a hard disk access LED, so your hard disk controller documentation may refer to this connection as optional.

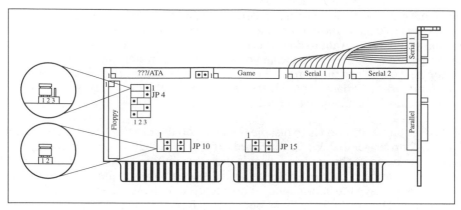

Figure 8-26: A typical diagram of a multi-I/O card.

Figure 8-27: The wiring from the hard disk LED is connected to the controller card.

Installing the new card

Install the new hard disk controller into the expansion slot you've determined to use. Choose the appropriate type of slot as close to the hard disk drive as possible so that the cables easily reach between the card and the hard disk drive. If you removed a hard disk controller card, and the new card uses the same type of expansion slot, you can install the new card in the same slot as the old card. If you're using a slot that hasn't been used before, you must remove the covering bracket and screw from the slot. Save this bracket and screw at least until you've completed the repair. (Hang on to them because they come in handy for closing up the opening if you remove something from this PC or another one.)

If you're installing a multi-I/O card, you may need to remove the screw and bracket from a slot adjacent to the one the card is in so that you can make the new ports accessible from the back of the PC.

To place the card into the slot, handle it by the edges and place it over the slot with the connectors down. Then with your open hand across the top of the card, press firmly straight down, without bending the card, until the card settles into the slot.

Changing the CMOS settings

At this point, you must check the BIOS settings to be sure that the parameters for the hard disk drive are correctly entered. After the card is installed, turn on the PC and enter the CMOS setup menu. Check the hard disk drive parameters and, if necessary, re-enter the parameters you copied down before you started the upgrade procedure. If parameters are already there, check them against the ones you recorded to be sure that they're the same. (Again, if you're not sure how to navigate the CMOS, check Chapter 1 and Chapter 5.)

After you've completed this step, exit the CMOS menu, saving the changes. The PC should restart, and your hard disk drive should boot as usual, but faster. Please note that unlike installing a new hard disk drive, if the drive parameters are the same as before the new card was installed, all the data on the drive should remain in tact, so you don't need to partition or format the drive.

Controller cards with their own BIOS

If you've installed a controller card with its own BIOS so that you can get all the available space from an existing hard disk drive, you can expect to lose all the data on that drive. This means that you have to repartition and reformat your hard disk drive. You must treat this like installing a new hard disk drive (see Chapter 5).

Setting the parameters in the CMOS

A controller card with its own BIOS self-detects the parameters of the hard disk drive and performs the necessary drive translation. You may, however, have to enter unusual CMOS settings that the card will be set to override in order to work. For example, some cards require you to set the drive as a Type 1, even though the parameters won't match the drive, while other cards require you to set the drive as "None" or "Not Installed." The particular setting you should use is in the documentation for the controller card.

When the PC boots, the BIOS in the controller card displays a message during the boot process. This message displays copyright information from the company that designed the card and the type of drives it's handling. You can expect a delay the first time you connect the hard disk drive to the new controller card. Also, be prepared to boot from a floppy disk drive, as explained in the instructions for setting up a new hard disk drive.

Installing a slave drive

If you have a slave drive with data on it, and it's a drive less than 540MB in size, you can override the automatic parameter settings of the BIOS of most controller cards and keep the data that's on the drive. This procedure is usually done via a cryptic and rather archaic DOS utility called DEBUG.

DEBUG allows you to go directly to a memory address or a hard disk location and manipulate data bit by bit. It also allows you to start a program by accessing its starting location in memory. That's how the BIOS of old controller cards was accessed to get to the program used to low-level format a hard disk drive before the IDE standard was introduced. IDE drives come with the low-level formatting already done.

Although you should follow the directions given to you by the documentation of the controller card, you may have to follow this procedure. You must copy DEBUG from your DOS directory to your bootable floppy diskette, unless you're running Windows 95 and have made a Startup disk. In the case of the Windows 95 Startup disk, the utility has been copied there for you.

For example, some controller cards with a BIOS have you start the BIOS program from its memory location by typing **A:\DEBUG G=C800:6** and pressing Enter. This command tells DEBUG to go to the memory address C800 and start the program there. When the program starts, it allows you to select the drive you want to enter parameters for, and it then allows you to manually enter the drive parameters (such as cylinders, heads, sectors per track, and so on). After that is done, you must save your changes and exit the program, and then reboot the PC. The drive should be available for access.

If you change the memory address location for your controller card, then you must be sure to use that new starting memory address instead of C800 when you start DEBUG.

Installation in review

To upgrade your hard disk controller card, follow these steps:

1. Look inside your PC to see what type of hard disk controller card you have now and what expansion slots are available.

2. Back up your system.

3. Make a bootable floppy diskette.

4. Purchase your new hard disk controller card.

5. Remove or disable the old hard disk controller card.

6. Remove or disable duplicate controllers and/or ports if necessary (multi-I/O cards).

7. Connect the necessary cables to the hard disk drive(s), and then to the floppy disk drives and ports if applicable.

8. Install the new hard disk controller card.

9. Restart the PC, enter the CMOS setup, and re-enter the values for the hard disk drive.

10. Test the hard disk drive, floppy disk drives, and peripherals, such as the modem, printer, and so on.

11. Place the screws in the brackets of the newly-installed card and any ports you've installed. Close up the case and restart the PC to be sure that everything works.

New multi-I/O card sparks faster PC performance

Yasmin heard that she could get better performance from her sluggish PC if she upgraded the hard disk controller card. She checked inside her three-year-old 486 clone machine equipped with an internal modem and discovered a multi-I/O card with a hard disk controller, a floppy controller, two serial ports, one parallel port, and a game port.

She went down to a local computer store and purchased a multi-I/O card recommended by the store (but not a brand she'd heard of) for less than $30. Surprisingly, she discovered from the documentation on the box that the card's serial ports were equipped with faster 16550 UART chips, so that was an encouraging sign. But frankly, she had her doubts that such an inexpensive card would give her any better performance.

That night, Yasmin backed up her entire system on her tape backup drive. The next day, Yasmin created a bootable floppy diskette and copied FDISK and FORMAT to the diskette. She also entered the CMOS setup and copied down the parameters for her 420MB hard disk drive. The only thing left to do was to install the card.

Yasmin put on her wrist grounding strap, and then she swapped the new card with the old one. She disconnected the printer cable, unscrewed the necessary screws, and was careful to handle both cards only by the edges. When the new card was installed, she checked to be sure that the card was seated properly and all the cables were connected. She went ahead and put the screw into the second bracket that holds the serial and game ports because it was not connected to a card and might fall backward onto the motherboard while she worked. She also reconnected the parallel port and the LED light for the hard disk drive.

Yasmin restarted the PC, entered the CMOS, and found that the settings had changed to Not Installed for her hard disk drive C. She copied the parameters she'd written down, saved and exited the CMOS, and watched while the PC rebooted. The PC booted without a problem off the hard disk drive, and Yasmin noticed right away that the boot sequence was faster. Windows also came up faster and appeared to run faster.

Knowing that she needed to test her installation, Yasmin put a disk in the floppy drive and was able to do a directory on the disk without a problem. She attempted to print, which went well, but when she tried to use her modem, the telecommunications software gave her an error message. She then remembered that she probably had both serial ports on the card enabled, and one was conflicting with the modem.

She checked the modem settings in the telecommunications software and discovered that the modem was set for COM2. She looked at the documentation on the new card to see how to disable COM2. Taking the card back out of the slot, she left the cables connected, but set the jumpers so that COM2 was disabled, and then she wrote down that she'd disabled COM2 and the date on the new card's documentation. She then reinstalled the card, checked the connections one more time to be sure that they were secure, and restarted the PC.

This time the telecommunications software worked fine. Yasmin turned off the PC, put the screw in the bracket for the card, closed up the case, and then ran her tests briefly one more time. This time the floppy drives, the printer, and the modem worked. Yasmin was pleased with the noticeably faster performance from her PC.

Software installation

Some controller cards come with software drivers designed to enhance the performance of the card. These drivers offer special functions, such as speeding up access to Windows or providing compatibility for use with networks such as Novell. You'll find installation instructions for these drivers in the documentation that comes with the card, but be aware that the installation of these drivers may modify your CONFIG.SYS or AUTOEXEC.BAT files. You want to be sure that you have backup copies of these two files before installing the new drivers.

Don't install these drivers if you don't have to, because the drivers take up memory space, and additional drivers add another layer of processing to what you already have. This addition creates an opportunity for problems to arise due to incompatibilities with other software and hardware later down the line.

If you do decide to install the drivers that came with the card, and things don't work out as expected, you'll be depending heavily on the backups and the bootable diskette you made earlier. Also, be very careful to look over any README files on the diskette before you install the software, because you may discover and avoid potential problems.

Troubleshooting

Hard disk controller cards either work or they don't. If you're having trouble, check here, and be sure to check the troubleshooting section in Chapter 5.

An error message says that the floppy disk drive and hard disk drive are not found. This error message may say something like No FD Found **or** No HD Found.

1. If both the floppy disk drive(s) and the hard disk drive are not recognized by the system, a problem may exist with the controller card. Be sure that the controller card is seated correctly in the expansion slot.

2. Be sure that you've disabled or removed all other hard disk controller cards.

3. Be sure that the connections are made correctly between the controller card and the hard disk drive, floppy disk drive, and so on.

4. Be sure that the CMOS settings are correct for the hard disk drive.

5. Try moving the card to a different slot, if you can. If all the slots of the type you want to use are full, trade the card with another card in the same type of slot.

6. Make sure that you've installed the card in the correct type of expansion slot.

7. A controller card with its own BIOS can overlap in memory with other devices, such as high resolution video cards or network cards. Reinsert and reconnect the old hard disk controller card and see if the system works. If the old card works, you may have a memory conflict problem. You may be able to change the memory address that the controller card uses via jumpers on the card, and if you can, the documentation that comes with the card tells you how. You may not have more than one or two other memory choices, so the best way to test is to set the card to each of the alternative memory address settings and then try again to see if it works.

The floppy disk drive appears to spin up and act normally at boot, but the error message No boot device available **appears, and the hard disk drive is not accessible.**

If you've installed a controller card with a BIOS to get all the capacity out of a large hard disk drive, you must partition and format the drive just as though you installed it for the first time. If you need the data off the drive and forgot to back it up first, reinstall your old controller card, re-enter the previous values, and then backup the drive. When you install the new controller card, you can repartition and reformat, and then copy the data back onto the drive.

Troubleshooting Practice: What's Wrong In These Photos?

Figure 8-28: See answer 1.

Figure 8-29: See answer 2.

Answers:

1. This card is inserted incorrectly and is not making proper contact with the slot.

2. Although this card may work, it is missing the screw that secures the card into the slot.

Summary

✦ A video card upgrade or a hard disk controller upgrade can significantly increase the performance of Windows.

✦ PCI and VL-bus expansion slots offer faster performance, but the cards that work in those slots usually cost more.

✦ Determine what type of video you have now to know what video card you can upgrade to.

✦ A software driver is required to make your video card talk to your monitor in Windows. Although Windows usually comes with video drivers, you often get better performance when you use the software driver that comes with the video card.

✦ You're likely to need your original Windows installation diskettes or CD-ROM in order to successfully perform a video card upgrade.

✦ If you have an on-board video adapter or hard disk controller, you need the documentation for your motherboard in order to upgrade so that you can disable the on-board devices.

✦ A backup is critical for adding a new video card or hard disk controller, but especially for the hard disk controller upgrade.

✦ It's best not to attempt both a video card and a hard disk controller upgrade at the same time. The best timing is to perform the two upgrades about a week apart so that any latent problems have time to surface.

✦   ✦   ✦

Fax/Modem Upgrades to Get You on the Information Superhighway

In This Chapter

✦ Getting the best modem

✦ Determining what COM ports and modems have in common

✦ Determining if you can add a modem to your system

✦ Testing your new modem under Windows 3.x and Windows 95

✦ Determining if a Plug and Play modem will work for you

✦ Discovering tricks the pros use to install modems

Tools Needed

✦ Phillips screwdriver

✦ Antistatic mat (recommended)

A modem is a cool piece of computer hardware. With it, you can chase a friend through mazes and dungeons, even though you are in a different location; identify a caller and have the caller's account information on-screen before you pick up the phone; talk to people on the other side of the planet; fax documents you create without printing them or physically handling them; and instruct your computer to take messages for you.

The capability to do all this depends on having a modem that supports features such as faxing, voice, simultaneous voice and data transfer, and Caller ID. You also need a phone line, software capable of taking advantage of the features of the modem, and, if you want to get on the Internet, an account with a "provider" so that you can connect to the information superhighway.

Most modems come with software and free trial time on services that allow you access to the Internet and the capability to send and receive faxes. However, you have to get phone service, and services such as Caller ID, from your local telephone company.

No matter what kind of modem you get, you have to install it before you can take advantage of its capabilities. This chapter focuses on purchasing a modem, installing the modem, connecting to the phone line, and using the software you have to test your new modem.

TIP

To prepare for this chapter, take a quick look at Chapter 8, especially at the sections on types of expansion slots, installing a card in a slot, and multi-I/O cards.

Preparation

Like most new hardware purchases, you must look at your system to determine what type of modem will work for you. In this section, you learn what a modem is and how it works, what to look for in your computer to determine the type of modem to get, and what to look for in purchasing a modem.

What is a modem?

The term *modem* is a composite word that comes from the two words *modulator* and *demodulator,* which refer to what the modem does. The modem takes the digital output from the computer and modulates it into tones that can travel across analog telephone lines. When a modem receives these tones from the phone line, it demodulates them back into a digital form that the computer can understand.

Fax machines work in much the same way, only they add an additional step. The additional step is turning the image on the paper into a digitized form that describes where the ink is on the page and then translating that digital signal into tones that can travel over the phone lines. On the other end, the receiving fax interprets the tones and puts the dots on the page in the order described. Fax machines were a take-off on modems, so it was a logical step for fax capability to be added to modems.

Modems are serial devices, which means that they can send or receive only one bit at a time. Parallel devices, such as printers and tape drives, can send and receive several bits (usually eight bits) at a time. Because of this, these devices normally use parallel ports to speed communication. Although serial ports can be used for printing or other activities, they are most efficiently used for communication.

Baud rate

The *baud rate* refers to how fast a modem can transmit data. Technically, the baud rate is the number of voltage or frequency changes that can be made in a second. At lower rates, baud rates are equal to the number of bits that can be transmitted per second, so one *baud* is equal to one *bit*. Often, the term *bits per second* or *bps* used instead of *baud*. However, new compression standards have been introduced so that a baud can be equal to two or more bits.

The baud rate standards are designated by the Consultative Committee for International Telephony and Telegraphy (CCITT) arm of the International Telecommunications Union (ITU). Because of this designation, you may see CCITT or ITU acronym on a baud rate standard, but it's essentially the same group.

The following table helps you determine the bits per second the modem can transmit, based on the CCITT standard.

CCITT Term	Bits per second
V.32	4,800 and 9,600
V.32 bis*	14,400
V.34	28,800
V.42 bis*	38,400

* The term *bis* means the second revision of the standard.

Most modems that can transmit at faster speeds can slow down to accommodate a slower modem on the other end of the connection. So the rule of thumb is simply to get the fastest baud rate modem you can afford. Of course, the actual speed at which you can receive data depends a good deal on the speed of the modem transmitting to you, the quality of the phone lines, and the speed of the serial port — especially if you're using an external modem.

Although these baud rates may seem particularly fast, and they are for communication over analog telephone lines, they are not as fast as you may think. To give you an idea, your floppy disk drive can deliver data to your PC at a baud rate of about 36,000 bps. If you've had to wait on a floppy disk drive to find and deliver your file, then you know that that's not particularly fast. Compare that speed to the V.42 bis speed of 38,400 bps, and you see that online communication is relatively slow.

Fax baud rates

Most faxes send and receive at 9,600 bps, although you see speeds from 4,800 to 14,400 bps. Group 3, a standard for faxes, is available in most fax compatible modems. It allows for speeds up to 14,400 bps but can adjust down to whatever rate the sending or receiving fax can handle.

What's a COM port?

Because serial ports are most frequently used for communication, they are known as COM ports. A COM port needs two things to work correctly in your PC — free space in memory and a way to get the CPU's attention when it needs work done. One of the things that helps the COM port do its job is the UART chip. You read about the UART, memory addresses, and IRQs in the next sections.

What's a UART?

UART stands for *Universal Asynchronous Receiver Transmitter.* A UART is a chip designed to convert data for transport through the serial port and for converting incoming data to a format the software can understand. The UART chip you hear the most about is the 16550 UART, because of its special capabilities for faster and more reliable data transmission.

Most UART chips interrupt the computer each time data enters the serial port so that it can be processed. During an *interrupt,* the CPU drops all other tasks and focuses on the incoming data and then returns to processing. At slower serial speeds, this interruption isn't usually a problem, because the CPU is fast enough that you don't notice it and no data gets lost. However, at faster speeds the CPU can fall behind and lose incoming data.

The 16550 UART chip's claim to fame is that it uses a buffer called a *FIFO (First In, First Out)* buffer so that it can store up to 16 characters before it has to interrupt the CPU. This buffer speeds things up quite a bit and allows for less data loss at higher transmission speeds. So, if you plan to do high-speed modem communications, you need the 16550 UART chip.

Interrupts

The COM port gets attention from the CPU through a direct line known as an *interrupt request line,* known simply as an *interrupt* or *IRQ.* There are 16 IRQs available on a PC, numbered 0 through 15. This means that only 16 devices on the PC can have an IRQ. Because hard disk drive controllers, mice, and other devices also depend on having an IRQ, these direct lines can become in short supply. Serial devices typically use IRQs 3 and 4, although they can use others. It is generally accepted that no serial device can use an IRQ higher than IRQ 7.

Memory (or I/O) addresses

In addition to IRQ shortages, another problem is getting free space in memory, known as an I/O (input/output) address. Memory is allocated in blocks. Although these blocks are small, devices cannot share a block of memory — it's an all or nothing proposition. Although COM1 and COM2 usually have space reserved in memory, there may not be memory space for COM3 and COM4. However, if you get a free IRQ, you can usually secure the memory needed for the COM port.

The location where the block starts is the *base* address. This is sometimes referred to as the *base I/O address*. These addresses are in hexadecimal (base-16) format, so sometimes you see them with the letter *H* before or after and sometimes with a zero in front. You may see an address for COM1 expressed as a base I/O of 03F8, 3F8, 03F8H, or 03F8h.

If you remember how memory is allocated on the PC from Chapter 6; then you remember that of the lower 1MB of memory (which is 1024 kilobytes or K), 640K is reserved for applications, and 384K is reserved for hardware devices on the PC to communicate with the CPU. The memory addresses for the COM ports fall into that 384K range.

Two devices cannot be set to use the same I/O address. This is called a *memory conflict.* Neither one will work, and the conflict could stop your system from working, as well.

IRQ sharing

As if things weren't confusing enough, IRQs can be shared in some cases. Although a COM port cannot share a memory address with another device on the PC, it can share an IRQ, provided the IRQ isn't in constant use by the other device. This means that a modem can share an IRQ with a sound card because the sound card won't use the IRQ if the modem is in use, but the modem cannot share an IRQ with a mouse. Because IRQs can be shared, common practice is to have COM1 and COM3 use the same IRQ, while COM2 and COM4 use the same IRQ.

Sharing doesn't always work, though, so you should not count on it. The best and most reliable scenario is if each device that needs the attention of the CPU has its own IRQ.

Standard memory addresses and interrupts for COM ports

The following table shows the standard memory addresses and interrupts for the four COM ports on the PC.

Serial Port	IRQ	Base I/O Address
COM1	IRQ 4	03F8
COM2	IRQ 3	02F8
COM3	IRQ 4,3 (5,7 alternate IRQ)	03E8*
COM4	IRQ 3,4 (5,7 alternate IRQ)	02E8*

* Note that some hardware and software products do not support COM3 or COM4.

It's also important to note that parallel ports, noted as LPT ports, usually use IRQ 7 for the first parallel port, or LPT1, and IRQ 5 for a second LPT port, or LPT2. Other devices that use IRQ 5 include sound cards, network cards, CD-ROM interface cards, tape backup interface cards, and SCSI controllers. Because IRQ 5 or 7 can sometimes be used as alternate settings doesn't mean that they are available.

The relationship between modems and COM ports

Because modems are used for communication, they either have COM port capabilities built in or they make use of an available COM port on your PC. Because modems and COM ports are tightly linked from an installation point of view, you must know about the existing COM ports on your PC before you can make decisions concerning the addition of a modem.

Why you should avoid COM3 and COM4

After seeing how many variables are involved in using COM3 or COM4 and how these COM ports can end up sharing resources, it's not too hard to see why some hardware and software manufacturers avoid supporting these ports altogether. Because of this avoidance, even if you get your modem working on COM3 or COM4, you may find that your software application won't talk to it unless it's on COM1 or COM2.

You may not have to deal with the problem of software that won't talk to COM3 or COM4, because installation software is smarter these days and attempts to choose COM1 or COM2 for a newly installed modem. However, if you have a choice, you should be like the pros and avoid using COM3 and COM4, precisely for the reasons I mention.

The bottom line is that you have to know what COM ports you have and what COM ports and IRQs are available in order to decide which ones you can use. You learn how to do that in the next section.

How to find out what COM ports you have

Before you consider a modem purchase, you should find out what COM ports are available on your PC. Although this may sound complicated, you're about to learn where to look and what to look for. Most PCs have two serial ports, so that's the place to start looking.

Finding your serial ports

The best place to start looking for COM ports is to look for the serial ports on the back of your PC. Serial ports usually come in either 25-pin male or 9-pin male connectors, and chances are you have one of each, as shown in Figure 9-1. (If you refer to Chapter 15 on printer upgrades, you see that parallel connectors are also 25-pin, but female instead of male.) If there are two serial connectors, it's a pretty safe bet that they are configured to be COM1 and COM2.

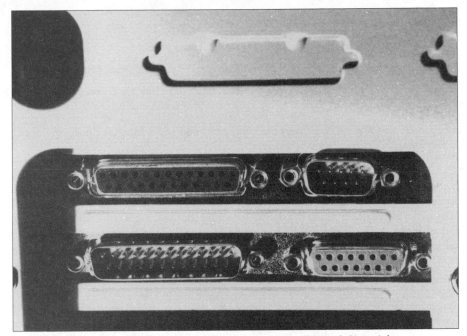

Figure 9-1: A 9-pin male (top right) and a 25-pin male (lower left) serial connector.

You may notice that your mouse is connected to one of the ports. This mouse would be a *serial* mouse which means that one of your COM ports is in use. If you're unsure if your mouse is a serial mouse or not, keep reading to learn how to find out.

If you see something that looks like Figure 9-15, then you already have a modem. You should still go on to the next step, because you may be able to determine what COM port your modem is set to.

Looking at your PC's BIOS configuration

Another place to look to determine what COM ports you have active is in the BIOS. You may be able to see this information displayed by the BIOS during the boot sequence, as shown by the AMI BIOS in Figure 9-2. The information is displayed in the order of the COM ports, so the first address would be the memory address for the first COM port available. As you can see, if you go back to the table shown earlier, the 3F8 address indicates that COM1 is active, and 2F8 indicates an active COM2 port. That doesn't mean these port addresses are not being used, but it does mean that they're available.

```
System Configuration (C) Copyright 1985-1990 American Megatrends Inc.,

Main Processor      : 80386          Base Memory Size  : 640 KB
Numeric Processor : None             Ext. Memory Size  : 7424 KB
Floppy Drive A:     : 1.44 MB, 3½"   Hard Disk C: Type : 47
Floppy Drive B:     : 1.2 MB, 5¼"    Hard Disk D: Type : 47
Display Type        : VGA/PGA/EGA    Serial Port(s)    : 3F8,2F8
ROM-BIOS Date       : 05/05/91       Parallel Ports(s) : 378
```

Figure 9-2: This AMI BIOS displays the serial port base I/O addresses during the boot sequence.

When the serial port settings are displayed in the BIOS menu, as in the example, the ports are controlled from a card inserted into one of the expansion slots in the PC. These cards are often multi-I/O cards, meaning that the same card has on it the hard disk controller, floppy disk drive controller, two serial ports, one parallel port, and a game port. This information could be useful to you, especially if you plan to install an internal modem. See Chapter 8 for more information on multi-I/O cards.

If you don't see anything regarding the COM ports or serial ports during the boot sequence, then enter the CMOS and look for serial port settings. You may have to look in an advanced settings menu or a submenu of the opening screen. Look for key phrases such as "chipset features," "peripheral configuration," or "port configuration."

When you find the reference to serial ports, you've found what you're looking for. As shown in the example in Figure 9-3, this Phoenix BIOS designates the serial ports as Serial Port A and Serial Port B. Either of these ports can have their COM port designation and address changed, or they can be disabled from the CMOS menu. The reference to the COM ports in the BIOS indicates that the ports are built-in to the motherboard, which happens to be the case in this particular example.

TIP

Sometimes you see a reference to an RS-232 port. The term *RS-232* has been used so much for serial port connections that it is understood to mean *serial,* and it is even used sometimes in place of the actual term *serial.*

```
                    ROM EISA BIOS (2B69DA09)
                     CHIPSET FEATURES SETUP
                     AWARD SOFTWARE, INC.

 CPU-To-PCI Write Posting  : Disabled     PCI Posted Write Buffer  : Enabled
 CPU Read Multiple PreFetch: Disabled     8 Bit I/O Recovery Time  : 11
 CPU Line Read Multiple    : Disabled     16 Bit I/O Recovery Time : 7
 CPU Line Read PreFetch    : Disabled
 CPU Line Read             : Disabled     Onboard FDC Controller   : Enabled
 CPU Burst Write Assembly  : Disabled     Onboard Serial Port 1    : COM1/3F8
 PCI-To-CPU Write Posting  : Disabled     Onboard Serial Port 2    : COM2/2F8
 VGA Performance Mode       : Disabled     Onboard Parallel Port    : 378/IRQ7
 Video Buffer Cacheable    : Disabled     Parallel Port Mode       : Normal

 DRAM Last Write to CAS#   : 2
 DRAM CAS# Hold Time       : 6
 CAS Address Hold Time     : 2
 Read CAS# Pulse Width     : 3
 Write CAS# Pulse Width    : 2
 CAS# Precharge Time       : 1          ESC : Quit          ↑↓→← : Select Item
 RAS# to CAS Address Delay : 2          F1  : Help          PU/PD/+/- : Modify
 RAS# to CAS# Delay        : 3          F5  : Old Values   (Shift)F2 : Color
 RAS# Precharge Time       : 5          F6  : Load BIOS  Defaults
                                        F7  : Load Setup Defaults
```

Figure 9-3: An example of a Phoenix BIOS that allows you to disable or assign addresses to the serial ports it designates as Serial Port A and Serial Port B.

Looking for a Plug and Play (PnP) BIOS

While you're in the BIOS, look for the terms *Plug and Play* or *PnP*. If you find those terms, you may find adding a modem to your system much easier, especially if you plan to add an internal modem. This ease of use is because your modem software installation program or Windows 95 can make adjustments to the BIOS settings for you to enable or disable the proper ports and configure your modem correctly. However, you still must note the current settings for the COM ports, as you may decide to use an external modem.

There are cases where the BIOS and/or Windows 95 doesn't pick up on the modem. This means that you may have to make the adjustments manually to both the BIOS and Windows 95. The modem documentation should give you an outline of the necessary information to make the adjustments, and so will this chapter.

 You can also use the Windows 95 Device Manager to see if you have a PnP BIOS. To start Device Manager, select Start⇨Settings⇨Control Panel⇨System⇨Device Manager. Be sure that View devices by connection is selected, as shown in Figure 9-4. You should see a reference to a PnP BIOS, as shown in the figure, if you have such a BIOS.

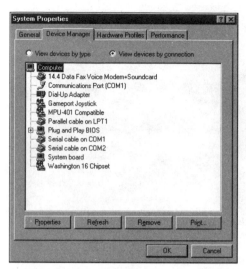

Figure 9-4: It's easier to see a PnP BIOS when View devices by connection is selected in the Windows 95 Device Manager.

How to use MSD under DOS/Windows 3.x

The next step to finding your COM ports is to discover what devices, if any, are using the COM ports, and what memory addresses and interrupts the COM ports are set to. If you have a PC diagnostic software tool that tells you the COM port settings, you should use it. If not, you can use the Microsoft Diagnostic (MSD) that comes with DOS 5.0 or higher.

To start MSD, exit Windows. From the DOS prompt, type **MSD** and press Enter. (MSD is in the DOS directory, so you may have to type **CD \DOS**, press Enter, type **MSD,** and press Enter again.)

Looking at the current COM Port settings

When MSD has finished examining your system, you can select COM Ports, and MSD displays the information it has found concerning the serial ports on your system. For example, Figure 9-5 shows the result when MSD was run on a system with two external serial ports. Notice that the port address is shown, as well as the baud rate of the serial port. To close the COM Ports window, click on OK or press Esc.

The type of UART chip you have is shown as well. Make a note of that for reference when you decide what type of modem to get.

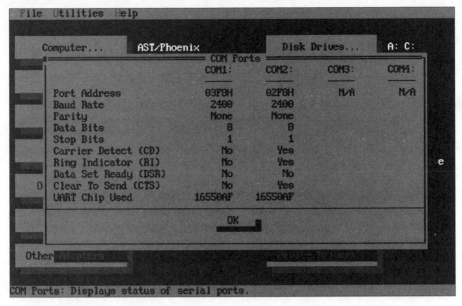

Figure 9-5: MSD shows the COM ports on a system with COM1 and COM2. N/A means that port designation is not being used.

Looking at the current IRQ settings

MSD also allows you to look at what interrupts are being used by which devices. Select IRQ Settings, and you see a screen similar to the one shown in Figure 9-6. In this example, not only are the IRQ's shown, but MSD has attempted to describe what kind of device is using the IRQ. Notice that COM1 is using IRQ 4 and that MSD believes there may be a serial mouse attached to that port, which is exactly the case. In this particular case, however, there was also an external modem attached to COM2 that MSD did not pick up. This is part of the reason why you must do a visual inspection of the PC's ports yourself and look at the BIOS settings as well.

How to use the Windows 95 Device Manager

Windows 95 offers Device Manager to allow you to see what ports are installed and to get information on those ports. To start Device Manager, select Start➪Settings➪ Control Panel➪System➪Device Manager. Be sure that View devices by type is selected, as shown in Figure 9-7. Select the plus (+) sign in front of Ports (COM & LPT) to display a list of available ports, as shown in the figure.

```
File  Utilities  Help
========================= IRQ Status =========================
 IRQ   Address   Description        Detected        Handled By

  0   144B:03F5  Timer Click        Yes             LOADRPM.COM
  1   144B:0414  Keyboard           Yes             LOADRPM.COM
  2   1249:0057  Second 8259A       Yes             Default Handlers
  3   1249:006F  COM2: COM4:        COM2:           Default Handlers
  4   1249:0087  COM1: COM3:        COM1:           Default Handlers
  5   1249:009F  LPT2:              No              Default Handlers
  6   1249:00B7  Floppy Disk        Yes             Default Handlers
  7   0070:06F4  LPT1:              Yes             System Area
  8   1249:0052  Real-Time Clock    Yes             Default Handlers
  9   F000:7FDB  Redirected IRQ2    Yes             BIOS
 10   1249:00CF  (Reserved)                         Default Handlers
 11   1249:00E7  (Reserved)                         Default Handlers
 12   1249:00FF  (Reserved)                         Default Handlers
 13   F000:7FCA  Math Coprocessor   No              BIOS
 14   1249:0117  Fixed Disk         Yes             Default Handlers
 15   F000:FF43  (Reserved)                         BIOS

                            OK

IRQ Status: Displays current usage of hardware interrupts.
```

Figure 9-6: MSD displays the IRQ assignments.

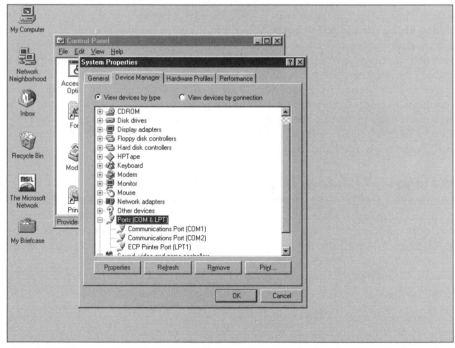

Figure 9-7: Be sure that View devices by type is selected when looking at ports using the Windows 95 Device Manager.

To view the memory address and IRQ information, highlight the port of interest and then select Properties⇨Resources. As shown in the example of a COM1 port in Figure 9-8, you see the address range the port uses; in this case, 03F8 to 03FF (so the base I/O is 03F8). The Interrupt Request (IRQ) line is number 4.

Look at the resources used for each port you have, even the parallel port(s), and make note of the base address and IRQ used for each port.

Points to consider when buying a modem

Now that you know what serial ports you have available, and the base I/O or memory address and IRQ for each one, you can make an educated decision on the type of modem to get. Here's what to look for.

How to decide between an internal or external modem

From an installation viewpoint, there are basically two types of modems — internal and external. An internal modem is simply a circuit board that can be inserted into an expansion slot in your PC. This modem has all the necessary chips and hardware for a serial port built-in, as well as the chips needed for modem and other functions. An external modem has its own housing and connects via a cable to a serial port already on the PC. Figure 9-9 shows both an internal and an external modem.

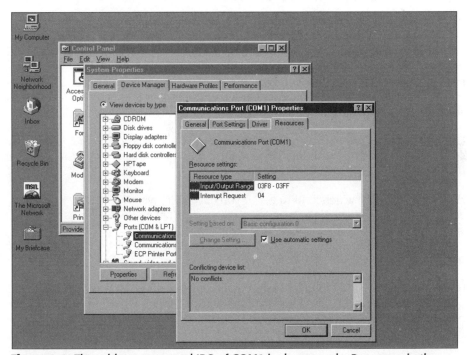

Figure 9-8: The address range and IRQ of COM1 is shown under Resources in the Communications Port Properties box.

Figure 9-9: An internal modem is a circuit board, while an external modem has a housing.

Internal modems offer the advantages of taking less space on the desktop and costing less than external modems. In addition, internal modems usually have the latest and fastest UART chips to help speed communications. Internal modems usually offer more features, such as voice mail, Caller ID, and other features that work if you have software designed to support these features.

External modems cost more and take up more space. They require that you have a serial cable (usually an additional expense), and they have a separate power supply that must be plugged in.

How do you decide which kind to get? If you have a PC system with a card that controls the ports, then it's easiest to install an external modem, because you use a serial port that is already configured. If your serial port has the 16550 UART chip, you're in even better shape, because your communications will go faster, with fewer bottlenecks between the serial port and the modem.

However, you may need to get an internal modem because of the special features it offers. If you have a Plug and Play BIOS, installing an internal modem will be easier, but you could be looking at more steps to installation. Here's why.

As mentioned earlier, the display of serial port information during the boot sequence, as shown in Figure 9-3, indicates that you probably have a card that controls the ports. You may also already have a COM1 and a COM2 port. So, in order to install an internal modem, you must disable one of the COM ports on your multi-I/O card to prevent a conflict with the modem.

Disabling the port on a multi-I/O card usually means that you have to physically adjust jumper settings on the card. To know which jumper settings you have to adjust, you must have the documentation for the card (see Chapter 8). But, unless you have the documentation or the jumper settings are silk-screened on the card, getting the documentation for a multi-I/O card is just about impossible. In this situation, the pros spend an extra few bucks and install a new multi-I/O card that has the documentation. Then they can disable the appropriate COM port on the card, set the internal modem to that COM port, and all is well.

If you decide on an internal modem, you must open up your PC and determine if you have an available expansion slot. You may need an ISA slot (see Chapter 8, if you haven't already, for information on expansion slots), but you must know if a slot is available for your new modem.

Plug and Play internal modems

Whether or not you have a Plug and Play (PnP) BIOS, many modems offer the benefit of software selectable settings, meaning that these modems do not have jumpers or switches you must adjust. Either the BIOS or the software that comes with the modem sets the COM port base I/O and IRQ settings for you.

Unfortunately, software selectable settings aren't always as automated as you'd like, which is why there's a preparation section in this chapter to help you find out for yourself what's being used and what's available. In addition, you may need to find out what those COM settings are if you install software later down the road that will make use of the modem or its features. But when PnP does work, it's a pleasure and certainly the easiest way to install a modem.

Fax/modem considerations

Most faxes send and receive at 9,600 bps; however, you see speeds of 4,800 bps and 14,400 bps. A fax is designed to adjust to the speed of the receiving fax, so it's better to have a faster fax modem than a slower one. The latest fax standard is the Group 3 (or Group III) standard, from the Electronics Industry Association and the Telecommunication Industry Association (EIA/TIA), so look for that one.

You may also see references to the Class 1 standard. The Class 1 standard defines the commands given to the fax/modem and is part of the Group 3 standard, so software that is Group 3 compliant should also be Class 1 compliant. The reason that you may see Class 1 mentioned separately is to place emphasis on compatibility.

Realistically, although you can receive faxes with your fax/modem, most people send only and use a separate fax machine or PC for receiving faxes. The decision to use a separate PC or fax for receiving is due to the fact that receiving a fax tends to demand much in the way of system resources, so your work may slow to a crawl or even a stand-still while your PC receives a fax.

Dual voice and data capability (DSVD)

Some modems now offer you the ability to transmit voice and data over the same phone line at the same time, a feature known as *digital simultaneous voice and data* (DSVD). Software programs are available that allow you and a friend to share documents while you talk it over or chase each other through a dungeon.

It's important to realize that the modems on both ends must have DSVD capability. A modem with DSVD capability will talk to one without it, but you cannot share voice and data over a single phone line unless both modems involved are DSVD. If you're buying two modems, get both from the same manufacturer, because DSVD is not firmly established as a standard; otherwise, you may get unreliable results with modems from two different manufacturers.

After you've decided on the features and type of modem your system can support, it's time for installation.

Installation

Installing an external modem is easier than installing an internal modem, but as I mention earlier, internal modems have more of the cool features in demand these days. Here's how to install either one, starting with the external modem.

Installing an external modem

You need the following five items to install an external modem:

1. The modem

2. A serial cable to connect the modem to the PC

3. A modular telephone cable

4. An available outlet in which to plug in the modem's power supply

5. An available telephone jack

Installing an external modem is straightforward, and you can do it quickly. Just watch for a few things. First, when you purchase the modem, be sure that you get a modular phone cord and a serial cable to connect the modem to the PC. As shown in Figure 9-10, the modem has a 25-pin female connector. Your PC should have a 25-pin male connector, so the cable must be a 25-pin female to 25-pin male serial cable. Serial cables are wired differently than parallel cables, so be sure that it's a serial cable. When you install the modem, be sure that the PC is off, and it's a good idea to be grounded, even though you won't be working inside the PC.

TIP

Install the modem to the 25-pin serial port, especially if it's a fax/modem. You can adapt a 9-pin serial port to a 25-pin serial cable with an inexpensive adapter, but there have been reports of problems receiving faxes when that arrangement is used.

Connect the cable to the PC, then to the modem. Be sure to secure the cable to the port and to the modem. After you connect the cable, you can connect the phone line. Most modems have two connectors, one to connect your phone for voice and another for connecting the modem to the phone jack.

After the phone line is connected, plug in the power connection to the modem and the other end to the power outlet so that your modem is receiving power. Turn the on/off switch on the top or back of the modem to on and look for a light indicating that the modem is receiving power. Now you can turn on your PC and skip down to the testing section to test your new modem.

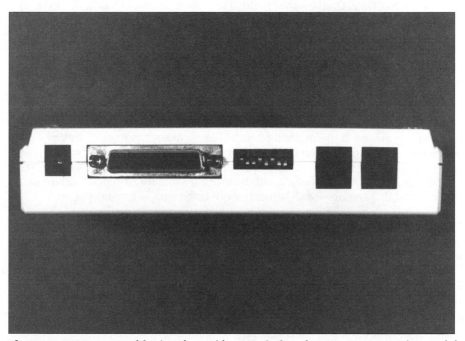

Figure 9-10: An external fax/modem with a 25-pin female connector. Note the modular phone connectors.

Installing an internal modem

You need the following five things to install an internal modem:

1. The modem

2. A Phillips screwdriver

3. A modular telephone cable

4. An available expansion slot inside the PC

5. An available telephone jack

Installing an internal modem requires that you insert the modem into a vacant expansion slot in your PC. You should have looked already to be sure that you had an available expansion slot. The instructions for inserting a card into an expansion slot are in Chapter 8, but here are a few additional helpful hints.

If you have a multi-I/O card, you may need to disable the unused COM port on the card. For example, if you have a mouse using the 9-pin serial port on COM1, but nothing is using the 25-pin serial port set to COM2, you can disable the 25-pin serial port. This frees the IRQ and memory space for your internal modem, which would then be set to COM2. On the other hand, if the mouse was on COM2, then you should disable COM1. Chapter 8 has information on installing multi-I/O cards, so if you don't have the necessary documentation to disable a COM port, then you may need to purchase another multi-I/O card to replace the one you have. Follow the directions to disable the appropriate COM port on the new multi-I/O card.

Now you must turn to your modem. If the modem is not a Plug and Play modem, then you must set the modem to use the settings of the COM port you disabled on the multi-I/O card. Figure 9-11 shows a PnP modem and a modem that has jumpers that must be set. You need the modem documentation to set the jumper settings, unless this information is printed on the front or back of the modem itself. For example, if you want to set the modem to use the standard settings for COM2, then set the jumpers or switches on the modem to base I/O 2F8 and IRQ 3. The standard memory address and IRQ settings for COM ports were listed earlier in this chapter.

After the modem is ready, install it in the PC in an expansion slot as far away from other cards in your PC as possible. This separation is because modems tend to be wider than other cards, so they may touch other cards, which could stop your PC from working. Also, modem cards tend to give off a little more heat than other cards. The best arrangement is moving it so that it's the farthest away from the power supply and has one or more free slots between it and the next card. If you have to move other cards to get the modem in the farthest position, then do so, being careful to get the cables and other connections properly reattached. Also, be sure not to touch any other cards with the modem card as you insert it.

Modem cards tend to be wider than other cards and give off slightly more heat, so it's best to install them as far away from the other cards in your system as possible.

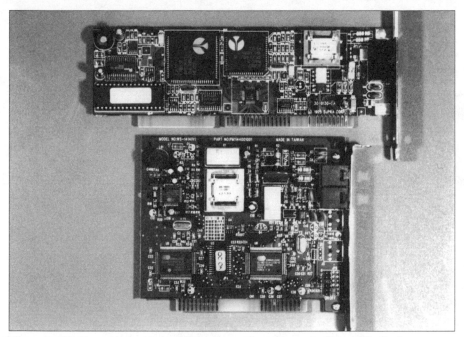

Figure 9-11: Here are two internal modems. The top one is PnP, while the bottom one has jumpers on the lower right for setting the I/O address and IRQ assignment.

Secure the card with the screw you removed from the bracket that held the case opening closed, because you're going to attach the phone lines to the card and you don't want it loose. Attach the phone line from the wall jack to the modem, and, if you want, you can attach a line to a regular phone so that you can dial out normally, as shown in Figure 9-12.

As with other hardware installations, when installing an internal modem it's best to leave the PC case open if you can during the initial testing phases to be sure that the card works. By leaving it open, you don't have to keep opening and closing the case whenever you need to make a change to the card.

If you're installing a PnP modem, there are no jumpers or switch settings. However, if you're installing a PnP modem to a PC with DOS or Windows 3.*x*, you need PnP manager software to configure the modem for you to the correct settings each time you start the PC. The manager software, which should come with the modem, comes in two parts. One part determines the modem settings, often with your help, and writes the settings to a data file on your PC. Then a second program is added to your environment files. Each time your PC starts, the second program reads the data file with the settings and sets the correct IRQ and memory address settings for the PnP card, which is called *configuring* the PnP card. A very detailed discussion of this process and a case study are included in Chapter 11.

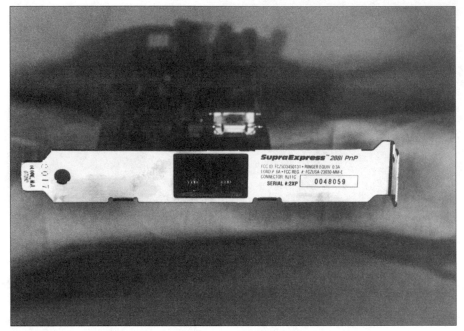

Figure 9-12: An internal modem offers modular telephone connectors.

Testing

There are a couple of ways to test a modem installation. The first is to install software that talks to the modem and determines if the software recognizes the modem. The second is to use the software to get the modem to dial and connect to a number. You want to perform each test. These tests are different under DOS and Windows 3.*x* than they are under Windows 95. I start with the DOS/Windows 3.*x* testing steps and then move to the Windows 95 testing steps.

DOS/Windows 3.*x* testing

When you purchased the modem, you receive software that enables you to use the modem to connect to a bulletin board or online service such as America Online, CompuServe, Prodigy, or others. A utility program comes with Windows 3.*x*, but it's tough to use and I don't recommend using it. The easiest way to accomplish this first testing step is to install the software and allow it to recognize the modem. The software should determine what base I/O and interrupt the modem is using, and it then configures itself to use those settings.

Most of the software is Windows 3.*x* compatible and should include instructions on how to start the installation program under Windows. Usually, you start in Program Manager, select File⇨Run, type in either **A:\SETUP** or **A:\INSTALL**, and click on OK. When the software starts, it looks for the modem, and it may report back to you the COM port where the modem was found.

What to expect when connecting to an online service for the first time

Now the second testing phase begins. You can test your modem by using one of the online services software programs you received with the modem from America Online, CompuServe, or Prodigy. Select an online service and try to connect to it. Some software finds the modem and configures itself to the correct COM port address and IRQ. Other software requires that you know what COM port the modem is connected to.

When the software you decided to use has found the modem and configured itself, you are asked to give your name and other information, as well as your phone number, including the area code. You also are asked to enter the code found on the packaging or documentation. And you are asked to provide bank account information for a direct debit of your account or a credit card number so that you can be billed for the service. (Even if you get free time initially, they want to be able to bill you when the free time is up.) The software attempts to make a connection via the phone line with its online service to get you an access number that is convenient for you. When it attempts that connection, you have your second test.

What you should hear before connecting

Your modem has a speaker, so when it comes time to actually dial and connect to a service, you should hear a dial tone and the phone being dialed by the modem. You also hear high-pitched tones as the modem that answers your call gets in sync with your modem, a process called *handshaking*. When you're connected, the software should say you're connected and the speaker on the modem should shut off so that you no longer hear the modem communication sounds.

Connecting to the Microsoft Download Service using Terminal

Test your modem by connecting to the Microsoft Download Service. Use the telecommunication utility that comes with Windows 3.*x*. To do this, select Accessories⇨Terminal (See Figure 9-13). When Terminal starts, you are asked for the default serial port, which means that you must tell Terminal what serial port your modem is using. Select the port and then set up the number to call by selecting Settings⇨Phone Number. Type in **1-206-936-6735** (unless you live in the 206 area code, and then leave out the *1-206-*) and click on OK. To dial the number you entered select Phone⇨Dial. You should hear the same things as described in the section "What you should hear before connecting." After you're connected, follow the instructions offered by the Microsoft Download Service.

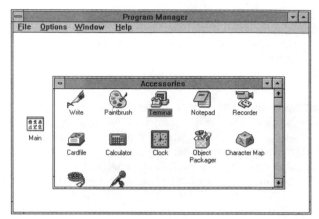

Figure 9-13: The Terminal utility in Windows 3.x enables you to test your modem.

Windows 95 testing

If your modem is correctly installed, Windows 95 should recognize it when you restart the computer and install the correct drivers. When it does this, Windows 95 tells you it has found new hardware on your system and is installing the drivers for the new hardware. It also presents you with the Dialing Properties dialog box, shown in Figure 9-14, so that you can enter your area code and perform functions such as dialing an access code for an outside line or turning off call-waiting.

Installing software for an online service

You can test your modem by using one of the online services software programs that you received with the modem from America Online, CompuServe, or Prodigy. Instructions should come with the programs from the online services for installation. The easiest way to install the instructions is to place the diskette from the service in the A drive, and then select Start➪Settings➪Control Panel➪Add/Remove Programs➪Install and let Windows 95 guide you through the installation steps. This step also places the software on the list of programs that are available when you select Start➪Programs.

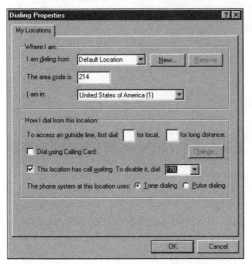

Figure 9-14: The Dialing Properties dialog box comes up when Windows 95 recognizes your new modem.

Connecting to the Microsoft Download Service using HyperTerminal

You may also test your modem by connecting to the Microsoft Download Service. Use the telecommunication utility that comes with Windows 95. To do this, select Start⇨Programs⇨Accessories⇨HyperTerminal (see Figure 9-15). Select Hypertrm.exe to start the HyperTerminal program. Type **Microsoft BBS** for the name of the new connection and then click on OK, as shown in Figure 9-18. For the area code, enter **206** and then **936-6735** for the phone number, and select OK⇨Dial (see Figure 9-16). You should hear the same things as described in the section "What you should hear before connecting." After you're connected, follow the instructions offered by the Microsoft Download Service.

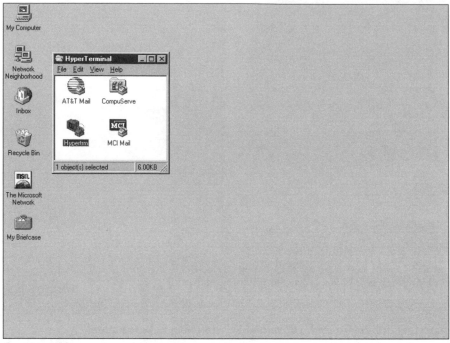

Figure 9-15: HyperTerminal is a utility in Windows 95 that you can use to test your modem. Select Hypertrm.exe to start the utility.

Figure 9-16: Enter the phone number and area code of the service you want to connect to using HyperTerminal.

Installation in review

To add a modem to your system, follow these steps:

1. Check the back of your computer for serial ports.

2. Check the BIOS configuration for serial port addresses and PnP.

3. Use a diagnostic software tool such as MSD or Device Manager to look at the ports.

4. Write down the base I/O and IRQs for each COM port.

5. Purchase a modem, including needed accessories, such as cables.

6. Install the modem, configuring the modem for the proper COM port if necessary.

7. Test to see if the software or the operating system recognizes the modem.

8. Test the modem by connecting to an online service.

Question: My phone doesn't ring anymore now that I've connected it to the back of my modem, but I can make and receive calls. What's happened?

Answer: The modem has disabled some of the functionality of your phone, so it is now a *dumb handset.* To make the phone ring again, you must connect it directly to the wall outlet. Get an inexpensive line doubler, and connect both your phone and the modem to the same incoming phone line.

Question: How do I use the voice, fax, and other capabilities of my modem?

Answer: When you have the modem installed and working, it's all in the software. In other words, you must install software that takes advantage of the features of your modem. You can use several software packages with the same modem, as long as you use them one at a time.

Question: Everytime I get an incoming call on my call waiting, my online session ends. What's going on?

Answer: Call waiting disrupts the session. You can turn off call waiting by placing the characters needed to turn off the service (usually *70). At the beginning of any phone number you have the modem dial. Many software packages offer the capability to turn off call waiting. Windows 95 allows you to turn off call waiting by selecting Start⇨ Control Panel⇨Modems⇨Dialing Properties. Check the box in front of "This location has call waiting. To disable it dial . . . " and pick the `disable call waiting` string off the list, or enter a new string.

Troubleshooting

Software doesn't recognize the modem.

1. If the modem is external, did you turn it on before you started the software? If not, exit the software, turn on the modem, and start the software again.

2. If the modem is external, check to see that it's correctly cabled.

3. If the modem is internal, check to see that it's placed in the correct expansion slot and that it is firmly in the slot. See the troubleshooting section of Chapter 8.

4. Make sure the software is set to the correct COM port. Look for a "configuration" or "modem settings" option to view the COM port setting.

5. If the modem is internal, you may need to go in and disable the port the modem is set to.

6. Check to see if the modem is in conflict with another device on the system. Look specifically for conflicts between your modem and a sound card, network card, CD-ROM interface card, tape backup interface card, or a SCSI controller.

   Try MSD if you're running DOS/Windows 3.x, and Device Manager if you're running Windows 95. Use the information under the section "How to find out what COM ports you have" earlier in this chapter, and look for two devices set to the same base I/O address or to the same IRQ. Check the BIOS settings. If the BIOS shows the serial port settings when it boots, and one setting is now missing, the conflict may be on that COM port. If the BIOS offers the capability to disable the ports from the CMOS menu, make sure that no ports conflict with the port settings on your modem.

   You can also check for conflicts using the Windows 95 Device Manager. If Device Manager shows a yellow circle with an exclamation point in it (as shown in Figure 9-17), a conflict exists. You may have to delete one of the ports to remove the conflict, but check the resources of the ports first to determine where the conflict lies before deleting anything.

   If Device Manager shows a red X on the port or other device (as shown in Figure 9-18), then it has been disabled. Check the properties of the device or port to determine why it was disabled. (See the Windows 95 multiple-boot configuration section of Chapter 13).

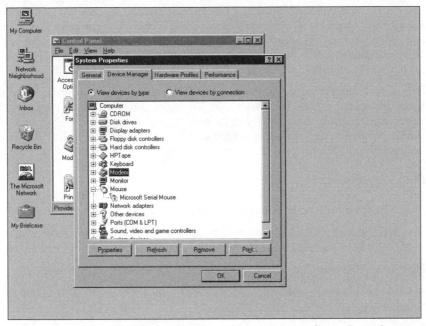

Figure 9-17: The yellow circle with the exclamation point shown in Device Manager indicates a conflict with that device; in this case, the mouse.

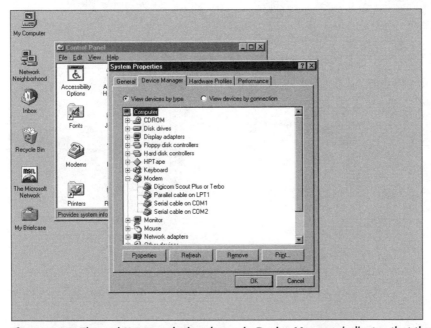

Figure 9-18: The red *X* over a device shown in Device Manager indicates that the device is disabled. In this case, the modem device driver is disabled.

7. Check the Modems Properties box for diagnostic information. Select Start⇨
Settings⇨Control Panel⇨Modems⇨Diagnostics. Highlight the port you want to
see more information about, and select More Info. Windows 95 provides you
with the base I/O, IRQ, baud rate, and even information on the UART chip, as
shown in Figure 9-19.

8. If you're running Windows 3.x, make sure that the port the modem is set to has
the same settings as those in Windows. To check the Windows settings for the
port from Program Manager, select Main⇨Control Panel⇨Ports. Highlight the
port of interest and then select Settings⇨Advanced to see or modify the base I/O
address and IRQ setting for that port.

"No dial tone" message.

1. Plug a telephone directly into the wall outlet, and be sure a dial tone is available.

2. Check to be sure that you connected the phone and the line from the wall outlet
to the correct plugs on the modem. Reverse the two plugs if you're not sure.

3. Make sure that the plugs connect firmly into the phone connections.

4. Make sure that there are no other software applications running that use the
modem.

5. Try another telephone line cord.

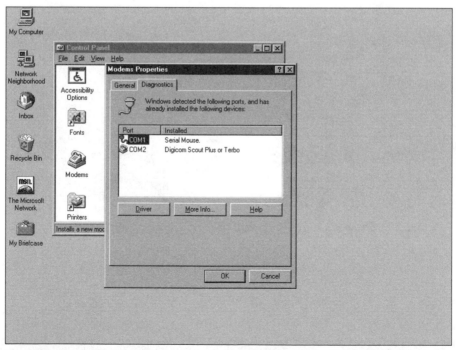

Figure 9-19: You can get diagnostic information about your modem in Windows 95.

No sound from the modem.

1. If you're using an external modem, check to see if there's a volume control on the modem to turn up the sound.

2. See also "No dial tone."

My PC won't boot.

1. This can happen if you installed an internal modem card and the card has physically touched one of the other cards in the system. Check to be sure that the card is away from other cards in the system.

2. Look for an IRQ conflict with another device on your system. See point 5 under "Software doesn't recognize the modem."

Windows will not start or Windows 95 says there's a conflict with a device on my system.

Look for an IRQ conflict with another device on your system. See point 5 under "Software doesn't recognize the modem."

Troubleshooting Practice: What's Wrong in This Photo?

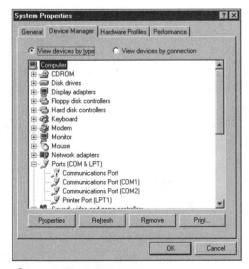

Figure 9-20: See answer.

Answer:

There is a device conflict here between the ports in this Windows 95 Device Manager display.

Summary

◆ You need software that takes advantage of the features of your modem. That software may come with the modem, or you may need to purchase it separately.

◆ The type of modem you install depends on the type of input/output (I/O) card you have on your system, the number of existing COM ports, and the type of BIOS you have.

◆ Internal modems usually offer more features than external modems, but they can be more difficult to install.

◆ It's best to install a modem on COM1 or COM2 and avoid COM3 and COM4.

◆   ◆   ◆

CHAPTER 10

Upgrading Your Power Supply or Battery

In This Chapter

✦ Understanding what your power supply and battery do

✦ Determining whether your system is underpowered

✦ Measuring the voltage output from your power supply

✦ Purchasing and connecting a new power supply

✦ Finding your PC's battery

✦ Testing the voltage in the battery

✦ Saving your CMOS settings

✦ Installing an easily replaceable battery

Tools Needed

✦ Wrist grounding strap

✦ Multimeter (digital multimeter recommended)

✦ Needlenose pliers

✦ Phillips screwdriver

✦ Wire cutters (optional)

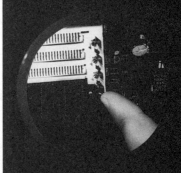

Although you wouldn't think so, power supply and battery upgrades are fairly common. You may not have heard much about these upgrades, because they're inexpensive and not as glamorous as other upgrades. However, these two critical components can make a big difference in the reliability of your PC. A battery upgrade can help stave off problems before they occur; a power supply upgrade is especially important if you plan to add multimedia or other components to your PC. In addition, the power supply is a component with moving parts and so it's one of the most frequently replaced items on a PC.

These components are together in this chapter because both deal with the power sent to critical components of your PC and both require the same tools to install and troubleshoot. This chapter is divided into two sections, one for power supply upgrades and one for the battery upgrades. Power supply upgrades are addressed first.

Power Supply Upgrades

The power supply is needed to provide the correct amount of voltage to your PC's components. If the power supply cannot meet the voltage demands placed on it by the components in your PC, you can experience problems that range from data loss to intermittent errors that you can't quite put your finger on. When you understand more about what a power supply does, you can see how upgrading it can help your PC.

What is a power supply?

The power supply, a large silver or green box, is one of the largest items inside your PC. Its job is to convert electrical current from the *alternating current* (AC) coming in from your electric company into two lines of *direct current* (DC) at much lower voltages. Technically, the power supply converts the 110 AC voltage to + 12 and -12 volts DC for the mechanical components of your PC, such as the motor that spins the floppy disk drive and the hard disk drive, and +5 and -5 volts DC to power the logical stuff that happens in the processor and circuit boards in your PC. It also produces a power good signal that starts the boot process on your PC.

If you know a little about the power supplied to you by your electric company, then you may know about the fluctuations in the voltage delivered to you. Spikes and valleys in the power are common and (for the most part) expected. Because of those ups and downs, the best situation would be to have your PC's power supply condition the incoming power so it maintains an even level of supply, minus the peaks and surges.

In the real world, however, you probably won't see many power supplies that condition the power to smooth out spikes and valleys, unless you have a special application or are a connoisseur of fine power supplies. They cost several times more than the average unit available through your local computer store.

The power supply has two components that are important to you: the fan and the power connections.

The fan

The fan is the one moving component in most power supplies. It gets the most attention because it can be heard; it's usually mounted inside the case,with an opening to the outside. Fan noise is a constant complaint among PC users; some fans are so loud that some users have replaced a power supply for that reason alone.

Contrary to popular belief, the fan in the power supply is not designed to cool the entire inside space of the PC. Instead, it is designed to cool only the power supply itself (though it does provide air movement within most PCs).

Cooling the power supply is a critical role; overheating can cause damage and keep the power supply from functioning properly, resulting in significantly lower power output levels, data errors, and unreliable performance of the PC.

It is possible to replace the fan in the power supply, but if it hasn't been doing its cooling job effectively, it possibly has caused irreparable damage. I would advise you to replace the entire unit, not merely the fan. Most power supplies cost under $100 (many are under $50); besides, dangerous components inside the power supply can harm you if you touch them, even if the unit is off.

If the fan in your power supply is making noise, or if the amount of noise is increasing, this is a clue that the unit has a problem, and you may have to replace it.

The power connections

A standard power supply delivers its 5 or 12 volts of power to components in the PC via 4-pin connectors that snake out like arms on an octopus from a single location on the box (see Figure 10-1). A pair of multiwire connectors (usually labeled P8 and P9) are the only exception; these two fit together on a specially designed power connector on the motherboard of the PC as shown in Figure 10-2.

Preparation

When you upgrade your power supply, you must learn the wattage of your existing unit; then you can determine what you need to get. I offer advice on how to test the voltage your power supply is putting out now so that you know if it's working as it should, and some rules of thumb to help you determine what kind of power supply to get.

Determining the wattage of your current power supply

Open your computer and look at the label on your power supply to determine its wattage, as shown in Figure 10-3. Power supplies vary in wattage from 150 to 320 watts or more. Most PCs come with a 200-watt power supply.

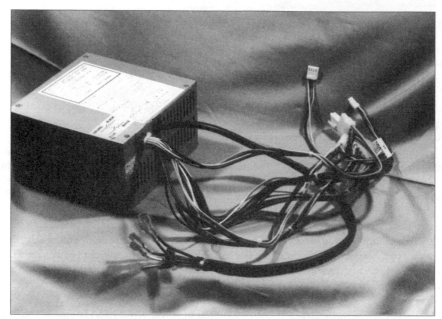

Figure 10-1: A typical PC power supply.

Figure 10-2: Standard power supplies have a pair of connectors sometimes labeled P8 and P9 that fit together on the motherboard.

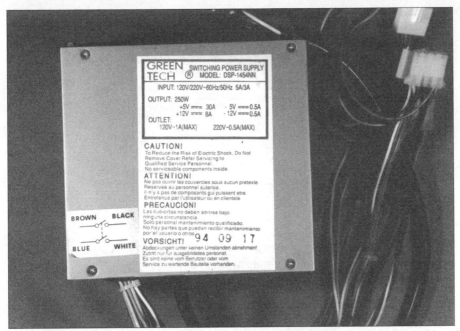

Figure 10-3: The wattage of the power supply is a three digit number followed by either the word *watts* or a W, as shown on this 250-watt unit.

Determining the wattage you need

Most PC makers put in a power supply adequate for the needs of the components installed in the machine — and no more. Therefore, if you plan to add components, consider upgrading to a larger power supply.

How big a unit should you add? You could examine each component, find the wattage numbers for each one, add up those numbers, and then determine whether your power supply can put out that wattage. It's easier, however, to use the following rules of thumb, understood as common sense in the PC business. For example, a 200-watt power supply is usually adequate for a system with a single hard disk drive and two floppy disk drives. However, a multimedia system (meaning a sound card and CD-ROM drive) should have a 230- to 250-watt power supply. A system loaded with components — several hard disk drives, two or more CD-ROM drives, network support, and other peripherals — should have at least a 300-watt power supply. Figure 10-4 offers a table of recommendations for power supply sizes with certain components.

If you are thinking of expanding your PC beyond what your current PC case can hold, you should know that it's standard practice to include a power supply with a new PC case. Such a unit is planned to be adequate to power all the devices you have room

If your system has the following components, your power supply should be...*

Component	Power supply
1 floppy disk drive 1 hard disk drive	200 watt
2 floppy disk drives 1 or 2 hard disk drives 1 CD-ROM drive 1 sound card	250 watt
More than 2 floppy disk drives or more than 2 hard disk drives or more than 1 CD-ROM drive	300 watt

*These are just guidelines. The power requirements for your system will vary.

Figure 10-4: This is a table of recommended power supply wattage for PC systems.

for in the case. So, if you buy the super-deluxe case that will hold four floppy drives, six hard disk drives, and so on, you're likely to get a 300-watt (or higher) power supply included.

What can happen if the system is underpowered

If your power supply is not adequate to feed the power demands of your system, you could experience symptoms ranging from boot problems to data loss. To understand why, you need to know what happens with a hard disk drive when the power supply is inadequate.

Remember that the hard disk drive rotates at a minimum of 3600 rotations per minute (RPM) the entire time your PC is on. (Some hard disk drives rotate at even higher speeds of 4200 RPM.) The 12-volt power keeps the motor in the hard disk drive spinning and moves the arm for the read/write heads. Commonly, there are variations in the power coming in, but if the 12-volt line falls below a certain point, that hard disk drive motor is not going to have the power to spin the platters fast enough or move the read/write heads to the correct point.

With several devices making demands on the power supply, if there's not enough power to go around, the most common scenario is intermittent errors. This causes random problems, such as the read/write head not making it to the right location before it starts writing data, or perhaps the platters were spinning slower so that the read/write head hit the platter, destroying data there, or perhaps there's not enough power for the read/write heads to read the boot information off the hard disk drive when the power first comes on. The likelihood of losing data that is important to you is high because the read/write heads are usually poised over data you've just accessed.

However, a power supply that can deliver more than your system needs is never a problem. You simply won't use the extra capacity, but you have plenty there for what you do need. You're always better off getting a larger power supply than you think you need.

Another factor is that newer components need less power. As the PC world moves to lower voltages and energy-saving devices, the demands on the power supply are fewer. If you're adding new components to a system, they are likely to use less power than the components currently in your system. You can always have power you don't use.

Testing the voltage

You can test to see whether your power supply is delivering the correct voltage. The easiest device to use in measuring voltage is a *digital multimeter,* available at almost any electronics store. Take one of the loose power leads, set the multimeter to DC, and insert the probes into the female pins. You should get something close to 12 volts on the right side, as shown in Figure 10-5, and close to 5 volts on the left as shown in Figure 10-6. Variances of .5 volts either way are not uncommon. On the 12-volt side, it's okay to see voltages between 11.5 and 12.5 volts; on the 5-volt side, readings between 4.5 and 5.5 volts are common. If either the 12-volt line or the 5-volt line drops below or goes above these thresholds, replace the power supply.

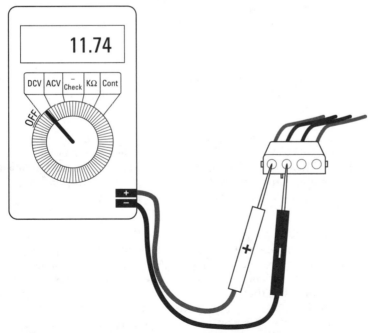

Figure 10-5: Measuring the voltage on the 12-volt line, the voltages can vary but should be within .5 volts either way.

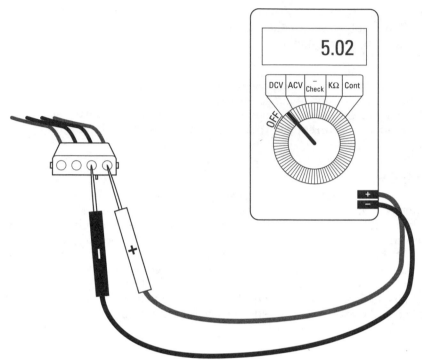

Figure 10-6: On the 5-volt line, measured voltages vary but should be within .5 either way.

Some power supplies can explode if they do not have a *load,* meaning that the power connectors must be attached to something when you turn the power supply on. You get your best test results if the power supply is at least connected to the motherboard and one other device (such as a floppy disk drive).

Of course, if the problems are intermittent, you may or may not identify them by testing your components this way. You can leave the multimeter connected, turn the PC off, and turn it back on to see what you're getting at boot up. You can also leave the case open and the multimeter connected, if that's practical for the way your PC is set up, and visually monitor the voltage while you're working.

Proprietary power supplies

One key to whether your system is proprietary is the type of power supply in your system. By proprietary, I mean that the manufacturer of your system has designed a power supply that has a special shape or special connectors. Sometimes this customizing is done because vendors feel that they can improve on the design of currently available power supplies. The power supply still delivers 12 volts and 5 volts and may connect to your components the same way, but the vendor has designed a custom power supply. Sometimes it's obvious that the power supply is proprietary, but other times there's some quirk (such as a special switch that is soldered into the power supply that reaches to the other side of the PC's case) that you won't notice until you attempt to remove the unit.

If you discover your power supply is proprietary, you have to get another power supply from the vendor or from someone who carries those specialized power supplies, which is going to cost you. Prices for these proprietary power supplies, assuming that you can get one, range from double to more than four times the price of the more widely used standard models. Figure 10-7 shows an example of a proprietary PC power supply.

Clues to help you spot a proprietary power supply:

1. The fan is outside the power supply in the case.

2. The connectors to the motherboard do not look like the connectors in Figure 10-2.

3. It's not "boxy" looking. If you're power supply is long and narrow, it's probably proprietary. (See Chapter 1.)

If you find out by examining your system that you have a proprietary power supply, you're probably better off calling around to computer suppliers before you remove the power supply. Have the manufacturer and model of your system handy when you call.

Figure 10-7: This proprietary power supply has a special built-in switch designed exclusively for this case.

Buying tips

Buying a power supply is not difficult, once you know what wattage you want. But here are a few helpful hints.

Take your old power supply with you when you buy a new one

Power supplies vary in exact size and shape depending on the case in which they're installed. For example, a power supply in a desktop PC can be different in size from a power supply in a mini-tower case, even if the wattage is the same. There aren't many variations, but there are enough that the only way for you to get a power supply that works in your system is to remove the old power supply and take it with you when you go to buy a new one. Then there's no guesswork. You simply go into the computer store and ask for a power supply like the one you have, but in the wattage that you require.

Also, be sure that you get the right number of small and large Molex power connectors. If you have the old power supply with you, it is easy to tell what you need and whether you need adapters. See Figure 10-2. (The illustrations in Chapters 4 and 5 also provide examples of these connectors and an explanation of the adapters.)

Check the power supply against the one you have before you buy

Sometimes a proprietary power supply looks like a standard one, but there's something proprietary about the power supply that isn't obvious until you get it out of the case. The following tip provides a list of checks to be sure your new power supply will fit your case.

To be sure that your new power supply will fit:

1. Compare the old and new power supplies for size. The sizes can be slightly different in some cases, but the screw holes for securing the power supply to the case should be in the same places or you won't be able to secure the new one into the case.

2. Compare the connectors for the power switch. Some power supplies have an on/off switch on the side. Most newer model power supplies have four wires with connectors that fit onto a switch for turning the PC off and on (see Figure 10-9 later in the chapter). If you have these types of wires, be sure that the wires are long enough to reach the switch.

3. In some desktop cases, the power supply is secured with hooks or mounting clips that slide into clips built into the bottom of the case. Turn the power supplies over and compare to be sure that the mounting clips are in the right places.

Installation

There are a few tricks to removing and installing a power supply, but the process can be done quickly and relatively easily. Here's how to remove the old power supply and install the new one.

Removing your old power supply

Obviously, it's important to turn the PC off. Ground yourself to the power supply so that you don't have to remove the power cord from the unit until the last moment. First remove the connections to the motherboard, then remove the power connections to the other drives, and then loosen the screws that hold the power supply to the case and lift it out.

Removing the power connectors from the motherboard

To remove the power connectors from the motherboard, take each one, pull straight up for about a quarter of an inch, then tilt the connector forward toward the power supply at a forty-five degree angle and pull it up and away from the motherboard, as shown in Figure 10-8.

Figure 10-8: It's easiest to remove the power supply connector by pulling it straight up for about a quarter inch, then tilting it forward at an angle to remove it.

Removing the power connectors from the drives

You may be able to remove the power connectors from the various drives in the system by pulling on them gently, but sometimes these connectors are stubborn. If they don't come loose easily, resist the urge to pull on the wires because you may pull one of the wires out of the connector. Instead, use needlenose pliers to grasp at the sides of the connector and pull it loose.

Removing the wires from the power switch

Some power supplies have a power switch built into the side, accessible from outside the case. Your power supply, however, may be connected via four colored wires to a switch mounted on the front of your PC. See Figure 10-9. Make note of the order of the wires on the switch, then remove the wires from the switch. You should be able to work the wires free by hand, but if they're stubborn, use your needlenose pliers. Try not to pull on the wires.

TIP

Be sure to make a diagram for yourself to determine which color wires go where so you can install the new power supply the same way. Because the wire order depends on the orientation of your switch, it is tough to get right if you don't write it down.

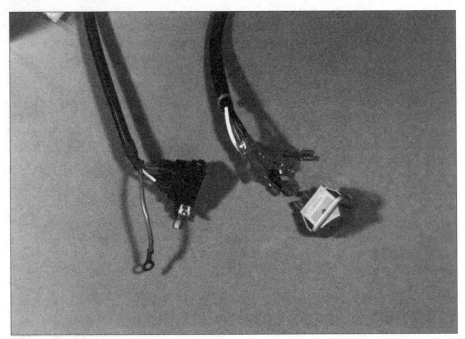

Figure 10-9: A couple of typical PC switches. The one on the left shows the switch with the four wires from the power supply connected.

Removing the screws that hold the power supply to the case

When you have the power cables free, take a screwdriver and remove the screws that hold the power supply to the case. There are usually four screws, which are most often accessible from the back of the PC case. Be sure to hang on to these screws because you need them to install the new power supply. If you lose one, tell the people at the store where you buy your power supply, because it's likely that they have some you can purchase.

Removing the power cord and sliding the power supply free

Now you can remove the power cord from the power supply. When you do, you are no longer grounded, so be careful not to touch any of the components of the PC.

If you remove the power supply from a desktop PC, be sure to slide it forward in the case, then lift it out. There are clips in the bottom of most desktop cases and mounting clips that fit those grooves in the power supply, so you must slide the power supply out of the clips in order to lift it from the case.

Installing the new power supply

When you've removed the old power supply and have taken it with you to get a new power supply, installing the unit is pretty much the opposite of removing it. Put the new power supply in the PC case, secure it with the screws you used to hold the old power supply, and connect the power cable to it. Avoid touching any of the other components of your system until the power cable is connected, and then be sure to ground yourself.

If you're working with a desktop case, slide the power supply in so that the mounting clips on the underside of the unit catch the clips in the bottom of the case. Then be sure to secure it with the screws you saved when you removed the old power supply. When the unit is securely mounted, attach the power cable and connect your grounding strap to it and to your wrist, as shown in Chapter 2.

When the power supply is connected, connect the P8 and P9 power connectors to the motherboard.

The black wires go together in the center when the P8 and P9 connectors are correctly connected, as shown in Figure 10-8. If you get this wrong, you can irreparably damage your motherboard.

When the motherboard connectors are on, reconnect power to the drives. The Molex connectors for the power go in only one way, which makes connection easier. The large Molex connectors have the corners rounded on the top, and the small Molex connectors have a notch to prevent improper insertion.

If you need more detailed illustrations for connecting the power cables to the drives, see Chapters 4 and 5.

The last task you may need to do is connect the power wires to the on/off switch. (If your on/off switch is on the power supply, then this is not an issue.) You should have already written down the wire order by color, so just reconnect the wires in the same way.

Now that your new power supply is connected, be sure to check that the ribbon cables are still securely connected to the drives and the cards. Sometimes things get pulled loose when you're grappling around inside your PC, and it's easier to catch it now than later. When you've checked things over, you're ready to fire up your PC and test your new power supply.

CASE STUDY

New power supply solves data loss

Henry's PC was behaving in an unusual manner. It wouldn't boot the first time he turned it on in the morning, but it would usually boot if he turned it off and back on again. Then he noticed an increasing volume of noise coming from the back of the PC.

Concerned, Henry consulted a friend, who mentioned that he should look into replacing the power supply. Henry was becoming increasingly convinced that the hard disk drive was at fault, as he began to notice that things he saved didn't appear to be there the next time he went in. Also, sometimes the PC would lock up in the middle of some task, and Henry would have to reboot several times to get it working again. This, of course, caused him more data loss, which concerned him enough to act.

Henry opened his PC at his power supply, noted that it had wires that attached to a switch in the front of his PC, and that it had four large and two small Molex connectors that powered his floppy disk drives and his CPU cooling fan. He went down to a local computer store to get a new power supply, but when they showed him the models they had, he realized he wasn't quite sure anymore about the size of his power supply.

When he returned, he opened up his PC and removed his current power supply. He had some trouble getting the power connections to the motherboard loose until he tilted the connectors forward, but everything else came loose fairly easily. He was careful to wear his grounding strap and remove the power cable last so that he was grounded while working. He also made careful notes about the color and position of the wires connected to the switch on the front before he removed those connections.

He took the old power supply down to his computer store and it took just a moment to match it to a new power supply. Henry decided to get a 230-watt power supply instead of the 200-watt he was replacing, because the cost was minimal and he was thinking about adding a second hard disk drive or an internal CD-ROM drive later.

Henry came back and installed the new power supply. He was cautioned at the computer store to be sure to put the black wires together when he placed the P8 and P9 connectors on the motherboard, and he was careful to do so. He was also sure to secure the new hard disk drive into the case and plug in the power cable, so he could ground himself while making the other connections.

When the new power supply was in, Henry checked the ribbon connections to the drives to be sure that nothing was loose, and then he turned on the PC. It booted immediately and looked fine, so he placed the cover back on the case. Henry was especially pleased as he noticed that next week that all the problems he'd been experiencing went away, including the bothersome fan noise.

Testing the new power supply

Most of the testing with a new power supply has to do with whether the PC works when you turn it on. If it boots normally, then it has passed the test. Although you can test the voltage output, most people don't until they're having a problem.

However, to make sure that your PC works, quickly test the floppy disk drive by putting a diskette in and reading it. You also can access any other hard disk drives installed other than the boot drive (that must be working or the system won't boot), just to be sure that you didn't accidentally pull a ribbon cable loose while you were inside. If everything works, then close up the case and congratulate yourself!

You can get more life out of your power supply if you follow the simple advice that follows.

The biggest enemy of the power supply is dust. Dust acts as an insulating blanket to keep heat in, and it can choke the performance of the fan. If you can remove the dust, you can often salvage a power supply that you thought you might have to replace.

Removing the dust is easy. You simply get a can of compressed air, available at any electronics store, open up the PC case, and blow the air through the power supply to blow the dust out. It's best to attempt to blow the dust through the power supply out of the PC if you can, but sometimes you have to blow the other way to blow dust off the fan. If you get dust in the case, then simply blow it out after you finish with the power supply.

If there's lots of dust and you get ambitious, you can take the power supply out (usually this can be done without disconnecting anything) and open it up to get the dust out. Be sure to disconnect the power cord that goes to your wall outlet and avoid touching anything inside the unit.

I've thoroughly cleaned several power supplies with compressed air and have gotten from a few months to several more years service. This kind of cleaning can reduce fan noise as well.

Installation in review

To upgrade your power supply, follow these steps:

1. Determine the wattage of your old power supply.

2. Determine the wattage you need.

3. Remove your old power supply. (Be sure to disconnect the power cable last because you want to stay grounded while you remove the other connectors.)

4. Install the new power supply.

5. Test the system by turning it on and attempting to access all the drives.

6. Close up the case.

Troubleshooting

If the new power supply didn't work and the system didn't come up when you started it, then here's a list of things to check.

Nothing happened when I turned on the power switch.

1. Check to make sure that you connected the power wires to the on/off switch, and be sure that you connected the wires correctly.

2. Make sure that the power cable is plugged into the power supply.

3. If you're using a surge protector, check it to make sure that it's on.

4. Make sure that you connected the P8 and P9 connectors to the motherboard correctly.

The floppy disk drive doesn't work.

You probably pulled one of the cables loose. Check the troubleshooting section in Chapter 4 on floppy disk drives.

The computer won't boot from the hard disk drive.

You probably pulled one of the hard disk drive cables loose. Check the hard disk drive troubleshooting section in Chapter 5.

Battery Upgrades

The battery in your PC offers many of the same functions as the battery in your watch. It maintains the time and date while the PC is off, and it supplies power to the CMOS so the information concerning the drive parameters as well as other CMOS settings are maintained. If the battery on your PC fails, your computer will forget the time, date, and even that it has a hard disk drive. If your battery is delivering too low a voltage or is installed backwards, it can cause the system to be finicky about booting up.

Rather than allowing the battery to fail at some unexpected moment, it's better to perform periodic checks to be sure that the battery is functioning at the required levels. If the battery's *service capacity* (meaning the amount of voltage it can deliver) drops below eighty percent or so, then it's best to simply replace the battery. This replacement can be done at your convenience, instead of in a crisis.

To give you an idea, an alkaline battery that simply sits on a shelf for two years can lose ten percent of its service capacity. So, if your PC is at least two years old, you should be checking your battery's capacity. Here's what you need to know to do that.

Preparation

In this section, you see the different types of batteries that are out there and how to spot the battery on your PC. You also see how to test the voltage by using a digital multimeter and what voltages are acceptable. Finally, you learn how you can make a copy of the CMOS information before you replace the battery, and how to restore the CMOS setup information.

Determining the type of battery you have now

As part of the preparation for a battery upgrade, you must determine the type of battery that's in your system now. Several types of batteries are used on motherboards. Some are lithium batteries that look like a small barrel and are soldered onto the motherboard as shown in Figure 10-10. Some are also the coin type batteries that can be either soldered (see Figure 10-11) or placed in a holder on the motherboard (see Figure 10-12). Some systems may have a battery pack of three AA or AAA alkaline batteries, such as the two packs shown in Figure 10-13. These batteries can be sold as a bundled pack or as a holder in which you can place standard alkaline batteries.

Figure 10-10: A lithium battery soldered into the PC motherboard.

Figure 10-11: A coin type battery soldered into the motherboard.

Figure 10-12: A coin type battery that's removable and easily replaced.

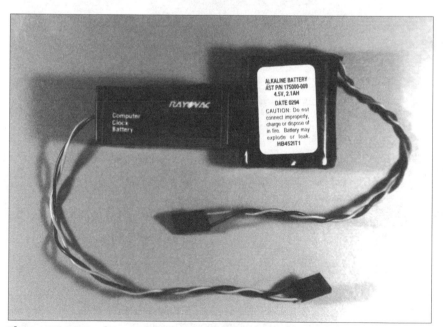

Figure 10-13: Replacement battery packs designed to fit into a special 3- or 4-pin male connector and be the external battery source on a motherboard.

The most reliable types are the real-time clock batteries and the Ni/Cad batteries. The real-time clock batteries look like a black rectangle and often have a small picture of a clock printed on top as shown in Figure 10-14. These can last up to ten years and if you have one, you can close up your PC and quit concerning yourself with your battery. You'll probably get tired of using the system before that battery fails.

The Ni/Cad batteries are not as reliable as the real-time clock batteries (Figure 10-15), but they do charge while the system is on, which means that you have less worry about failure. They can, however, wear out and corrode, so you must check them periodically.

Proprietary batteries

Some proprietary batteries have been designed by system manufacturers for certain name-brand PC systems. If you don't see a battery like the ones mentioned previously, you may have a system with a proprietary arrangement. This chapter helps you however, because the system designer may have built in a way to override the proprietary battery arrangement so that you can use a standard battery pack, or some some other way to upgrade the battery may exist. As usual, you need detailed system documentation, but much of what you read in the following pages still applies.

Figure 10-14: A real-time clock battery. These batteries can last as long as ten years, so if you have one, then there's no need to worry about the battery.

Figure 10-15: This Ni/Cad battery looks much like the barrel-shaped lithium battery, but it is recharged while the PC is in operation.

How to measure the voltage from your battery

To measure the service capacity of the battery you need your digital multimeter and a battery that has the positive and negative terminals available. Set the multimeter to DCV for direct current voltage, and place the red probe on the positive side and the black probe on the negative side. Usually there will be a plus and minus sign on each end. Look at the voltage readout and compare it to the voltage listed on the battery. Most PC batteries are 3.6-volt, although that can vary. (If you get it backwards, you get the voltage displayed as a negative value.)

How to determine if you should replace the battery

The rule of thumb is that if the measured voltage is lower than 20 percent of what the rating is on the battery, then you should replace the battery. For example, if the battery is a 3.6-volt battery, and you get less than 2.8 volts when you measure, then you need to replace the battery. Obviously, this is a judgment call. At 20 percent, you still have some time to replace the battery, but you should do so as soon as you can.

If you have a battery pack with individual batteries or a group of batteries together, it's going to be difficult to measure the voltage. Some battery packs, such as the one shown in Figure 10-13, have a date printed on them. If that date is more than two years old, you should just replace the pack. With batteries that fit into a holder, it's harder to tell, so if your PC is two years old, you should just plan to replace those batteries.

What to look for if the battery is soldered onto the motherboard

Most motherboards with batteries soldered on have an external battery connection that consists of two to four pins, as shown in Figure 10-10. These pins accommodate a battery pack, such as the ones shown in Figure 10-13. The rub is that sometimes you have to tell the system that the new battery pack is available. The battery on the motherboard is referred to as the *internal* battery, and the battery pack that attaches to the pins is called the *external* battery.

Some motherboard makers are considerate and provide the settings for you. Look for silk-screened jumper settings and labels for both the external battery pin connection and the jumper location and settings, as shown in Figure 10-16. However, some do not mark these for you, as shown in the example in Figure 10-17. Yet, when you know what you're looking for, it's fairly obvious that the jumper and the 3-pin male connection shown in Figure 10-17 are meant to handle an external battery.

When you understand a little about the conventions in this industry, it becomes easier to figure out the external battery connection. Even the manual that comes with the motherboard shown in Figure 10-17 doesn't document the J1 jumper and the J2 connection. But notice that the jumper and the 3-pin male connection are in physical proximity to the battery and power supply. Also note that the battery is labeled BT1. With these clues, you can assume that removing the shunt from the J1 jumper enables the J2 external battery connection.

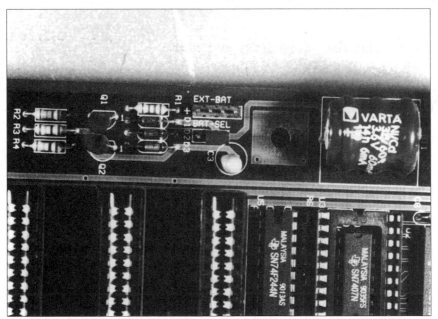

Figure 10-16: The external battery connection and the jumper to select the external battery are clearly marked. To change to the external battery, simply move the shunt on the jumper to the other side.

Figure 10-17: On this 486 motherboard, the external battery connection and the jumper setting are undocumented in the manual.

Some motherboards have no jumper near the battery at all, but have only a 3- or 4-pin male connection for an external battery. In cases such as these, the act of attaching an external battery usually disables the internal battery.

If you don't have the documentation for the jumper settings, and it's not silk-screened on the motherboard, the only thing you can do is make an educated guess. Failure of the internal battery is one of the top reasons people replace motherboards.

Of course, cases do exist where there is no external battery connection at all. In these cases, you can pay a technician to come out and solder in a connection for a battery pack that uses standard batteries, but it's usually cheaper to just replace the motherboard. (See Chapter 12 for how to replace the motherboard.)

Recording your CMOS settings

CMOS settings can be rather complicated, and if you remove your battery without a record of what those settings were, your system may never be the same. (You should have a record of these settings anyway, as mentioned in Chapter 1.)

You can print the CMOS settings. Enter the CMOS and, as you view each screen, press the Print Screen key on your keyboard to send the screens to the printer. Some strange looking symbols and shapes will appear, but you'll get the settings.

If you have a laser printer, you must have a full page of information before the printer will print. If you get to the end and there's still a page in the print buffer of your printer, you can send a page eject character to the printer.

To do this, get to the DOS prompt. Sending a page eject character to the printer will work from the DOS prompt in Windows as well. The MS-DOS Prompt icon is in the Main group in Windows 3.x, and in Windows 95, select Start⇨Programs⇨MS-DOS Prompt.

At the DOS prompt, type **ECHO ALT-12 > LPT1** and then press Enter. (To type Alt-12, be sure that the Num Lock is off, hold down the Alt key, type the number **12** on the numeric keypad, then let up on the Alt key. This generates the character that tells the laser printer to eject the page.) If you have the printer set to a different port, such as COM1, then substitute that port designation for LPT1.

Shareware and commercial programs exist that have save and restore utilities for the CMOS. The program reads the CMOS, stores the information to a file, and restores it from the file when you're ready. If you happen to have one of these utilities or have access to one, you may want to use it. The only way to be certain that you can restore the CMOS, however, is to have the settings on paper.

Battery buying tips

When you know the type of battery you have and whether you have external battery connectors, then you can shop for a replacement battery. Most PC batteries with the external battery connectors use three AA or AAA 1.5-volt batteries for a total of 4.5 volts, although you may be upgrading a 3.6-volt battery. One thing to watch for is that some of the external replacement battery packs have only two or three holes for pins in the molded plastic shunt that goes over the pins. This isn't a big crisis, because you can usually take a sharp object and easily poke through the plastic to make the additional holes you need. It's easier, however, if you have a 4-pin connector to get a battery pack that has four holes in the connector.

If you're replacing a coin battery be sure to write down the voltage, manufacturer, and any numbers on the battery itself. You may even want to take it with you so you're sure you get a replacement with the right size and thickness. When you have the battery you need, you can proceed with installation.

Installation

Installation of a battery upgrade is not difficult or time consuming, but it varies depending on the type of battery to which you're upgrading. Here you read about both the coin batteries and the external battery packs.

Installing a coin battery

Installation of a new battery is obvious when you're installing a coin battery into a holder. Just be sure to install the coin battery with the plus side up and be sure that it's securely placed into the holder.

Installing the battery pack upgrade

Most battery replacements require an upgrade to the external battery pack discussed in the preparation section. When you're upgrading to an external battery from an internal battery, there are a few things you have to watch for. One is making sure that you get the external battery connected to the pins so the polarity is correct. Another is getting the jumper settings changed so the external battery is the power source for the CMOS. You also need to secure the battery inside the case by using the Velcro patch supplied on the battery pack.

Correct connection of the battery pack

When connecting the battery pack shunt over the pins, one rule of thumb is that the red wire or positive lead should always be farthest from the power supply. If you have a connection where the pins are perpendicular to the power supply, so one pin is obviously farther from the power supply than the others, then this rule is easy to implement.

Testing for the ground pin

If the pins are parallel to the power supply, so no one pin is closer or farther away, then you must find the pin that's the ground and make sure that the black wire (or the negative lead) is over that pin. The sure-fire way to test for the ground is to take your multimeter and set it to the Continuity setting. Then place the negative or black test lead on the power supply (be sure that the power supply is not on, but is plugged in), and then put the red lead on each of the two outside pins (see Figure 10-18). When the multimeter beeps, then you know that the pin you touched is the ground and the black wire side of the battery pack connector should be on that side.

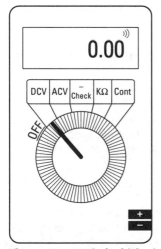

Figure 10-18: Find which pin is the ground using a digital multimeter in continuity mode. When you touch the correct pin, the multimeter beeps.

Setting the jumpers to the external battery setting

You need the documentation on the motherboard to know how to set the jumpers if the jumper settings aren't silk-screened onto the motherboard. You may find that there's one jumper near the battery connection, and you simply remove the shunt to "open" the jumper so that it doesn't make contact in order to switch to the external battery. Some jumpers have three pins, and you simply change the shunt to the other pair of pins to change to the external battery, as you can see in Figure 10-16. This may be documented as "1-2," meaning that the shunt goes over pins 1 and 2, or "2-3," meaning that the shunt goes over pins 2 and 3. There should be a small number 1 for pin one near that pin as a frame of reference.

If you don't have the documentation, and there's none silk-screened on the motherboard, then you can look for a jumper near the connection and try changing it to see whether it works. More than likely, that is the jumper you need to change. Just remember how it was so you can set it back if it doesn't work.

Securing the battery pack to the PC case or power supply

Most battery packs come with a Velcro tape attached that has a sticky tape on one side. The Velcro allows you to attach the battery to the side of the power supply or to the back of the case. Secure attachment of the battery pack is important because you don't just want the battery lying on the motherboard, and you want it out of the way.

Restoring the CMOS settings

When the battery is in, it's time to restart the PC and enter the CMOS menu to restore the settings. If you're fortunate, you may find that the CMOS settings are unchanged and you can simply verify the information. However, you may have to restore the settings from the printed material you made before you started this operation. Be sure to change the time and date settings in the CMOS to the correct settings before you leave, and be sure to save your changes.

When you finish, you can let the PC reboot normally. Everything should come up the way it was before you started.

The acid test

To begin the acid test (whether your battery installation was successful), turn the PC on. When you've confirmed that the system is working, turn it off, wait 5 to 10 seconds, and turn it on again. If the battery has backed up the CMOS settings, then the PC should boot normally.

Removing the internal battery (optional)

Some technicians feel as though it is bad practice to leave an internal battery still soldered to the motherboard. Old batteries are notorious for leaking acid that destroys the circuit boards to which they originally supplied power. You can take a pair of wire cutters and snip off the old battery and dispose of it. Just be sure that the power is off and you're grounded while you perform this operation.

Installation in review

To upgrade your PC battery, follow these steps:

1. Open the PC and determine the type of battery you have. If you have a battery pack, it should be replaced every two years. If you have a real-time clock, you don't need to go any further.

2. Measure the voltage. If the voltage is lower than the service capacity listed on the battery, it should be replaced.

3. Check the motherboard for an external battery connector if the battery you have now is soldered onto the motherboard.

4. Check the motherboard and the documentation for your system for the jumper that disables the internal battery, if you have a soldered battery.

5. Print the CMOS settings.

6. Purchase a new battery.

7. Install the new battery. Change the jumper settings to enable an external battery, if you've installed one.

8. Restart the system and restore the CMOS settings. Exit saving the changes and allow the system to boot.

9. Turn the PC off, wait 5 to 10 seconds, and turn it on again to see whether the battery is maintaining power to the CMOS.

10. Close the PC case.

Some BIOSs have a password-protection feature for the CMOS menu. If you lose the password to the CMOS, one way to gain access again is to disable or remove the battery for about 24 hours. (Remember that you can usually disable an internal battery by changing a jumper setting.) Of course, the CMOS forgets everything, but it also forgets that there was a password and lets you back in.

Incorrect battery installation causes intermittent problem

Cecil had a new clone PC that he bought from a friend, but after a short time, he found himself with a troublesome problem. The PC wouldn't boot consistently each time he started it. But when the machine booted, it appeared to run fine. Cecil quickly learned how to restore the CMOS settings, because sometimes the settings were gone when he rebooted the machine.

Cecil took the PC to several computer repair facilities, but he was unable to duplicate the problem when he had the machine on-site. Being interested in computer repair anyway, Cecil decided to take a computer repair course.

During the course, students were invited to bring in their PCs that needed attention, so Cecil brought in his. The instructor said it appeared to be a problem with the battery. Cecil had an external battery pack in his PC, so the instructor suggested that he replace the external battery pack with a new one. Cecil removed the external battery pack and was careful to note the position of the wires so that he could install the new battery pack the same way.

But the problem persisted, and the instructor suggested a continuity test on the pins for the battery pack to be sure that it was installed correctly. The instructor turned off the PC, made sure that it was plugged in, removed the battery connection from the pins, and then showed Cecil how to use the digital MultiMate for the continuity.

The instructor had Cecil set the MultiMate on CON, and then Cecil touched the black (or negative) probe to the power supply as a ground while touching the red (or positive) probe to pins of the external battery connection. When touching one of the pins, the tester emitted a beep, so then the instructor told Cecil that he could be sure that that pin was the ground pin.

Cecil realized he'd placed the new battery in backwards, so he reinstalled the battery, placing the black wire side of the connection so that it made contact with the ground pin. He then restarted the PC, and it booted without a problem. He also remembered that he'd been careful to connect the new battery the same way as the old battery, and he realized that this had been a problem from the beginning. Cecil was skeptical that something fixed so easily could be the only problem, but after a week of no problems, he was convinced.

Troubleshooting

Here are some common scenarios that can occur after a battery replacement and some help for you to uncover and correct the problem.

The PC won't boot.

1. Check to be sure that the battery is installed correctly. Coin batteries can sometimes be difficult to get back in so they make good contact, so check this carefully. Be sure that the negative wire from the battery pack is connected to the ground pin of the battery connection.

2. Check to be sure that the jumper settings are correct.

The PC boots sometimes and not others.

This can be a tell-tale sign that the battery was installed backwards so the positive and negative are reversed. See number 1 under "The PC won't boot."

Troubleshooting Practice: What's Wrong in These Photos?

Figure 10-19: See answer 1.

Figure 10-20: See answer 2.

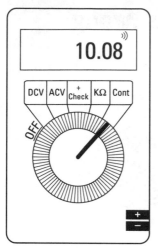

Figure 10-21: See answer 3.

Answers:

1. The power connector to the motherboard is backwards! The black wires should be together in the center. This arrangement can toast the motherboard if the PC is turned on!

2. The internal battery is corroded and has leaked acid onto the motherboard. This usually requires replacement of the motherboard.

3. This power supply's 12-volt line only measures 10 volts output. Even if the 5-volt line measures within normal parameters, this power supply should be replaced.

Summary

✦ If you plan to add multimedia or several other components to your PC, you should consider adding a higher wattage power supply as well.

✦ Proprietary power supplies can be difficult to find. Even if your power supply is not proprietary, you should take it with you when purchasing an upgrade so you can be sure that the new power supply fits.

✦ Many PC motherboards have an option that allows you to install an external battery and disable the one soldered onto the motherboard.

✦ Be sure to back up your CMOS before installing a new battery.

✦   ✦   ✦

Multimedia Upgrades

In This Chapter

✦ Determining the correct multimedia hardware for your system

✦ Uncovering barriers to your upgrade before you start

✦ Getting Plug and Play hardware working in DOS/Windows 3.*x*

✦ Installing a CD-ROM drive

✦ Saving cash on a multimedia upgrade

Tools Needed

✦ Phillips screwdriver

✦ Antistatic mat (recommended)

I f you haven't seen anything about multimedia lately, you haven't been paying attention. *Multimedia* is a combination of sound and pictures, usually involving animation and video. From an upgrade viewpoint, multimedia is the addition of a sound card, speakers (which connect to the sound card), and a CD-ROM drive. With a sound card, you have the capability to listen to and record your own sounds, including voices and music. In addition, a CD-ROM drive opens up a whole world of software that was too cumbersome to be distributed on floppy diskettes, such as encyclopedias, games, and complex software. It also opens the door for interactive help and tutorials for training.

Adding multimedia capability to your PC can be less expensive than you may think. This chapter covers the installation of the components you need for multimedia. It explains the components themselves and how they interact, as well as how to install, test, and troubleshoot them. It also covers the installation under DOS, Windows 3.*x*, and Windows 95.

To help you prepare for this chapter, read Chapters 4, 5, 8, 11, and 13. Chapter 4 (adding a floppy disk drive) and Chapter 5 (hard disk drive upgrades) help you with the CD-ROM drive installation portion of this chapter. You'll also find Chapter 8 helpful for the explanation of the various expansion slots in the PC and how to install cards into your PC. The information in Chapter 9 on fax/modem upgrades helps you familiarize yourself with the concept of interrupts (IRQs) and memory addresses. Because a multimedia upgrade almost always involves changes to your PC's environment files, you find an explanation in Chapter 13 as to what the environment files are and how to edit these files should the need arise. You also find information on how to create a rescue diskette.

Preparation

Because a multimedia upgrade *will* make changes to your environment files, one of the first preparation steps you need to take is creating a rescue diskette.

In addition, a multimedia upgrade is like three upgrades in one, because often you're installing a sound card, a CD-ROM drive, and a game port. Rather than attempting to deal with all three components at once, take them one at a time — beginning with the sound card.

The sound card

A sound card is a circuit board that fits into an expansion slot on your PC. It can take analog signals such as those from a microphone or other recording device and deliver them to the PC in a digital input that can be stored, usually on the hard disk drive. The sound card can also reverse the process, taking digital signals recorded in the proper format and translating them into audio.

Sound terminology

Sound cards are categorized by the number of notes they can play back simultaneously. Designations of 8-bit, 16-bit, and 32-bit mean the sound card can play back 8 notes, 16 notes, or 32 notes simultaneously. Don't confuse this capability with the physical interface of the card to the computer, such as 8-bit cards that fit into an 8-bit or XT slot on the motherboard, or 16-bit cards that fit an ISA slot. A 32-bit sound card can play 32-bit sound even if it fits into a 16-bit ISA slot.

Sound card jacks and connectors

If you have a cassette recorder or a portable cassette player, you recognize the jacks on the back of the sound card, as shown in Figure 11-1. These jacks use the standard audio connectors found on devices such as microphones, speakers, and CD players. This sound card has two input jacks and two output jacks. The card also has a 15-pin female *musical instrument digital interface (MIDI)* connector to which you can connect a joystick or a MIDI device such as an electronic keyboard.

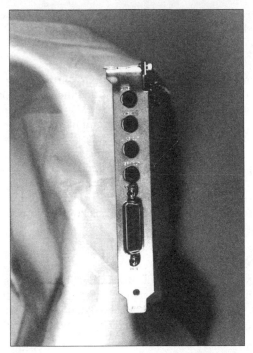

Figure 11-1: Most new sound cards have four jacks and a MIDI port.

Sound card memory address and IRQ issues

As you may remember from Chapter 9, every device that requires attention from the CPU must have a memory address and an *interrupt request line (IRQ)* so it can interrupt the CPU. Because only 16 interrupts exist on a PC, the number of devices that you can add with your own IRQ is limited.

Most sound cards use IRQ 7 or IRQ 5; as you may remember from Chapter 8, these two interrupts are used most often by parallel (LPT) ports. Because most sound cards are Plug and Play, the software that comes with the sound card attempts to find a free IRQ for you. You should, however, check for a free interrupt to use with your sound card if you have a second parallel port, a modem, or a network card. You can do this with MSD, as shown in Chapter 9.

You can also see the IRQs in use under Windows 95 by selecting Start➪Settings➪ Control Panel➪System➪Device Manager. Make sure that View devices by type is selected, and then highlight Computer in the window and select Properties. When the Computer Properties window opens, select Interrupt Request to see the IRQs.

Software drivers for the sound card

For the sound card to work, you must load a *driver* that will handle the interaction between the operating system and the sound card. Load the driver via the environment files. Load the sound card drivers either in the AUTOEXEC.BAT or CONFIG.SYS file, depending on the installation software. The installation also adds several statements to the AUTOEXEC.BAT file to set up the environment for the sound card.

Upgradeable sound cards

Several vendors place emphasis on the upgradeability of their sound cards. These upgrades include adding memory or adding a daughterboard. Added memory boosts the performance of the sound card. Usually it takes the form of SIMMs placed directly into SIMM slots on the card. For more information about SIMMs and memory upgrades, see Chapter 6.

A daughterboard is installed in a slot parallel to the sound card and connected to the card via a ribbon cable. Most daughterboards add wave-table synthesis and MIDI playback capability. These daughterboards are often called *wave* or *wave-table* boards. The addition of a wave-table board enables you to synthesize and play back the sounds made by various musical instruments.

Sound cards with an IDE interface

Sound cards have been available that would support a CD-ROM drive, but this has always been tempered by incompatibilities among the various types of CD-ROM drive interfaces. You had to be careful what CD-ROM drive you purchased; often you were limited to multimedia upgrade kits. A typical such kit included the sound card and the CD-ROM drive it would support.

That limitation preceded the development of CD-ROM drives that met the AT-Attachment Packet Interface (ATAPI) for *integrated drive electronics* (IDE) drives. This advancement solves the problem of incompatible CD-ROM drives; as long as the drive is ATAPI/IDE-compatible, it works with a sound card that has an ATAPI/IDE interface. The ATAPI/IDE standard also allows CD-ROM drives to be connected to standard IDE controllers.

As with any IDE interface, the IDE interface on a sound card also requires an IRQ. This IRQ is usually IRQ 10 or 11, although the hardware can use other IRQs.

Audio out

Most sound cards, with or without an IDE interface, have an audio connector for the CD-ROM drive. By using the cable that comes with the CD-ROM drive, you can connect the audio output that would normally come out of the jack in front of the CD-ROM drive. With this new connection, audio output comes out through your PC speakers via the sound card. Using the software that controls the sound card, you can treat the CD-ROM drive like an audio CD player and play music from your PC speakers. Some sound cards offer several cable connections for audio output from the CD to support the most widely used CD-ROM drives. These connections are sometimes labeled "audio input" or "CD in."

The CD-ROM drive

CD-ROM stands for *compact disc read-only memory* and is sometimes called a *laser disc* drive. A CD-ROM drive uses a beam of light (the laser) to read data sealed into tough, plastic discs. The biggest advantage to a CD-ROM disc is that it can hold upwards of 600MB of data on one side.

The problem with CD-ROM drives was, at first, speed. Much slower than hard disk drives, CD-ROM drive speeds are designated in multiples of the original data transfer rate (150 kilobytes per second), which is known now as a *single-speed* drive. Double-speed drives (or 2X drives) are faster at 300 kilobytes per second; triple-speed drives (or 3X drives) run at 450 kilobytes per second, quad drives (or 4X drives) at 600 kilobytes per second, 6X drives at 900 kilobytes per second, and 8X drives at 1,200 kilobytes per second. Other speed measurements exist for CD-ROM drives (such as average access time), but drive speeds are fastest and are used for comparison.

The CD-ROM drive interface

The majority of CD-ROM drives sold now have an *integrated drive electronics (IDE)* interface— the same interface used for your hard disk drive. Now you can install and treat your CD-ROM drive as you would a hard disk drive. Most of these drives are also internal and fit nicely into a 5 1/4-inch drive bay — which means you need such an opening on your PC case to install the CD-ROM drive (see Chapter 4).

You may be able to install the CD-ROM drive to an existing IDE controller on your system. This idea is especially good if you have two IDE hard disk controllers on your system; you can use the second controller for your CD-ROM drive. Installation of the CD-ROM drive onto the second IDE controller is the preferred method; a CD-ROM drive on the same controller as a hard disk drive can slow down the access time of the hard disk drive. Also, using the second IDE controller avoids master/slave issues with the CD-ROM drive and eliminates the need for an IDE interface on your sound card.

If you don't have a spare 5 1/4-inch drive bay, you can obtain an external CD-ROM drive, but you have trouble finding an external IDE CD-ROM drive. You also have to obtain a special controller card for such a drive — and you need to install it separately from the sound card. Although you should follow the instructions on the external drive you obtain, much of the information here still helps with the installation.

Direct memory access (DMA)

Most mass-storage devices on a PC, such as hard disk drives, bypass the CPU via a channel directly into memory called *direct memory access* (DMA). Fewer DMA channels exist than IRQs. In fact, most PCs have between three and five DMA channels; these are often used by disk drives, network cards, optical scanners, and CD-ROM drives. Although there is such a thing as a shared DMA channel (known as *virtual* DMA), most DMA channels are not shared.

CD-ROM drives usually use DMA channel 1 (the low DMA) or DMA channel 3 (the high DMA). Without diagnostic software built for looking at DMA channels, you cannot easily tell what DMA channels are being used if you're running MS-DOS or Windows 3.1. However, you can guess that one or more DMA channels are in use if your system is running an optical scanner or a network card. Most software used for installing a CD-ROM drive under DOS or Windows 3.1 looks for a free DMA channel; you have to rely on it to find one. If, however, you're running Windows 95, you can easily see the DMA channels in use.

You can look at the DMA channels in use with Windows 95. To do this, select Start⇨Settings⇨Control Panel⇨System⇨Device Manager. Make sure that View devices by type is selected, highlight Computer in the window, and select Properties. The Computer Properties window opens. Select Direct Memory Access and then the View Resources tab to see what is currently being used, as shown in Figure 11-2.

Software drivers for the CD-ROM drive

CD-ROM drives require not one, but two drivers loaded in the environment files, one in the CONFIG.SYS file and the other in the AUTOEXEC.BAT file. The driver loaded in CONFIG.SYS is provided by the drive's manufacturer. A second driver in AUTOEXEC. BAT is usually the Microsoft driver, MSCDEX.EXE. Although the manufacturer of the CD-ROM drive may provide a driver instead of MSCDEX.EXE, this driver is easier to use and install and is highly compatible with software applications. Use it if you have a choice.

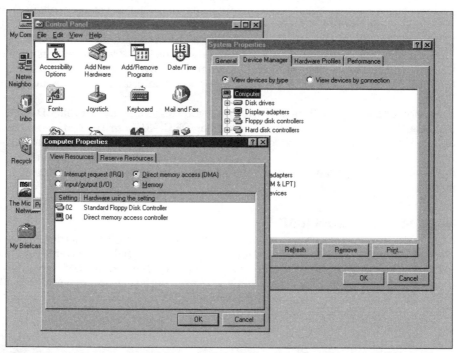

Figure 11-2: Windows 95 enables you to view the DMA resources of your system.

The driver loaded into the CONFIG.SYS file is a *real-mode* driver that requires use of the lower 1MB of memory on your PC. The AUTOEXEC.BAT driver is a *protected-mode* driver — you can load it into high memory. Although the roles of these drivers are changing, use of the term *real mode driver* frequently refers to the driver supplied by the vendor and loaded in the CONFIG.SYS. The term *protected-mode driver* usually refers to the driver in the AUTOEXEC.BAT. This protected-mode driver can be supplied by the vendor, or you can use MSCDEX.

The majority of the time, these drivers are loaded for you by the installation software that comes with the CD-ROM drive. You should allow the installation software to load the drivers, as this usually requires setting several parameters in the command line.

The CD-ROM driver dynamically allocates a drive letter to the CD-ROM drive during the boot sequence. That drive letter is the last drive letter available, and it changes only if you add another hard disk drive to your system.

Because Windows 95 handles memory differently, it can load the real-mode driver from the CONFIG.SYS file into high memory; it supplies its own protected-mode driver. Thus, although it doesn't need the MS-DOS MSCDEX driver normally loaded in the AUTOEXEC.BAT file, it still allocates a drive letter to the CD-ROM drive in the same way.

Windows 95 handles CD-ROM drivers differently

Randi upgraded to Windows 95 on a PC with a Sony CD-ROM drive. She was curious and a little nervous about how Windows 95 would handle her CD-ROM drive and drivers. She wanted to keep her old MS-DOS 6.22 and Windows 3.1, so she created a multiple-boot configuration. The Sony CD-ROM drive used a second IDE interface on the system board.

After she created a rescue diskette and backed up her system, Randi created the multiple-boot configuration by starting the Windows 95 installation from inside Windows 3.1; she used the File⇨Run command in Program Manager. When she got the chance to do so during the installation, she directed Windows 95 to be installed in the C:\WIN95 directory instead of the C:\WINDOWS directory.

After the installation, Randi started SYSEDIT to see how Windows 95 had changed her environment files. What she saw, shown in Figure 11-3, was that Windows 95 had loaded her real-mode CD-ROM driver into high memory and commented out (using the REM command) her MSCDEX driver altogether. Upon testing the drive, however, she found it worked fine. In fact, it started some of her CD-ROM-based programs when she inserted the CD into the drive. She later discovered that this was due to a special program, the AUTORUN.INF file, on these CDs that worked in combination with a setting in Windows 95.

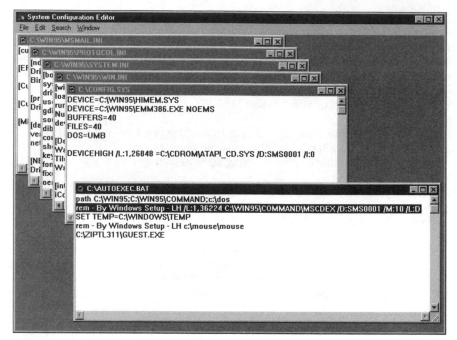

Figure 11-3: Windows 95 handles the CD-ROM drivers in a DOS/Windows 3.1/Windows 95 multiple-boot configuration.

But now Randi's big concern was whether her CD-ROM drive would still work in Windows 3.1, now that the driver was commented out. She restarted the computer, pressed F8 when she saw the `Starting Windows 95` message, and chose her previous version of MS-DOS from the list of options. She typed **WIN** to start Windows 3.1, which started just as it had before. She then tried to access her CD-ROM drive and found that she could do so with no problem. When she looked at her environment files, the device drivers were present, with no REM statement in front of the driver in the AUTOEXEC.BAT file. Randi was impressed that Windows 95 handled her CD-ROM drivers so deftly.

The MIDI connector

Most sound cards come with a 15-pin female connector known as the *musical instrument digital interface* (MIDI) connector or *joystick/MIDI connector*. This connector is the same one shown in Figure 11-1. It can be used to attach a joystick, two joysticks (using a *Y* adapter), or a MIDI device such as an electronic keyboard. With the correct software, and with a MIDI-equipped electronic keyboard attached to this port, you can do things such as play music on the keyboard that your PC transforms into sheet music (or vice-versa).

Sometimes this connector is called a *Gameport* because you can attach a joystick to it. If this port is not on a sound card, however, it is not a MIDI port and cannot be used for MIDI applications.

If you want to use a joystick, you must purchase one. When the sound card is working, you can attach the joystick to the port and it should work as well.

Looking inside your system

By this time, you should be familiar with taking a look inside your system before you purchase a component. In this case, you're looking for free expansion slots into which you can place your sound card. You're also looking for enough case space for a 5 1/4-inch CD-ROM drive and a second IDE controller. If you've looked over Chapters 4, 5, and 8, then you know what to look for in terms of expansion slots, drive space, and that second IDE controller.

If you have a second IDE controller, you have decisions to make. You can purchase a sound card without an IDE interface and use the second IDE controller on your motherboard for the CD-ROM drive. If you get a sound card with an IDE interface, you probably won't have the system resources available for adding a *third* IDE controller to your system. This means that you have to either disable the IDE controller on the sound card or the second controller on your motherboard. If you prefer to use the IDE controller on your sound card, it will probably be easier to get the CD-ROM drive working with the second IDE controller on your motherboard first, then switch the CD-ROM drive to your sound card IDE and disable the second IDE on your motherboard.

You can probably disable the second IDE controller through the BIOS or through jumpers on the motherboard. The easiest way is through the BIOS; look at your CMOS menu for that second controller and find out how to disable it. Don't disable it until you must. If you have a Plug and Play BIOS, the installation process may do the disabling for you.

Make sure you have a power cable for the CD-ROM drive. If not, get a splitter and split the power for the CD-ROM drive from one of the floppy disk drives, instead of a hard disk drive.

Buying tips

Almost any sound card you buy is going to be much like the ones shown in Figure 11-4; an IDE CD-ROM drive looks like the one shown in Figure 11-5. Look for a sound card and CD-ROM drive that fit your needs and the components in your system. If you're running Windows 95, you probably want to get a Plug and Play (PnP) sound card that Windows 95 can configure for you. (You find more information on PnP cards later in this chapter.) You can expect to pay $80 to $150 for a sound card with an IDE interface, and $50 to $200 for a CD-ROM drive, depending on the speed of the drive.

Figure 11-4: Two PnP sound cards with IDE interfaces are shown. One is a Sound Blaster and the other is a clone that's Sound Blaster-compatible.

Figure 11-5: Here's a Sony internal IDE CD-ROM drive.

Software requirements

As with any other software, multimedia software titles have hardware requirements printed on the box. A multimedia title you want to run may require a 4X CD-ROM drive and 16-bit sound. It works better with a faster CD-ROM drive and a 32-bit sound card, but it probably won't run as well or at all with less than those requirements. So, if you have software in mind when performing your upgrade, make sure you're adding components to meet or exceed the software's requirements.

Most multimedia upgrade kits contain a sound card with an IDE controller on the card, an internal CD-ROM drive, a set of speakers, and usually multimedia software titles. Before you buy, compare prices; are the kits really cheaper than buying the individual items separately, especially if the software titles in the kits do not interest you?

Compatibility

Plenty of companies are making sound cards, but unless you have some special need for especially high-quality sound, your best bet is to get a sound card that is Sound Blaster Pro-compatible. Sound Blaster is a product of Creative Labs and is the most widely supported card in the PC industry. So, you should look on the box of the card you want to buy to see whether it's Sound Blaster-compatible.

Windows 3.*x* and Windows 95 both have software drivers for the most popular sound cards. These drivers should work on any card that says it's compatible with a card supported by Windows. Software drivers should come with the card as well, although it's less trouble to use the drivers in Windows.

CD-ROM purchase tips

When you purchase an internal CD-ROM drive, you need a 40-pin cable (such as a hard disk drive cable), an audio connector, and rails and screws to secure the drive into the case, depending on the type of case you have. The cables—both the 40-pin and the audio—should come with the CD-ROM drive. You may have to purchase a rail kit to get the screws and rails to install the drive into a drive bay.

You should also get a disk with the manufacturer's software driver and installation routine on it.

Plug and Play advice

The industry is getting away from *legacy* cards — that is, add-on cards with jumpers or switches for IRQ, DMA, and memory address assignments. Instead, the PC world is moving toward software selectable settings known as *Plug and Play* (PnP). This move enables an operating system designed for PnP, such as Windows 95, to dynamically allocate resources each time the system starts.

PnP also enables you to install a new sound card or other PnP cards, and then simply start the PC and allow Windows 95 to find your new hardware and set it up. Such an arrangement does require that you have the diskettes or CD-ROM used to install Windows 95, but if you have the resources free for the card you want to install, the process is nearly painless.

Previous versions of MS-DOS and Windows 3.x don't dynamically allocate resources; neither does the MS-DOS mode in Windows 95. Dealing with PnP cards can be more difficult in these environments.

If you're not running Windows 95, but you have a PnP card, you must still specify the settings for that card each time the system boots up. Making the settings requires a driver in the CONFIG.SYS file. For the driver in the CONFIG.SYS file to know what the settings are, you must run a utility program when you install the PnP card that sets up a file with the configuration information the driver uses each time the system reboots.

The most popular driver for configuration is the *Intel Configuration Manager,* known as *ICM,* and its counterpart utility for setting up the configuration is the *ISA Configuration Utility* (ICU). You may find these files on your PC or distributed on the diskettes with your sound card. If ICM has been used previously to set up PnP hardware on your system, you know because a C:\PLUGPLAY directory is on your hard disk drive and the following statement appears in your CONFIG.SYS file:

```
DEVICE=C:\PLUGPLAY\DRIVERS\DOS\DWCFGMG.SYS
```

Due to conflicts with the BIOS of some systems and the ICM and ICU utilities, several vendors have come up with their own configuration driver and configuration utility for their PnP cards. Using these can add yet another device line to your CONFIG.SYS file to configure PnP cards from a particular vendor.

The bottom line here is that it's easier to run Windows 95 if you're going to use PnP hardware. If you cannot run Windows 95, then you should seriously consider getting a sound card with jumpers or switches. If you cannot do that, you should check with the vendor of the PnP card you're considering to see whether the vendor offers a driver and utility for that particular card. The best place to check is online. Access the vendor's homepage on the Internet or contact a BBS so that you can download these tools.

Return policy

As with any purchase, you should find out what the store's return policy is before you buy. It should be written down. If the written policy is different from what the salespeople tell you, get them to write down what they're telling you on your receipt and initial it.

Question: If I have a Plug and Play (PnP) BIOS, do I have to get a PnP sound card?

Answer: No, although you'll probably be hard-pressed to find a new sound card that's not PnP.

Question: If I don't have a PnP BIOS, can I still use a PnP sound card?

Answer: Yes, but the most important part of Plug and Play is a PnP operating system such as Windows 95. If you're not running Windows 95, it's easier to either upgrade to Windows 95 or avoid PnP cards.

Installation

You've looked over your system. You've bought your sound card, CD-ROM drive, and all the necessary cables. Now you're ready to begin installation.

Installing the sound card and CD-ROM drive

You should review Chapter 8 so that you know how to install a card in a system. If your sound card has an IDE interface to which you're cabling a CD-ROM drive, you may find it easier to attach the ribbon cable and the audio cable to the card before you install the card into the expansion slot. When you have attached the ribbon cable and audio output, your sound card should look like the one shown in Figure 11-6.

Figure 11-6: A sound card with the IDE CD-ROM drive cabled to it and the audio cable attached.

If you're installing a sound card with jumpers or switches, set those now. You should know which system resources are free, such as the IRQs (although you may not know the DMA settings or memory addresses that will work if you're running DOS/Windows 3.*x*). You may have to pull the card out, change the settings, and reinsert the card several times to find the correct settings. When you do find them, write them down in the documentation that came with the card; add the date, and then file the documentation away for reference when you complete the installation.

As soon as you set any jumpers or switches, attach the speakers to the sound card. Frequently, PC speakers connect to each other with a single stereo connector to the sound card. Be sure to connect the speakers to the correct jack, or you won't get the sound output.

TIP

You can use amplified speakers without power or batteries with most sound cards. Simply plug the jack into the speaker out jack. Be sure that the speakers are turned off or they won't work this way. If you have amplified speakers with power, you can connect them to the line out jack.

Watch for the same issues when attaching the ribbon cable to the CD-ROM drive as you do in Chapter 5 with a hard disk drive, including watching for pin 1. Attach the audio output cable to the CD-ROM drive from the sound card. Attach a power cable from the power supply to the CD-ROM drive. With the ribbon cable, audio output, and power cable attached, the CD-ROM drive should look something like the one shown in Figure 11-7. As with a hard disk drive installation, don't secure the CD-ROM drive into the case until you're sure it's going to work.

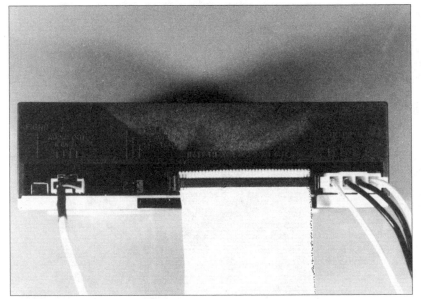

Figure 11-7: An IDE CD-ROM drive with the ribbon cable, audio out cable, and power cable attached.

Fortunately, with the installation of a CD-ROM drive, you do not have to go into the BIOS and set parameters as you do with a hard disk drive. If you're installing the card to a second IDE controller on your motherboard, be sure the controller is enabled in the CMOS menu.

Installing the software under DOS/Windows 3.x

Start with the installation of the CD-ROM software, because some sound cards require that you use the CD-ROM drive to install software included with the sound card. After you've tested the CD-ROM drive and it's working, you can go on to the sound card software installation.

As for the CD-ROM drive, Windows 3.x recognizes the drive after it is correctly configured under DOS. The INSTALL or SETUP program (found on the diskette that came with the CD-ROM drive) guides you through the installation and modifies the appropriate environment files for you.

If you're installing a PnP sound card, you must first install a configuration manager and a utility before you run the actual sound card installation program. You're most likely to run into the ICM and ICU. (Be aware that the ICU does not work in a system with an EISA bus.)

ICM creates a PLUGPLAY directory on your hard disk drive and copies files into that directory. It also adds the configuration device driver to your CONFIG.SYS file that sets up your PnP card each time the system boots. The driver is a line in your CONFIG.SYS file that looks something like this: `DEVICE=C:\PLUGPLAY\DRIVERS\DOS\DWCFGMG.SYS`. The ICU creates a data file, ESCD.RF, in the root directory of your hard disk drive that the configuration device driver uses to set up your PnP cards each time you reboot your system.

When you have completed this step, you can go on with the installation of the actual sound card driver. As with the CD-ROM installation, you run the INSTALL or SETUP program from the diskette that configures the sound card for you. If you have not set up ICM and ICU, the installation informs you and does not allow you to continue.

In addition to the environment files, have a copy of the ICM and ICU — as well as a copy of the ESCD.RF file and any other utilities or device drivers used to set up your sound card — on a new rescue diskette. (That's the rescue diskette you're going to create after you get all this set up and working.)

Installing a sound card under Windows 95

If you've installed a PnP sound card and a CD-ROM drive, the easiest thing to do is start Windows 95 with your installation CD-ROM or diskettes ready. Windows 95 is pretty good at recognizing and configuring sound cards, CD-ROM drives, and even game ports.

If the card is not PnP and Windows 95 didn't set it up when it started, you must start Windows 95, select Start⇨Settings⇨Control Panel⇨Add New Hardware, and follow the instructions you find there. Have these items handy: the switch/jumper settings, the diskette that came with the sound card, and the Windows installation diskettes or CD-ROM.

Follow the installation instructions, but when Windows asks whether you want it to detect your new hardware, select No⇨Next. On the list of hardware devices, select Sound, Video and Game Controllers⇨Next, and then choose the manufacturer and model of your sound card from the list. If your sound card is not listed, you can select Have Disk or choose a manufacturer and model that your sound card is compatible with.

Testing

To test the CD-ROM drive, you must see whether the drive is recognized by the system. From Windows 3.x, you can select Main⇨File Manager and see whether the CD-ROM drive is listed with the other drives. You should also place a CD in the drive (not an audio CD) and see whether File Manager shows you the contents of the CD.

Under Windows 95, you can test to see whether the CD-ROM drive is recognized by placing a CD in the drive, selecting My Computer, and looking for the CD-ROM drive. You can see the files on the CD by selecting the CD ROM icon in My Computer.

To test the sound card, you must start software that makes sound. The sound card installation program should have helped you complete that testing during the installation process. Also, if you're running Windows 3.x or Windows 95, you should hear sound when the program starts.

You can deliberately cause sounds in Windows 3.x by selecting Main⇨Control Panel⇨Sounds, highlighting a sound, and selecting Test.

Under Windows 95, you can hear sounds by selecting Start⇨Settings⇨Control Panel⇨Sounds. Highlight a sound from the list and select the play button to hear the sound.

Securing the CD-ROM drive into the case

When you're sure everything works, you can secure the CD-ROM drive into the case. Do so as you would with any 5¼-inch drive. If you need instructions, refer to Chapter 4.

Performing a system-wide test

When you've secured the CD-ROM drive into the case, do a final check of the system before you close the case. Restart the system, check that the hard disk drive and floppy drives work, that the CD-ROM drive works, and that the sound card, modem, and other components work. When you've verified that everything is working, close the case.

Installation in review

To add a sound card and CD-ROM drive to your system, follow these steps:

1. Check your IRQs and DMA channels, if possible. Look for devices that may create conflicts (such as a second parallel port, an optical scanner, or a network card).

2. Look for expansion slots inside the PC, a second IDE controller, and power for the CD-ROM drive.

3. Determine the sound card and CD-ROM drive to purchase. Be sure to get speakers, all necessary cables, rails, and screws.

4. Install the sound card. Connect the speakers.

5. Connect the CD-ROM drive to the IDE connector, either on the sound card or on the motherboard. Connect the audio cable from the CD-ROM drive to the sound card.

6. Under DOS/Windows 3.*x*, restart the computer. Start the installation software for the CD-ROM drive, and follow the instructions. When the CD-ROM drive is working, start the installation for the sound card. Under Windows 95, restart the computer and have the Windows 95 installation diskettes or CD-ROM handy.

7. Test the sound card. Test the CD-ROM drive.

8. Install the CD-ROM drive into a drive bay.

9. Test the sound card, CD-ROM drive, and other drives to be sure that everything is working before closing the system unit's case.

Configuration of a PnP sound card in DOS/Windows 3.*x*

Bob wanted to install a sound card for his PC that already had a CD-ROM drive. His PC was running DOS 6.22 and Windows 3.11. When he went to shop for a sound card, the only card he could find outside of a multimedia kit was a Sound Blaster Pro Plug and Play 16-bit sound card with a built-in IDE CD-ROM drive. He wasn't sure if a PnP card would work in his system, but the store assured him that the card could be returned within 30 days if he couldn't get it to work. So Bob bought the card and a set of speakers.

Bob installed the card into a free ISA slot, connected the speakers, and looked through the four diskettes that came with the card for the installation disk. Of the other three diskettes, two were labeled disk 1 and disk 2 of a Plug and Play Configuration Manager program; the other was labeled Accessories. Two books came with the sound card, but Bob decided to try the installation without reading through the books.

He viewed the directory on the installation diskette, found an INSTALL.EXE, and typed A:\INSTALL to begin. The installation program started, asked him about which directory to install the sound programs to, to confirm his Windows directory, and in what drive was the boot drive. It looked like the installation was going to work, but then it suddenly halted and a message appeared saying that the Configuration Manager would have to be installed first and then the installation could be restarted.

Bob got out the two Configuration Manager diskettes, put the first one in the A drive, and typed A:\INSTALL. This installation program was much like the first one, but it was from Intel, which piqued Bob's interest. It made a modification to his CONFIG.SYS file and asked him to reboot.

When he rebooted, Bob saw a lengthy error message. He rebooted and pressed the F8 key to make the statements in the environment files execute one line at a time. The first line of the CONFIG.SYS file was DEVICE=C:\PLUGPLAY\DRIVERS\DOS\ DWCFGMG.SYS and was obviously added by the configuration software. When that line executed, Bob saw a message that the Plug and Play Configuration Manager was loading, the version number, the Intel copyright, and the following error message:

```
ERROR: Could not read NVS. Error=FFFFFFFFh.
```

Bob tried running the Configuration Manager installation again, but the same error message appeared when he rebooted. He decided to try the installation program for the sound card software again, but he got error messages there as well.

What he really wanted was for the sound card to work in Windows, so he started Windows and attempted to configure the sound card. He selected Main⇨Control Panel⇨Drivers⇨Add, highlighted the Creative Labs Sound Blaster 1.5 driver from the list, and clicked on OK. He was asked for a diskette from his installation disks and then another menu asked for a port (or memory address) setting and an IRQ. He looked at the documentation and selected 220 for the port and 5 for the IRQ (the default settings for the sound card). But when he clicked on OK, an error message appeared saying that those settings were not a match for the sound card settings.

Bob tried another combination of settings and another, each time getting the message that the settings were incorrect. He decided that the sound card wasn't configured at all and, therefore, it didn't matter what settings he selected. He exited Windows and attempted to contact Creative Labs customer support.

While he was waiting on the phone, he found an address to the company's Internet site. Bob had access to the Internet. Rather than stay on hold, he decided to look for help there.

Bob looked at anything that may have contained troubleshooting help for his sound card. In searching, he ran across information that the Intel configuration software doesn't work with every BIOS. In a sub-sub-menu, Bob found that Creative Labs had its own configuration management software.

The software came in a self-extracting .EXE file, which Bob downloaded to his computer. He created a directory for the software, copied the program into the directory, and started the program, which uncompressed into a number of files. In reading a README file that was among the uncompressed files, Bob discovered that there was a Creative PnP Configuration Manager (CTCM) and a Creative PnP Configuration Utility (CTCU) that would configure his sound card for him. There were also updated drivers for the sound card as well. In addition, he discovered that he'd downloaded this configuration software, and to use it, he needed to install it.

Bob started the INSTALL program from the newly downloaded configuration utility directory. This INSTALL program looked very much like the Intel Configuration Manager software, and it too added instructions to his CONFIG.SYS and AUTOEXEC.BAT files. To avoid any possible conflicts with the Intel driver, which wasn't working anyway, Bob started the DOS EDIT program and placed an REM statement in front of the Intel device driver statement so it would not be executed. Then he rebooted the computer.

This time, he got a different message from the Creative Labs Plug and Play Configuration Manager, which said:

```
Found Creative Plug and Play card: Creative SB16 PnP
Successfully configured 3 of 3 Creative Plug and Play devices.
```

Bob had to think for a moment to come up with three devices, but he realized that the software had configured the sound card, IDE CD-ROM drive controller, and the MIDI interface port.

But as the boot proceeded, Bob got another error message. He executed the environment files one line at a time, and he found that the line DEVICE=C:\CTCM\CTCM in the CONFIG.SYS file was the one that successfully configured the card. However, the line C:\CTCM\CTCU /S /W=C:\WINDOWS was producing the following error message:

```
Not enough memory to run CTCU
Free some memory and try again
```

Bob ran the MEM command and discovered (with all the drivers loading) that was only 540K of lower memory available, although he had 16MB of RAM. He decided to reboot and use the F8 line-by-line execution to stop some device drivers from loading, especially those needed by Windows. He did this, but got the same error message from the CTCU program. While checking the memory resources, he found that he had 657K of free lower memory, which should have been plenty.

Bob was getting ready to give up, but he went back to the README file and also found a MANUAL.TXT file. He discovered that the CTCU program was simply for providing information about *legacy* cards — that is, cards that are not PnP. Because he'd received the message that the sound card devices had been successfully configured, he decided to go back into Windows and try again to set up the sound card drivers.

He went back to the Drivers menu in the Control Panel and went through the steps again. This time, when he chose the default settings for the sound card and clicked on OK, he got a message from Windows saying the driver had been successfully configured and that he should contact Creative Labs for an updated driver. He clciked on OK, and Windows asked him whether he wanted to restart to make the settings active. He chose to restart, and when Windows came back up, he heard sound from his speakers.

He went into the Sounds menu in the Control Panel and tested the sounds. Each sound worked, although he found himself adjusting the volume up on his speakers. Bob decided to see whether the configuration would last if he rebooted the computer, so he exited Windows and rebooted. Windows came up with sound again.

To clean up, Bob deleted the Intel Configuration Manager device driver from his CONFIG.SYS file and the line that started the CTCU from the AUTOEXEC.BAT file. He left the CTCM line in the CONFIG.SYS file, however, and was careful to create a new rescue diskette with these drivers on it.

Later, Bob discovered that the Intel configuration utility has problems with some BIOSs, as does the Creative Labs configuration software. He was just glad it had worked on his system.

Troubleshooting

Here's a list of things to check if the sound card or CD-ROM drive doesn't work.

No sound.

1. Are the speakers connected? Are they connected to the right jack? Do they have power? If the sound card has a volume knob near the jacks, is that knob turned up? Have you checked the volume controls on the speakers themselves?

2. If this is a PnP card, has it been configured correctly, or at all? If you're attempting to install the card under DOS/Windows 3.*x*, have you installed the Configuration Manager software? Have you checked with the manufacturer of the card to see if there's updated Configuration Management software?

3. If you're running Windows 95, was the card recognized when Windows 95 started? If not, you must add the card to the Windows 95 configuration manually. This can happen if you have a *legacy* card (which has jumpers or switches) rather than a PnP card. Follow the instructions under "Installating a sound card and CD-ROM drive."

4. Look for conflicts between the modem and another device on the system. Some sound card vendors offer diagnostic utilities for this purpose, so look on the diskettes that came with your sound card. Also, check any README files or files that end with the extensions .TXT or .DOC for information.

 Under Windows 95, you can look for conflicts using Device Manager. To get to Device Manager, select Start⇨Settings⇨Control Panel⇨System⇨Device Manger. A conflict is indicated by a yellow circle with an exclamation point in it. A red *X* indicates that the device has been disabled.

If a conflict exists, you can attempt to resolve it by highlighting the device with the conflict icon and then select Properties⇨Resources. Make sure the Use Automatic Settings box is selected. If that box is already checked, look at the Conflicting Devices List box for components that Windows 95 has listed in conflict. Check the Resources of those conflicting devices the same way you checked the resources of your sound card to be sure that the Use Automatic Settings box is checked there as well. Then restart Windows 95 so it can dynamically allocate the system resources again.

5. Is the sound card installed correctly? Check the troubleshooting section of Chapter 8.

6. If you're getting an error message, try pressing the F8 key when you see `Starting MS-DOS` or `Starting Windows 95` to execute the environment files one line at a time. Doing so enables you to isolate the source of the error message and determine where to look for an answer.

7. Do you have a second parallel port, a network interface card (NIC), or optical scanner on your system? A trick the pros use is to remove all but the essential cards and the new card, and then add the other cards one at a time until you find the card that's causing the conflict.

CD-ROM drive is not recognized.

1. Is the CD-ROM drive correctly cabled? Is the drive getting power? Check the troubleshooting section of Chapter 5.

2. Are the drivers for the CD-ROM drive installed? A trick the pros use is to add the /V switch to the MSCDEX driver loaded in the AUTOEXEC.BAT file. This makes the line look something like this:

```
C:\DOS\MSCDEX.EXE /D:MSCD0001 /M:20 /V /S
```

The /V switch is for *verbose* and instructs the driver to print on-screen information about memory usage while the driver is loading.

My PC won't boot.

A memory conflict or IRQ conflict can cause this. See the troubleshooting tips under "No sound."

Windows won't start or Windows 95 says there's a conflict with a device on my system.

Look for an IRQ conflict with another device on your system. See the troubleshooting tips under "No sound."

Troubleshooting Practice: What's Wrong in These Photos?

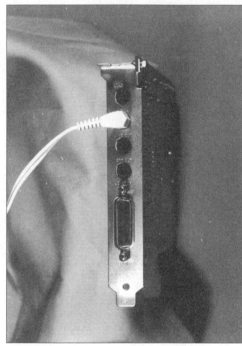

Figure 11-8: See answer 1.

Figure 11-9: See answer 2.

Answers:

1. The speakers are plugged into the wrong jack.
2. The cable is connected backwards to the IDE interface on the sound card. The stripe should be on the side where the pin 1 is designated.

Summary

✦ You can purchase a sound card with an IDE interface that supports an IDE CD-ROM drive.

✦ An IDE CD-ROM drive works better if you put it on its own controller.

✦ Both sound cards and CD-ROM drives require that drivers be installed in the environment files to get these components to work.

✦ Look to see whether you have a second IDE controller before you purchase a sound card with an IDE controller. If you do have a second IDE controller, see whether you can disable it in the BIOS.

✦ It's much easier to install Plug and Play sound cards with a CD-ROM drive under Windows 95 than to do so under DOS or Windows 3.x.

✦   ✦   ✦

Replacing Your Motherboard

In This Chapter

◆ Getting the best motherboard

◆ Removing your old motherboard

◆ Installing your motherboard using tricks from the pros

Tools Needed

◆ Wrist grounding strap

◆ Antistatic mat (recommended)

◆ Needlenose pliers

◆ Phillips screwdriver

◆ Wire cutters

◆ Rubber cement (recommended)

Replacing your motherboard makes a great deal of sense sometimes, and other times it is the only option. A motherboard upgrade makes sense when you can move most of the hardware in the PC you want to upgrade to the new motherboard. Motherboard upgrades are also a popular way to get a BIOS that offers drive translation so that you can use a hard disk drive larger than 540MB. Further, a motherboard replacement is a must when the battery that's soldered onto the motherboard fails and cannot be replaced with an external battery.

Although an intermediate user can perform this procedure, it is best performed after you've had some experience with other upgrades in the earlier chapters of this book. In other words, don't make a motherboard replacement your first upgrade experience with a PC.

Although I've designed this book so that you can simply turn to a chapter and perform an upgrade, this chapter is an exception. In order to successfully replace your motherboard, you need to read the chapters preceding this one. The terminology used in this chapter is fully explained in the preceding chapters.

Also, this type of upgrade requires you to remove just about everything from your PC, which means you have to reinstall everything. That leaves much room for error, so I help you minimize potential problems by presenting a systematic approach, as I've done in the other chapters. The troubleshooting help for each component is detailed in the chapter that covers that specific part, and in the "Installation in review," I direct you to the specific chapter.

As far as what it will cost you, you can expect to pay $100 to $300 or more for a new motherboard.

In this chapter, I focus on the specifics of installing a new motherboard. Starting with what to look for in your system, I cover choosing a new motherboard, removing the components from your old motherboard, removing the old motherboard itself, installing the new motherboard either in your case or in a new case, getting the system running again, and troubleshooting advice. I begin with the preparation.

Preparation

The only way to accomplish a successful motherboard upgrade is to do your homework first. You need to know what a motherboard is and what it does, and then you need to decide what kind of motherboard will fit in your case (or if you need a new case), what components you want to reuse, and what type of motherboard makes sense for your system.

What is a motherboard?

Also called the *system board* or *main board,* the motherboard is the backbone of your PC. Everything that happens from the time you turn on your PC until you turn it off happens through the motherboard. The motherboard is the physical connection for all the components that make up your PC.

The motherboard is a large circuit board made of reinforced plastic. It is built in multiple layers of circuits, called *traces,* that are so slim they are silk-screened onto each layer of the board, in much the same way a design is silk-screened onto a T-shirt. The layers are glued together, the circuits are connected from layer to layer where appropriate, and components are soldered on. Needless to say, bending or stretching this board can produce failure that can be difficult, if not impossible, to repair. Due to the complex nature and the plummeting cost of motherboards, replacing a motherboard is cheaper than spending the money diagnosing and repairing it.

Motherboards are relatively inexpensive to design. Although the components on the board need to meet certain standards to be compatible with other components, users with a few thousand dollars in their pockets can have their own motherboards designed and produced. Large companies that produce PCs often have motherboards produced to fit custom cases that also are specially designed. Part of your preparation work in determining what you need to replace your motherboard is determining if your case and motherboard are customized in this way.

Determining if a new motherboard will work in your PC's case

You need to determine if you can install a new motherboard in the case you have. The first step in that process involves looking at the case from the outside. Look to see if the ports are lined up along the bottom or across one side of the case, as shown in Figure 12-1. If they are, then the ports are probably built into your motherboard, which means the case is probably specially designed as well, and you need to purchase a new case. If the ports are coming out of the expansion slot openings, as shown in Figure 12-2, then you probably can reuse the case you have for your new motherboard.

Figure 12-1: These ports are not in the expansion slot openings; instead, they are in special openings in the case. This indicates that you may need to replace your case when you upgrade your motherboard.

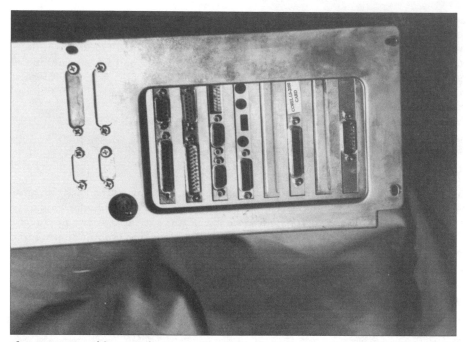

Figure 12-2: In this case, the ports are available through expansion slot openings, which indicates that you can reuse this case with a new motherboard.

TIP

Purchasing a new case when you purchase a new motherboard is always a safe move. Whoever sells you the case and the motherboard is able to help you make sure the motherboard fits the case. You also can expect to receive documentation with the case that helps you connect small items to the motherboard, such as the speaker and the reset button. A new case should also include a new power supply.

Considerations when buying a motherboard

After you've determined whether or not you need a new case, you need to decide what kind of motherboard you want. The decision depends heavily on the type of processor you use, the chipset you choose, whether you decide to get integrated controllers and ports on-board, the number of expansion slots, and the features of the BIOS. You also want to make sure you get the proper materials for the installation of the motherboard.

Processor

Much of what you decide is determined by the processor you want to use, which is the first question you'll be asked when you purchase a motherboard. These days, the processor is sold separately from the motherboard, so if you have a processor you want to reuse, you need to identify it. If you want a new processor, you have to decide which one and at what speed. Chapter 7 contains the information you need to identify your current processor or decide on a new one.

Chipsets

If you've looked at your motherboard, notice that, besides the processor, there are a number of chips that have the name of a manufacturer on them. One of the most popular is Intel, as shown on the Pentium motherboard in Figure 12-3. This group of chips works together and is known simply as the *chipset*. These chips are responsible for housekeeping functions of the motherboard, such as control logic, clock signals, control of the bus, direct memory access (DMA), and interrupt control. Chipsets used to contain a number of chips, but these days you may see only two or three chips in a chipset.

Figure 12-3: This Pentium motherboard uses a chipset made by Intel and has an Award BIOS.

Your biggest concern is compatibility, so you want to buy a motherboard with a chipset that's fairly well-known. Well-known manufacturers include Intel, Chips and Technologies (or C&T), Opti, SiS, IDC, Toshiba, Texas Instruments, and UMC. Other reliable chipset manufacturers can and will enter the market, but if you see a motherboard with a chipset you don't recognize, you should ask how long the chipset manufacturer has been around.

Integrated controllers and ports

You need to integrate the standard controllers and ports onto a motherboard. These integrated boards may have only the hard disk and floppy disk drive controllers on-board, or they may include the drive controllers as well as two serial, one parallel, and one game port. Some boards include two integrated hard disk drive controllers for controlling up to four hard disk drives. The board with the Intel chipset shown in Figure 12-3 has an integrated PCI hard disk controller and a standard IDE hard disk controller, each of which can support two drives.

If you opt not to get the controllers and ports on the motherboard, or that option is not available to you, you may need to purchase a multi-I/O controller. You also may need a multi-I/O controller if you opt for a new case, because your current serial and parallel ports are physically built into the motherboard. As explained in Chapter 8, you can get a single card that provides you with a hard disk drive controller that supports two hard disk drives, a floppy disk drive controller that supports two floppy disk drives, and two serial, one parallel, and 1 game port. Of course, you need an expansion slot for this type of card, and you need to decide what type of expansion slots you want on your new motherboard.

Expansion slots

Your choice of expansion slots probably will be between PCI or VL-bus slots on the motherboard, along with ISA slots. As I mentioned in Chapter 8, the PCI and VL-bus are competing standards, although PCI is usually faster. If you opt for an Intel chipset, you're also choosing PCI, because Intel developed and is promoting the PCI standard. (If you need to see these different types of expansion slots, turn to the photos in Chapter 8.)

You need to assess the number and type of expansion slots you need and want. Adding a modem, a CD-ROM drive, and a sound card could take up as many as three slots. In addition, a multi-I/O card can take two slots, and a video card can take another slot. That's six slots.

TIP

Remember that several PCI cards, such as multi-I/O cards, require a daughterboard to be inserted into an adjoining ISA slot and attached to the PCI card via a ribbon cable. These cards are often aimed at the use of a "shared slot."

You also want to make sure that the case you have or purchase has at least the same number of expansion slot openings as there are expansion slots on your motherboard. If you're reusing a case, you need to count the expansion slots and make sure they equal the number on the new motherboard. If not, you need to either purchase a new case or switch to a different motherboard.

BIOS features to look for

The BIOS has the last word as to what is supported, especially where drives are concerned. If you purchase a multi-I/O card that supports four hard disk drives, but only two are supported in the BIOS, then you can add only two hard disk drives, unless the multi-I/O card has its own BIOS.

In addition, you may want to look for a BIOS that offers drive translation so that you can install a hard disk drive that's bigger than 540MB. The details on this limitation are found in Chapter 5. Although there are other ways around this limit, the easiest and most efficient way is to have the BIOS handle the translation. Because you're purchasing a new motherboard anyway, you may as well get this drive translation feature.

The documentation that comes with the motherboard tells you the manufacturer and version of the BIOS, as well as whether or not the drive translation feature (sometimes known as LBA mode) is available. You also can look for the BIOS chip on the motherboard, as shown in Figure 12-3.

Materials for installation

You need a handful of materials for installing your new motherboard. These materials help secure and support the motherboard in the case. They include plastic stand-offs, brass stand-offs, screws that fit into the brass stand-offs, and heavy paper washers. These materials are shown in Figure 12-4.

All these materials are probably being used now to secure your current motherboard to the case, but you may need new ones if you damage one when you remove your current motherboard. Most of the time, these materials come with a new case, and most computer stores carry these inexpensive items as a matter of course and can supply you with as many as you need.

To be on the safe side, you probably should have a minimum of eight plastic stand-offs, six brass stand-offs, six screws that fit the brass stand-offs, and six heavy paper washers. The washers are probably the hardest to find, but you can either make them yourself out of 40 to 60 pound paper (the weight paper that is used for the flyers that hang on your door knob to advertise pizza), or you can purchase them at any electronics supply store.

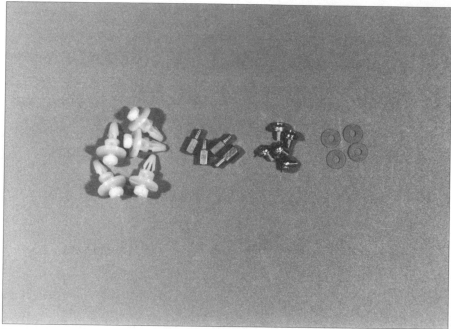

Figure 12-4: Plastic stand-offs, brass stand-offs, screws that fit into the brass stand-offs, and heavy paper washers are the materials you need to secure your motherboard into the case.

Buying a new case

If your current case does not accommodate the motherboard you want, you can purchase a new case. If you're buying a new case, you may as well get one that's easy to work in. My favorites are the minitower or full-tower cases because I think they offer much more elbow room and are easier to get into and out of.

You can expect to get a power supply with the case that's large enough to accommodate the various components the case is designed to hold. For example, if you purchase a case that holds one floppy disk drive and one hard disk drive, then the power supply you get is going to be in the 200 watt or lower range. If you purchase a deluxe case that holds six hard disk drives and four floppy disk drives, you can expect to get a 300+ watt power supply. If you're confused about power supplies and the wattage, Chapter 10 contains all the information you need.

The case also should come with a speaker, LEDs indicating that the PC is on and hard disk access, a reset switch, and perhaps an on/off switch as well. All the necessary screws and stand-offs for attaching the motherboard should be included. (Photos are included in the installation section.)

Motherboard purchase checklist

1. Does your motherboard have the features you want? Does it come with documentation?

2. Does your motherboard fit into your current PC case, or do you need a new case? Does the case have the same number of expansion slot openings as the motherboard has expansion slots?

3. Do you have the plastic stand-offs, brass stand-offs, and heavy paper washers for installation?

4. Do you have the processor and a CPU cooler?

5. Do you need any additional memory or SIMM adapters?

6. Do you need a multi-I/O card?

In addition, you can expect to get documentation, which usually consists of one small sheet of paper. However, this paper tells you which wires go to which component of the case, such as the speaker, reset button, and so on. These items must be connected to pins on the motherboard in order to work. This documentation is very helpful if this is your first time installing a motherboard in a case.

Installation

The installation of a new motherboard into an existing case involves removing the old components, removing the old motherboard, installing the new motherboard, and reinstalling the old components. If you purchase a new case, you can skip ahead to installing the new motherboard.

Removing the old components

If you're installing your new motherboard into a new case, you don't need to remove the old components you plan to reuse until you get the new motherboard installed in the new case. At that point, you want to remove the components one at a time from your old PC and install them into your new computer.

Disconnecting peripherals

However, if you're reusing the case you have now, you need to remove most of the components in your PC, especially those that use an expansion slot. Removing components means disconnecting any peripherals, such as the printer. You should remove all the external cables, including the one to the keyboard, with the exception of the power cable to the power supply. (Remember, you need the power supply cable attached so that you are grounded while you're wearing your wrist grounding strap, which is connected to either the case or the power supply.) You may want to label the cables with masking tape as you remove them and write on the tape what the cable connects to.

Disconnecting ribbon cables inside the PC

You need to remove any ribbon cables that connect these cards to various drives in your computer. However, disconnect the cable from only the card it goes to and not from the drive. Leaving the cable connected to the drive or port and removing it from only the card helps you when you reinstall everything. If you have to disconnect the ribbon cables completely, labeling the cables with masking tape will help you reconnect the cables.

Removing cards in expansion slots

After the cables are removed, you can begin removing the cards from their expansion slots. An antistatic mat now comes in handy; lay the cards you've removed on the antistatic mat. You can purchase one at retail outlets that carry computers. You can also use antistatic foam (be sure it's antistatic foam and not just plain foam) or antistatic bags to lay the cards on as you remove them.

Be sure not to lay the cards on top of each other. Some cards, such as internal modem cards, have chips that hold an electrical charge that can damage other cards on contact.

The removal of other components depends on the design of the case. You may not have to remove the drives or the power supply to get the motherboard out. This is a judgment call, but if you're reusing the case and can fit the new motherboard in without removing these components, then by all means, don't remove them.

Disconnecting wires to case switches

The last items to disconnect are the wires to the power supply and the wires to various devices attached to the motherboard. These wires include the speaker wire, the reset switch wire, the turbo switch wire, the keyboard-lock wire, and so on. You may want to make masking tape labels for these wires so that you can identify them when you need to make these connections on the new motherboard.

The turbo switch adjusts the clock speed. When it is off, the PC's clock speed is slower than when it is on. Most users leave the turbo switch on, but leaving it off can be useful for slowing down the PC if it is responding too fast for a certain situation. However, the turbo switch has been phased out of Pentium-based systems.

The keyboard lock is not available in every case, but it is very common. The lock is attached to a switch that instructs the motherboard not to accept commands from the keyboard or mouse, so it essentially locks all users out of the system. The small, round, silver keys that come with most computer systems are used in the lock. These keys are pretty common, so they're not much of a deterrent to someone who really wants to get into your PC.

Removing the old motherboard

The old motherboard is held to the case by screws that fit into brass stand-offs in the case. These screws are usually above the expansion slots on the same side of the motherboard that the power cable connection is on, as shown in Figure 12-5. Some motherboards are held with more than two screws, so you want to look for others, but two screws is the norm. When you locate the screws, remove and hang onto them for use when you install your new motherboard.

Other support for the motherboard commonly comes in the form of plastic stand-offs that fit through special holes in the case and expand on the other side of the hole, as shown in Figure 12-6. Sometimes, you can remove these stand-offs by squeezing the top of the stand-off with a pair of needlenose pliers while you pull up gently on the motherboard. Sometimes you have to cut the stand-offs from underneath the case in order to remove the motherboard. On a minitower case, you can usually get to the back of the stand-off and cut off the back part with a pair of wire cutters. After the stand-offs and screws are removed, you should be able to simply lift the motherboard out of the case.

Figure 12-5: The screws that hold the motherboard are usually near the expansion slots.

Checking the settings on the new motherboard

Checking the settings on a motherboard is easiest when you have it out of the case. You want to make sure the motherboard is set for the correct video you're using (usually VGA or simply color) and set to accept the processor you plan to use. If you're unfamiliar with how to check this, look back at Chapters 7 and 8.

Installing the new motherboard

When you install a new motherboard, you must first position the stand-offs that will hold the motherboard. If you've removed a motherboard from an existing case, the brass stand-offs that held the screws should still be in place. However, just because the stand-offs are in place doesn't mean that they are correctly positioned for installing the new motherboard.

Most cases these days are made to accommodate several sizes in motherboards. You need to hold the new motherboard up to the case and, based on the location of the holes in the motherboard, determine where the brass and plastic stand-offs should go. The idea is to give the motherboard even support and hold it in place.

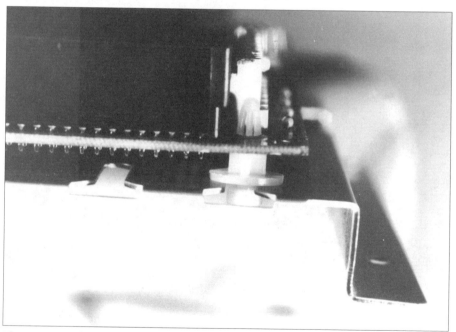

Figure 12-6: The plastic stand-off acts as support and contributes to holding the motherboard in place.

TIP

Two rules of thumb when placing the motherboard are

1. The expansion slots should go toward the back of the case (where the expansion slot openings are).

2. The power connector on the motherboard should be on the same side as the power supply or as near the power supply as possible.

As I mentioned earlier, two brass stand-offs are usually placed a few inches apart near the expansion slot openings toward the back of the case. Figure 12-8 shows how to screw these stand-offs into the case. The brass stand-off is designed to accommodate the small, round-top Phillips screw (shown in Figure 12-7) that secures the motherboard in place.

The plastic stand-offs slide into slots in the case, as shown in Figure 12-6. These stand-offs are used mainly for support, so don't expect an exact fit. You want to put a plastic stand-off everywhere you can to support the board, although some boards offer more holes for the stand-offs than other boards. If you have a place for a plastic stand-off but no hole in the motherboard, you can cut the top off the stand-off so it simply supports the board, as shown in Figure 12-8.

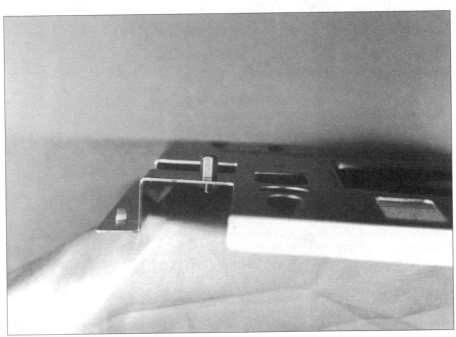

Figure 12-7: The threaded brass stand-offs screw into the case.

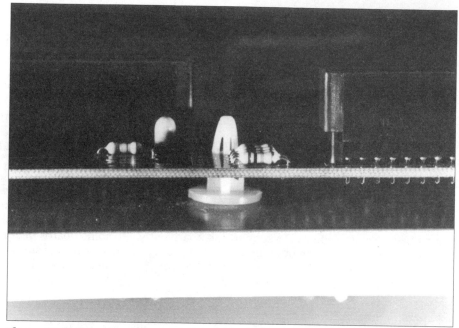

Figure 12-8: You can cut the top off a plastic stand-off so that it can be used merely to support the motherboard if a hole is not present but support is needed.

Occasionally, you run into situations in which there are brass stand-offs or holes for brass stand-offs, but nothing is in place where the motherboard obviously needs support. Remember that you're pushing cards into the expansion slots; you want the motherboard to have enough support so that it doesn't bend under the pressure.

In this case, you have a couple options. One is to hunt down a plastic stand-off that screws into the case the way a brass stand-off does. They're out there, but difficult to find. The other option is to put some material between the stand-off and the motherboard to allow for support but prevent direct contact. I've seen things such as transparent tape and a scrap of 40 pound paper used for this. Although paper is better than transparent tape, I highly recommend hunting down a special plastic stand-off or trying to remove the brass stand-off and using a regular plastic stand-off in a nearby location for support.

After you have the brass stand-offs and plastic stand-offs in place, it's time to put the paper washers in place. Your goal is to get the paper washers on both sides of the motherboard, as shown in Figures 12-9 and 12-10. This is important because the traces in the motherboard may be too close to the coating placed around the holes. If the screw makes contact through the coating with the traces, it can create a circuit to the case of the PC, which in turn could cause shorts and errors in the operation of the motherboard.

Figure 12-9: This view shows the paper washers on the top of the motherboard under the screw.

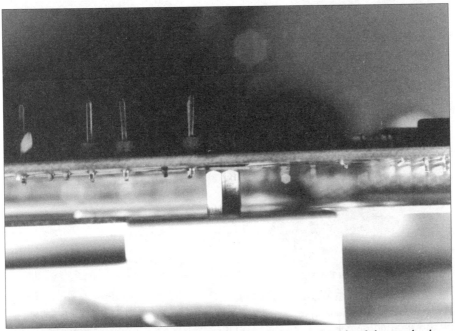

Figure 12-10: This view shows the paper washer on the underside of the motherboard on top of the brass stand-off.

You need to place the paper washers that go underneath the motherboard onto the brass stand-offs before you put the motherboard in the case. To get each washer to stay in place for the few minutes it takes to get the motherboard settled, use a little rubber cement on one side of the washer.

After the stand-offs and washers are in place, lower the motherboard carefully down over the stand-offs and press it into place. The plastic stand-offs should pop into place through the holes, but you may need to maneuver each one slightly into the proper position before you can press it through the hole. You then can place the washers onto the round Phillips screws and secure the motherboard in place. Tighten the screws until they are secure — don't overtighten. The motherboard may still seem less than totally secure, but after you get the cards into the expansion slots and tightened into the case, this arrangement becomes very solid.

Connecting the case switches

When the motherboard is in the case, but before you've added all the cards to the expansion slots, is the easiest time for you to connect the case switches, including the speaker, to your new motherboard. The documentation for your motherboard should tell you where the connections are for the reset switch, the speaker, the keyboard lock, the turbo switch, and so on. In addition, many motherboards have these connections labeled right on the board, as shown in Figure 12-11. As you can see in the figure, pin 1 is usually labeled with a small number 1, although sometimes a + sign is used.

Figure 12-11: The speaker, reset, keyboard lock, and turbo connections are labeled on this motherboard. Pin 1 is indicated on the speaker connection, so you can assume that pin 1 is on the same side on the other connections.

The positive lead on the connection goes to pin 1, but sometimes the leads are hard to distinguish. Instead of using red and black for positive and negative, these connectors have many colors. One way to find pin 1 is to look at the plastic connector. A small arrow on one side indicates pin 1. The documentation for the case may help you as well.

You may be tempted to skip this step until you see if the motherboard works, but if you don't at least make the speaker connection, you won't hear the beep codes. Without the beep codes, troubleshooting is much more difficult.

Installing the basic components

Now that the motherboard is in place, you want to install only the components that are absolutely necessary to test it and make sure that it's working. These components are the processor (if it's not already installed), the memory, the power supply, the floppy and hard disk drives, the video card, the keyboard, the mouse (if the motherboard has a built-in mouse port), and the monitor. (Actually, you need only the A drive and the C drive, but you may as well install whatever floppy and hard disk drives are at hand.)

After the basic components are installed, you need to start the computer, enter the CMOS, and enter the type of floppy disk drive and the hard disk drive parameters. You can expect an error message the first time you start the computer, before you get a chance to enter the CMOS, because the computer's self-test tells it that the CMOS settings don't match what it detects is installed. In fact, the computer may suggest that you enter the CMOS, or it may simply dump you into the CMOS to make the changes needed. Be sure to save the settings when you exit the CMOS.

If you need help installing the basic components, check the Steps-to-Success later in the chapter for the component you need help with. You will be directed to the chapter that covers that component.

Testing

At this point, your test is simply to see if the computer boots and you can access all the drives you have installed. If you can, then you're probably a genius; almost everyone forgets something at this point. After you figure out what component you forgot to connect, see the Troubleshooting section of this chapter and of the chapter that pertains to the component. Be sure to test again until everything you've installed to this point is connected and working correctly.

Installing the rest of the components, one at a time

You're now brimming over with confidence and probably want to slap the remaining stuff in the case and get it over with. The problem with this is that you won't know which component is creating a conflict if you have a problem. If you install and test each remaining component one at a time, then you know which component is responsible if you have a problem. The only exception is installing a CD-ROM drive and sound card, because both may work off the same card, depending on what type of CD-ROM drive you have.

If you run into problems, check the Troubleshooting section of the chapter that covers the component. (At this point, you don't need to bother with the Troubleshooting section of this chapter.)

Question: Some people say that the paper washers are not necessary in motherboard installation because the traces are designed to make a wide path around the holes in the motherboard. Placing these paper washers is a hassle, and the systems of people who don't use them work just fine. Why should I do it?

Answer: Figure 12-12 shows a motherboard where the traces are touching the metal coating around the hole. Figure 12-13 shows a motherboard where the internal battery is soldered to the metal coating around a screw hole.

Motherboards are mass produced, and although designers mean well, preventing the types of errors displayed in Figures 12-12 and 12-13 can be difficult and costly. Although you may think you can look at a motherboard and tell if the screw holes will be a problem, in multilayer boards such as these, you simply can't tell because you can't see all the layers.

Figure 12-12: The traces appear to be in contact with the metal coating around the screw hole in the motherboard.

Figure 12-13: You can see that the internal battery is soldered onto the metal coating around the screw hole.

Even if the system works when you don't use the paper washers, it potentially may not work later. I've seen people take shortcuts such as using transparent tape instead of paper washers or placing transparent tape over a brass stand-off that is used simply as a support. You can often get by using transparent tape for a while, but if the system is moved and the board shifts a little or the tape wears through, then suddenly a problem occurs that is seemingly inexplicable — one of those "mysterious" errors that makes the computer start producing errors and eventually stop working altogether for "no reason."

Why take the chance? All you have to do is place two paper washers on the top and bottom anywhere a metal screw holds a motherboard to a metal stand-off.

Question: What if I'm using this book to build a new PC? How do I get the computer going if I have a new hard disk drive with nothing on it to boot from?

Answer: You need a copy of DOS or Windows 95. Each operating system has a diskette that you can use as a boot disk to boot the computer from the A drive. You then can proceed with the installation of the hard disk drive, as presented in Chapter 5. Windows 95 calls this diskette the *startup* disk.

Testing again

This final test involves turning off the computer and waiting 5 to 10 seconds before turning it back on again. You'll know if the video is working, but make sure you can access each of the drives, including the CD-ROM drive, test the modem, try the mouse, try to print something, try the tape drive, and start up a couple of your favorite programs and make sure they look the same. If everything works as it should, then close up the case and give yourself a pat on the back.

Installation in review

To upgrade your motherboard, follow these steps:

1. Open the case and determine what type of motherboard you have now, including the type of processor. (See Chapter 7.)

2. Determine if a new case is needed.

3. Determine if a multi-I/O card is needed.

4. Determine if memory is needed, and if so, what kind. (You may be able to reuse the memory in your current system. See Chapter 6.)

5. Purchase the motherboard and extra stand-offs.

6. Purchase the processor, memory, case, and multi-I/O card, if needed. (See Chapters 6, 7, and 8.)

7. Record the CMOS settings.

8. Remove the components from the old PC (only if you haven't purchased a new case).

9. Make sure the motherboard settings are correct for the type of video, processor, and so on that you plan to use.

10. Install the new motherboard.

11. Install the processor, memory, floppy disk drive(s), hard disk drive(s), power supply, and video card. Then attach the monitor and keyboard. (See Chapters 3, 4, 5, 6, 7, 8, and 10.)

12. Configure the new CMOS using settings recorded earlier. (See Chapters 4 and 5.)

13. Test.

14. Install the remaining components, such as the mouse, modem, CD-ROM drive, sound card, printer, and others, one at a time. Test after each installation. (See Chapters 3, 9, 11, and 15.)

15. Test once more.

16. Close the case.

Missed stand-off causes malfunction

Nancy wanted a new motherboard that would support the 1.6GB hard disk drive she planned to install. She purchased an inexpensive 486 motherboard that supported the 486-66 MHz processor she owned and that also had the BIOS drive translation feature. She backed up her system, prepared a boot disk just in case, put on her grounding strap, and began installing the new motherboard in her existing case.

She didn't have to remove the drives or the power supply from her minitower case. As a pleasant surprise, her case had a feature that enabled her to lower the motherboard out of the case on hinges after the expansion cards were removed so that she could work on the motherboard more easily.

Nancy removed the old motherboard, placed the SIMMs from the old motherboard into the first bank on the new motherboard, installed and configured the motherboard for the 486 processor, and then proceeded to install the new motherboard. She was careful to use paper washers on both sides of the screws that went into the brass stand-offs at the top. She connected the speaker and switches from the case and the power cables. She then installed the drives, video card, monitor, and keyboard.

When Nancy started the computer to test it, she was surprised to get an almost continuous beeping noise and an error message concerning the video, although she could see the message on the screen. Nancy checked over the installation and noticed something she didn't see the first time. A brass stand-off was installed in the case toward the bottom of the motherboard as a support. Nancy checked and saw the brass stand-off was making direct contact with the motherboard.

Nancy removed the components she'd installed, the motherboard, and the brass stand-off, and she placed a plastic stand-off with the top cut off nearby for support in the same location. She then put everything back together and tested the computer again. This time it worked. Nancy breathed a sigh of relief that she caught the problem before it had a chance to do permanent damage to her motherboard.

Troubleshooting

A few failures are common to motherboard installation, which I discuss in this section. However, if you're getting a specific error message, check the troubleshooting section of the chapter covering that component.

There is no boot and no video.

1. Did you install the power cables from the power supply to the motherboard? Is the power on? Check Chapter 10 for help.

2. Did you install the memory? Did you install the memory the way the motherboard requires it installed? You must often fill the first bank of memory with the same size and capacity SIMMs. Check Chapter 6 for help.

I get video, but the computer doesn't get far in the boot process.

Make sure the processor is installed correctly. See Chapter 7.

I get many beeps and an error message.

This could indicate a short in the motherboard. Did you install the paper washers so that the screws don't make contact with the brass stand-offs and the motherboard? Do you have a brass stand-off somewhere else in the case making direct contact with the motherboard?

The computer appears to boot OK, but I don't hear a beep when it boots.

Check to see if you connected the PC speaker to the motherboard. If so, check to see if you got the connection backwards. Look for pin 1 on the motherboard connection and pin 1 on the speaker connector, as described under the "Connecting the case switches" section earlier in this chapter.

Troubleshooting Practice: What's Wrong in These Photos?

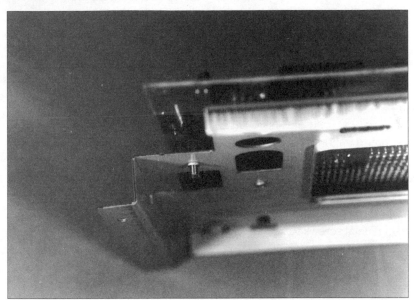

Figure 12-14: See answer 1.

Figure 12-15: See answer 2.

Answers:

1. A brass stand-off is making direct contact with the motherboard from underneath. This should have been replaced with a plastic stand-off to provide support for the motherboard without causing a potential malfunction.

2. No washer is protecting the traces of the motherboard from potential contact with this screw. This situation is also an opportunity for a short or other malfunction.

Summary

✦ A motherboard upgrade isn't difficult, but it is something you should attempt only after you've had some experience with other PC upgrades.

✦ You may need to purchase a new case, especially if your current motherboard has the ports on-board.

✦ You want to prevent accidental shorts or malfunctions by using paper washers when using metal screws to secure the motherboard.

✦ Make sure the motherboard is properly supported by non-conductive materials.

✦   ✦   ✦

Operating System Issues, Upgrades, Dual Boots, and Multiple-Boot Configurations

In This Chapter

✦ Defining and manipulating environment files

✦ Determining whether you're a good candidate for a Windows 95 upgrade

✦ Setting up dual boots to get the most from your PC

Entire books have been written on just DOS or just Windows. That's not the purpose of this chapter. If you don't understand something about directories and filenames or how to navigate Windows, you need to get yourself a good introductory book such as *DOS For Dummies, 2nd Edition*, *Windows For Dummies*, or *Windows 95 For Dummies*.

This chapter is a cut-to-the-chase approach to what you need to know about the operating system to perform *any* upgrade, and then specifically about operating system upgrades. First, you get an introduction to the basics of working with the operating system from the point of view of PC upgrades. Then, you learn helpful information about what to expect in an operating system upgrade, and how to fix it if something goes wrong. This chapter also offers operating system tips and tricks that are practical in real-life situations, such as dual-boot configurations with DOS/Windows 3.x and Windows 95, as well as multiple-boot configurations under DOS and Windows 95.

Many hardware and software upgrades modify critical operating system files and can leave you high and dry if you don't know anything about those modifications. You must know how to make boot diskettes and backups to avoid being left high and dry. This chapter covers how to make boot diskettes and backups, as well as the tricks the pros use in troubleshooting new installations.

The chapter also covers preparation information on what the operating system does; the role of the environment files; creating a boot diskette, or *rescue diskette,* for DOS, Windows 3.x, and Windows 95; upgrading DOS or Windows 3.x to a new version of DOS or Windows 95; editing and troubleshooting environment files; setting up a dual boot with DOS/Windows 3.x and Windows 95; and setting up a multiple-boot configuration in DOS or Windows 95.

Preparation

The operating system is an integral part of the PC environment. The hardware and the software work together to allow you as the user to control the actions of the PC. Many operating systems will run on a PC, including DOS, Windows 3.x, Windows 95, Windows NT, UNIX (in a variety of flavors), XENIX, and a number of more obscure systems. However, because this discussion is limited to the most common upgrades, it only covers DOS, Windows 3.x, and Windows 95.

To understand the significance of the operating system from the point view of adding PC hardware, you must understand a few specifics: What the operating system is, how it interacts with the PC hardware during the boot process, and how the environment files are involved in the process.

What's an operating system?

The operating system is a go-between. It interprets the commands given to it by the software you install to the PC hardware and, in turn, interprets the hardware feedback to the software you use. The two tasks of the operating system you're probably most familiar with are handling housekeeping functions (such as the storage, retrieval, and deletion of data on the PC drives) and the display of information on your monitor.

As operating systems become more sophisticated, they take on more housekeeping; Windows is a prime example. Windows has taken on the management of the PC's memory resources for you (the user), so, theoretically, you can run more than one program at a time. In addition, rather than having to tell each software program you install what type of monitor and printer you're using, programs designed for Windows allow Windows to handle those tasks. When Windows takes on more housekeeping, the PC user no longer has to deal with the idiosyncrasies of each software program when it comes to printing and screen displays.

DOS version issues

DOS is at the center of the PC world; analysts refer to the entire PC market as the "DOS market," even when referring to Windows. Whether you can see it or not, DOS is beneath every version of Windows, including Windows 95. One of the most critical questions you must be able to answer when you start dealing with PC upgrades is *What version of DOS are you using?* The version tells whose DOS it is and how recently it was released.

DOS is at the helm of those PCs that run DOS itself, Windows 3.*x,* or Windows 95. Microsoft is the largest and most prevalent supplier of DOS in the form of MS-DOS. IBM has a version called PC-DOS, and Novell also has a version. Subtle differences exist in the various versions; unless you're technically skilled or have to change versions for some reason, stay with MS-DOS. The vast majority of PCs runs it, which means the vast majority of software is designed to work with it as well. You only create headaches for yourself if you switch.

Software is designed to operate with certain versions of DOS. The convention in the PC industry is that any software should work with a *later* version of DOS than it was designed for. For example, if you buy a software product that says it works with DOS 5.0, and you have DOS 6.22, then the software should run with your version of DOS.

Before Windows 3.*x* can be installed, a version of DOS must be installed. You can upgrade your DOS version under Windows 3.*x* if you want. Windows 95 does not require that you have a stand-alone version of DOS (although technically it does have MS-DOS 7.0 built in, Microsoft has no plans to release that version commercially). The latest version of MS-DOS available is 6.22. Of Windows, it's Windows 95, which is sometimes referenced in technical manuals as Windows 4.0. Windows version 3 came in three versions, Version 3.0, Version 3.1, and Version 3.11. Versions 3.1 and 3.11 are considered the first multimedia versions of Windows.

One more wrinkle you must know about is that Microsoft does license its MS-DOS to various large computer manufacturers. These companies modify MS-DOS with special functions to talk to special hardware features built into proprietary PCs. Compaq, Dell, and others are known for their own versions of DOS; this practice is especially prevalent in laptop computers. What this means to you is that if you buy a PC with a special version of DOS on it (such as Dell's DOS 6.0), then you cannot upgrade to a later version of DOS without getting that later version from Dell. For example, you cannot upgrade to MS-DOS 6.22 from Dell's version of MS-DOS 6.0. Upgrading to a later version of MS-DOS on a PC with a proprietary DOS version creates a mess.

What happens when the PC boots

When you turn on your PC, the BIOS checks over the hardware and then is programmed to look at track 0, sector 0 (the *boot sector*) of disks A and C to locate the operating system *kernel*. The diskette on which the operating system is found is called the *boot diskette*. In the DOS world, the kernel consists of three files:MSDOS.SYS, IO.SYS, and COMMAND.COM. It loads these three files into memory and then searches for the environment files CONFIG.SYS and AUTOEXEC.BAT. Although the files that make up the kernel must be there, the environment files do not have to be present to boot the PC.

Two of the three files, MSDOS.SYS and IO.SYS, are hidden *system files* — that is, if you call up the root directory of the boot drive, these files won't show up on-screen. However, if you type **ATTRIB** (for attribute) and press Enter, these files are listed with an *H* for hidden and an *S* for system.

IO.SYS and MSDOS.SYS have been actual programs in the past. Under Windows 95, however, MSDOS.SYS is a text file that sets up parameters for how Windows 95 is to be run. The file has to be a certain length; antiviral software checks the length of the MSDOS.SYS file to make sure it hasn't been piggybacked by a virus. If the file's length changes, antiviral software will report that a virus is present. To keep the file length the same, it is filled at the end with random characters so that its length matches that of MSDOS.SYS when it was a program.

The role the environment files play

The environment files, CONFIG.SYS (short for *configure system*) and AUTOEXEC.BAT (short for *automatically executed batch file*), set up the PC's environment for that session. The CONFIG.SYS is executed first, and it basically establishes parameters for how memory is used and configured and loads device drivers so that the operating system can talk to add-on hardware such as CD-ROM drives. After it runs, the AUTOEXEC.BAT file performs commands you could type yourself at the DOS prompt if you wanted to. The AUTOEXEC.BAT also specifies the directories in which the PC will look for the commands you type (written on one line, they form the *path statement*), and it is the place where programs can be automatically started each time the PC boots. If there's an antivirus program you want to start each time before you boot Windows 3.*x,* then you can load a command to start it into the AUTOEXEC.BAT; make sure it precedes the command to start Windows.

Windows has *environment files* as well. These files end with the extension .INI; the two most critical are the WIN.INI and SYSTEM.INI. In a later section on editing environment files, you learn an easy way to take a look at these files.

The operating system kernel and the environment files are what you need to successfully start your PC. If these elements become lost or damaged, your life can get very difficult. The good news is that it's easy to create a diskette you can boot from that will have all the critical files you need.

Creating a rescue diskette

As previously mentioned, you can boot the computer from a floppy diskette that contains the essential operating system files known collectively as the *DOS kernel*. However, such a *rescue diskette* is more than just a bootable floppy diskette. It should also contain your system's environment files and any device drivers that are loaded in those environment files. Here's how to create a rescue diskette for DOS, Windows 3.*x*, and Windows 95.

 There may be an option in your BIOS that enables you to skip the search for the DOS kernel on the A drive at boot-up. After all, checking the A drive simply puts unnecessary wear and tear on it and slows down the boot process; normally, you want to boot from your C drive anyway.

Your computer needs to look at the A drive for the operating system in order for you to boot from the your rescue diskette, should the need arise. If your computer doesn't look at the A: drive for the operating system, you can change it so it look at the A drive. Enter the BIOS, and look for something like "boot options," "floppy drive seek at boot", or "system boot sequence." Look in the advanced CMOS setup menu or a submenu to find this option. Then set the computer to search the A drive first. You may have to enable the "floppy drive seek at boot" option. You also may need to change a "system boot-up sequence" option from "C:, A:" to "A:, C:." In some cases, you may have to both enable the "floppy drive seek at boot" option and change the "system boot-up sequence."

Creating a DOS rescue diskette

The minimum you should have is a bootable floppy diskette. However, what you should have is a rescue diskette that contains your environment files and the drivers loaded in those environment files.

There are three steps to the creation of a rescue diskette. The first is to create a bootable diskette by using the DOS format command, the second is to copy the environment files to the diskette, and the third is to copy any drivers loaded in the environment files to the diskette.

Creating a bootable diskette

The first thing to do when creating a rescue diskette is to find out what version of DOS you're using so you can label the diskette. At the DOS prompt, type **VER** and press Enter to have DOS display the version.

Under DOS, you create a bootable diskette by typing **FORMAT A: /S** and pressing Enter. Because system files have a special attribute that does not allow them to be copied, adding the /S parameter to the format command moves the system files to the diskette in the drive specified; in this case, the diskette in the A drive. You can also use the SYS command to move the kernel to a diskette that is already formatted (if you're using DOS 5.0 or higher) by typing **SYS A:** and pressing Enter.

At the end of the formatting, DOS moves the kernel and informs you that it's moved with the message `System transferred`. Then you are asked for a label of 11 characters for the diskette; spaces are not permitted, so use the underline character instead. Label the diskette as a boot diskette, and add the version of DOS, like this: `BOOT_DOS622`.

Copying critical programs to the diskette

Under DOS and Windows 3.*x*, you must copy programs used by DOS to perform critical functions to install new drives or troubleshoot problems to the rescue diskette. These programs are found in your DOS directory on the hard disk drive and include FDISK, FORMAT, SYS, SCANDISK, EDIT, MEM and ATTRIB.

To copy these files, type at the DOS prompt: **COPY C:\DOS\FDISK.* A:** and press Enter. (The asterisk {*}, or DOS wild card character, is made by holding down the Shift key and selecting the number 8.) For each subsequent file, substitute the filename for FDISK in the command until you've copied all the files. These files are critical to the installation of a new hard disk drive or recovery of a drive from disaster; be sure to have them on hand.

Copying the environment files to the diskette

When you've made the bootable diskette, create a directory on the diskette for the environment files. Type **MD A:\ENVRNMT** and press Enter. Then type **COPY C:\AUTOEXEC.BAT A:\ENVRNMT** and press Enter. Use the copy command again; type **COPY C:\CONFIG.SYS A:\ENVRNMT** and press Enter. Now you have a copy of the PC's environment files on the boot diskette.

You could bypass the directory creation on the A drive and copy the environment files to the root directory of the A drive. If you do that, you get error messages when you use the bootable diskette to restart your computer. The computer tries to execute the commands in the CONFIG.SYS and AUTOEXEC.BAT, but those command files and directories are not be available on the A disk. Changing the environment files to work on the A drive is a lot of work for nothing. You either can ignore the error messages or put the files in a directory so that they're not executed at boot time. Because error messages tend to frighten users, place them in a directory on the A drive.

Copying the drivers to the bootable diskette

Look at your CONFIG.SYS file for lines that say `DEVICE=` or `DEVICEHIGH=`. These commands are loading device drivers for control of hardware devices, such as your CD-ROM drive. You must have these drivers to get your CD-ROM drive working, especially if you have installed your operating system from a CD-ROM disc.

CONFIG.SYS device driver examples

For example, here's a typical CONFIG.SYS file from a multimedia PC:

```
DEVICE=C:\DOS\HIMEM.SYS
DOS=HIGH,UMB
DEVICE=C:\DOS\EMM386.EXE NOEMS I=B000-B7FF
FILES=99
BUFFERS=40
STACKS=0,0
FCBS=1
DEVICEHIGH=C:\MOUSE\MOUSE.SYS
DEVICEHIGH=C:\NEC_CD\NEC_IDE.SYS /D:MSCD0001
```

Notice that four device drivers are loaded here: HIMEM.SYS, EMM386.EXE, MOUSE.SYS, and NEC_IDE.SYS. Notice also that the location of each device driver on the hard disk drive is listed as well. For example, the HIMEM.SYS driver is in the WINDOWS directory on the C: drive. The first two device drivers are memory managers; they're not critical to copy to your rescue diskette (you restore them when you restore your operating system). But to be on the safe side, you may want to copy them as well.

However, of the next two device drivers, one is the mouse driver and the other is the CD-ROM drive device driver. Of the four, the most important is the CD-ROM driver because it is not part of the operating system; it came from an installation diskette that probably came with the CD-ROM drive. Without this driver, you probably won't be able to get the CD-ROM drive working should something happen to the copy of the driver that's on your hard disk drive.

Make a directory on the rescue diskette by typing **MD A:\DRIVERS** and pressing Enter. Then use the Copy command to move each of the drivers to the DRIVERS directory. For example, to move the CD-ROM driver in the example, type **COPY C:\NEC_CD\NEC_IDE.SYS A:\DRIVERS** and press Enter.

AUTOEXEC.BAT driver examples

Here's a typical AUTOEXEC.BAT file from a multimedia PC:

```
@ECHO OFF
C:\SOUND144\UTILITY\AZCAL.EXE
PROMPT $P$G
PATH C:\VIEWER;C:\WINDOWS;C:\WINDOWS;C:\
LH C:\DOS\MSCDEX.EXE /D:MSCD0001 /M:20 /S
C:\WINDOWS\SMARTDRV.EXE 1024 512 /X
SET TEMP=C:\TEMP
SET BLASTER=A220 I5 D1 T4
SET GALAXY=A220 I5 D1 K10 P530 T6
SET SOUND=C:\SOUND144
```

In this case, the second line shows you a driver for a sound card, AZCAL.EXE, being loaded. This driver is one you should copy. Also, the CD-ROM driver from Microsoft, MSCDEX.EXE, is being loaded and configured. You want a copy of that driver on your rescue diskette because the CD-ROM drive won't work without it. It wouldn't hurt to have a copy of SMARTDRV.EXE on your rescue diskette as well, although if you reload Windows, you get this driver as part of Windows.

Some Pentium computers are so fast, that if you set the computer to boot from the A drive, the poor floppy disk drive couldn't answer fast enough, and you'd get the error message No boot device available. In anticipation of this problem, some BIOS manufacturers have placed a function in the CMOS setup menu that enables you to choose a lower speed for the PC during the boot process. This usually slows down the PC in general, but it helps you boot from a floppy diskette on a very fast PC. Look for a function such as *boot speed* or *turbo speed* in the CMOS setup menu.

Don't forget to change the setting back when you finish booting from your floppy diskette, however, or you may wonder if your fast PC is broken.

Labeling the bootable diskette

You must label the diskette as *bootable*, indicating what version of DOS you used, what PC it came from, and the date. The date is especially important, as you should make one of these diskettes each time you make a major change to your system, such as adding new hardware, new software, or upgrading your operating system. The date on the diskette helps you choose the most recent diskette to use when you restore your data in a crisis situation.

Creating a Windows 3.x rescue diskette

To create a Windows 3.x rescue diskette, you must follow all the steps in creating a DOS rescue diskette, with a few additions. Exit Windows and follow the steps you use to create the DOS diskette. When you copy the environment files, you must add the files that create the Windows 3.x environment as well. These are the WIN.INI and SYSTEM.INI files found in the Windows directory on the hard disk drive.

You can also use the Windows 3.x File Manager to create your rescue diskette. To make a bootable floppy diskette, place a diskette in the A drive and select Main⇨File Manager⇨Disk⇨Make System Disk. To make directories on the new bootable diskette, select the A drive, then select File⇨Create directory. To copy files, highlight the file, select File⇨Copy, and enter the location on the A drive to which you want the file copied.

Be sure to label the diskette with both the version of DOS and the version of Windows (either 3.0 or 3.1) that you're running. Don't forget to copy the drivers from the CONFIG.SYS and AUTOEXEC.BAT files.

Creating a Windows 95 startup diskette

Windows 95 has made creation of a rescue diskette much easier by offering a utility that creates a *startup* diskette. This utility does much of the copying for you; all you need to add are your environment files and any critical device drivers.

To create this startup diskette in Windows 95, place a diskette in the A drive, and then select My Computer⇨Control Panel⇨Add/Remove Programs⇨Startup Disk⇨Create Disk. Windows 95 asks you for your original Windows diskettes or CD-ROM. In Figure 13-1, Windows 95 is requesting installation diskettes from which to copy.

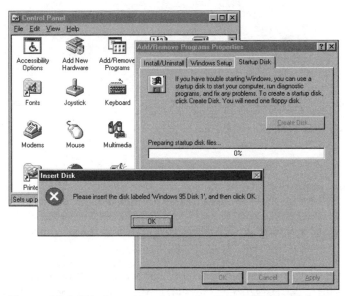

Figure 13-1: Windows 95 asks you for the installation diskettes or CD when you make a startup diskette.

If you don't have them, just click on OK anyway; the Add/Remove Programs Properties box comes up, offering you the option to change where Windows 95 finds the system files (and other files it needs to create the startup diskette). Just click on the down arrow and select the drive on which Windows is installed (usually drive C). As Windows looks for various files, it will stop and ask you the location. Your best bet is to try the C:\WINDOWS directory or the C:\WINDOWS\COMMAND directory.

If all else fails, and because Windows is a multitasking environment, leave the startup disk utility running and switch to the Windows Explorer to find the location of the needed file. Select Start⇨Programs⇨Windows Explorer⇨Tools⇨Find⇨Files or Folders. Enter the name of the file and let Explorer find its location for you. When you find it, switch back to the startup disk utility by minimizing Explorer and entering the location of the file.

Windows 95 takes over from there and creates a diskette, adding many of the programs I've encouraged you to add, and a couple extra ones, as shown in Figure 13-2.

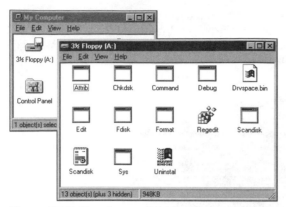

Figure 13-2: Here is a peek at the files on a Windows 95
startup diskette.

Next, create a directory on the diskette for the environment files and call it
ENVRNMNT. With the diskette in the A drive, select My Computer⇨A:⇨File⇨New⇨
Folder. Name the new folder *ENVRNMNT*. Copy the AUTOEXEC.BAT, CONFIG.SYS,
WIN.INI, SYSTEM.INI, and a new file called SYSTEM.DAT. The SYSTEM.DAT file is the
Windows 95 *registry* — a very important file.

To copy these files, select My Computer⇨C: and highlight the file you want to copy.
Then hold down the control (Ctrl) key while holding down the left mouse button; drag
the file to the ENVRNMNT folder on the A drive. The file should have a plus sign (+) on
it to indicate that it's being copied, not moved. Be sure to look for the plus sign shown
in Figure 13-3 so that you copy the file without moving its location.

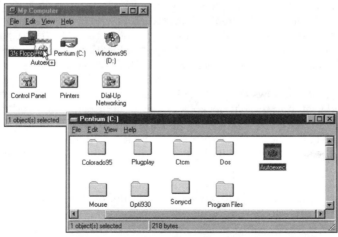

Figure 13-3: A file being copied by using drag and drop has
a plus (+) sign on it, as shown. If there's no plus sign, the file is
being moved.

When it's time to copy the drivers, you may find yourself with too many files for one diskette, so you may want to start a second diskette. Then copy the drivers from the AUTOEXEC.BAT and CONFIG.SYS files. As examples, here are the two typical environment files from earlier, but this time they are from a Windows 95-based PC. Note that there is no DOS directory. Instead you'll see the C:\WINDOWS and C:\WINDOWS\COMMAND directories as locations for drivers supplied by Microsoft with Windows 95.

Here's a sample Windows 95 CONFIG.SYS file from a multimedia PC:

```
DEVICE=C:\WINDOWS\HIMEM.SYS
DOS=HIGH,UMB
DEVICE=C:\WINDOWS\EMM386.EXE NOEMS I=B000-B7FF
FILES=99
BUFFERS=40
STACKS=0,0
FCBS=1
DEVICEHIGH=C:\WINDOWS\MOUSE.SYS
DEVICEHIGH=C:\NEC_CD\NEC_IDE.SYS /D:MSCD0001
```

Here's a sample Windows 95 AUTOEXEC.BAT file from a multimedia PC:

```
@ECHO OFF
C:\SOUND144\UTILITY\AZCAL.EXE
PROMPT $P$G
PATH C:\VIEWER;C:\WINDOWS;C:\WINDOWS\COMMAND;C:\
LH C:\WINDOWS\COMMAND\MSCDEX.EXE /D:MSCD0001 /M:20 /S
C:\WINDOWS\SMARTDRV.EXE 1024 512 /X
SET DIRCMD=/O
SET TEMP=C:\WINTEMP
SET WINPMT=[WINDOWS] $P$G
SET BLASTER=A220 I5 D1 T4
SET GALAXY=A220 I5 D1 K10 P530 T6
SET SOUND=C:\SOUND144
```

Notice that the same device drivers are loaded as in the DOS example, including those for a sound card and a CD-ROM drive, but the locations of the files are different.

After you've completed your startup diskette(s), be sure to label them as Windows 95 startup diskettes and include what PC they're from and the date. If you have two diskettes, it's a good idea to indicate that by labeling them "Disk 1 of 2" and "Disk 2 of 2."

Pentium boots too fast for startup diskette

Elija was a new Windows 95 user, and he decided he should use an uninstall program he'd bought for Windows 3.1 to remove a program from his Pentium PC running Windows 95. This caused his PC to lock up. When he attempted to reboot, Windows 95 would not come up.

However, Windows 95 gave him a message that said he should boot from his startup diskette. Fortunately, Elija had made a startup diskette, so he placed the diskette in the A drive and rebooted the computer. It appeared, however, that the computer would not boot off the diskette. Elija called a friend, who suggested that he look in the CMOS setup menu for an option that might disable the floppy drive boot. He found one, and the PC went to the floppy disk drive, but he still got the message "no boot device available."

Elija remembered seeing something about another boot setting in the CMOS setup, so he went back in to look. He found a setting that allowed him to switch between a fast boot or a slow boot; it was set to Turbo. He set it to the only other setting, which was De-Turbo, and exited the CMOS.

This time the PC booted from the floppy diskette, and Windows 95 walked him through the steps to restoring itself. However, when it was done, Elija noticed that everything the computer did took more than twice as long as it used to. Elija looked through all the Help files in Windows to see whether there was something he could set differently, but he couldn't find anything. He also compared the environment files on his startup diskette with the Windows 95 startup files, but he couldn't find anything there, either.

Then he remembered the De-Turbo setting in the CMOS. Elija entered the CMOS and set the boot speed back to Turbo. While he was at it, he turned off the "floppy drive seek at boot" he'd en-abled earlier. Elija was delighted to discover that when he exited the CMOS, the PC booted at normal speed. He made a note on the uninstall program's box that it should *not* be used with Windows 95, and he thanked himself for being smart enough to have the startup diskette handy.

Installation in review

To create a rescue diskette under DOS or Windows 3.x, follow these steps:

1. Place a floppy diskette in the A drive. Under DOS, create a bootable diskette in the A drive using the format command with the /S parameter.

2. Copy FDISK, FORMAT, SYS, SCANDISK, EDIT, MEM, and ATTRIB from the DOS directory to the hard disk drive.

3. Copy the CONFIG.SYS and AUTOEXEC.BAT environment files to a subdirectory on the diskette. Under Windows 3.x, add the WIN.INI and SYSTEM.INI files to the subdirectory.

4. Look at the CONFIG.SYS and AUTOEXEC.BAT files, and copy drivers for the CD-ROM drive, mouse, and so on to a subdirectory on the diskette.

Steps to create a startup diskette under Windows 95:

1. Place a floppy diskette in the A drive. Select My Computer⇨Control Panel⇨Add/Remove Programs⇨Startup Disk.⇨Create Disk.

2. Copy the environment files to a subdirectory on the diskette. These files include the AUTOEXEC.BAT, CONFIG.SYS, WIN.INI, SYSTEM.INI, and SYSTEM.DAT.

3. Look at the CONFIG.SYS and AUTOEXEC.BAT and copy drivers for the CD-ROM drive, mouse, and so on, to a subdirectory on the diskette. You may need two diskettes if the first one is full.

When you've created the diskette(s), label them with the version of the operating system, the PC used to make it (them), and the date. Then store your diskette(s)for safekeeping.

Editing environment files

One of the tasks you often run across in performing PC upgrades is editing environment files. The *environment files* are simply text files that contain commands that DOS, Windows 3.*x*, and Windows 95 know how to interpret. Most technical support personnel and PC troubleshooting texts assume that you know how to edit environment files and that all you need to be shown is what to add or look for. Most intermediate PC users, however, have little or no background in editing environment files, although most have used a word processor.

The stickiest problem in editing environment files is that most inexperienced PC users forget to make a copy of the files at two critical points. The first such point is *before any PC upgrade is begun*. The second is *before any editing is done*. Any pro will tell you that the way you keep yourself out of trouble is to make sure you can roll back to what you had before you started making changes. Never be so foolhardy as to assume that you'll remember what's there or that you don't need a copy.

The second sticky problem in editing environment files is choosing an editing tool. Although you can use a word processing program to create and edit these files, do so very carefully; word processors add *formatting* — the command codes that tell the printer where and how to place text on the page. Word processors are designed to insert these codes, which in turn are designed to be invisible to you so you get the results you want from your printer. However, if these codes are inserted into environment files, you're going to have problems.

To use a word processing program to edit environment files, you must know how to save the program so that no printer formatting is included with the text. This will be found under your Save options in your word processing program and is known by many terms, including: unformatted text, text only, ASCII (pronounced *ask-ee*) text, and plain text.

Rather than go through the pain and frustration of attempting to pull formatting out of environment files, use a couple of editing tools you already have that were created just for this purpose. You learn about these tools next.

How to use EDIT under DOS

If you're at a DOS prompt, even after exiting Windows 3.*x* or Windows 95, you can use the program EDIT.COM. Edit is known as a *text editor* — it adds no formatting to any file, but it lets you perform basic functions, such as adding and changing text, copying, pasting, searching for text strings, and saving files.

Figure 13-4 shows the EDIT screen with an AUTOEXEC.BAT file loaded. Start EDIT by typing **EDIT** and pressing Enter at the DOS prompt. Then you can open a file by selecting File⇨Open and choosing the file you want.

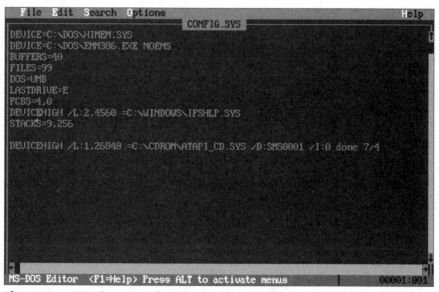

```
  File  Edit  Search  Options                                    Help
                          CONFIG.SYS
DEVICE=C:\DOS\HIMEM.SYS
DEVICE=C:\DOS\EMM386.EXE NOEMS
BUFFERS=40
FILES=99
DOS=UMB
LASTDRIVE=E
FCBS=4,0
DEVICEHIGH /L:2,4560 =C:\WINDOWS\IFSHLP.SYS
STACKS=9,256

DEVICEHIGH /L:1,26848 =C:\CDROM\ATAPI_CD.SYS /D:SMS0001 /I:0 done 7/4




MS-DOS Editor  <F1=Help> Press ALT to activate menus          00001:001
```

Figure 13-4: EDIT is a text editor that comes with DOS 5.0 and higher for the purpose of editing environment files.

EDIT makes use of a mouse, but if you don't have a mouse available, you can activate the menu options at the top of the screen by holding down the Alt key. To open the File menu, hold down the Alt key and press F. Use the up and down arrows to select menu items (or you can press the first letter of the menu item, such as O for Open). When you're in submenus, such as the Open menu, you can use the Tab key to move around from field to field.

EDIT comes with DOS in Version 5.0 and higher; it's available under Windows 3.x, and it comes with Windows 95. In fact, it's one of the utility programs Windows 95 copies for you when you create a startup diskette.

TIP If you want to edit environment files in Windows, don't use EDIT in a DOS Window. Windows write-protects those files; if you try to edit them, none of the editing you do will "take," and you'll be back where you started. The best way to edit environment files under Windows is to use the SYSEDIT command, discussed next.

How to use SYSEDIT under Windows 3.x and Windows 95

If you must edit the environment files, and you're running Windows, the easiest way to do so is to use the SYSEDIT command. There's a version of SYSEDIT for Windows 3.x and one for Windows 95.

Under Windows 3.x, you start SYSEDIT by selecting File⇨Run, then typing in **SYSEDIT** (as shown in Figure 13-5) and clicking on OK. The System Configuration Editor starts and brings you all the relevant environment files for Windows, including the AUTOEXEC.BAT and CONFIG.SYS files, in a cascade format so that you can simply click on the file you want and begin editing (see Figure 13-6). When you've made the changes you want to make, you can save them by selecting File⇨Save from the System Configuration Editor menu.

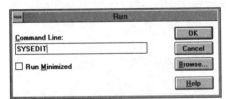

Figure 13-5: Under Windows 3.x, select
File⇨Run, type **SYSEDIT,** and click on OK.

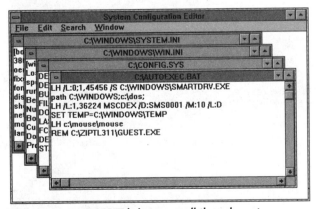

Figure 13-6: SYSEDIT brings you all the relevant
Windows 3.x environment files for editing.

TIP

The System Configuration Editor has no Save As option; you must have a copy of the environment files before you begin editing them.

Under Windows 95, select Start⇨Run, type in **SYSEDIT** (as shown in Figure 13-7), and then click on OK. The System Configuration Editor brings you all the relevant environment files, including the AUTOEXEC.BAT and CONFIG.SYS files, as shown in Figure 13-8.

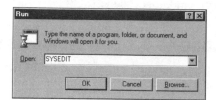

Figure 13-7: Under Windows 95, select Start⇨Run, and then type **SYSEDIT** and click on OK.

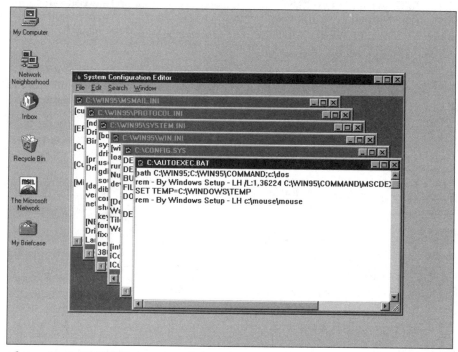

Figure 13-8: SYSEDIT brings you all the relevant Windows 95 environment files for editing.

Tricks for troubleshooting environment files

Some problems you encounter when you attempt to get something to work are caused by conflicting drivers or conflicting settings in the environment files. You don't have to be a DOS expert to find the source of the problem, though you may need some help to fix it. When you know the specific lines that generate the error messages you're getting, you'll spend much less time hunting down the answer to the problem. Since MS-DOS Version 5.0, a couple of tricks have been carried on into Windows 95 that you'll find very useful in this type of troubleshooting.

Clean boot

Some troubleshooting situations and some programs require no other commands or environment settings be loaded when these programs execute. This is called a *clean* boot. To get one, press F5 when you see the message `Starting MS-DOS` or `Starting Windows 95` and the computer skips execution of the environment files altogether.

Executing the environment files one line at a time

To have the environment files execute one line at a time, press the F8 key when the message `Starting MS-DOS` or `Starting Windows 95` appears on the monitor.

When you press F8, you must confirm each line with a *Y* for yes or a *N* for no before that line will execute. This confirmation is a big help in troubleshooting; you can determine where the problem is if you're getting an error message during boot-up.

You can also use this capability to skip the execution of one or more lines of an environment file. This capability is especially useful if you suspect one driver is creating a conflict with another driver. If you skip the execution of the line that's suspect, and the new software or hardware works, then you know that line is the problem.

"Comment out" commands

Another way you can troubleshoot environment files is to *comment out* commands in these files so a particular line is not executed. To do so in the AUTOEXEC.BAT and CONFIG.SYS files, type the characters **REM** and a space in front of the line, that you do not want to execute, as shown in Figure 13-9. REM stands for *remark* and tells DOS not to execute the command. The following is an example CONFIG.SYS file with a driver commented out.

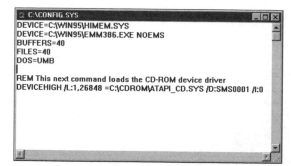

Figure 13-9: Placing REM and a space turns the line into a comment that is not executed by DOS, as shown in this CONFIG.SYS file.

In the Windows .INI files, you comment out commands by using the semicolon (;). A semicolon at the beginning of a line tells Windows not to execute that line. Also, Windows stops execution of a line from the point of a semicolon onward; you can follow a command with a comment on the same line.

TIP Commenting is a way you can place notes to yourself in these files. You may find these comments useful later, especially if you plan to install several new devices. Here's an example of a comment placed in a SYSTEM.INI file by IOmega's Ditto Tools, a tape drive utility program. Notice that the installation program for the tape drive software "commented out" the next device driver that was being loaded by the SYSTEM.INI file.

```
[386Enh]
DEVICE=C:\QBWIN\VFINTD.386 ;line added by Ditto Tools
;device=vcdremap.vxd
pbIRport=2
```

This is a polite way for the software installation to handle removing a conflicting device driver while adding its own. In this case, if you decided that you wanted to remove the Ditto Tools driver, you could simply remove the line this driver added, and then remove the semicolon from the previous device driver. In this way, restoring the previous settings is much easier than trying to go back and figure out which driver Ditto Tools removed if it had not simply commented out the offending driver. (If you've made copies of your environment files, including WIN.INI and SYSTEM.INI, you can copy the old file back over the revised .INI file to restore your previous settings. This is a lifesaver if you must remove a utility or program that's causing havoc.)

Researching back to the source of the command

When you determine which line or lines in your environment files are causing problems, you must look up what those lines do. That is, you have to go to the program that generated a command to find out what the command does — and then what, if anything, you can do to change it.

The first step is to find the source of the command. Usually the path to the command tells you what the source of the command is. For example, take the sample AUTOEXEC.BAT file for Windows 95 that you had earlier:

```
@ECHO OFF
C:\SOUND144\UTILITY\AZCAL.EXE
PROMPT $P$G
PATH C:\VIEWER;C:\WINDOWS;C:\WINDOWS\COMMAND;C:\
LH C:\WINDOWS\COMMAND\MSCDEX.EXE /D:MSCD0001 /M:20 /S
C:\WINDOWS\SMARTDRV.EXE 1024 512 /X
SET DIRCMD=/O
SET TEMP=C:\WINTEMP
SET WINPMT=[WINDOWS] $P$G
SET BLASTER=A220 I5 D1 T4
SET GALAXY=A220 I5 D1 K10 P530 T6
SET SOUND=C:\SOUND144
```

Notice that the @ECHO OFF command doesn't have a path, indicating that it is a DOS command. In this case, that command means *Don't print (or echo) the remaining commands to the monitor as they are executed.* Because DOS is under Windows 95, you'd find this type of command in the Windows 95 documentation. If Windows 95 were not running, it would be necessary to find the command and its function in a DOS manual. In DOS versions 5.0 to 6.22, you can find the DOS commands by typing **HELP** at the DOS prompt, which brings up a list of DOS commands. In Windows 95, you can find help by selecting Start⇨Help.

If you see a command started with DEVICEHIGH, HIGH, LOADHIGH, or LH, the driver that's being loaded into memory is being loaded into memory above the 640K barrier by a device driver that was activated in the CONFIG.SYS file.

The next command in the example AUTOEXEC.BAT gives the full path to the driver being loaded. (It's easy to tell that line loads a driver for a sound card.) If a problem with that line created an error situation, the place to start looking for help would be in the directory where the driver is found. The first step would be to look in the C:\SOUND144 directory or the C:\SOUND144\UTILITY directory for information. Specifically, look for a README file or a file that has the extension .TXT or .DOC that indicates that the file is a document. The second place to look would be in any written documentation that came with the program or hardware. In this case it would be the sound card's hardware documentation. A third option is to contact the vendor of either the computer or the sound card and see whether a faxback service, bulletin board service, or an Internet site offers troubleshooting help.

Notice that several of the other drivers are being loaded from the C:\WINDOWS directory, a dead giveaway that these are Windows commands. Help for these commands can be found in the Windows' documentation or online help.

Upgrading to Windows 95

Microsoft has released two versions of Windows 95. One version is aimed at those with new PC installations, and the other is an upgrade version. The upgrade requires that you have Windows 3.0, 3.1 or 3.11, Windows for Workgroups 3.1, MS-DOS, or an OEM version of MS-DOS (OEM-DOS) 3.2. Each upgrade is available either on diskettes or on CD-ROM, but the CD-ROM version installs faster and offers additional features.

If you're installing Windows 95 as an upgrade to Windows 3.0, the Windows installation instructions won't work. You must proceed with the installation following the instructions for installation from the DOS prompt as though you didn't have Windows 3.0 installed; install Windows 95 to your Windows 3.0 directory.

The Windows 95 upgrade has gone without incident for the vast majority of users who have tried it so far. The biggest attraction to Windows 95 is that DOS programs that wouldn't run under Windows 3.x now run successfully under 95, including games. Before you upgrade, however, here are a few items that can cause you difficulty in installing Windows 95.

Hardware requirements

You can run Windows 95 on a 386-based (not a 386SX) PC with about 50MB of free hard disk space and 8MB of RAM. However, you'll be much happier with at least a 486-based PC, 16MB of RAM, and a 100MB or more of free disk space. In addition, Windows 95 will not work with anything less than a VGA video display at 640 x 480 resolution.

To make sure the Windows 95 installation picks up all your existing program groups in Windows 3.x, Microsoft recommends that you start the upgrade from within Windows 3.x. To do so, select File⇨Run. Then type **A:\SETUP** for the diskette version and **D:\WIN95\SETUP** if you have the CD-ROM version (substitute the letter of your CD-ROM drive for D). If you follow the installation, you'll end up replacing your current Windows 3.x installation with Windows 95. If you want to keep your existing DOS/Windows 3.x installation, see the section on dual-booting DOS/Windows 3.x and Windows 95.

Watch out for antivirus software and RAM-doubling utilities

The two most prevalent causes of problems in an upgrade to Windows 95 are antivirus software and RAM-doubling utilities. The problem with antiviral software has to do with the fact that Windows 95 changes the DOS kernel, which antiviral software tends to protect. Actually, anything that write-protects the DOS kernel interferes with the installation of Windows 95; although antivirus software is the most likely culprit, scattered BIOSs do exist that include functions that write-protect the boot sector of the hard disk drive.

If you attempt to install Windows 95 with the DOS kernel write-protected, the installation will fail, and you'll get a message that says something like `Windows was unable to update your system files`. If you're not sure antiviral software is being loaded, here are a few indicators.

If your PC is automatically loading antiviral software, you may get a message from the antiviral software at boot-up, and you are likely to sit through a session of virus-checking activity. This indicates that one of the environment files is loading the antiviral software. You can also look over your environment files for a command that loads antiviral software. All you have to do is disable the software until after the Windows 95 installation. Usually you can place the REM command in front of the command line that loads the software, as discussed earlier.

Another persistent type of software problem occurs when the software manipulates RAM (especially true of RAM-doubling programs). You probably know whether RAM-doubling software is present; you either installed it or had someone else install it for you. Microsoft says that RAM doubling software, particularly SoftRam version 1.03 in combination with Windows 95, will make the system "unstable," which is one of those amusing understatements technical people like to make. *Unstable* can mean anything from data corruption to a total system crash. There's not any reason to take that kind of risk.

Setting up a DOS/Windows 3.x and Windows 95 dual boot

You can keep your existing DOS/Windows 3.x installation and add Windows 95. When this is accomplished, you can choose to start Windows 95 or your previous version of DOS, in which you can run Windows 3.x as you did before.

To accomplish this installation, you must have Windows 3.x running, and then follow the directions above for starting the installation of Windows 95. However, when the installation gets to the point where you choose the directory in which to install Windows 95, you'll have a choice between C:\WINDOWS and OTHER. Choose OTHER, and the installation then asks what directory you want to install to. Type **WIN95**, although you can choose any 8 character name you'd like. Windows 95 then installs to that directory, leaving your Windows 3.x installation in the C:\WINDOWS directory.

When you have Windows 95 installed, you can boot to your previous installation by pressing F8 when you see the `Starting Windows 95` message during boot up. You're then presented with a list of options, including `Previous version of DOS`. Choose that option and start Windows 3.x, if necessary.

The dual boot configuration comes with a couple of disadvantages. One is the obvious fact that it simply takes more disk space. The other is that you may have to reinstall all your software packages to get them to work with Windows 95. You can usually reinstall them to the same directory as before, but these applications won't make it into Windows 95 without re-installation.

Setting up a multiple-boot configuration

Earlier, you read how the operating system controls the communication of software with the hardware. Some PC software designers, however, have chosen to talk directly to the PC hardware with their software, by-passing the operating system. These programs are termed *ill-behaved* in the programming world, and they often cause conflicts with other software.

There are reasons for bypassing the operating system, and most of them have to do with performance. Adding another layer of processing, such as an operating system to interpret commands, slows things down. If you're a game designer or are designing a software tool that requires high performance from the PC to work, the only way you may be able to deliver the performance needed to make your software work is to cut through the layers and talk to the hardware yourself. If the operating system is talking, and the PC hardware (such as the video card) and another program are trying to control the same hardware at the same time, then the system locks up or crashes. Because the memory is the communication channel where instructions are picked up and received by the hardware, these types of conflicts are often called *memory conflicts.*

Setting up a multiple-boot configuration in DOS

What do you do if you have one PC and two programs that you need to run that won't run together? For example, what if you want to use an optical scanner, but when you installed the optical scanner drivers, you discovered that you no longer had the lower memory to run an accounting package on which you're dependent? Or, what if you find out that you need the DOS network driver SHARE to run the multimedia version of Microsoft Works for Windows, but SHARE seems to cause conflicts with another program? It'd be great to have two PCs in these cases like these, but that's not always possible. The next best thing is a multiple-boot configuration.

This is a common practice, and it's used in a variety of situations, not only for situations where software or hardware drivers are in conflict, but also for when two different people are using the computer. One instance that stands out is a university facility that has a limited number of PCs, and has set up these computers so that students with various handicaps who need special hardware can reboot the PC and choose their own configuration tailored to their special needs.

Under MS-DOS 6.0 and higher, you can have two or more configurations, with the option of choosing between them at boot time. Here are a couple of examples of how this is done.

Example 1 shows the first set of sample CONFIG.SYS and AUTOEXEC.BAT files for a multi-boot configuration. In this case, to save lower memory to run a game under DOS, there's a separate boot configuration for GAMES and one for WINDOWS. The first configuration is vanilla, only loading the necessary drivers (which include a mouse driver) for playing games and avoiding Windows to save lower memory. The WINDOWS configuration starts Windows.

Example 1 shows the environment files for this GAMES/WINDOWS configuration.

CONFIG.SYS MULTI-BOOT EXAMPLE 1

```
[MENU]
MENUITEM=GAMES
MENUITEM=WINDOWS

[GAMES]
FILES=99
BUFFERS=40
STACKS=9,256
DOS=HIGH

[WINDOWS]
FILES=99
BUFFERS=40
DEVICE=C:\WINDOWS\HIMEM.SYS
STACKS=9,256
SHELL=C:\DOS\COMMAND.COM C:\DOS /P /E:256
```

AUTOEXEC.BAT MULTI-BOOT EXAMPLE 1

```
GOTO %CONFIG%

REM This starts the games configuration and Windows is not loaded
:GAMES
PATH=C:\;C:\DOS;
C:\MOUSE\MOUSE.EXE
PROMPT GAMES CONFIGURATION $_$P$G
GOTO END

:WINDOWS
PATH=C:\;C:\DOS;C:\WINDOWS
SET TEMP=C:\WINDOWS\TEMP
C:\MOUSE\MOUSE.EXE
PROMPT WINDOWS CONFIGURATION $_$P$G
WIN
GOTO END

:END
```

The setup for the multiple-boot configuration is in the first three lines of the CONFIG.SYS file. These lines tell DOS that it should offer a menu when this file is executed that allows you to pick either GAMES or WINDOWS. When you boot your system with this configuration, you see the multiple boot configuration menu that looks something like this:

```
MS-DOS 6.22 Startup Menu

  1. GAMES
  2. WINDOWS

Enter a choice:
```

By choosing 1, you set the variable %CONFIG% equal to the characters GAMES. DOS then looks for the term GAMES in square brackets and executes all the commands there until it gets to the next square bracket.

Then DOS starts the AUTOEXEC.BAT file, and the GOTO %CONFIG% command directs DOS to look for a colon with the characters *GAMES* after it. DOS executes the instructions until it reaches another GOTO statement or the end of the file. In this case, the second GOTO statement is set equal to the characters *END*, so DOS must look for a colon and the characters *END*. The characters *END* are the last line in the file, so DOS quits executing commands at that point.

When you choose option 2, the same thing happens, only this time %CONFIG% is set equal to the characters *WINDOWS,* and the commands after WINDOWS are executed instead.

Although you can have several multiple-boot configurations, you should set up as few as possible because it can become a headache, especially if you plan to install new software later. For each boot configuration, you must specify a menu item with a unique name. In addition, set the DOS PROMPT command so that it displays the configuration you loaded. In example 1, the DOS prompt appears like this:

```
GAMES
C:\>
```

And the Windows configuration has this prompt:

```
WINDOWS
C:\>
```

If you have the DOS prompt change with each boot configuration, then you know at a glance which configuration is loaded.

Also, notice that the path for C:\WINDOWS is not in the PATH statement of the GAMES configuration. This absence helps prevent someone from typing **WIN** and starting Windows when your PC is not correctly configured to run Windows.

To make a multi-boot successful, the file COMMAND.COM must be in the C:\DOS directory, as well as in the C directory (or root directory) of the hard disk drive. COMMAND.COM should already be in both of those places, but if you have trouble making this work, you should check.

Here's a more complex example of a multiple-boot configuration. In this example, a CD-ROM driver is loaded in one configuration, and an optical scanner is loaded in the other.

CONFIG.SYS MULTI-BOOT EXAMPLE 2

```
[MENU]
MENUITEM=CDROM
MENUITEM=SCANNER
```

```
[CDROM]
DEVICE=C:\DOS\SETVER.EXE
STACKS=9,256
DOS=HIGH,UMB
FILES=99
BUFFERS=40
SHELL=C:\DOS\COMMAND.COM C:\DOS\ /P
REM This Corel CD-ROM driver must load before the high memory
       drivers
DEVICE=C:\CORELDRV\CUNI_LS2.SYS /ID:? /N:1 /D:MSCD001
DEVICEHIGH=C:\DOS\HIMEM.SYS
DEVICEHIGH=C:\DOS\EMM386.EXE RAM

[SCANNER]
DEVICEHIGH=C:\DOS\HIMEM.SYS
DEVICEHIGH=C:\DOS\EMM386.EXE RAM
DEVICE=C:\DOS\SETVER.EXE
STACKS=9,256
DOS=HIGH,UMB
FILES=99
BUFFERS=17
SHELL=C:\DOS\COMMAND.COM C:\DOS\ /P
REM This is the optical scanner driver
DEVICEHIGH=C:\DRIVERS\SCANDEVB.SYS
```

AUTOEXEC.BAT MULTI-BOOT EXAMPLE 2

```
@ECHO OFF
GOTO %CONFIG%

:CDROM
LOADHIGH C:\DOS\SMARTDRV.EXE
SET MOUSE=C:\MOUSE1
C:\MOUSE1\MOUSE.EXE /Q
C:\DOS\PRINT /Q:32 /D:LPT1 /B:1024 >NUL
SET TEMP=C:\DOS
REM This is the Microsoft CD-ROM driver
C:\DOS\MSCDEX /V /D:MSCD001 /M:10
REM Initialize the CD-ROM drive
DIR E:
PATH C:\DOS;C:\;C:\WINDOWS;C:\VIEWER;C:\NDW;
PROMPT CDROM CONFIGURATION $_$P$G
GOTO END

:SCANNER
LOADHIGH C:\DOS\SMARTDRV.EXE
SET MOUSE=C:\MOUSE1
C:\MOUSE1\MOUSE.EXE /Q
C:\DOS\PRINT /Q:32 /D:LPT1 /B:1024 >NUL
SET TEMP=C:\DOS
REM **** SCANNER — CALERA path ****
```

```
C:\CALERA\BIN\INPATH C:\CALERA\BIN
IF ERRORLEVEL 1 GOTO CALERA_OK
PATH C:\DOS;C:\;C:\WINDOWS;C:\CALERA\BIN;%PATH%;:CALERA_OK
PROMPT SCANNER CONFIGURATION $_$P$G
GOTO END

:END
```

In Example 2, each set of commands for the CDROM and SCANNER configurations includes all the commands as if they were stand-alone environment files. I could have placed some commands that are common to each configuration at the top of each environment file above the CDROM variable, but if the commands have been optimized to use memory more efficiently by the way they're loaded, then you lose that optimization.

Plus, it's easier to just create a multi-boot configuration by simply allowing an installation program to modify the environment files (you have copies of the originals, of course). Then you can simply copy the newly modified environment files to the appropriate section of a new multi-boot environment file, and replace the old environment files with the new ones.

If you need further help creating these multi-boot configuration files, online help is available. Type **HELP MULTI-CONFIG** at the DOS prompt.

Common mistakes checklist

1. No copy the original file is made before editing starts.

2. Substituting the uppercase letter *O* for the number zero (0) when typing commands. Although *O* and zero look alike, each character is represented to the computer by a unique number, so your PC sees these two characters as completely different.

3. Typographical errors. Double- and triple-check your commands to be sure that they're right. A spelling checker won't help, because these words are limited to eight characters, which makes for some awkward spelling.

4. Using a word processor that inserts formatting into these text files. The best way to ensure that this doesn't happen is to use EDIT or SYSEDIT, as described earlier in this chapter.

5. Attempting to set up environment files for new devices or programs manually. Make a copy of the environment files, let the installation program for the new device modify the files for you, get the device or software working, make a copy of the modified file, and *then* set up your multiple-boot configuration.

6. Making more than one change at a time. If you make more than one change, you could have fixed one problem but created another. You can only know what a change has done if you limit yourself to one change.

Setting up a multiple-boot configuration in Windows 95

Windows 95 calls multiple-boot configurations *hardware profiles* because it is limited to enabling or disabling hardware. Unlike DOS, however, much of the work is done for you, making it easier to accomplish.

You won't need a multiple-boot configuration as much in Windows 95, because Windows 95 is better at memory management, so lower memory is available for your DOS programs and games. However, you may find *hardware profiles* useful for PCs on a network; network cards can dig heavily into resources that you could be using for other functions when you don't need to be connected. Also, portable PCs that connect to docking stations have special hardware drivers that can be disabled when the PC is used away from the docking station. Creating new hardware profiles can be useful.

Creating a new hardware profile

To create a new hardware profile, copy your current hardware profile to a new profile with a different name, and then make changes. To copy your current hardware profile, select Start⇨Settings⇨Control Panel⇨System⇨Hardware Profiles⇨Copy. In the Copy Profile box, type a name for the new profile you want to create, and click on OK. In Figure 13-10, the new hardware profile is called No Network to indicate that no network drivers are loaded in this profile.

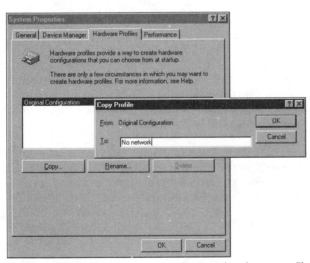

Figure 13-10: Type a name for the new hardware profile.

Modifying the new hardware profile

All the hardware available in your old profile is available in this new profile. Your job now is to disable the hardware you don't want in this current profile. To do so, select the Device Manager tab at the top of the screen, and make sure that View devices by type is selected, as shown in Figure 13-11.

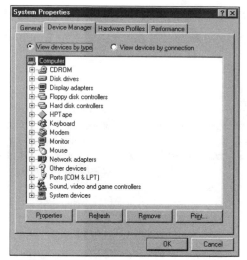

Figure 13-11: You can choose hardware devices to remove from (or add to) your hardware profile from the Device Manager box. Be sure that View devices by type is selected.

If you selected OK one too many times when you created the new hardware profile, then you found yourself at the Windows 95 desktop. To get to the Device Manager, select Start⇨Settings⇨Control Panel⇨System⇨Device Manager.

Select the plus sign next to the device you want to disable, highlight the specific hardware, and click on Properties. The Properties dialog box for that device comes up, as shown in Figure 13-12. You can disable the device in any hardware profile that is available by selecting the check in the box to remove it.

After you select the hardware you want enabled or disabled in each profile, you must exit Windows 95 to make the changes take effect. Select Start⇨Shut Down⇨Restart. When Windows 95 restarts, it presents you with a menu from which you may select the hardware profile you created, which will look something like this:

```
Select one of the following:

1. Original Configuration
2. No Network Drivers
3. None of the above

Enter your choice:
```

Now you can choose which hardware profile is booted and proceed with your Windows 95 session.

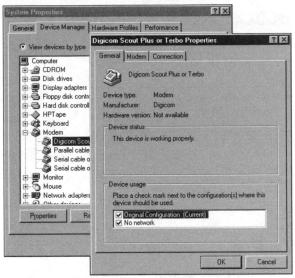

Figure 13-12: After you select the hardware, select Properties to open the Properties box so that you can pick the hardware profile in which the device is to be active.

Deleting a hardware profile

You can remove a hardware profile at any time. Select Start⇨Settings⇨Control Panel⇨System⇨Hardware Profiles. Highlight the profile you want to delete, and select Delete. When you are down to only one hardware profile, you will no longer be given a choice of hardware profiles when you boot your computer.

Windows 95 does not allow you to delete the hardware profile you are using for the current session.

The Futz Factor

A group of analysts known as the Gartner Group gets credit for the term *Futz Factor,* which refers to the time you spend getting new things on your PC to work. Multiple-boot configurations are especially "futz-prone"; you can expect to boot and reboot, making changes and "tweaking" until you're free of error messages and everything works.

What this means is that you don't want to pick a high-pressure situation or a time when you're under a tight schedule to attempt this type of operation. If that 200-page report is due tomorrow morning, it would be a bad idea to start a multi-boot configuration this afternoon. Allow yourself time to "futz around." And when you do get it working, be sure to make a new rescue diskette or startup diskette.

Troubleshooting Practice: What's Wrong in These Photos?

```
AUTOEXEC.BAT
    %CONFIG%

    REM This starts the games configuration and Windows is not loaded
    :GAMES
    PATH=C:/;C:/DOS;
    C:/MOUSE/MOUSE.EXE
    PROMPT GAMES CONFIGURATION $_$P$G
    GOTO END

    :WINDOWS
    PATH=C:/;C:/DOS;C:/WINDOWS
    SET TEMP=C:/WINDOWS/TEMP
    C:/MOUSE/MOUSE.EXE
    PROMPT WINDOWS CONFIGURATION $_$P$G
    WIN
    GOTO END

    :END
```

Figure 13-13: See answer 1.

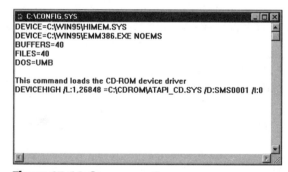

Figure 13-14: See answer 2.

Answers:

1. The GOTO command has been left off the %CONFIG% statement in this AUTOEXEC.BAT file from a multi-boot configuration.

2. Note the comment in this CONFIG.SYS file without REM in front of it. This comment will produce an error message such as `Bad command or filename` when the PC is rebooted.

Summary

✦ Besides a backup of your system, you should have a bootable diskette that contains the environment files and any device drivers called by the two main environment files.

✦ The environment files determine how the PC is configured. The two main files are AUTOEXEC.BAT and CONFIG.SYS. Under Windows, additional environment files are WIN.INI and SYSTEM.INI; Windows 95 adds the SYSTEM.DAT.

✦ You must remove or disable antivirus utilities and RAM-doubling software to make your Windows 95 upgrade successful.

✦ You can add special commands to the DOS environment files under DOS 6.0 or higher that allow you to choose which drivers are loaded. This feature can allow you to use your PC as if it were two separate PCs.

✦ You can choose which drivers are loaded under Windows 95 and use hardware profiles to enable or disable specific hardware.

✦   ✦   ✦

Connectivity on the Cheap

In This Chapter

✦ Linking two PCs for the price of a cable

✦ Sharing resources between the two linked PCs

✦ Synchronizing files between two PCs using My Briefcase

Tools Needed

✦ Parallel or serial cable

When you have more than one computer, especially if you use a laptop when you travel, moving data from one computer to the other can be a problem. Floppy diskettes become inadequate quickly, especially if you're working on very large files.

Powerful programs are available that enable you to transfer files between PCs using your modem or using a special cable, but you must be prepared to spend some money. Some of these programs even enable you to operate one PC from another. If, however, you want a cheap way to exchange data between PCs and keep your data synchronized, nothing's less expensive than Windows 95's Direct Cable Connection coupled with the My Briefcase function. For the price of a parallel or serial cable, you can connect two PCs running Windows 95, share resources, and even synchronize files between the two machines.

This chapter covers how to set up the Direct Cable Connection to share files between two PCs and how to use My Briefcase to synchronize files. The first portion covers Direct Cable Connection, and the second portion covers how to set up My Briefcase to synchronize files between two PCs.

Direct Connection Using Windows 95

You can connect two PCs directly using a parallel or serial cable under Windows 95 so that you can share files, printers, and other resources. This connection is a little finicky to set up, but after you've done so, it's easy to use. Read on to learn what you need to perform a direct connection, how to set it up, and how to restart it after you've done it the first time.

Requirements for direct connection

Obviously, you must have two PCs, each running Windows 95. You can connect them by using the parallel or serial ports, but you must use the same port designations on both PCs. For example, you can't use COM1 on one and COM2 on the other. You must use COM1 on both, COM2 on both, or LPT1 on both PCs. (If you need a refresher about parallel and serial ports, check the information and illustrations in Chapter 9 and Chapter 15.)

If you decide to use the parallel ports, you must be sure that both LPT ports are set to the same type of data transfer mode. Newer PCs enable you to configure the parallel port in the BIOS setup in one of several ways. Your choices may include the AT mode (also sometimes known as *compatible* or *single direction*), the bidirectional mode (sometimes referred to as *PS/2 mode*), the Extended Capabilities Port (ECP) mode, and Enhanced Parallel Port (EPP) mode. EPP is not widely supported, AT mode is slow, and ECP requires a special cable, so use bidirectional mode if you decide to use the parallel ports.

You can get special parallel cables by mail order from vendors such as Parallel Technologies Direct. (See Appendix A for contact information.) A much less expensive approach is to use bidirectional mode and standard parallel cables. Just be sure to use a real parallel cable; other types of cables are wired differently.

You can get an adapter that converts the Centronics connector to a 25-pin male connector; doing so lets you simply disconnect your printer cable, connect the adapter, and plug into the parallel port on another PC. It's also easy and inexpensive to purchase a parallel cable with 25-pin male connectors, a serial cable with 25-pin female adapters at each end, or a serial cable with 9-pin female adapters at each end. Such cables come in varying lengths to meet your needs.

Looking for the Direct Cable Connection utility

You need the Windows 95 Direct Cable Connection utility. Check to see whether this utility is available by selecting Start⇨Programs⇨Accessories and then looking for Direct Cable Connection, as shown in Figure 14-1. If it is not there, add it by following the steps in the next section.

Figure 14-1: If Direct Cable Connection is installed, you find it under Accessories.

How to install the Direct Cable Connection utility

To add the Direct Cable Connection utility, select Start⇨Settings⇨Control Panel⇨ Add/Remove Programs⇨Windows Setup. In the box, you see several Windows components. Highlight Communications and then select Details. Select Direct Cable Connection, and then click on OK to go back to the Add/Remove Properties menu. Click on OK again, and Windows prompts you for a Windows 95 installation diskette from which to copy the utilities.

If you want to perform the installation from a CD instead, click on OK without placing a diskette in the floppy drive. The Copying Files menu appears; from it you can use Browse to select the WIN95 directory on your CD-ROM drive. When the utility is copied, Windows informs you that it will restart your PC so the changes can take effect.

How to configure for connection

To configure your PCs for connection, you must determine which PC is to be the guest and which should be the host, connect the cable between the two computers, configure the guest and host PCs for the connection, set up shared resources on the host so that the guest PC will have something to access, and enable the connection.

Determining the host and guest PCs

You must first determine which PC should be the host and which should be the guest. File copying and resource sharing only go one way, from host to guest, so you need to configure the PCs so that the one with the files you want to share is the host and the one to receive files is the guest. For example, if you have a laptop and you want to move files from it to the desktop, configure the laptop as the host and the desktop as the guest. If you want to switch their roles, you can do so with a couple of extra steps after the systems are configured correctly.

Connecting the cable

When you decide which PC to make the host and which to make the guest, you must configure the Direct Cable Connection utility on each PC. The first part of the configuration process is to connect the cable between the two PCs. For this example, assume that I've connected the cable between the LPT 1 (parallel) ports of two PCs running Windows 95.

Configuring the guest PC

It's easiest to begin by configuring the guest PC. Start the Direct Cable Connection utility on the guest by selecting Start⇨Programs⇨Accessories⇨Direct Cable Connection ⇨Guest. This starts a Windows 95 *Wizard* that attempts to guide you through the configuration process.

If any network utilities or other options must be installed, the Wizard prompts you for the necessary installation diskettes or CD. You may also have to restart the computer (after the installation of the necessary network utilities is accomplished), and then start the Direct Cable Connection utility again.

You are prompted again to choose Guest or Host. Select Guest⇨Next. Direct Cable Connection prompts you for the port you plan to use. For this example, I selected LPT1, as shown in Figure 14-2. Highlight the port you want to use and select Next. (You should already have your cable installed.) Direct Cable Connection prompts you to set up the host computer.

Leave this screen on your guest PC and go set up the host computer, because when you select Finish, Direct Cable Connection attempts to access your host PC.

Configuring the host PC

Configuring the host PC is much like configuring the guest PC. You start the Direct Cable Connection utility, as you would when configuring the guest PC, but you select Host instead of Guest when given a choice.

In addition, Windows 95 may ask you whether you want to enable file and printer sharing, as shown in Figure 14-3. You must do this in order for the Direct Cable Connection to work.

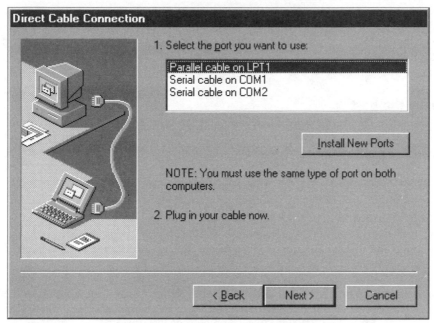

Figure 14-2: Direct Cable Connection asks you for the port to use.

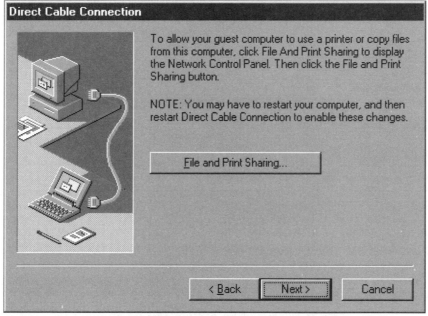

Figure 14-3: You are prompted to set up File and Print Sharing on the host.

To enable file and printer sharing, select File and Print Sharing⇨File and Print Sharing. (Yes, you select it twice — once in the Direct Cable Connection box and once in the Network box.) Then select "I want to be able to give others access to my files" and "I want to be able to give others access to my printer(s)", and click on OK twice. Expect to restart the computer to enable this functionality.

Naming the host

If you're setting up the host, you may need to click on the Identification tab at the top of the Network menu and give your host a name. You may be asked for the name of the host when attempting to make the connection between the two computers. When you're finished, click on OK. Windows requires you to restart your PC before these settings can take effect.

Setting up shared resources on the host

Resources that the guest PC can use must be available on the host. Now that you've enabled file and printer sharing, you can select the resources you want to make available to the guest PC.

From the desktop, open My Computer and highlight a resource, such as a hard disk drive. In this case, I've highlighted drive C on the host computer. Select File⇨Sharing, select Shared As, and give the resource a name (see Figure 14-4). You must enter a filename that follows the DOS filename rules: no spaces, colons, and so on are allowed. You are not required to enter a comment, although a comment may help you identify the shared resource when you're working at the guest PC.

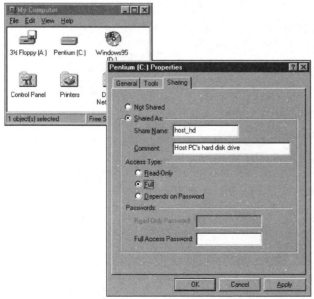

Figure 14-4: To share a resource, you must enable sharing for that resource, which in this case is the C drive on the host PC.

If Sharing isn't available in the File menu, then you haven't enabled file and printer sharing as described under "Configuring the Host PC" in this chapter.

Notice that you can choose the type of access and password protect the drive with passwords. Read-only access allows files to be opened or copied, but not changed. Full access allows changes, additions, or removal of the files to be accomplished from the guest computer.

The password feature is for restricting others' access to your data; if you're the only one using this feature, you don't need a password. If that is the case, simply leave the password fields blank; that way no password is required.

When you finish with the Sharing menu, click on OK. After you click on OK, a hand appears under the icon of the resource you've selected to share, indicating that it is a shared resource.

Printer sharing is available, but it won't do you much good if your printer isn't connected — and it won't be if you're using the parallel port for Direct Cable Connection. If you're using a different port for your printer, setting up your printer for sharing can be a big convenience. To do so, select the printer's folder, highlight the printer you want to share, and then select File⇨Sharing. Although the menu for sharing printers is a little different, it also requires that you select Shared As and name the printer. When you finish, click on OK. The printer icon changes to indicate that it is shared (see Figure 14-5).

Figure 14-5: Both the C drive and the HP printer have hands underneath to indicate that they are shared resources.

You may change the sharing status of the resources on your host PC by following this procedure again, limiting or expanding access as needed.

Connecting for the first time

If you left your guest computer waiting for you to select Finish, now is the time to do so. If not, you must start Direct Cable Connection on both your host and guest PCs. During the connection process, you are informed about the status of the connection. On the guest PC, you may be asked for the name of the host computer. When you enter the name of the host, a window appears with the name of the host at the top and any shared resources (such as hard disk drives). Figure 14-6 shows an example.

Figure 14-6: Shared resources on the host appear in a window on the guest.

Restarting Direct Cable Connection

After you've been through the configuration the first time, reconnecting is much easier. Simply select Start⇨Programs⇨Accessories⇨Direct Cable Connection and follow the prompts.

Changing the host and guest designations

After the initial configuration, you can change the host and guest designations by starting Direct Cable Connection and selecting Change. You may then change the guest to a host or vice versa. Be prepared to go through the steps to configure the host, name the host, and set up shared resources on the host. The same is true of changing a host to a guest, except fewer steps are needed because there's no resource sharing on a guest computer.

Troubleshooting

If no connection is established, review the following list:

1. Are the PCs configured to use the same port?

2. Is the cable securely connected to the correct port on each PC?

3. Do you have the correct cable? Try another parallel cable.

TIP

Probably the most common mistake in setting up Direct Cable Connection is using the wrong cable. So check carefully.

4. Is one PC the host and the other the guest?

5. Do the ports work? If you're using the parallel port, does the printer work when you connect it to that port? See the troubleshooting section of Chapter 9 for information on locating problems with serial ports.

6. Is File and Print Sharing enabled? If it isn't, there's nothing to share.

7. Have you set up a shared resource on the host?

8. Are both PCs using the Microsoft File and Print Sharing Protocol? (That's the Microsoft Internetwork Packet Exchange/Sequenced Packet Exchange or IPX/SPX protocol.) The easiest way to explain protocol is to liken it to a language. Both PCs have to be using the same protocol or speaking the same *language* to communicate. You can check whether the Microsoft IPX/SPX protocol is available by selecting Start⇨Settings⇨Control Panel⇨Network. The IPX/SPX protocol should be in the list of installed network components, and the Primary Network Logon should be Client for Microsoft Networks.

If you don't see the IPX/SPX protocol there, you can add it. From the Network properties menu, select Add⇨Protocol⇨Add⇨Microsoft⇨IPX/SPX-compatible protocol (see Figure 14-7) and click on OK. If Windows needs one of your installation diskettes, it asks you for it. After you do this, the Microsoft IPX/SPX protocol should be available in the Network properties box.

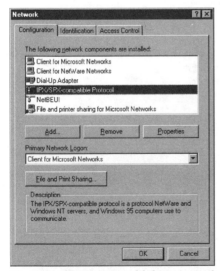

Figure 14-7: You can add the Microsoft IPX/SPX protocol if it is not already available.

9. Is the Microsoft IPX/SPX protocol bound to the Dial-Up Adapter? The Dial-Up Adapter is used for the Direct Cable Connection, and the protocol should have been bound to the adapter when it was added. Here's how to check whether this was done. Select Start⇨Settings⇨Control Panel⇨Network, highlight the Dial-Up Adapter, and select Properties⇨Bindings.

Make sure that there's a check in the box in front of the IPX/SPX-compatible protocol to indicate that it is bound to the Dial-Up Adapter. If no check mark is in the box, the protocol is not bound. You must select the IPX/SPX-compatible protocol to bind it, and then click on OK⇨OK to get back to Control Panel. Windows 95 restarts your computer so the change can take effect.

Updating Files between Two PCs

The easiest way to update files between two PCs is to get the Direct Cable Connection established and then use the Windows 95 My Briefcase to make sure that you have the most up-to-date version of the file on both PCs (see Figure 14-8). Each time you start the Direct Cable Connection, you can start Briefcase and have the file or files updated to the most recent version on both PCs. That way, you always have the most recent version of critical files, and you don't have to keep track of when you last worked on a file to make sure you get it copied. You can just start Briefcase and let it check for you.

Figure 14-8: The Windows 95 My Briefcase is available on the desktop.

TIP The Briefcase is designed to handle several individual files, but not entire directories (or folders). If you're working with entire directories, you'd be better off copying those items from the guest to the host and back again instead of using Briefcase.

To set up Briefcase to synchronize files between two PCs, you must have (1) Direct Cable Connection working between the two PCs as explained earlier in this chapter, (2) the Briefcase function on the PC that is the guest, and (3) the program that created the file on both PCs. What I mean by having the program that created the file on both PCs is that if you're using Microsoft Word for Windows to create your file, then you must have a copy of Microsoft Word for Windows on both your host and guest PCs.

How to add files to Briefcase

For this approach to work, you must add files that reside on the host to the Briefcase on the guest. This addition is done on the guest PC by using Direct Cable Connect.

When you're ready to add files to the Briefcase on the guest PC, make sure the Direct Cable Connection is running between the host and the guest, and then simply select the files from the host and "drag and drop" the files over to the Briefcase icon on the guest desktop, as shown in Figure 14-9.

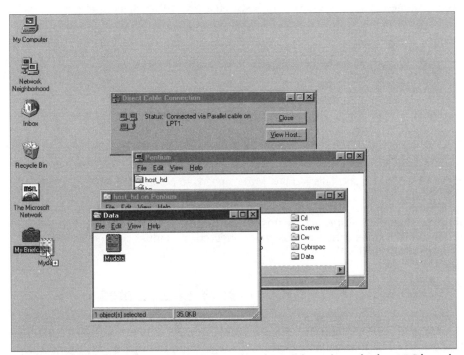

Figure 14-9: The Mydata file is being moved to the Briefcase from the host PC by using drag and drop.

Drag and drop works like this: You highlight the file, hold the left mouse button down, and while holding the button down, begin moving the mouse. A "shadowy" version of the file you've chosen appears on-screen under your mouse pointer, and it stays with the mouse pointer until you "drop" it — that is, you release the left mouse button. You want to drop the file onto the Briefcase icon, as shown with the file Mydata.

When the file is moved, you may check the Briefcase to see whether the file is there by selecting My Briefcase. As you can see, Mydata is in the My Briefcase window.

How to edit Briefcase files on the guest

When you've added the file from the host to the Briefcase on the guest, then you can edit the file by opening my Briefcase and double-clicking on the file. Windows 95 brings up the application that created the file, and you can work on the file just as you would if it was on the host PC.

How to tell whether your Briefcase files need to be synchronized

One of the slick things about Briefcase is that it checks your files to see whether any have changed. If so, it alerts you in the Briefcase window. Select the My Briefcase icon, and it informs you if files need to be updated, as shown in Figure 14-10.

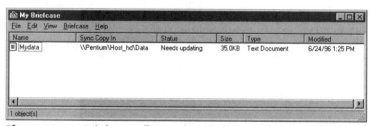

Figure 14-10: Briefcase tells you that Mydata needs to be updated.

If the file has been edited on the host, then there's no way the guest PC's Briefcase can know about it unless the two PCs are connected. You must connect the PCs to synchronize the files that have been changed on the host.

How to synchronize (update) Briefcase files

To synchronize the files, start My Briefcase on the guest and select Briefcase. If Briefcase has determined that the file exists in a more recent version, it will have the Update All selection available. Select Update All, and the Update My Briefcase window appears, showing both versions of the file and asking you whether you want to replace the older version of the file that is in the Briefcase with the newer version of the file. Select Update to replace the previous version of the file with the most recently changed version from the host PC (see Figure 14-11).

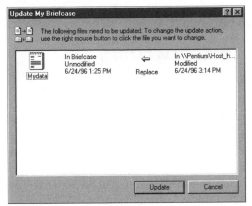

Figure 14-11: When you choose an update option, Briefcase shows you each file and asks you to confirm the update.

If you want to replace the newer version of the file with the older version, you may do that as well. Simply place your mouse cursor over the older file and click the right mouse button. A list of options appears; one of them changes the direction of the arrow so that the older file is replaced with the new one, and another option skips the replacement.

To see the location of each file, hold your mouse cursor over the file for a few seconds, and the path appears.

Splitting files and orphans

Briefcase works by making a copy of any file placed in it and placing that copy in a special directory on your hard disk drive. Briefcase creates and maintains a link between that copy and the original file, which it constantly updates whenever possible. You can break that link so that each file is independent, an action called *splitting* the files. After a file is split, it becomes an *orphan*.

You may want to split a file if you placed new material in the version of the file in the Briefcase on the guest and different new material in the file on the host. If you simply update, the file with the most recent date and time stamp overwrites the other, and you lose some information. If you split the file in the Briefcase on the guest, then you can add the file on the host to the Briefcase again. You have two versions of the file, but this allows you to cut and paste between the two files by using the guest PC so that you don't lose any data.

To split the file, open Briefcase on the guest PC, highlight the file, and select Briefcase⇨Split file from Original. You are asked to confirm the split. After the file is split, it is an orphan (as shown in Figure 14-12) and no longer can be linked to the original file.

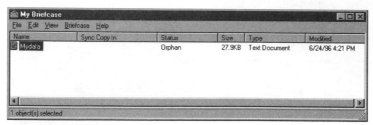

Figure 14-12: This file has been split and is an orphan.

Splitting a file is not reversible. If you want a linked file again, you have to add the original to the Briefcase again.

Troubleshooting

If My Briefcase says the file is write-protected, go to the host PC where the original file is located and make sure you've enabled full sharing for that file. See "Setting up shared resources on the host" under the "How to configure for connection" section in this chapter. Read-only sharing doesn't allow you to properly update the file.

Troubleshooting Practice: What's Wrong in These Photos?

Here are some common problem situations. Can you tell what's wrong?

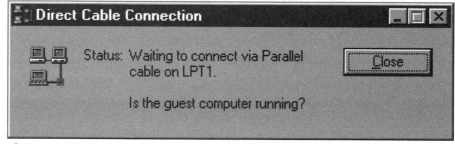

Figure 14-13: See answer 1.

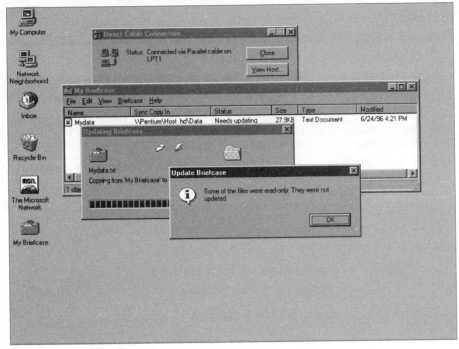

Figure 14-14: See answer 2.

Answers:

1. The host PC is not communicating properly with the guest. This is frequently a cable problem.

2. The file is not properly set up for sharing on the host PC. Either the file is not set up for sharing at all, or it is set up for read-only sharing. Full-sharing must be enabled.

Summary

✦ After it is set up, the Windows 95 Direct Cable Connection is a simple and elegant way to connect two PCs to transfer data.

✦ The two PCs must be connected using the same port on each, though you can use either the serial or parallel ports. For example, if you choose to use LPT1 on one PC, then you must use LPT1 on the other.

✦ Printer sharing is possible, but you have to connect the printers by using a port other than the port connected to the printer on the host.

✦ My Briefcase requires Direct Cable Connection to update files between a guest and host PC.

✦ If you add the host files to My Briefcase on the guest, then you can update the files anytime changes are made on either the host or guest PC.

✦   ✦   ✦

Printer Upgrades

In This Chapter

✦ Installing printers successfully

✦ Decoding printer terms and port terms

✦ Setting up a printer in Windows 3.x and Windows 95

✦ Troubleshooting tips and solutions

✦ Connecting two printers to one PC or vice versa

Tools Needed

✦ Wrist grounding strap (for memory upgrades)

✦ Small Phillips screwdriver

✦ Small flathead screwdriver

If you are like most people, you are not looking for advice on purchasing a printer. Most people know what they want in a printer because they either have seen output from someone else's printer or have worked with a printer they like. You probably know what you want, what your budget will allow, and that before you get anything, you should shop around. (If you *are* looking for advice on purchasing a printer, however, you would be better off checking out monthly and weekly publications such as *PC World*, *InfoWorld*, or a number of others that specialize in covering new products and issues that face the computer user.)

So, if you are not looking for advice on what to buy, then what *are* you looking for? More than likely, you are looking for help on getting that new printer to work with your system. This may include information about how to connect the printer, how to get your software to talk to the printer, and perhaps how to get two PCs to successfully use one printer. You even may want to keep your old printer connected to your PC while adding a new model or adding more memory to a laser printer. That information is the focus of this chapter.

In this chapter, I talk about the essential things you need to know about each type of printer, including how to get the proper connections and software for the printer you decide to buy, how to connect your new printer and install your printer driver software, the steps involved for testing your printer, and things to look for if you have problems.

Preparation

Although the preparation in getting a new printer to work is minimal, you must do it in order for your printer to function. Frankly, printer details can be boring, but a few essential facts about different printers will help you set up one. You also may need some information on how to get the right cable for, and how to set up the printer software drivers that you get with, a new printer so that it works in DOS, Windows 3.x, and Windows 95.

What to know about each type of printer

I talk about three types of printers in this chapter: laser printers, inkjet printers, and impact printers. I divided the printers into two categories, however, for the purpose of discussing how to upgrade printers. Those categories are (1) laser printers and (2) everything else.

Laser printers

Adding a laser printer is almost like adding another computer to your PC, but don't let that fact scare you. Laser printers are easy to understand and use after you know a few facts about them.

Laser printers are a cross between a computer and a photocopier (see Figure 15-1). They have their own microprocessors and memory, but they use toner and heat to print items. The mechanical process of printing involves a rotating drum that attracts the toner particles to the paper rolled across it, at which point heat is applied to fuse the toner to the paper. Internally, the microprocessor builds the entire image of a single page in memory, using the data sent from your PC, and then sends the image of that page to the mechanical portion of the printer, where it is printed. As a result, if there is not enough memory to hold the image of the entire page, the laser printer cannot print the page.

Some laser printers come with built-in fonts, but if you work much with graphics or page design, the program you use to create the image must send the font or the description of the character styles that you are using (along with the image) to the printer. This process is called *downloading* the font to the printer. The reason why you need to know about this process is because it uses even more of the laser printer's memory.

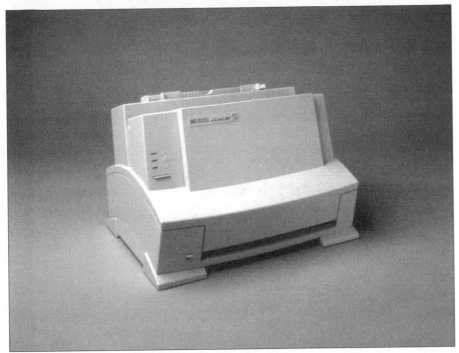

Figure 15-1: The HP LaserJet 5L printer.

TIP

What are fonts? *Fonts* (sometimes called *type styles*) are sets of letters of the alphabet that have a certain design. You can see your fonts under Windows 3.*x* by selecting Main⇨Control Panel⇨Fonts. If you're using Windows 95, you can see your fonts by selecting Start ⇨Settings⇨Control Panel⇨Fonts. In the most technical sense, a font is defined by the type of character, the character size, and other characteristics such as bold or italic. For example, Times New Roman in a 12-point size technically is a different font from Times New Roman in a 13-point size or Times New Roman in 12-point italics.

Keep in mind two important facts about fonts. First, the larger the font, the more memory it uses in your printer. Second, the more fonts you use in a document, the more memory your laser printer needs to print your pages.

So, using and adding memory is an issue for laser printers in much the same way as it is for PCs. Most of the new laser printers come with at least 2MB of memory and a number of fonts already built into them. These specifications usually are more than adequate for the average computer user. However, if you are planning to print large graphic images or are planning to use a number of fonts that are not built into the printer, then you should consider adding memory to your laser printer.

Other types of printers

For the purposes of upgrading, inkjet printers and impact printers (such as dot matrix or daisy wheel printers) work in the same way. These printers require a very small memory space, usually called the *print buffer,* to store data coming in from the computer. These printers require little memory because they only print a line or a small section of a page at a time rather than the entire page simultaneously (like laser printers).

Your biggest concern when upgrading to these types of printers is to make sure that you have the right software driver so that the information can be correctly sent to the printer. This brings me to the subject of the software that you should use for printers.

Software drivers for printers

Printers receive instructions from your computer on how to print what you sent to it. Not all printers speak the same language, however. Some printers, especially laser printers made by Hewlett-Packard, speak Printer Control Language (PCL), whereas others speak PostScript, and still others speak other languages.

To convert the commands sent out by your software into printer control codes that your printer can use, you need a piece of software called a *printer driver.* Most new printers come with a diskette that contains such software drivers. The drivers found there are your best bet because they are designed by the manufacturer to take advantage of your new printer's features.

DOS, Windows, and printer drivers

With DOS, you are required to define a printer for every software application that you install. The beauty of Windows is that you have to set up the printer driver only once. All your Windows-compatible software applications (and any new, Windows-compatible applications that you install) know to use the software driver that you've already defined. If you have the driver from the manufacturer, you can set up any version of Windows to use that driver.

Situations exist, however, in which the drivers from the manufacturer are not available. For example, the diskette may be lost, the printer may be an older type that did not come with a diskette, or the printer may be a used printer. To cover these circumstances, Windows 3.x and Windows 95 offer a set of printer drivers for your use. In the "Installation" section later in this chapter, I show you how to set up the drivers in both programs.

When a new operating system such as Windows 95 comes along, many printer manufacturers offer updated drivers. If you upgrade to Windows 95 and have trouble with your printer, you should check with the manufacturer to see if an updated driver geared toward Windows 95 is available. You often can get these drivers on disk for a nominal charge, or you can download the drivers from the manufacturer's Internet site or bulletin board service.

Emulation

A few brands of printers lead the market, such as those made by Hewlett-Packard (HP), Epson, Citizen, and IBM, to name a few. Any other manufacturer that wants to sell printers designs its printer to accept the same commands as a printer leading the market. When a printer is designed in such a way, it is said to be compatible with, or to *emulate,* a popular printer. This means that even if your printer is not a name brand one, if you can find out which printer it emulates, you can use the printer driver for that printer.

After you have a basic understanding of how your printer communicates with your PC, and you also have a software driver for your printer, you need to turn your attention to actually connecting your printer to your computer. You accomplish this task by using a printer cable. The following information can help you avoid several trips to the computer store to get the right cable.

Get the right cable

The vast majority of people set up their printers to use the PC's parallel port because that port is the most efficient one for the printer to use. Most parallel ports are bidirectional, which means that the computer can send data to the printer and the printer can respond to it at the same time. The printer's capability to respond is important because it enables the printer to say things such as it is not ready yet or that it has all the data it can handle right now and that the PC should wait a minute before sending more. This feature also enables the printer to signal when it is ready for more data. To get this feature, you probably want a cable that has a male, 25-pin parallel port connector on one end for connecting to your PC's parallel port.

The other end of the cable — the end that connects to the printer — is the one that you really need to be concerned about. This end may or may not be a connector like the one on your PC, so compatibility is an issue. This can be confusing, because many printers have both a 25-pin serial connector and a Centronics parallel connector, as shown in Figure 15-2. A common mistake is to get a cable that connects the parallel port on the computer to the serial port on the printer. That seems to make more sense to most people because the parallel cable on the computer is a 25-pin female and the serial port on the printer is a 25-pin male connector. The Centronics connector doesn't look like any port on the PC, so it's difficult for most people to imagine that they need this strange-looking connector on one end of the cable to connect the printer to their parallel port.

Because today's printers are sold in retail outlets by sales people with little knowledge of computing (much less cabling), you can find yourself with little or no assistance in finding the right cable. A demonstration model of your printer or a manual that you can look at typically is available, however, if you ask. Figure 15-3 shows you what to look for.

Figure 15-2: A printer with both a 25-pin female serial port and a Centronics parallel port.

The most common connectors found on the printer side are the Centronics parallel connector and the 25-pin parallel connector. Both are shown in Figure 15-3. If your printer has the Centronics parallel female connector on the back, as shown in Figure 15-2, you need to get a parallel cable with a male Centronics connector, such as the one shown in Figure 15-3.

 If you need a cable with 25-pin male connectors on each end, make sure that you buy a parallel printer cable, not a serial printer cable. The two cables may look identical, but they are wired differently. The packaging for the cable should say whether the cable is parallel or serial.

Centronics to serial mix-up

Jeff bought a new, color inkjet printer to replace his old dot matrix printer. He bought the printer and a parallel printer cable and then installed the printer on his PC. When he tested the printer, all it printed was gibberish. Jeff checked the connections, made sure he had the right printer driver, made sure the printer was online, and finally called the computer store. The store's personnel were at a loss regarding the source of the problem as well. Jeff was about to take the printer back to the store, but then he decided to call a computer consultant he knew and ask what might be wrong.

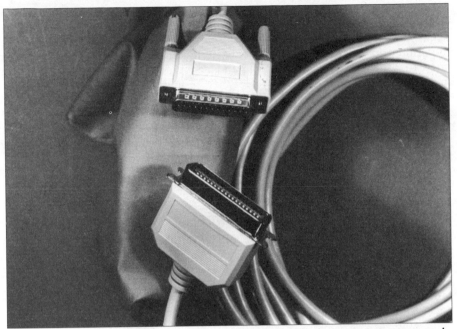

Figure 15-3: A parallel printer cable with the Centronics male connector on one end and the 25-pin male connector on the other.

After asking the standard questions, the computer consultant asked Jeff what port he had connected the printer to. Jeff told the consultant that he had connected the cable to the parallel port. The consultant then asked what type of cable Jeff was using. Jeff described the cable as having a 25-pin male connector on each end. The consultant then asked Jeff to describe the ports on the back of the printer.

One printer port was a 25-pin female port, whereas the other port turned out to be a Centronics female port. The Centronics port was the parallel port, and the 25-pin female port was the serial port. Jeff had the parallel port on the PC connected to the serial port on the printer. Jeff went back to the store and got a parallel printer cable with the Centronics male connector on one end and the 25-pin male connector on the other end, reconnected the printer, and was able to get everything to work.

Know your ports

You need to know the names that the computer uses for the ports in order to set up your printer correctly. Parallel ports are designated as LPT (which stands for logical port and is sometimes written in lowercase — *lpt*). If you have only one parallel port, it is designated as LPT1; if you have two, the second parallel port is designated LPT2; and so on. Most PCs have only one parallel port, although some PCs have two.

If you have two parallel ports and they are not labeled, the easiest way to determine which one is which is to do this test: Simply connect your printer to one port, and when you set up the printer in Windows, tell Windows that you want to use LPT1. If the printer doesn't work, switch the cable to the other parallel port. If it works, you know that the port that works is LPT1 and, conversely, that the other parallel port must be LPT2.

TIP Remember that the parallel ports on your PC tend to be female, 25-pin ports. Serial ports are usually male and have either 25 pins or 9 pins. Game ports are female, but they usually have 15 pins. Figure 15-4 shows the various ports so that you can see the differences.

Installation

After you have the correct cable and, hopefully, the software drivers, you can begin the installation process. The first thing that you should do, before you connect a new printer or plug it in, is make sure that it has the supplies that it needs in order to print. This may mean installing a toner cartridge or ink cartridge or putting a ribbon in the printer. This is not a time to wear your best clothes. You need to do this task according to the manufacturer's instructions, which vary from printer to printer.

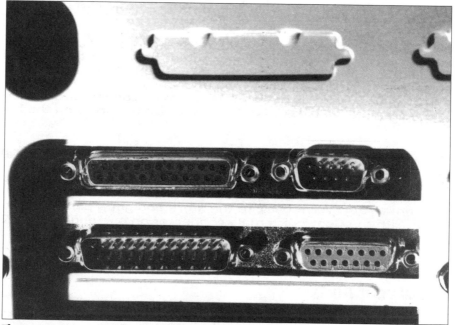

Figure 15-4: A 25-pin female parallel port, a 9-pin male serial port, a 25-pin male serial port, and a 15-pin female game port are shown.

After the toner, ink, or ribbon is installed in the printer, connect the cable from the parallel port on your computer to the parallel port on the printer. Most printer cables come with screws that you can tighten by hand to secure the connection to the parallel port. Some screws require you to use a small Phillips or flathead screwdriver. If you have a similar connector on your printer, you can secure the connection in the same way. If you have a Centronics connector, it uses clips to secure the connector.

After the cable is secure, connect the power cable to the printer, plug it in, and turn on the computer and the printer. You need to set up the printer in a software application, and the easiest and most productive place in which to do that is Windows. The printer driver installation instructions for Windows 3.x and Windows 95 are detailed in the next two sections.

Windows 3.x printer driver installation

If you have a printer driver diskette that came with your new printer, you want to keep it handy now. If not, you still can install the printer, but you need your Windows installation diskettes.

To set up a new printer in Windows 3.x, go to the Main group and select Control Panel⊏❯Printers⊏❯Add. Choose your new printer from the list presented. After you highlight your printer, select Install and tell Windows which drive contains your printer installation diskette or insert the Windows installation diskette requested. (See Figure 15-5.) Windows installs the driver for your new printer.

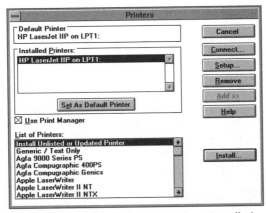

Figure 15-5: The Windows 3.x printer installation screen.

If you need to designate a port other than the standard LPT1, make sure that the printer you want to connect is highlighted in the Installed Printers dialog box. Then select Connect from the Printers menu, pick the port from those available and then click on OK (see Figure 15-6). The printer you selected should show the port change after you exit the Connect menu.

If you want to designate the new printer as the printer you use most of the time, you need to set up the new printer as the *default printer,* as shown in Figure 15-6. Highlight your printer in the Installed Printers dialog box and then select the Set as Default Printer option to make your printer appear in the Default Printer dialog box. To finish, click on Close.

The last step is to test the printer. Before you start testing it, though, make sure that the printer has paper. You can use your word processor (if one is installed) or the Windows Write program in the Accessories group to print a test document. In Windows Write, select File⇨Open and look for a file with the .WRI extension. The best place to look is in the Windows directory. Look for a file such as README.WRI, because those files typically use fonts and formatting that are clearly visible on your screen, which makes it easier to determine that your printer is printing correctly. After you have correctly printed a document, you can be confident that your printer is working.

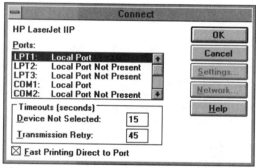

Figure 15-6: The Windows 3.*x* Connect menu enables you to select a different port for your printer.

You can change the paper orientation, the size of the paper that the printer is using, and a number of other options by following a couple of methods in Windows 3.*x*. The first way is to select File⇨Printer Setup in any application that you are using. The second way is to open the Main group and select Control Panel⇨Printers⇨Setup.

Windows 95 printer driver installation

To install a printer driver in Windows 95, you need the diskette that came with your new printer or your Windows 95 installation diskettes or CD-ROM. To set up the printer driver in Windows 95, select Start⇨Settings⇨Printers⇨Add a Printer, which starts the Add Printer Wizard. Select Next⇨Local Printer (if you are not adding a printer to a network), highlight the manufacturer of your printer from the box on the left, and then choose your specific model from the box on the right. If you have the diskette from your new printer, select Have Disk and tell Windows the disk drive where you are inserting the printer diskette (see Figure 15-7). Windows 95 then installs the printer driver, adding an icon for the new printer in the Printers group.

If you do not have the diskette from the printer manufacturer, you can use the printer drivers included on the Windows 95 installation diskettes or CD-ROM. After you have selected your printer manufacturer and model, click on Next and choose the printer port you want to use with this printer, as shown in Figure 15-8.

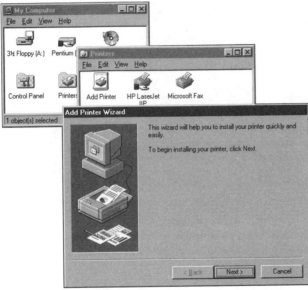

Figure 15-7: The Windows 95 Add Printer Wizard.

After you choose the port, Windows 95 asks you if you want to make this new printer the default printer (the main printer). Indicate your preference (you can change it later) and then click on Next to choose your last option, which is to print a test page. You definitely should print a test page. After you have printed the test page and you see that the printer is working, you have finished installing your new printer, so you can click on Finish to exit the Add Printer Wizard.

TIP

If you want to make changes to the settings you have selected for your printer, select Start⇨Settings⇨Printers, highlight the printer you want to change and then click the right mouse button. From the menu that opens (see Figure 15-9), you can view the print queue by selecting Open, change the default status of the printer by selecting "Set As Default," or view the printer's properties by selecting Properties. The Properties menu includes a number of different options for the printer, but the one that you'll probably use the most is the capability to change the size and orientation of the paper (see Figure 15-10).

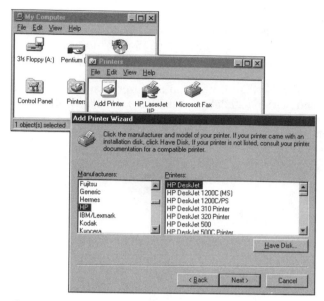

Figure 15-8: In Windows 95, you pick your printer manufacturer in the left windows, which narrows the list of printer models in the right window.

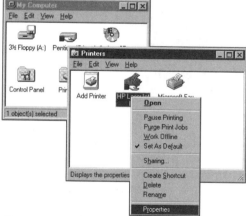

Figure 15-9: Clicking the right mouse button on the printer brings up a menu for that printer.

You need at least 2MB of free disk space to print in Windows 95.

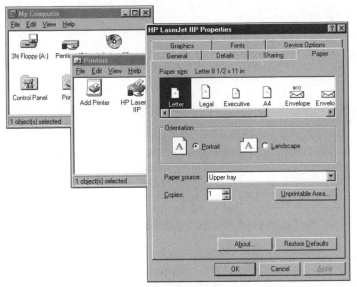

Figure 15-10: The printer properties in Windows 95 include a number of options, including the paper settings.

What to do if your printer is not listed

If your printer is not listed in the printers available in Windows, and you do not have a diskette, then you need to see if your printer emulates a printer that appears on the list. If so, install the driver for that printer and follow the instructions in your printer documentation to adjust your printer for emulation, if necessary. This buys you time to contact the manufacturer of the printer so that you can get the proper driver for your printer that enables you to take advantage of features that may be specific to your particular printer.

Installation in review

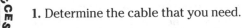

To upgrade to a new printer, follow these steps:

1. Determine the cable that you need.

2. Look for the software drivers that should have come with the printer.

3. With the computer and printer off, connect the printer by using the parallel cable.

4. Connect the power cable to the printer and plug it in.

5. Install the ink cartridge or toner cartridge, or put a ribbon in the printer, by following the manufacturer's instructions.

6. Turn on the computer and printer.

7. Install the software driver in Windows.

8. Test the printer.

9. Configure the printer in your other software programs.

Question: I have a short (6 foot) printer cable, and I'd like to put my printer farther away. I've heard that I cannot use a parallel cable longer than 8 feet. Is that true?

Answer: No. If the parallel cable is properly shielded, you can use a cable as long as 50 feet. Some specially designed cables can even go farther. Just keep the cable away from strong electromagnetic or magnetic fields, such those generated by refrigeration equipment, fluorescent lighting, large motors, and other such devices.

Question: Why does Windows list my fax drivers with the printers?

Answer: Windows considers a fax/modem to be a printing device. To the PC, sending a fax is the same as printing to the fax/modem, although it requires a different software driver. Hence, the software drivers for your fax programs are listed with the printer drivers.

Troubleshooting

If you have problems getting your new printer to work, here is a list of the most common problems and possible answers.

The printer won't print at all.

1. Is the printer on?

2. Is the printer plugged in? Is the outlet that it is plugged into working? Plug something else that you know works (such as a lamp) into the outlet to be sure.

3. Is the printer's power switch on? Look on the back or sides of the printer for the power switch.

4. Is the printer online? Here, *online* means that the printer is accepting communication from the computer. Most printers have an online button with a light next to it that indicates whether the printer is online. If the light is not lit, the printer is not online. Some printers also have a display that tells you whether or not the printer is online, so check the display as well.

5. Is there paper in the printer? Is there paper stuck in the printer? A light on the printer may be blinking to indicate that the printer is out of paper or that the paper is jammed. If the printer has a display, check to see if it tells you what the problem is.

6. Did you remember to install a toner cartridge, ink cartridge, or ribbon? Check the installation instructions again to make sure that you installed these materials correctly. (One common mistake with some laser printer toner cartridges is that users sometimes forget to remove the sealing tape before the toner is installed.)

7. Do you have the correct printer driver installed?

8. Is the printer set to use the correct port? Some printers with two ports allow you to set what port to use. You should check your printer settings (look in your printer documentation for how to do this) to make sure that the printer is set to use the port you've selected.

9. If you are running Windows 95, do you have at least 2MB of free hard disk space? You need at least that much for the printer to work.

The printer seems to be on, but it won't print.

Will the printer run a self test? If this works, you can be sure that you have a communication problem between the printer and your PC. It could be a wrong driver, a problem with a port, or the wrong cable.

The printer acts like it's receiving data, but won't print.

1. Do you have the right printer driver?

2. Does the printer have paper? Is the paper positioned so that the printer can sense it? Remove the paper and reinsert it to see if that helps.

3. Does the printer have the right size paper?

4. Is the paper jammed? Check to be sure the paper path is clear according to the instructions in your printer's documentation.

5. Is it a laser printer? Laser printers require a special page eject character to be sent at the end of less than a full page of information. Otherwise, the printer holds the data until it gets enough to print a full page. This tends to happen if you are attempting to use the Print Screen key on the keyboard to print what you see on the computer screen. Try using a word processor for printing or sending more than one page of data to the printer. You also can type a command line at the DOS prompt to send the page eject character to the printer. (The page eject character is generated when you hold down Alt, type **12** on the numeric keypad, and then release Alt; this action is represented as Alt+12.) The command line is ECHO ALT-12 > LPT1. If you have the printer set to a different port, such as COM1, then substitute that port designation for LPT1.

6. Do you have the right cable? Make sure that you have a parallel cable if you are using parallel ports, or a serial cable if you are using serial ports. Also, make sure that you are not running a cable from the parallel port on the PC to the serial port on the printer or vice versa.

The printer prints gibberish.

1. Do you have the right cable? Make sure that you have a parallel cable if you are using parallel ports, or a serial cable if you are using serial ports. Also, make sure that you are not running a cable from the parallel port on the PC to the serial port on the printer or vice versa.

2. Do you have the right printer driver?

Adding Memory to a Laser Printer

If you purchase a laser printer from a computer reseller, you may be able to get the reseller to put additional memory in your computer for you if you purchase the memory around the same time. But if you buy the laser printer at one of the many retail outlets that do not offer technical support for the products they sell, or if you need to upgrade memory in a printer you currently have, then you can add the memory yourself.

Many new laser printers, such as the Hewlett-Packard LaserJets (starting with the Model 4), enable you to add memory in the form of single, in-line memory modules (SIMMs) in much the same way that you would add memory to your PC. Most of these printers have internal SIMM slots. (See Chapter 6.) You plug standard SIMMs into those slots in the same way that you would add memory to your PC. You need to look at your documentation for your particular printer and then refer to Chapter 6 (which covers memory upgrades) to get the information you need for adding more memory to your printer.

You may find yourself adding memory to an existing printer or to one that uses a more proprietary memory system, however. For example, the HP IIP uses memory "cards" populated with DRAM chips (called DIPs) to add memory. These cards easily plug into the back of the laser printer. Memory cards are simple to install and are available through mail-order sources as well as in retail computer stores. Those companies specializing in laser printer toner refill and laser printer repair also should be able to help you determine the memory you need for your laser printer.

Whether you are using memory cards or SIMMs to upgrade the memory in your laser printer, you still need to wear a wrist grounding strap to protect your hardware. Also, you can expect the printer to automatically recognize the new memory after it is installed correctly. You can ensure that the additional memory is available by running the printer's self test, which gives you a report that includes the amount of memory installed. A button or switch typically is available on the front of the printer that is labeled "test" or "self-test."

Multiple PCs and Printers

You can keep your old printer and your new printer connected to the same PC. You also may want to connect two PCs to the same printer. I cover the most commonly used methods for connection here.

Using switch boxes

The most common way to connect multiple PCs or multiple printers is to use a switch box. (You can set up a peer-to-peer network to share resources between PCs, which is covered in Chapter 14.) Switch boxes come in manual and electronic versions. Manual switch boxes require you to physically change a switch, but electronic switch boxes sense the signal coming in and direct it without you having to do anything. Both kinds are inexpensive and popular. You can find switch boxes specially designed for connecting two PCs to a single printer and for connecting two printers to a single PC.

You should be aware that manual switch boxes can contribute to the failure of your printer in certain circumstances. If the manual switch box doesn't entirely break one connection before it makes another connection, and if there is a difference in the voltage of the ground between one device and another, the difference in voltage can blow out the port on the printer or the PC. This type of accident is not one that your printer warranty or PC warranty will cover. Fortunately, this situation does not occur frequently, but it is something you may see referenced in your printer documentation.

Connecting a second printer by using the serial ports

Some printers offer you the option of using both the parallel and serial ports at the same time. This means that you can connect two PCs to the printer by using both ports. In that case, the printer has the capability to handle the input from both PCs. Of course, this requires you to use the serial port and a serial cable from one of the PCs to connect to the printer.

If you plan to install a printer by using a serial port, then you have to determine which serial port is which on the PC to which you are connecting. Serial ports are designated as *COM ports* (short for communications, which is sometimes written in all lowercase — *com*). Some PCs have as many as four COM ports, with the first serial port designated as COM1, the second as COM2, and so on. If you have a modem or a fax/modem on your PC, it uses one of those COM ports. The trick is finding out which port is which and if any are available. The information you need to identify serial ports is in Chapter 9.

After you have your serial port identified, you need to be sure to get a serial cable with the correct connectors on each end to connect the PC to the port. Then you can install the printer. When you set up the printer in Windows, be sure to designate the COM port that the printer will be using.

Summary

✦ To successfully upgrade your printer, be sure to get the right cable and know the designation of the port you plan to connect to.

✦ The software drivers from the manufacturer of the printer are the best to use.

✦ Printers often emulate other, more popular brands, and you can use that information to install a printer.

✦ You need the installation diskettes or CD-ROM to install a printer in Windows if you don't have a diskette that came with the printer.

✦ Memory upgrades are common in laser printers and often use standard SIMMs.

✦   ✦   ✦

Resources for Tools and Products

Here is contact information for companies listed in the book, as well as for popular vendors of PCs and PC products. I emphasize technical support numbers, BBS numbers, and Internet addresses where you can find troubleshooting help and download software drivers. Of course, this information has been checked, but it is subject to change without notice.

Acer
OEM of PC systems
2641 Orchard Parkway
San Jose, CA 95134
Phone: (408) 432-6200
BBS: (408) 428-0140
Internet home page: http://www.acer.com

Adaptec
Manufacturer of I/O cards
691 Milpitas Blvd.
Milpitas, CA 95035
Phone: (408) 945-8600
Technical support: (800) 959-7274
Faxback: (408) 957-7150
BBS: (408) 945-7727
Internet home page: http://www.adaptec.com

Advanced Micro Devices (AMD)
Manufacturer of processors for PC systems
PO Box 3453
Sunnyvale, CA 94088
Phone: (408) 732-2400
Automated technical support: (800) 222-9323
Faxback: (800) 222-9323
Internet home page: http://www.amd.com

American Megatrends, Inc.
BIOS manufacturer
6145-F Northbelt Parkway
Norcross, GA 30071
Phone: (770) 246-8600
Sales: (800) 828-9264
Fax: (770) 246-8790
Faxback: (770) 246-8787
Internet home page:
http://www.megatrends.com

AMP
Computer components and accessories,
including voltage regulator interposers
P.O. Box 3608 — m/s 038-003
Harrisburg, PA 17105-3608
Phone: (905) 470-4425
Toll-free: (800) 522-6752
Faxback: (800) 522-6752
Internet catalog: http://connect.amp.com

AST Research, Inc.
OEM of PC systems
16215 Alton Parkway
Irvine, CA 92619
Toll-free: (800) 727-1278
Service and support: (800) 876-4278
Service and support: (714) 727-9292
Technical support: (800) 758-0278
Faxback: (800) 876-4278
Internet home page: http://www.ast.com

Autotime/Memorytime Corporation
Manufacturers of SIMM Adapters
6605 S.W. Macadam Avenue
Portland, OR 97201
Phone: (503) 452-8577
Fax: (503) 452-8495
Autofax 24 hours: (503) 452-0208

Award Software
BIOS manufacturer
777 East Middlefield Road
Mountain View, CA 94043-4023
Phone: (415) 968 4433
Fax: (415) 968 0274
BBS: (415) 968 0249
Internet home page: http://www.award.com

Cameleon Technology, Inc.
Manufacturers of SIMM adapters called
SIMMVerters
816 Charcot Avenue
San Jose, CA 95131
Phone: (408) 436-8681
Fax: (408) 436-8685

Colorado Memory Systems (CMS),
a subsidiary of Hewlett-Packard
Manufacturers of tape backup drives
2403 4th Avenue
Greeley, CO 80631
Toll-free: (800) 469-5150
BBS: (970) 635-0650
Internet file site: ftp://ftp.hp.com

Compaq
OEM of PC systems
PO Box 692000
Houston, TX 77269
Phone: (713) 370-0670
Faxback: (800) 345-1518
Internet home page:
http://www.compaq.com

Computer Discount Warehouse (CDW)
Catalog of computer parts and accessories,
including upgrade components
1020 E. Lake Cook Road
Buffalo Grove, IL 60089
Call for free catalog toll free in U.S.:
(800) 313-4239
Outside U.S. fax: (312) 527-2798
Internet: http://www.cdw.com

Conner Peripherals, merged with Seagate in
February, 1996. *See Seagate*.

Creative Labs
Manufacturer of multimedia kits
and sound cards
1901 McCarthy Blvd.
Milpitas, CA 95035
Phone: (408) 428-6600
Internet home page: http://www.creaf.com

Cyrix
Manufacturer of processors for PC systems
PO Box 850118
Richardson, TX 75085
Phone: (214) 994-8388
Technical Support: (800) 46-CYRIX
Faxback: (800) 462-9749
BBS: (214) 968-8610
Internet: http://www.cyrix.com

Data Comm Warehouse
Catalog of computer parts and accessories,
including upgrade components
1700 Oak Street
P.O. Box 301
Lakewood, NJ 08701-9885
Call for free catalog toll free in U.S.:
(800) 328-2261
Outside U.S. fax: (908) 363-4823
Internet home page:
http://www.warehouse.com

Dell Computer
OEMs of PC systems
2214 West Braker Lane, Suite D
Austin, TX 78758-4053
Technical support: (800) 624-9896
Faxback: (800) 950-1329
BBS: (512) 728-8528
Internet home page: http://www.dell.com

Dynamic Learning Systems
Publisher of PC repair newsletters
PO Box 805
Marlboro, MA 01752
Phone: (508) 366-9487
Fax: (508) 898-9995
BBS: (508) 366-7683
Internet home page:
http://www.dlspubs.com/

Epson
OEMs of PC systems
PO Box 2842
Torrance, CA 90509
Technical support: (800) 922-8911
Faxback: (310) 782-4214
BBS (310) 782-4531
Internet home page:
http://www.epson.com

Gateway 2000
OEMs of PC systems
PO Box 2000
North Sioux City, SD 57049
Technical support: (800) 846-2301
Automated technical support:
(800) 846-2118
Internet home page: http://www.gw2k.com

Global Computer Supplies
Catalog of computer parts and accessories,
including upgrade components
1050 Northbrook Parkway, Department 71
Suwanee, GA 30174
Call for free catalog toll free in U.S.:
(800) 845-6225
Outside U.S. phone: (779) 339-9999

Hayes
Manufacturer of modems
World Headquarters
5835 Peachtree Corners East
Norcross, GA 30092
Phone: (770) 441-1617
Fax: (770) 449-0087
Faxback: (800) 429-3739
BBS: (770) 446-6336
Internet home page:
http://www.hayes.com

Hewlett-Packard
A manufacturer of printers, PCs, and
peripherals
3000 Hanover Street 20BX
Palo Alto, CA 94304
Printer support: (208) 323-2551
Vectra PC products support: (800) 626-6535
Faxback: (800) 333-1917
BBS: (208) 344-1691
Internet home page: http:\\www.hp.com

IBM PC Company
OEMs of PC systems
3039 Cornwallis Drive, Bldg. 203
Research Triangle Park, NC 27709
Phone: (919) 517-0001
Technical support: (800) 772-2227
BBS: (919) 517-0001
Faxback technical support: (800) 426-3395
Internet home page:
http:\\www.pc.ibm.com
Internet page for IBM Surepath BIOS:
http:\\www.surepath.ibm.com

Insight
Catalog of computer parts and accessories,
including upgrade components
1912 West 4th Street
Tempe, AZ 85281
Toll-free: (800) 610-4444
Fax: (602) 902-1161
Internet home page:
http://www.insight.com

Intel
Manufacturers of the most popular
processors for PC systems
2200 Mission College Blvd.
Santa Clara, CA 95051
Technical support U.S.: 800-321-4044
Technical support UK: +44-1793-43-11-44
Faxback in U.S.: (800) 525-3019
Internet: http://www.intel.com

Iomega Corporation
Manufacturer of tape backup drives
and the ZIP drive
1821 West Iomega Way
Roy, UT 84067
Phone: (801) 778-1000
Toll-free: (800) 697-8833
Faxback: (801) 778-5763
BBS: (801) 778-5888
Internet home page:
http://www.iomega.com

Jensen Tools
Distributor of tools and test equipment
for PCs. Free catalog available.
7815 South 46th Street
Phoenix, AZ 85044
Phone: (602) 968-6231
Toll-free: (800) 426-1194
Fax: (800) 366-9662

Kingston Technology Corporation
Manufacturers of memory products
17600 Newhope Street
Fountain Valley, CA 92708
Toll-free: (800) 337-8409
Internet home page:
http://www.kingston.com

Maxtor, subsidiary of Hyundai Electronics
of America
Makes hard disk drives
2190 Miller Drive
Longmont, CO 80501
Phone: (303) 651-6000
Technical support: (800) 262-9867
Customer service: (800) 486-3472
Fax: (303) 678-2260
Faxback: (303) 678-2618
BBS: (303) 678-2222 (English and Spanish)
Internet home page:
http://www.maxtor.com

Media Vision
Manufacturers of multimedia kits and
sound cards
1435 McCandles Drive
Milpitas, CA 95035
Phone: (510) 770-8600
Fax: (408) 934-8459
Internet home page: http://www.dell.com

Micro House
Maker of software for hard disk drive
installation and translation. Supplier of
technical specifications for computer
hardware.
4900 Pearl East Circle, Suite 101
Boulder, CO 80301
Phone: (303) 443-3388
Toll-free: (800) 926-8299
Fax: (303) 443-3323

Microid Research
BIOS Manufacturer (MR BIOS)
2336-D Walsh Avenue
Santa Clara, CA, 95051
Phone: (408) 727-6991
Internet home page:
http://www.mrbios.com

Micron Technology
Manufacturer of memory products
8000 Federal Way
P.O. Box 6
Boise, ID 83707-0006
Phone: (208) 368-4000
Fax: (208) 363-4431
Internet home page:
http://www.micron.com/mti

Microsoft
Maker of DOS and Windows operating
systems
1 Microsoft Way
Redmond, WA 98052
Phone: (206) 882-8080
BBS (download service): (206) 936-6735
Internet home page:
http://www.microsoft.com

NEC Technologies, Inc.
Manufacturers of CD-ROM drives, monitors,
disk drives, and PCs
1280 North Arlington Heights Road,
Suite 500
Itasoa, IL 60143
Toll-free: (800) 632-4636
Phone: (508) 264-8000
CD-ROM products: (800) 632-4667
Desktop systems: (800) 632-4565
Customer service: (800) 388-8888
Faxback: (800) 366-0476
BBS: (508) 635-4706
Internet home page: http://www.nec.com

Ontrack
Maker of Disk Manager
6321 Bury Drive
Minneapolis, MN 55346
Phone: (612) 937-1107
Toll-free: (800) 752-1333
Fax: (612) 937-5815
BBS: (612) 937-0860
Internet home page:
http://www.ontrack.com

OsoSoft
Maker of Burn-In, shareware for PC testing
1472 Sixth Street
Los Osos, CA
Phone: (805) 528-1759
Fax: (805) 528-3074
BBS: (805) 528-3753

Packard Bell NEC
OEMs of PC systems
5701 Lindero Canyon Road
Westlake Village, CA 91362
Phone: (818) 865-1555
BBS: (801) 250-1600
Internet home page:
http://www.packardbell.com

Parallel Technologies Direct
A source for "Smart" parallel or Universal
Connection Mode (UCM) cables
4240 B Street
Auburn, WA 98001
Phone: (206) 813-8728
Toll-free: (800) 789-4784
E-mail on the Internet: sales@lpt.com

PC Zone, The Catalog of computer parts
and accessories, including upgrade
components
15815 SE 37th Street
Bellevue, WA 98006-1800
Call for free catalog toll free in U.S.:
(800) 258-2088
Outside U.S. fax: (206) 603-2550
Internet: http://www.internetMCI.com/
marketplace/mzone

Phoenix Technologies Ltd.
BIOS manufacturers
World Headquarters
2770 De La Cruz
Santa Clara, CA 95050
Phone: (408) 654 9000
Fax: (408) 452 1985
Internet home page: http://www.ptltd.com

Quantum
Manufacturer of hard disk drives
500 McCarthy Boulevard
Milpitas, CA 95035
Phone: (408) 894-4000
Technical support: (800) 826-8022
Faxback: (800) 434-7532
BBS: (408) 894-3214
Internet home page:
http://www.quantum.com

Seagate (now merged with Conner Peripherals)
Manufacturer of hard disk drives
920 Disk Drive
Scotts Valley, CA 95066
Phone: (408) 452-2000
Technical support: (800) 732-4283
Tape sales: (800) 626-6637
Disk sales: (408) 438-8111
Customer service: (800) 486-3472
SeaFAX: (408) 456-4903
BBS: (408) 456-4415 up to 14.4 N-8-1
Internet home page:
http://www.seagate.com

Storage Dimensions
Maker of Drive Pro and EZ-Drive software
for hard disk drive installation and
software drive translation
Worldwide Headquarters
1656 McCarthy Boulevard
Milpitas, CA 95035
Phone: (408) 954-0710
Toll-free: (800) 765-7895
Fax: (408) 944-1200
Technical support: (408) 894-1325
Internet home page:
http://www.storagedimensions.com

Supra Corporation, a Diamond Multimedia Company
Manufacturer of modems
7101 Supra Drive Southwest
Albany, OR 97321
Toll-free: (800) 774-4965
Fax: (503) 967-2401
Faxback: (541) 967-0072
Internet home page:
http://www.supra.com

Symantec
Maker of Norton Utilities PC diagnostic software
World Headquarters
10201 Torre Avenue
Cupertino, CA 95014
Phone: (408) 253-9600
Fax: (408) 253-3968
Internet home page:
http:\\www.symantec.com

Touchstone Software
Maker of Check It PC diagnostic software
2124 Main Street
Huntington Beach, CA 92648
Phone: (714) 969-7746
Fax: (714) 969-4444
Internet home page:
http:\\www.checkit.com

U.S. Robotics
Manufacturer of modems
8100 North McCormick
Skokie, IL 60076
Technical support: (847) 982-5151
Fax: (847) 676-7314
Faxback: (800) 856-1045 US
Faxback outside U.S.: (303) 727-7079
Internet home page: http://www.usr.com

Western Digital Corporation
Manufacturer of hard disk drives,
controller cards, CD-ROM drives
8105 Irvine Center Drive
Irvine, CA 92718
Phone: (714) 932-4900
BBS: (714) 753-1234
Technical support: (714) 932-4900
Internet home page: http://www.wdc.com

Glossary

2DD — Double-sided, double-density diskette, either a 360K
5^1/$_4$-inch diskette or a 720K 3^1/$_2$-inch diskette.

2HD — Double-sided, high-density diskette, either a 1.2MB,
5^1/$_4$-inch diskette, or a 1.44MB, 3^1/$_2$-inch diskette.

ASCII — *American Standard Code for Information Interchange*
(pronounced *ask-ee*). A scheme that represents the characters of
the alphabet and the numbers 0 – 9 by digital values that are
stored by the computer as binary zeros and ones.

AT parallel mode — A single directional mode sometimes
known as the *compatible* mode used for transmission of data
between a PC and peripherals.

ATAPI — *AT-Attachment Packet Interface* for IDE drives. Sometimes referred to as ATAPI-IDE, this term is used mostly in
reference to CD-ROM drives that can be run from the standard
IDE controller interface to the computer used by hard disk
drives.

auto answer — A modem feature that allows the modem to
detect and answer an incoming call.

baud rate — The number of voltage or frequency changes that
can be made in a second. At lower speeds, the baud rate is equal
to the bps.

BBS — *Bulletin Board System*. A host system that receives calls
from other modem-equipped computers and provides services
such as electronic mail, uploading and downloading files,
chatting with other callers, and providing information.

bezel — See *faceplate*.

bi-directional mode — A mode for parallel ports that allows data
to exchange both ways. It is sometimes referred to as the *PS/2*
mode.

bis — Used with the CCITT (now called ITU) communication standards aimed at modem communication, this term denotes that the bps rate is achieved through data compression. The term itself is French for "two" or "second."

bit — A bit or binary digit is the smallest amount of data a computer can store.

bps — Bits per second.

buffer — A temporary memory storage area used during I/O operations.

byte — A group of eight bits.

cache — (Pronounced *cash*.) A reserved section of high-speed memory used to improve computer performance.

CCITT — Consultative Committee for International Telephony and Telegraphy. An arm of the ITU responsible for setting international standards for electronic communications.

CGA — *Color Graphics Array.* A low-resolution color video standard.

CHS — *Cylinder/Head/Sector.* A technique used to address information on most current hard drives by sending the cylinder number, head number, and sector number to the drive controller. Has been replaced by LBA (logical block addressing), which simply sends an absolute sector number to the controller.

CODEC — A Coder/Decoder circuit involved in the conversion of sound (such as voice or music) into digital signals and vice-versa.

CPU — *Central Processing Unit.* The "brain" of the computer.

CRC — *Cyclical Redundancy Check.* An error detection technique used for data transfers.

daisy-chaining — The connection of several devices to a single port or interface.

DAT — Digital Audio Tape.

daughterboard — Technically, a daughterboard plugs directly into other boards. But this term is usually used for any board or expansion card for the PC that attaches to another card via a ribbon cable or by plugging in directly to the other card. The purpose of the daughterboard is to provides expanded features to the functions of the card to which it is attached.

DIN — *Duetsche Industrie Norm* (translated as German Industrial Norm). The committee that sets the German industrial standards. DIN is used in reference to keyboard and pointing device connectors.

diskette — Popular use of this term means a floppy disk although, technically, a 5¹/₄-inch size disk is a diskette, while the 3¹/₂-inch size is a microdisk.

DMF — Microsoft's *Distribution Media Format.* Formats 3 ¹/₂-inch diskettes at 1.77MB.

DOS — *Disk Operating System.* The most well-known are Microsoft MS-DOS and Microsoft Windows.

download — The act of receiving a file from an electronic source, such as a BBS.

drive translation — Technically, drive translation is a means of shuffling the cylinder, sector, and head numbers on an IDE drive. This term is often used as a synonym for *LBA.* See *LBA.*

DSHD — Double-sided, high-density.

DSVD — *Digital Simultaneous Voice and Data.* Refers to the ability of modems to transmit voice and data at the same time over a single phone line.

DTR — *Data Terminal Ready.* A signal generated by a modem to indicate that it is ready to receive data from the computer.

ECHS — *Enhanced Cylinder/Head/Sector.* A translation mode so that drives larger than 500MB can be used on a DOS-based PC.

ECP — *Extended Capabilities Port.* A parallel port standard for data transfer.

EDO — *Extended Data Out.* A type of RAM used in PCs that is heralded for its performance.

EGA — *Extended Graphics Array.* A color video standard for PCs.

EIDE — *Enhanced IDE.* A standard developed by hard disk drive manufacturer Western Digital to handle issues involving drive translation of large hard disk drives. See *IDE.*

environment files — Special files that contain the settings that determine how the PC will use the available memory and other hardware settings. In DOS, those files are the CONFIG.SYS and the AUTOEXEC.BAT. In Windows, the environment files include the WIN.INI and SYSTEM.INI.

EPP — *Enhanced Parallel Port.* A parallel port standard for data transfer that is heralded for allowing "daisy-chaining" of parallel devices.

ESD — *Electrostatic Discharge.* Also known as *static electricity.*

extended character set — A set of figures used for formatting and control codes to hardware in the PC world. It is used in addition to the ASCII character set.

faceplate — A cover used for cosmetics to cover the opening around or in front of a component, such as a floppy disk drive.

fast paging memory — A type of RAM used in PCs.

FIFO — *First In, First Out.* See *UART.*

form factor — The physical size of a drive. This term is popularly used to describe the width of the drive, such as a $3^{1}/_{2}$-inch 1.2GB hard disk drive.

FPU — A *floating processor unit* also known as a *math coprocessor.*

full-height — A measurement of height in floppy and hard disk drives. Full-height drives are no longer manufactured, but the measurement of about $3^{1}/_{2}$-inches is still widely used as a gauge for PC case and drive design. See *half-height.*

GB — *Gigabyte.* 1024 megabytes (MB).

half-height — A measurement of the height of a floppy or hard disk drive. This measurement is understood in the PC industry to be about 1.7 inches. See *full-height.*

hardware profile — The Windows 95 term for a multiple boot configuration.

hercules — A monochrome graphics video standard.

IDE — *Integrated Drive Electronics.* A standard for hard disk drives in which the "intelligence" necessary for the drive's operation is built into the drive instead of the controller card.

IPX/SPX — *Internetwork Packet Exchange/Sequenced Packet Exchange.* These are actually two network protocols that work together to create, maintain, and terminate connections. IPX moves information across the network and SPX works on top of IPX and adds commands.

ITU — The *International Telecommunications Union*, of which the CCITT is a part. See *CCITT.*

K — *Kilobyte.* 1,024 bytes.

kHz — *Kilohertz.* A thousand electrical vibrations or cycles (hertz) a second. This term is used in reference to scan frequencies in monitors and for comparing performance in sound cards.

LBA — *Logical Block Address*. A mode that allows a hard disk drive larger than 540MB to be used under DOS.

LCC — *Leaded Chip Carrier*. A type of socket used mostly for 286 chips.

LED — *Light Emitting Diode*. A type of display used frequently in computers and other electronic devices.

LIF — *Low Insertion Force*. A type of processor socket that does require you to push on the processor chip to insert it.

math coprocessor — See *FPU*.

MB — *Megabyte*. 1024 kilobytes (K).

MFM — *Modified Frequency Modulation*. An encoding method for data storage on hard disk drives that has been replaced by IDE.

microdisk — A $3^1/_2$-inch floppy diskette.

microprocessor — See *processor*.

MIDI — *Musical Instrument Digital Interface*. A protocol for information exchange between musical instruments, computers, and synthesizers.

MNP — *Microcom Network Protocols*. Protocols used for error correction in modem data transfers.

modem — A device that modulates or changes the digital signals of the computer to tones that can be sent over analog telephone lines and demodulates the tones it receives.

monochrome — A single color video display, usually white, green, or amber.

MPC — *Multimedia Personal Computer*. Also refers to the council of computer companies that define standards for multimedia.

multiple-configuration menu — The menu DOS 6.0 or higher displays to choose which configuration to use when a multiple boot configuration is set up in the DOS environment files.

multiple boot configuration — A way to select what drivers and environment settings get used. You can set this up yourself by making changes to the environment files in DOS or by using the hardware profile feature in Windows 95.

ns — *Nanosecond.* One billionth of a second.

paddle board — See *daughterboard.*

PCL — *Printer Control Language.* A page description language used by laser printers.

PGA — *Pin Grid Array.* A type of socket where a high number of pins can be connected in a small space. Used extensively in upgradeable microprocessors, and sometimes known as the "bed of nails."

pickoff — This term describes the connectors on cables. It's used mostly in reference to the connections on ribbon cabling supplied with internal tape back up drives and floppy disk drives.

pipeline burst cache — A type of cache known for its performance. See *cache.*

PLCC — Plastic Leaded Chip Carrier. See *LCC.*

postscript — A page description language used by printers.

processor — See *CPU.*

protocol — A set of rules, conventions, and procedures for communicating data between two devices. Protocols can be thought of as the "languages" of computers. Each computer must use the same protocol or speak the same "language" in order for two computers to communicate.

PS/2 parallel mode — See *bi-directional mode.*

read/write precompensation — See *write precompensation.*

real-time clock — A clock on the PC. This term is usually used when referencing a certain type of PC battery and clock that can last as long as 10 years.

RLL — *Run Length Limited.* A type of MFM (see *MFM),* RLL was used in hard disk drives for data storage but has been replaced by IDE.

RPC/WPC — Read Precompensation/Write Precompensation. See *write precompensation.*

RS-232 — A 25-pin connector, which can be either serial or parallel. The term *RS-232* has been used so much for serial port connections that it is understood to mean serial and is even used sometimes in place of the actual term *serial.*

SCSI — *Small Computer Systems Interface.* Known for allowing *daisy-chaining* of devices.

service capacity — The potential voltage output left in a battery.

SPT — *Sectors Per Track*. A term referencing the way hard disk space is divided for data storage.

SVGA — *Super VGA*. A high-resolution color graphics standard. See *VGA*.

telecommunications — The realm of using a modem and the phone lines to connect two or more computers to share information.

traces — The wiring or circuits that connect components on a printed circuit board. Usually this term is used in reference to the circuits on a motherboard.

UART — *Universal Asynchronous Receiver Transmitter*. A UART is a chip on the serial port or internal modem card that converts outgoing data from parallel (usually eight bits at a time) to serial (one bit at a time) for passage through the serial port. It also converts serial data coming in to your computer through a serial port to parallel data that your software can understand. The chip usually referred to when the term *UART* is used is the 16550 UART chip, which has a FIFO buffer to help reduce load on the CPU.

UCM — *Universal Connection Mode*. Cables or "smart" parallel cables that can adjust to different parallel connection modes.

upload — The act of sending a file to an electronic source, such as a BBS.

v.22 — A CCITT standard for modem communications at 1200 bps.

v.22 bis — CCITT standard for modem communications at 2400 bps.

v.32 — CCITT standard for modem communications at 4800 and 9600 bps.

v.32 bis — CCITT standard for modem communications at 14,400 bps.

v.34 — CCITT standard for modem communications at 28,800 bps.

v.42 bis — CCITT standard for modem communications at 38,400 bps.

VBE — *VGA BIOS Extension*. A Video Electronics Standards Association video display standard that is gaining popularity.

VESA — *Video Electronics Standards Association*. A group of PC graphics vendors responsible for defining much of the high resolution video and multimedia display standards. VESA is responsible for the *local bus* or *video local bus* standard, aimed at multimedia, and designed to speed the movement of large amounts of data through the PC bus.

VGA — *Video Graphics Array.* A widely-used color video standard for PCs.

WPC — See *write precompensation.*

write precompensation — A way of compensating for "drift" of the magnetic information written on the disk. Many BIOS's provide a way for you to enter a value for the cylinder on the hard disk drive at which this precompensation should start. Traditional settings are 0 (zero) or 65535. Because IDE drives handle this themselves, you can leave this value blank. If the BIOS requires you to put a value, put zero.

XGA — *Extended Graphics Array.* A very high resolution color video graphics standard.

ZIF — *Zero Insertion Force.* A type of processor socket that does not require you to push on the processor chip to insert it.

Index

Numbers

2DD, defined, 459
2HD, defined, 459
5-pin DIN connector, 38
6-pin mini-DIN connector, 38
9-pin male serial connector, 285
9-pin male serial port, 48, 50, 442
9-pin serial connector, 45
15-pin female game port, 442
15-pin female VGA port, 230
15-pin male VGA port, 230
25-pin female parallel port, 50, 442
25-pin female printer connector, 440
25-pin male serial connector, 285
25-pin male serial port, 50, 442
30-pin SIMMs, 171, 175
68-pin SIMMs *versus* 72-pin SIMMs, case study, 184
72-pin SIMMs, 171, 176, 184
640K memory barrier, 167
    Windows 95, 169

A

adapters
    9-pin to 25-pin serial port, 50
    Centronics to 25-pin male, 420
    keyboard, 5-pin DIN to 6-pin DIN, 38–40
    pointing devices
        25-pin to 9-pin, 49–50
        PS/2 mouse to serial port, 47–49

SIMMs (Single In-line Memory Modules), 184–185
three-and-a-half inch drive to five-and-a-quarter inch opening, 69
video on motherboard, 239
See also cables
See also connectors
American Standard Code for Information Exchange (ASCII), defined, 459
antistatic mat, 28
antistatic spray, 28
ASCII (American Standard Code for Information Exchange), defined, 459
AT parallel mode
    defined, 459
    parallel port mode, 420
ATAPI (AT-Attachment Packet Interface), defined, 459
AT-Attachment Packet Interface (ATAPI), defined, 459
ATTRIB command, 390
auto answer, defined, 459
AUTOEXEC.BAT file, 390

B

backing up data, 91
    overwriting disk during restore, 99
    overwriting previous backups, 99
    unable to use floppy disk drive while, 91
Basic Input/Output System (BIOS)
    See BIOS (Basic Input/Output System)

batteries
   buying tips, 332
   CMOS settings
      printing, 331–332
      restoring, 334
   coin type, 326–327
   determining current type, 325–328
   determining need to replace, 329
   external connection, 330–331
   incorrect installation, case study, 335–337
   installing, 332–334
   internal, 330
   jumper settings, 334
   lithium, 326
   measuring voltage, 329
   most reliable, 328
   Ni-Cad, 329
   proprietary, 328
   real-time clock, 328
   removing, 334
   service capacity, 325
   setting jumpers, 334
   soldered to motherboard, 330–331
   testing for ground pin, 333
   testing new, 334
   troubleshooting, 336–338
battery pack, 326
baud rate, defined, 459
BBS (Bulletin Board System), defined, 459
bezel
   See faceplate
bi-directional mode, defined, 459
bidirectional parallel port mode, 420
BIOS (Basic Input/Output System)
   COM ports, 285–287
   copyright date, 127
   data loss after update, 17
   defined, 15–16
   Flash, defined, 15–16
   hard disk controllers, 271–272
   hard disk drive, 125
   Plug and Play, 287–288
   second floppy disk drive, 69–71, 82

BIOS chip, 15
bis, defined, 460
bit, defined, 460
bootable diskettes
   creating, 391–392
   See also rescue diskette
   See also startup diskette
bps, defined, 460
Briefcase
   adding files to, 429–430
   editing files on the guest, 429–430
   orphans, 431–432
   splitting files, 431–432
   synchronizing files, 430–431
   troubleshooting, 432–433
   updating files between PCs, 428–429
   viewing file locations, 431
buffer, defined, 460
Bulletin Board System (BBS), defined, 459
byte, defined, 460

C

cables
   CD-ROM drive, 352
   floppy disk drive
      34-pin, 75–77
      installing a second, 75–77
      swapping A for B, 89–90
   hard disk drive, 132
      installing a second, 145–146
   mail order source, 420
   printer
      cable mixup, case study, 440–441
      maximum length, 448
      parallel, 441
   ribbon
      40-pin, 145, 269
      on a controller card, 149
      installation, 83
   sound card, 351
   transferring files between PCs with, 422
   See also adapters
   See also connectors

cache, defined, 460
case studies
   68-pin SIMMs *versus* 72-pin SIMMs, 184
   adding memory, 168–169
   Alps Glidepoint Keyboard Installation,
      57–59
   CD-ROM drives under Windows 95, 345–346
   CPU upgrade, 211–213
   disaster recovery, 100–101
   display problems, 260–261
   DOS upgrade halts tape backup, 104–105
   improper standoff installation, 383
   incorrect battery installation, 335–336
   installing a second hard disk drive, 150–155
   installing tape backup drive, 92–94
   keyboard adapters, 40
   memory upgrade, 189–191
   Microsoft Mouse Manager, 54
   multi-I/O card, 273–274
   new power supply, 322–323
   Pentium too fast for startup diskette,
      397–398
   Plug and Play sound card in DOS/
      Windows 3.*x*, 355–358
   processor upgrade, wrong size cooling
      fan, 220
   setting clock speed, 397–398
   swapping mouse/keyboard connections,
      46–47
   turbo switch, 397–398
   video card upgrade, 252–254
   Zip drive on a network, 108–110
CCITT (Consultative Committee for Interna-
      tional Telephony and Telegraphy),
      defined, 460
CD-ROM drives
   buying tips, 347, 349
   device drivers, 344–345
   DMA (direct memory access), 343–344
   finding slots for, 347
   installing, 351–354
   interface, 343
   internal, 348
   mounting, 354
   Plug and Play, 349–351
   software requirements, 349
   Sound-Blaster compatibility, 349
   testing, 354
   troubleshooting, 360–362
   Windows 3.*x* won't start, 360
   under Windows 95, case study, 345–346
central processing units (CPUs)
   See CPUs (central processing units)
Centronics parallel port printer
      connector, 440
CGA (Color Graphics Array), defined, 460
CHS (Cylinder/Head/Sector), defined, 460
circuit tester, 27
clock cycles
   See clock speed
clock speed
   adjusting, 372
   defined, 198
   setting, case study, 397–398
CMOS (Complementary Metal-Oxide
      Semiconductor Technology)
   accessing settings, 16–17
   battery settings
      printing, 331–332
      restoring, 334
   defined, 15–16
   exiting, 19
   floppy disk drive, installing a second,
      69–71
   hard disk controllers, 267, 271–272
   hard disk drives
      installing a second, 149
      replacing, 125, 132–135
   settings disappear, 335–336
   setup screen, 17–18
   swap floppies function, 88–89
CODEC, defined, 460
Color Graphics Array (CGA), defined, 460

COM ports
   avoiding COM3 and COM4, 284
   BIOS configuration, 285–287
   current settings, 284–291
   defined, 282
   disabling unused, 293, 296
   interrupts for, 283
   MSD under DOS/Windows 3.*x*, 288
   Plug and Play BIOS, 287–288
compatible parallel port mode, 420
Complementary Metal-Oxide Semiconductor
     Technology (CMOS)
   See CMOS (Complementary Metal-Oxide
     Semiconductor Technology)
CONFIG.SYS file, 390
connectors
   9-pin male serial, 442
   15-pin female game port, 442
   25-pin female parallel, 442
   25-pin male serial, 442
   25-pin parallel, 440
   25-pin serial *versus* 25-pin parallel, 49–50
   Centronics parallel, 440
   Molex, 77
   pass-through, 102
   pickoffs, 92
   power supply, 77–78
   RS-232 standard, 49
   See also adapters
   See also cables
Consultative Committee for International
     Telephony and Telegraphy (CCITT),
     defined, 460
controller cards
   buying tips, 368
   floppy disk drives, 79–80
   hard disk drives, 120
   incorrect installation, 276–277
   integrated, 263
   ribbon cable, 149
   tape backup drive, internal, 91
   See also hard disk controllers

cooling fans
   CPUs (central processing units), 201
     installing, 216
     in PGA sockets, 214–215
     power supply, 219–220
   on Pentium processor, 209
   power supplies, 311
   wrong size, case study, 220
CPUs (central processing units)
   bus speed, 204
   cache, 201–202
   clock cycles, 198
   clock speed, 198
   cooling fans, 201, 214–215
     installing, 216
     power supply, 219–220
     wrong size, 220
   defined, 460
   determining current, 206–209
   energy saving, 223
   heat generation, 199–201
   heat sinks, 201
   identifying, 206–209
   inserting the wrong one, 223
   interposers, 201
   jumper settings, 214, 220–221
   low voltage processors, 199–201
   math coprocessors, 198–199
   names of, 198
   nonremovable, 207
   performance, 198
   pin 1, 218
   reading chip numbers, 209
   removing, 215–216
   seating in a socket, 217–219
   SL, 223
   SLC, 223
   sockets
     interchangeability, 223
     LCC (leaded chip carrier), 210
     LIF (low insertion force), 210, 219
     overdrive, 211

PGA (pin grid array), 210
PLCC (plastic leaded chip carrier), 210
soldered, 210
ZIF (zero insertion force), 210, 217–219
testing, 222
third party, 222
troubleshooting, 223–226
upgradeable, 202–204
upgrading
286 and 386 processors, 211
486 processors, 213
Pentium Pro processors, 223
Pentium processors, 213–214
voltage-regulator daughterboard, 201–202
CRC (Cyclical Redundancy Unit), defined, 460
cross-linked files, 100
Cyclical Redundancy Unit (CRC), defined, 460
Cylinder/Head/Sector (CHS), defined, 460

D

daisy-chaining, defined, 460
damage to equipment, risk of
See warnings
danger
See warnings
DAT, defined, 460
Data Terminal Ready (DTR), defined, 461
daughterboard, defined, 460
DEBUG program, 272
Deutsche Industrie Norm (DIN), defined, 460
device drivers
CD-ROM drives, 344–345
copying to rescue diskette, 392–394
fax, listed with printer drivers in Windows, 448
pointing devices, wired, 51–52
DOS, 52–54
Microsoft Mouse Manager, 53–54
MOUSE.COM, 53
MOUSE.SYS, 53
switch settings, 53–54
Windows 3.x and Windows 95, 52

printer
Windows 3.x, 443–444
Windows 95, 438, 444–447
protected-mode, 345
real-mode, 345
sound cards, 341–342
tape backup drive, external, 103–104
video cards
DOS, 246
Windows 3.x, 240–242, 246–247
Windows 95, 240–241, 247–248
digital multimeter, 315
Digital Simultaneous Voice and Data (DSVD), defined, 461
DIMMs (Dual In-line Memory Modules), 170
DIN (Deutsche Industrie Norm), defined, 460
DIPs (Dual-inline Packages), 170–171
Direct Cable Connection utility
changing host/guest designations, 426
configuring, 421–426
configuring guest PC, 422
configuring host PC, 422–424
determining host and guest PCs, 422
finding, 420–421
installing, 421
naming host PC, 424
passwords, 425
requirements for, 420
restarting, 426
sharing host resources, 424–425
troubleshooting, 426–428
disaster recovery, case study, 100–101
disk drives
See floppy disk drives
See hard disk drives
Disk Operating System (DOS)
See DOS (Disk Operating System)
diskettes
capacity, 67–68
cost, 67–68
defined, 461
sizes, 67–68

display problems, case study, 260–261

Distributed Media Format (DMF),
    defined, 461

DMF (Distributed Media Format),
    defined, 461

DOS (Disk Operating System)
    defined, 461
    dual boot, 408–412
    editing environment files, 400–401
    proprietary, causing data loss, 389
    rescue diskettes, 391–394
    shortcut from Windows boot, 85
    upgrade halts tape backup, case study,
      104–105
    versions of, 389–390
    video resolution, setting, 255

download, defined, 461

DRAM (dynamic random access memory)
    buying tips, 186–187
    defined, 169
    testing, 186–187
    video cards, 233

drive translation, defined, 461

drivers
    See device drivers

DSHD, defined, 461

DSVD (Digital Simultaneous Voice and Data),
    defined, 461

DTR (Data Terminal Ready), defined, 461

Dual In-line Memory Modules (DIMMs), 170

Dual-inline Packages (DIPs), 170–171

dynamic random access memory (DRAM)
    See DRAM (dynamic random access
      memory)

E

ECHS (Enhanced Cylinder/Head/Sector),
    defined, 461

ECP (Extended Capabilities Port)
    defined, 461
    parallel port mode, 420

EDO (Extended Data Output)
    defined, 461
    versus Fast Paging Mode, 176

EGA (Extended Graphics Array), defined, 461

EIDE (Enhanced IDE), defined, 461

EISA expansion slots, 236

electricity
    circuit tester, 26–27
    danger of injury by, 24
    earth ground, 25–26
    power surge protectors, 28
    See also ESD (electrostatic discharge)

electrostatic discharge (ESD)
    See ESD (electrostatic discharge)

Enhanced Cylinder/Head/Sector (ECHS),
    defined, 461

Enhanced IDE (EIDE), defined, 461

Enhanced Parallel Port (EPP)
    defined, 461
    parallel port mode, 420

environment files, 390
    copying to rescue diskette, 392
    defined, 461
    in DOS/Windows 3.*x*, 390
    editing with
      EDIT under DOS, 400–401
      SYSEDIT under Windows, 401–402
      text editors, 400
      word processors, 399–400
    troubleshooting
      clean boot, 403
      commenting out commands, 403–404
      editing, 412
      executing one line at a time, 403
      source of commands, 404–405

EPP (Enhanced Parallel Port)
    defined, 461
    parallel port mode, 420

error messages
    See troubleshooting

ESD (electrostatic discharge)
    antistatic mat, 28

antistatic spray, 28
component damage, 22
protection devices, 26–28
transportation protection, 29
voltage, 22
worse in cold weather, 22
wrist grounding strap, 22–25
expansion slots
8-bit PC/XT, 235
defined, 234
EISA, 236
identifying, 365–366
ISA, 236–237
PCI, 237
sharing, 238
Extended Capabilities Port (ECP)
defined, 461
parallel port mode, 420
extended character set, defined, 462
Extended Data Output (EDO), 176
defined, 461
Extended Graphics Array (EGA), defined, 461
Extended Graphics Array (XGA), defined, 466
external fax/modem connector, 295

F

faceplate, defined, 462
fans
See cooling fans
fast paging memory, defined, 462
Fast Paging Mode, 176
fax drivers, listed with printer drivers in
Windows, 448
FDISK command, partitioning a hard disk,
135–136
FIFO (First In, First Out)
See UART
figures
5-pin DIN connector, 38
6-pin mini-DIN connector, 38
9-pin male serial connector, 285

9-pin male serial port, 48, 50, 442
9-pin serial connector, 45
15-pin female game port, 442
15-pin female VGA port, 230
15-pin male VGA port, 230
25-pin female parallel port, 50, 442
25-pin female printer connector, 440
25-pin male serial connector, 285
25-pin male serial port, 50, 442
30-pin SIMMs, 171
30-pin SIMMs of varying speeds, 175
72-pin SIMMs, 171
72-pin SIMMs compared to a proprietary
SIMM, 184
72-pin SIMMs of varying speeds, 176
adapters
9-pin to 25-pin serial port, 50
PS/2 mouse to serial port, 49
three-and-a-half inch drive to
five-and-a-quarter inch opening, 69
video on motherboard, 239
banks on a motherboard, 172
batteries
coin type, 326–327
external connection, 330–331
incorrect installation, 337
lithium, 326
Ni-Cad, 329
real-time clock, 328
battery pack, 326
CD-ROM drive, internal, 348
Centronics parallel port printer
connector, 440
circuit tester, 27
controller cards, incorrect installation,
276–277
cooling fan on Pentium processor, 209
CPU coolers, 219
DIP, 171
expansion slots
8-bit PC/XT, 235
EISA, 236

expansion slots *(continued)*
  identifying, 365–366
  ISA, 236–237
  PCI, 237
external fax/modem connector, 295
external modems, 292
floppy disk drives
  with 34-pin male connector, 77
  combination, 69
  connector on a multi-I/O card, 80
  determining A or B designation, 81
  with edge connector, 76
  incorrect installation, 111–114
floppy diskettes, 68
hard disk drives
  IDE controller, 120
  incorrect installation, 161–163
  integrated controllers, 263
  ISA controller, 120
  jumpers, 147–148
  LED wiring, 270
  parameters, 133
IBM PS/2 Model 70, 11
jumpers
  saving shunts, 221
  settings printed on motherboard, 205
keyboard adapters, 39
keyboard connectors on motherboard, 39
LIF socket, 203
memory, incorrect installation, 194, 225
memory configuration tables, 180
Microsoft Natural Keyboard, 36
modems, internal, 292, 297
modular phone connector, 295, 298
motherboard
  Pentium, 367
  pin 1, 378
  screws holding, 373
mouse, 43
MSD menu, 14
multi-I/O card, 264, 268, 270
multimedia, incorrect installation, 361–362

Ni-Cad, 329
nonremovable processors, 207
paper washers, 370
  on motherboard, 377
  omitted from motherboard, 380–381
parallel port, 102
parity chips, 175
pen-mouse, 43
Pentium motherboard, 367
Pentium OverDrive processor, 202
Pentium processor with cooling fan, 209
pin 1 on floppy disk drive, 82
Plug and Play sound cards, 348
pointing device connectors, 45
pointing devices, 43
power supplies, 312–313
  connector, 78
  proprietary, 317
  removing, 319
power switches, 320
processor, pin 1, 218
processor extraction tool, 216
processors, 207–208
proprietary hardware, 11
PS/2 connectors, 45–46
shunts, saving, 221
SIMMs
  adapter boards, 185
  inserting, 189
  removing, 187–188
sound card jacks, 341
standoffs, 370
  incorrect use of, 385
  supporting motherboard, 374–376
system boards, 182
tape backup units, 103
trackball, 43
video cards, 236–238
  removing, 243
video port, 48
Windows 95, Mouse Properties menu,
  55–57

wrist grounding strap, 23–25
ZIF socket, 203
    pin 1, 218
    release lever, 217
files
    AUTOEXEC.BAT, 390
    CONFIG.SYS, 390
    cross-linked, 100
    erasing from backup tape, 99
    hidden, listing, 390
    IO.SYS, 390
    MSDOS.SYS, 390
    transferring between PCs
        See Direct Cable Connection
    updating between PCs
        See Briefcase
    See also environment files
First In, First Out (FIFO)
    See UART
Flash BIOS, defined, 15–16
floating processor unit (FPU), defined, 462
floppy disk drives
    34-pin male connector, 77
    adding a second
        BIOS, 69–71, 82
        burning in, 85–86
        cabling the controller card, 79–80
        cabling the disk drive, 80–81
        case space, 72–75
        CMOS setup, 69–71
        determining proper drive type, 67
        installing the case, 84–85
        mounting, 84–85
        power supply, 77–78, 81–82
        purchase checklist, 78
        testing, 83–84
    combination, 68–69
    connector on a multi-I/O card, 80
    controllers, integrated with hard disk
            controllers, 263
    determining A or B designation, 81
    edge connector, 76

five-and-a-quarter inch, 67
form factor, 67
full-height, 67
half-height, 67
incorrect installation, 111–114
swapping A for B
    built-in function in CMOS, 88–89
    CMOS setup, 88–89
testing, 96
three-and-a-half inch, 67
writing to lower-density diskettes, 68
fonts, downloading to laser printers, 436–437
form factor, defined, 462
FPU (floating processor unit), defined, 462
full-height, defined, 462
Futz Factor, 415

G

GB (gigabyte), defined, 462
gigabyte (GB), defined, 462

H

half-height, defined, 462
hard disk controllers
    buying tips, 266
    changing memory addresses, 272
    CMOS setup, recording, 267
    defined, 262
    determining current, 265
    drive translation, 264
    hardware installation
        cabling, 269–270
        CMOS setup, 271–272
        controllers, setting, 268–269
        expansion slot, 271
        ports, setting, 268–269
        potential problems, 265–266
    integrated with floppy disk controllers,
            262–263
    ISA, 120

hard disk controllers *(continued)*
   multi-I/O cards, 264, 267
      conflicts with internal modems, 268
      preparation, 267
   with own BIOS, 271–272
   removing, 268
   slave drives, 272
   software installation, 274–275
   troubleshooting
      no boot device, 275–276
      no FD found, 275
      no HD found, 275
      practice exercise, 276–277
hard disk drives
   500MB barrier, 126
   burning in, 139
   capacity, 126
   capacity smaller than expected, 143
   cold boot, 137
   drive geometry, 126
   drive translation software, 142–143
   dual master mode, 157
   formatting as system disk, 136–137
   IDE, problems with two together, 144
   incorrect installation, 161–163
   installing a second
      cabling, 148, 159–160
      case space, 144
      case study, 150–155
      CMOS settings, 149
      mounting, 155
      mounting hardware, 145
      testing, 149–150, 155–156
   landing zone, 134
   LBA (Logical Block Addressing), 126
   LED wiring, 270
   master/slave settings, 143, 146–148, 157
   parameters, 133
   partitioning, 135–136
   pre-formatted, 142
   pre-partitioned, 142
   replacing
      BIOS setup, 125
      bootable floppy disk, 123–125
      cabling, 131–132
      capacity, 122
      case space, 129–130
      clusters, 121
      CMOS setup, 125, 132–135
      cylinders, 121
      EIDE, 122
      head crashes, 119
      how they work, 118–119
      IDE, 122
      landing zone, 119
      MBR (master boot record), 121
      mounting, 138
      parking the heads, 119
      SCSI, 122
      sectors, 121
      tracks, 121
   restoring data to, 138–139
   single master mode, 157
   standard master mode, 157
   swapping drive assignments, 158–160
   testing, 137
   translation, 126–127
   troubleshooting
      cannot create partition, 141
      common mistakes, 160–163
      fixed disk configuration error, 140
      hard disk installation, 140–142
      HDD controller failure, 141
      invalid configuration information, 140–141
      jumper settings, 157–158
      no boot device available, 142
      no fixed disks present, 141
   write precompensation, 134
hardware
   interchangeability, 10–12
   proprietary, 10–12
hardware profile, defined, 462
hercules, defined, 462
hexadecimal addresses, 252
hidden files, listing, 390
HyperTerminal, 301–302

I

IBM PS/2 Model 70, 11
ICM (Intel Configuration Manager), 350
ICU (ISA Configuration Utility), 350
IDE hard disk controller, 120
IDE (Integrated Drive Electronics), defined, 462
injury, risk of
    See warnings
input devices
    defined, 31
    See also keyboards
    See also pointing devices
Integrated Drive Electronics (IDE),
        defined, 462
Intel Configuration Manager (ICM), 350
International Telecommunications Unit
        (ITU), defined, 462
Internetwork Packet Exchange/Sequenced
        Packet Exchange (IPX/SPX),
        defined, 462
interrupt request lines (IRQs)
    See IRQs (interrupt request lines)
IO.SYS file, 390
IPX/SPX (Internetwork Packet Exchange/
        Sequenced Packet Exchange),
        defined, 462
IRQs (interrupt request lines)
    current settings, 289
    sharing, 283
    sound cards, 341
    tape backup drive, external, 107
    viewing settings, Windows 95, 341
ISA Configuration Utility (ICU), 350
ITU (International Telecommunications
        Unit), defined, 462

J

jumpers
    determining existing settings, 159
    on a hard disk drive, 147–148

hard disk master/slave settings, 147, 157
master/slave setting, 159–160
saving shunts, 221
settings
    battery, 334
    CPUs (central processing units), 214,
        220–221
    hard disk master/slave, 147, 157
    master/slave, 159–160
    printed on motherboard, 205
settings printed on motherboard, 205
undocumented, 157–158

K

K (kilobyte), defined, 462
keyboards
    adapters, 38–40
    carpal tunnel syndrome, 34
    connectors, 38
    connectors on motherboard, 39
    double crush stress, 34
    ergonomic, 34–36
    installing, 40
        case study, 57–59
    key placement, 33–34
    key shortcuts, 35, 37
    Microsoft Natural Keyboard, 36
    noise level, 33
    pointing devices, built-in, 37
    stereo speakers, built-in, 37
    swapping mouse/keyboard connections,
        case study, 46–47
    troubleshooting, 41
    Windows 95, 35
    Windows 95 function key, 37
    wrist rests, 34
kHz (kilohertz), defined, 462
kilobyte (K), defined, 462
kilohertz (kHz), defined, 462

L

laser disc drives
    See CD-ROM drives
LBA (Logical Block Address), defined, 463
LCC (Leaded Chip Carrier), defined, 463
Leaded Chip Carrier (LCC), defined, 463
LED (Light Emitting Diode), defined, 463
legacy cards, 349
LIF (Low Insertion Force), defined, 463
LIF socket, 203
Light Emitting Diode (LED), defined, 463
Logical Block Address (LBA), defined, 463
Low Insertion Force (LIF), defined, 463

M

math coprocessor
    See FPU
MB (megabyte), defined, 463
megabyte (MB), defined, 463
memory
    640K barrier, 167
        Windows 95, 169
    adding, case study, 168–169
    addresses, hard disk controllers, 272
    base, 167
    on board, 183
    configuration, 173–177
        system requirements for, 178–179
        tables, 179–181
    conflicts caused by modems, 283
    contacts, 171
    conventional, 167
    defined, 166
    determining current amount, 177–178
    DIMMs (Dual In-line Memory
        Modules), 170
    DIPs (Dual-inline Packages), 170
    DRAM (dynamic random access memory),
        169, 233
    DRAMs
        buying tips, 186–187
        testing, 186–187
    EDO (Extended Data Output), 176
    fast paging, defined, 462
    Fast Paging Mode, 176
    hexadecimal addresses, 252
    incorrect installation, 194, 225
    nanoseconds as measure of speed, 171
    parity chips, 172–173
    printer, 436–437, 450
    proprietary, 183
    requirements for tape backup drive, 107
    ROM (Read-Only Memory), defined, 15–16
    SIMMs (Single In-line Memory
        Modules), 170
        adapter boards, 184–185
        bent pins, 192
        installing, 188–189
        making room for, 184–185
        mixing speeds, 192
        reading capacity of, 174–176
        removing, 187–188
        sockets, banks, and connectors, 171
    SIPs (Single-Inline Packages), 170
    sound card address, 341
    speed, 171
    sticks of, 186
    testing, 191
    tips, 171
    troubleshooting, 192–194
    upgrade, case study, 189–191
    upgrading, case study, 189–191
    video card
        blocking out, 259
        reserved, 231–233
        VRAM (video random access
            memory), 233
    virtual, 167
memory configuration tables, 180
MFM (Modified Frequency Modulation),
    defined, 463

Microcom Network Protocols (MNP),
    defined, 463
microdisks, 67
    defined, 463
microprocessor, defined, 463
Microsoft Diagnostic (MSD)
    See MSD (Microsoft Diagnostic)
Microsoft Mouse Manager, case study, 54
Microsoft Natural Keyboard, 36
MIDI (Musical Instrument Digital Interface)
    connectors, 346–347
    defined, 463
MNP (Microcom Network Protocols),
    defined, 463
modems
    base I/O addresses, 283
    baud rate, 281
    COM ports, 282
        avoiding COM3 and COM4, 284
        BIOS configuration, 285–287
        current settings, 284–291
        disabling unused, 293, 296
        interrupts for, 283
        MSD under DOS/Windows 3.*x*, 288
        Plug and Play BIOS, 287–288
    defined, 463
    DSVD (digital simultaneous voice and
        data), 294
    external, 292
    external fax/modem connector, 295
    fax baud rate, 281
    faxes, 293
    handshaking, 299
    heat generated by, 296
    how they work, 280
    installing
        external, 294–295
        internal, 296–298
    internal, 292, 297
        conflicts with multi-I/O cards, 268
    internal *versus* external, 291–293
    I/O addresses, 282–283
    IRQs, 282

current settings, 289
    sharing, 283
memory conflicts, 283
Microsoft Download Service
    Windows 3.*x*, 299–300
    Windows 95, 301–302
modular telephone connectors, 298
online services
    connecting to, 299
    installing software for, 300
Plug and Play internal, 293
sounds during connection, 299
testing
    DOS/Windows 3.*x*, 298–299
    Windows 95, 300–302
troubleshooting
    call waiting interrupts session, 303
    no dial tone, 306
    no sound from modem, 307
    PC won't boot, 307
    phone doesn't ring, 303
    practice exercise, 307–308
    software doesn't recognize modem,
        304–306
    Windows device conflict, 307
    Windows will not boot, 307
UART, 282
Modified Frequency Modulation (MFM),
    defined, 463
modular phone connector, 295
monitors
    damage from swapping monitor port and
        serial port, 47
    dot pitch, 251
    identifying to Windows 95, 248–250
    interlaced *versus* non-interlaced, 231
monochrome, defined, 463
motherboards
    banks on, 172
    buying tips
        BIOS features, 369
        chipsets, 367–368
        expansion slots, 368–369

motherboards *(continued)*
  buying tips *(continued)*
    installation materials, 369–370
    integrated controllers, 368
    integrated ports, 368
    processor, 367
  checking settings, 374
  finding space for, 365–366
  how they work, 364–365
  installing, 374–379
  keyboard lock, 372
  new case for, 370–371
  paper washers
    defined, 369
    necessity for, 380
  Pentium, 367
  pin 1, 378
  purchase checklist, 371
  removing, 371–373
  screws holding, 373
  standoffs, 369–370
    improper installation, 383
  testing, 379, 382
  traces, 364–365
  troubleshooting
    beeping and error messages, 384
    no beep on boot completion, 384
    no video, 384
    PC won't boot, 384
    practice exercise, 385–386
mouse
  swapping mouse/keyboard connections,
    case study, 46–47
  Windows 95 shortcut, 44
  See also pointing devices
mouse pad, 42
MPC (Multimedia Personal Computer),
    defined, 463
MSD (Microsoft Diagnostic), 13–15
  displaying video setup, 233–234
  menu, 14
MSDOS.SYS file, 390
multi-I/O cards
  case study, 273–274
  floppy disk drive connector, 80
  hard disk controllers, 264
    conflicts with internal modems, 268
  replacing, 267
multimedia
  defined, 339
  incorrect installation, 361–362
Multimedia Personal Computer (MPC),
    defined, 463
multiple boot configuration, defined, 463
multiple-configuration menu, defined, 463
Musical Instrument Digital Interface (MIDI)
  See MIDI (Musical Instrument Digital
    Interface)
My Briefcase. *See* Briefcase

N

nanoseconds (ns)
  defined, 464
  memory speed, 171
Ni-Cad battery, 329
ns (nanoseconds)
  defined, 464
  memory speed, 171

O

OEM (Original Equipment Manufacturer),
    12, 251
operating systems
  AUTOEXEC.BAT file, 390
  boot process, 390
  CONFIG.SYS file, 390
  DOS versions, 389–390
  environment files, 390
    copying to rescue diskette, 392
  IO.SYS file, 390
  kernels, 390
  MSDOS.SYS file, 390
  purpose of, 388–389
  special versions of, 12
  system files, 390
  Windows 95 versions, 389–390

Windows versions, 389–390
Original Equipment Manufacturer (OEM),
    12, 251

P

paddle board
    See daughterboard
paper washers, 370
    on motherboard, 377
    omitted from motherboard, 380–381
parallel ports
    bidirectional mode, 420
    compatible mode, 420
    ECP (Extended Capabilities Port)
        mode, 420
    EPP (Enhanced Parallel Port) mode, 420
    AT mode, 420
    PS/2 mode, 420
    single direction mode, 420
    versus serial ports, 102
parity chips, 172–173, 175
partitioning a hard disk, 135–136
    troubleshooting, 141
PCI slots, bus master, 251
PCL (Printer Control Language), defined, 464
pen-mouse, 43
Pentium motherboard, 367
Pentium OverDrive processor, 202
Pentium processor with cooling fan, 209
PGA (Pin Grid Array), defined, 464
phone connectors, modular, 295, 298
pickoff, defined, 464
pin 1 on floppy disk drive, 82
Pin Grid Array (PGA), defined, 464
pipeline burst cache, defined, 464
PLCC
    See LCC
Plug and Play
    BIOS (Basic Input/Output System), 287–288
    CD-ROM drives, 349–351
    COM ports, 287–288
    configuration managers, 350, 353

internal modems, 293
sound card in DOS/Windows 3.x, case
        study, 355–358
sound cards, 348
Windows 95, 349–351
PLUGPLAY directory, 353
PnP
    See Plug and Play
pointing devices, wired
    adapters
        25-pin to 9-pin, 49–50
        PS/2 mouse to serial mouse, 47–49
    adapting PS/2 mouse to serial port, 47–49
    connectors, 45
        bus mouse, 45
        PS/2 mouse, 44–47
        serial mouse, 47
    device drivers, 51–52
        DOS, 52–54
        Microsoft Mouse Manager, 53–54
        MOUSE.COM, 53
        MOUSE.SYS, 53
        switch settings, 53–54
        Windows 3.x and Windows 95, 52
    installing hardware, 51
    installing software, 51
        tools in DOS/Windows 3.x, 54
        tools in Windows 95, 55–57
    mouse, 43
    pen mouse, 43
    resolution, 43–44
    sensitivity, 43–44
    trackball, 43
    troubleshooting, 60–61
    types of, 42–43
pointing devices, wireless
    installing, 61–62
    troubleshooting, 62–63
ports
    9-pin male serial, 48, 50, 442
    9-pin to 25-pin serial adapter, 50
    15-pin female game, 442
    15-pin female VGA, 230

ports *(continued)*
  15-pin male VGA, 230
  25-pin female parallel, 50, 442
  25-pin male serial, 50, 442
  damage from swapping monitor and
      serial, 47
  integrated, buying tips, 368
  parallel
    bidirectional mode, 420
    compatible mode, 420
    ECP (Extended Capabilities Port)
        mode, 420
    EPP (Enhanced Parallel Port) mode, 420
    AT mode, 420
    PS/2 mode, 420
    single direction mode, 420
    versus serial ports, 102
  printers, 441–442
  serial
    defined, 47
    printer connections, 451
    PS/2 mouse connection, 47–49
    versus parallel ports, 102
  video, male *versus* female, 48
postscript, defined, 464
power supplies
  buying tips, 318
  connector, 78
  connectors, 311
  cooling fan, 311
  current wattage, 311–313
  dusting, 323–324
  exploding, 316
  how they work, 310
  installing, 321–322
  needed wattage, 313–314
  proprietary, 316–317
  removing, 319–321
  replacing, case study, 322–323
  testing, 323–324
  testing voltage, 315–316
  troubleshooting

    floppy disk drive doesn't work, 324
    no power, 324
    PC won't boot from hard disk, 325
power surge protectors, 28
power switches, 320
Printer Control Language (PCL), defined, 464
printers
  cabling, 439–440
  changing settings, 445–446
  connecting to serial port, 451
  emulation, 439
  impact, 438
  inkjet, 438
  installing, 442–443
  laser
    adding memory, 436–437, 450
    downloading fonts to, 436–437
  multiple PCs per, 451
  multiple per PC, 451
  not listed in Windows, 447
  ports, 441–442
  print buffers, 438
  printer drivers, 438
    Windows 3.*x*, 443–444
    Windows 95, 444–447
  sending page eject commands to, 332
  setting a default, 444
  switch boxes, 451
  testing, 444
  troubleshooting
    printer prints gibberish, 450
    printer won't print, 448–449
processor extraction tool, 216
processors
  See CPUs (central processing units)
proprietary hardware, 11
protocol, defined, 464
PS/2 connectors, 45–46
PS/2 parallel mode
  See bi-directional mode

R

RAM parity error, 193
README files, 13
Read-Only Memory (ROM), defined, 15–16
read/write precompensation
    See write precompensation
real-time clock
    batteries, 328
    defined, 464
REM command, 403
rescue diskettes
    creating, 19–20
    DOS, 391–394
    Windows 3.*x,* 394
    Windows 95, 394–397
    See also bootable diskette
    See also startup diskette
RLL (Run Length Limited), defined, 464
ROM (Read-Only Memory), defined, 15–16
RPC/WPC
    See write precompensation
RS-232, defined, 464
Run Length Limited (RLL), defined, 464

S

SCSI (Small Computer Systems Interface),
    defined, 464
Sectors Per Track (SPT), defined, 465
serial ports
    9-pin male, 48, 50, 442
    25-pin male, 50, 442
    adapters, 47–50
    connecting printers to, 451
    defined, 47
    versus parallel ports, 102
service capacity, defined, 465
shunts
    See jumpers
SIMMs (Single In-line Memory Modules)
    adapter boards, 184–185

bent pins, 192
defined, 170
inserting, 189
installing, 188–189
making room for, 184–185
mixing speeds, 192
reading capacity of, 174–176
removing, 187–188
sockets, banks, and connectors, 171
single direction parallel port mode, 420
Single In-line Memory Modules (SIMMs)
    See SIMMs (Single In-line Memory
        Modules)
Single-inline Packages (SIPs), 170
SIPs (Single-Inline Packages), 170
Small Computer Systems Interface (SCSI),
    defined, 464
SMRAM good message, 192
software drivers
    See device drivers
sound cards
    address, 341
    amplified speakers, 352
    audio output to PC speakers, 342
    device drivers, 341–342
    IDE interface, 342
    installing, 351–354
    IRQ issues, 341
    jacks and connectors, 340–341
    memory address, 341
    testing, 354–355
    types of, 340
    upgradeable, 342
    wave boards, 342
    wave-table boards, 342
speakers
    amplified, 352
    audio output to, 342
    built-in to keyboard, 37
SPT (Sectors Per Track), defined, 465

standoffs
    improper installation, case study, 383
    incorrect use of, 385
    supporting motherboard, 374–376
    types of materials, 370
Startup Disk, 124–125
startup diskettes
    creating, 394–397
    See also bootable diskette
    See also rescue diskette
Super VGA (SVGA), defined, 465
surge protectors
    See power surge protectors
SVGA (Super VGA), defined, 465
swap files, 167
system, listing components of
    DOS/Windows 3.*x*, 13–14
    Windows 95, 14–15
system boards, 182
system files, 390

T

tables, Intel processor family, 200–201
tape backup drive, external
    device drivers, 103–104
    installing hardware, 102–103
    installing software, 103–104
    pass-through connector, 102
    troubleshooting
        distance from monitor, 107
        IRQ conflicts, 107
        memory requirements, 107
        practice exercise, 110–115
        shoeshining, 108
        slow tape, 108
        sound card interference, 107
        tape speed *versus* computer speed, 108
    Windows 95 support for, 105–106
tape backup drive, internal
    erasing files on the tape, 99
    installing, case study, 92–94
    installing hardware
        cabling, 91–92
        case space, 90
        controller card, 91
        mounting, 96
        power supply, 91
    installing software, 94–96
    running programs from tape, 99
    testing, 94–96
    troubleshooting, 98–99
    unexplained tape movement, 95
    Windows 95 special instructions, 96–98
telecommunications, defined, 465
Terminal program, 299
terminate but stay resident (TSR)
        programs, 60
text editors, 400
touch pads, 43
traces, defined, 465
trackball, 43
troubleshooting
    batteries, 336–338
    Briefcase, 432–433
    CD-ROM drive, 360–362
        no sound, 359–360
        PC won't boot, 360
        practice exercise, 361–362
        Windows 3.*x* won't start, 360
        Windows 95 device conflicts, 360
    CMOS settings disappear, 335–336
    CPUs (central processing units), Intel,
        223–226
    Direct Cable Connection, 426–428
    disk cannot be formatted, 87–88
    diskette drive failure, 87
    diskette read failure, 87
    drive seek errors, 83
    editing environment files, 412
    environment files
        clean boot, 403
        commenting out commands, 403–404
        executing one line at a time, 403
        source of commands, 404–405
    external tape backup drive, 107–108
    hard disk controllers

no boot device, 275–276
no FD found, 275
no HD found, 275
practice exercise, 276–277
hard disk drives
cannot create partition, 141
fixed disk configuration error, 140
hard disk installation, 140–142
HDD controller failure, 141
installing, 160–163
invalid configuration information, 140–141
jumper settings, 157–158
no boot device available, 142
no fixed disks present, 141
installing a second floppy disk drive, 87–88
invalid configuration information, 87
keyboards, 41
memory
RAM parity error, 193
SMRAM good message, 192
modems
call waiting interrupts session, 303
no dial tone, 306
no sound from modem, 307
PC won't boot, 307
phone doesn't ring, 303
practice exercise, 307–308
software doesn't recognize modem,
304–306
Windows device conflict, 307
Windows will not boot, 307
motherboard
beeping and error messages, 384
no beep on boot completion, 384
no video, 384
PC won't boot, 384
practice exercise, 385–386
non-bootable disk in drive, 87
parameters not supported by drive, 88
PC won't boot, 335–336
pointing devices, wired, 60–61
pointing devices, wireless, 62–63

power supply
floppy disk drive doesn't work, 324
no power, 324
PC won't boot from hard disk, 325
printers
printing gibberish, 450
won't print, 448–449
seek error, 87
tape backup drive, external, 107–108
distance from monitor, 107
IRQ conflicts, 107
memory requirements, 107
practice exercise, 110–115
shoeshining, 108
slow tape, 108
sound card interference, 107
tape speed *versus* computer speed, 108
tape backup drive, internal, 98–99
updating files between PCs, 432–433
video cards
display is smaller than screen, 258
error messages during boot, 255
flicker, 260
garbled image, 255
no display, 254–255
Windows boots into DOS prompt,
258–259
Windows 95 upgrade, 416
unable to update system files, 407
Windows 95 upgrade unable to update
system files, 407
TSR (terminate but stay resident)
programs, 60
turbo switch, 372
case study, 397–398
type styles
See fonts

U

UART (Universal Asynchronous Receiver
Transmitter), defined, 465

UCM (Universal Connection Mode), defined, 465
UL-listed, 28
Universal Asynchronous Receiver Transmitter (UART), defined, 465
Universal Connection Mode (UCM), defined, 465
upload, defined, 465

V

v.22, defined, 465
v.22 bis, defined, 465
v.32, defined, 465
v.32 bis, defined, 465
v.34, defined, 465
v.42 bis, defined, 465
VBE (VGA BIOS Extension), defined, 465
VESA (Video Electronics Standards Association), defined, 465
VGA BIOS Extension (VBE), defined, 465
VGA (Video Graphics Array)
  defined, 466
  displays, identifying, 229
video cards
  buying tips, 239
  defined, 228
  determining current setup, 233–234
  device drivers
    DOS, 246
    Windows 3.x, 240–242, 246–247
    Windows 95, 240–241, 247–248
  DRAM (dynamic random access memory), 233
  expansion slots, 234–239
  expansion slots for, 236–238
  flicker, 230–231
  graphics accelerator card, 233
  installing, 243–244
  interlaced vs. non-interlaced monitors, 231
  memory, blocking out, 259
  number of colors, 229

PCI cards, 244
picture elements, 229
pixels, 229
refresh rates, 230
removing, 240–241, 243
reserved memory, 231–233
resolution, 229
scan rates, 230
testing, 244–245
troubleshooting
  display is smaller than screen, 258
  error messages during boot, 255
  flicker, 260
  garbled image, 255
  no display, 254–255
  Windows boots into DOS prompt, 258–259
upgrading, case study, 252–254
video resolution standards, 229
VRAM (video random access memory), 233
Video Electronics Standards Association (VESA), defined, 465
Video Graphics Array (VGA)
  defined, 466
  displays, identifying, 229
video ports, male versus female, 48
video random access memory (VRAM), 233
virtual memory, 167
VRAM (video random access memory), 233

W

warnings
  data loss or corruption
    after BIOS update, 17
    bootable disks, 108
    inadequate power supply, 314–315
    rescue disks, 96
    restoring from backup tape, 96, 108
    splitting power to the hard disk drive, 81

storing backup offsite, 108
Windows installed over proprietary
    DOS, 389
equipment damage
    blocked air vents, 85
    cards touching cards, 372
    dust, 323
    ESD (electrostatic discharge), 21
    exploding power supplies, 316
    heat generated by modem cards, 296
    improper insertion of processor chip, 223
    improper power supply connections, 321
    mismatched scan rate, 255
    mismatched scan rates, 231
    swapping keyboard and mouse
        connections, 45
    swapping monitor port and serial
        port, 47
    touching the contacts, 188
    voltage surges, 28
personal injury
    electrical shock, 24
    exploding power supplies, 316
Windows 95
    booting with an empty hard disk, 381
    Briefcase, 428–432
    CD-ROM drive handling, 345–346
    creating a startup diskette, 394–397
    Device Manager, 287–291
    Direct Cable Connection utility, 420–428
    disk space required for printing, 445–446
    displaying video setup, 234
    ejecting a printer page, 332
    installing a sound card, 353–354
    Mouse Properties menu, 55–57
    mouse shortcut, 44
    MS Backup missing, 94
    Plug and Play, 349–351
    previewing sounds, 354
    printer drivers, 438
    restoring to a new hard disk, 138–139
    safe mode, 242

scan rate, checking, 258
testing CD-ROM drives, 354
transferring files between PCs
    changing host/guest designations, 426
    configuring, 421–426
    configuring guest PC, 422
    configuring host PC, 422–424
    determining host and guest PCs, 422
    finding, 420–421
    installing, 421
    naming host PC, 424
    passwords, 425
    requirements for, 420
    restarting, 426
    sharing host resources, 424–425
    troubleshooting, 426–428
updating files between PCs, 428–429
    adding files to, 429–430
    editing files on the guest, 429–430
    orphans, 431–432
    splitting files, 431–432
    synchronizing files, 430–431
    troubleshooting, 432–433
    viewing file locations, 431
upgrading to
    antivirus software, problems with,
        406–407
    dual boot, 407
    dual boot, DOS, 408–412
    dual boot, Windows 95, 413–415
    hardware profiles, 413–415
    hardware requirements, 406
    RAM-doubling software, problems with,
        406–407
    troubleshooting, 416
    unable to update system files, 407
video resolution, setting, 257
viewing IRQ settings, 341
work-arounds, 13
WPC
    See write precompensation
wrist grounding strap, 22–25
write precompensation, defined, 466

X

XGA (Extended Graphics Array),
        defined, 466

Z

ZIF (Zero Insertion Force)
  defined, 466
  sockets
    with 486 processor, 203
    pin 1, 218
    release lever, 217
Zip drive on a network, case study, 108–110

IDG BOOKS WORLDWIDE REGISTRATION CARD

RETURN THIS REGISTRATION CARD FOR FREE CATALOG

Title of this book: **Upgrading Your Own PC**

My overall rating of this book: ❏ Very good [1]   ❏ Good [2]   ❏ Satisfactory [3]   ❏ Fair [4]   ❏ Poor [5]

How I first heard about this book:

❏ Found in bookstore; name: [6]

❏ Advertisement: [8]

❏ Word of mouth; heard about book from friend, co-worker, etc.: [10]

❏ Book review: [7]

❏ Catalog: [9]

❏ Other: [11]

What I liked most about this book:

What I would change, add, delete, etc., in future editions of this book:

Other comments:

Number of computer books I purchase in a year: ❏ 1 [12]   ❏ 2-5 [13]   ❏ 6-10 [14]   ❏ More than 10 [15]

I would characterize my computer skills as: ❏ Beginner [16]   ❏ Intermediate [17]   ❏ Advanced [18]   ❏ Professional [19]

I use ❏ DOS [20]   ❏ Windows [21]   ❏ OS/2 [22]   ❏ Unix [23]   ❏ Macintosh [24]   ❏ Other: [25]_____
(please specify)

I would be interested in new books on the following subjects:
(please check all that apply, and use the spaces provided to identify specific software)

❏ Word processing: [26]

❏ Data bases: [28]

❏ File Utilities: [30]

❏ Networking: [32]

❏ Other: [34]

❏ Spreadsheets: [27]

❏ Desktop publishing: [29]

❏ Money management: [31]

❏ Programming languages: [33]

I use a PC at (please check all that apply): ❏ home [35]   ❏ work [36]   ❏ school [37]   ❏ other: [38] _____

The disks I prefer to use are ❏ 5.25 [39]   ❏ 3.5 [40]   ❏ other: [41]_____

I have a CD ROM: ❏ yes [42]   ❏ no [43]

I plan to buy or upgrade computer hardware this year: ❏ yes [44]   ❏ no [45]

I plan to buy or upgrade computer software this year: ❏ yes [46]   ❏ no [47]

Name: _____   Business title: [48] _____   Type of Business: [49] _____

Address (❏ home [50] ❏ work [51]/Company name: _____)

Street/Suite# _____

City [52]/State [53]/Zipcode [54]: _____   Country [55] _____

❏ **I liked this book!** You may quote me by name in future
IDG Books Worldwide promotional materials.

My daytime phone number is _____

IDG BOOKS

THE WORLD OF
COMPUTER
KNOWLEDGE

BUSINESS REPLY MAIL
FIRST CLASS MAIL   PERMIT NO. 2605   FOSTER CITY, CALIFORNIA

NO POSTAGE
NECESSARY
IF MAILED
IN THE
UNITED STATES

IDG Books Worldwide
919 E Hillsdale Blvd, STE 400
Foster City, CA 94404-9691

☐ **YES!**

Please keep me informed about IDG's World of Computer Knowledge.
Send me the latest IDG Books catalog.